SWING UNMA

THE AGRICULTURAL RIOTS
OF 1830 TO 1832
AND THEIR WIDER IMPLICATIONS

edited by

MICHAEL HOLLAND

FACHRS Publications
Milton Keynes

Published by
FACHRS Publications
Family & Community Historical Research Society Limited
No 4, 5 West Hill, Aspley Guise, Milton Keynes MK17 8DP

© FACHRS Publications 2005

ISBN: 0954818088 (pbk)

Cover illustration
From an original drawing by Wendy Ingle

Cover design and typesetting
Angela Blaydon Publishing Limited
2 Elm Close, Ripley, Surrey GU23 6LE

Set in Times New Roman 10 pt

Printed by Alden Group Limited, Osney Mead, Oxford OX2 0EF

CONTENTS

Preface   iii

List of Tables   iv

List of Figures   iv

List of Illustrations   v

List of Maps   vi

Coinage Conversion Table   vii

Coinage Terms   vii

Swing Riot Prices at Today's Values   vii

Acknowledgements   viii

    List of Swing Researchers   viii

    List of Contributors   viii

List of Abbreviations   ix

I.   The Captain Swing Project - *Michael Holland*   1

II.   Swing Riots in Surrey - *Judy Hill and Mary James*   26

III. Fire the Farms - When the Shadow of Captain Swing
        Reached Shropshire - *James S Leach and Norman Davies*   62
    Appendix III.A: Extracts from the *Shrewsbury Chronicle*   82
    Appendix III.B: Adoption of Farm Machinery, 1772-1880   83
    Appendix III.C: Valuation of Property Destroyed in the Fires, 1830-31   84
    Appendix III.D: Last Confession of James Lea   85

IV. Burn up the *Pashnidge* - The Swing Riots in Essex - *Michael Holland*   87

V.   Swing in Derbyshire - *Clive Leivers*   118

VI.   'Down with Machinery!' - An Investigation into the
       Wycombe Paper Mill Riots of 1830 - *Vanessa Worship*   126

VII.   Between the Lines - *Valerie Batt-Rawden*   150
       Appendix VII.A: *Rural Queries* for Berkshire   168

VIII. The Life and Death of Richard Nockolds, Hand-loom
       Weaver of Norwich - *Stella Evans*   170

IX.   The British Cholera Riots of 1832 - *Sean Burrell and Geoff Gill*   184

X.   The Reverend Swing! - *Clive Leivers*   229

XI.   Transportation of Prisoners and the Settling of Sydney Cove - *Reay*
       Ferguson   241
       Appendix XI.A: Officers, Men and Passengers Sailing with the First Fleet   250
       Appendix XI.B: Family Tree of Ann Forbes or Butler or Huxley   254

Appendix I: List of Offenders, Date of Offence and Parish   261

Appendix II: List of Victims of Swing Protest   281

Consolidated Bibliography   295

Surname Index   299

Subject Index   303

CD-ROM

PREFACE

Swing Riots - Disturbances Post-Napoleonic Wars
Returning heroes but no jobs

During the Napoleonic wars men had been drafted into the Army and Navy, thus creating a serious shortage of manpower. The farming community was particularly hard hit and so forms of, for example, threshing machines were invented to replace manpower. When Waterloo had been won, soldiers and sailors were discharged in large numbers. They returned to their homes only to find machines doing their work. The situation was fertile ground for protest, and protest is fertile ground for research.

The Family & Community Historical Research Society is a Society formed to provide the opportunity for its members to carry out research on a national scale through projects.

The Swing Riots were selected as an important subject for research. With Michael Holland of Essex University as academic adviser and Jacqueline Cooper, and later Stella Evans, as Project Organiser, the project was under way.

From a variety of sources researchers discovered much new material, which is of value to historians and sociologists studying post-Napoleonic-War Britain. It was decided to publish so the results of the research would be widely available.

On behalf of the Society my thanks go to Michael Holland, Jacqueline Cooper, Stella Evans and all the researchers, who have made contributions to the project, and those who recorded their findings in essays.

The final word of appreciation is made to the Publications Sub-Committee of Angie Blaydon, Jacqueline Cooper and Clive Leivers, who, with Michael Holland, have done so much to bring this book to fruition.

Michael Kemp
Chairman
Family & Community Historical Research Society

LIST OF TABLES

Table I.I.	All Swing offences	5
Table I.II	Non-agricultural incidents	7
Table I.III	Recipients of anonymous threatening letters	11
Table I.IV	Non-agricultural-labourer protesters	15
Table I.V	Occupations of victims	17
Table I.VI	Perceptions of protest from *Rural Queries*	21
Table II.I	Incidents of protest in Surrey, 1830-1832	33
Table IV.1	Wage riots in Essex	93
Table IV.II	Machine-breaking in Essex	95
Table IV.III	Anonymous threatening letters	98
Table IV.IV	Incendiarism and attempted incendiarism in Essex	102
Table VI.I	The Wycombe paper-mill rioters	144
Table IX.I	Cholera cases and deaths in Britain, 1831-1832	188
Table IX.II	Chronology and locations of the Liverpool Cholera Riots, 1832	197
Table IX.III	Civil disturbances in Britain, 1812-1848	220
Table X.I	Offences involving clergymen	229
Table XI.I	Age in years of women sentenced and transported in First Fleet	241
Table XI.II	Place of sentencing of convicts on the First Fleet	243
Table XI.III	Occupations of women transported in the First Fleet	244

LIST OF FIGURES

Fig. I.1	Wages riots by county	9
Fig. I.2	Occupational status of tithe rioters	9
Fig. I.3	Age range of male protesters	16
Fig. I.4	Sentencing patterns	16
Fig. I.5	Capital sentencing patterns	16
Fig. I.6	Principal causes of protest (*Rural Queries*)	20
Fig. IV.1	Essex Swing incidents, September 1830-March 1831	106

LIST OF ILLUSTRATIONS

Illustration I.a	Hand threshing	2
Illustration I.b	Bradwell reward notice	3
Illustration I.c	Loan document	4
Illustration I.d	Hawkwell letter	12
Illustration II.a	Poster, Guildford, 1830	54
Illustration II.b	Handbill, Dorking, 1830	55
Illustration III.a	Dearnford Hall, 2003	80
Illustration III.b	Dearnford Hall farm buildings, rebuilt after the fire	80
Illustration III.c	Twemlows Farm, *ca* 1960	81
Illustration III.d	St Alkmund's Church	81
Illustration VI.a	High Street, Wycombe	126
Illustration VI.b	Resolutions of a meeting held at the Windmill Inn, 17 November 1830	128
Illustration VI.c	Announcement of a meeting to be held on 26 November 1830 at the Guild Hall, Chepping Wycombe	129
Illustration VI.d	Snakely Mill, Loudwater	132
Illustration VI.e	Resolutions of a meeting held at High Wycombe, 3 December 1830	134
Illustration VI.f	Calendar of prisoners in His Majesty's Gaol at Aylesbury, 10 January 1831	136
Illustration VI.g	Letter from George Maule to the Home Office, dated 11 January 1831	139
Illustration VI.h	Petition signed by Wycombe paper manufacturers on behalf of Blizzard and Sarney	141
Illustration VII.a	Man wearing a smock frock	155
Illustration VIII.a	Weavers' 'cottages' with high lofts, Magdeline Street, Norwich	172
Illustration VIII.b	Setting up a Draw Loom	173
Illustration VIII.c	Cottages, Barrack Street, Norwich, *ca* 1796	175
Illustration VIII.d	Copy of graffiti at Norwich Castle	182
Illustration IX.a	The 'blue stage of cholera'	185
Illustration IX.b	A Court for King Cholera	186
Illustration IX.c	16 August 1832: The last cholera corpse buried in Bartholomew yard	208
Illustration IX.d	A cholera riot in Exeter	210
Illustration X.a	John Coke, High Sheriff of Nottinghamshire	231
Illustration X.b	Reverend William Bowerbank's advertisement for Mansfield Grammar School, 1794	233
Illustration X.c	Extract from Pleasley parish register, 1817, showing Bowerbank as curate	236
Illustration XI.a	Bunks holding three or four women on each platform, three storeys' high	243
Illustration XI.b	Drawing of Sydney Cove, 1788	245

LIST OF MAPS

Map I.i	The true extent of Swing	6
Map I.ii	Attacks on non-agricultural machinery	8
Map I.iii	Tithe riots	10
Map I.iv	Food riots	10
Map I.v	Letters leading to incendiarism	13
Map I.vi	*Rural Queries* responding counties	19
Map II.i	Swing in Surrey	40
Map III.i	Incendiary events in Shropshire, 1830-32	77
Map III.ii	Incendiary incidents 1830-32 in the parish of Whitchurch	78
Map IV.i	Location of the County of Essex	88
Map IV.ii	Incidents in Essex, 1830-32	90
Map V.i	Incidents of Swing in Derbyshire	119
Map VI.i	Map showing the five mills on the River Wye where machinery was destroyed	130
Map IX.i	Cholera map of Leeds	204

COINAGE CONVERSION TABLE

6d	=	2.5p
1s	=	5p
2s	=	10p
5s	=	25p
10s	=	50p
240d	=	100p
20s	=	£1

COINAGE TERMS

Guinea (£1 1s 0d)	=	£1-5p
Crown (5s)	=	25p
Half crown (2s 6d)	=	12.5p
Florin (2s)	=	10p
Bob (1s)	=	5p
Tanner (6d)	=	2.5p

SWING RIOT PRICES AT TODAY'S VALUES

There are a number of references to sums of money in the essays within this volume. The sum of five pounds in 1830 would have the purchasing power of considerably more by today's standards. It is felt that a simple conversion table might be beneficial to readers of this book.

For the period 1830 to 1832, the pound sterling had the purchasing power of approximately £53 by today's values. In order to calculate the 21st century value of a sum of money quoted in 1830, simply multiply that sum by fifty-three to arrive at an approximate modern-day value, as follows:

In 1830 a land agent donated £5 cash towards the setting up of a watch. How much would £5 equate to by today's values?

5 multiplied by 53 equals 265. Therefore, £5 in 1830 can be said to be worth £265 today.

£100 would be worth £5,300, and so on.

ACKNOWLEDGEMENTS

LIST OF RESEARCHERS

Bob Allen
Anne Andrews
Valerie Batt-Rawden
Robert Brown
Ann Burke
Jacqueline Cooper
Cynthia Coultas
Barry Dackombe
Rosemary Davies
Anne Earl
Reay Ferguson
Shirley Firth
Jackie Gore
Noel Grimmet
John Hargreaves
Trevor Hill
Michael Hodgson
Hazel Hunt
Dick Hunter

Mary James
Christine Jones
Clive Leivers
John Loosley
Shirley Maile
Diana Mehew
Rhianydd Murray
Pauline Napier
Paul Newton Taylor
Diana Rau
John Robins
Michael Skidmore
Mary Varley
Margaret Vaudrey
Kate Weedon
Clare Wilkins
Vanessa Worship
Jean Wright

LIST OF CONTRIBUTORS

Valerie Batt-Rawden
Sean Burrell
Norman Davies
Stella Evans
Reay Ferguson
Geoff Gill

Judy Hill
Michael Holland
Mary James
James Leach
Clive Leivers
Vanessa Worship

ABBREVIATIONS

BPP	British Parliamentary Papers
BRO	Berkshire Record Office
CBS	Centre for Buckinghamshire Studies
CEAS	Centre for East Anglian Studies
ERO	Essex County Record Office, Chelmsford
FACHRS	Family & Community Historical Research Society
FM	Fitzwilliam Museum, Cambridge
NRO	Norfolk Record Office
SHC	Surrey History Centre, Woking
SRRC	Shropshire Records and Research Centre
TNA	The National Archives (formerly the Public Record Office)
VCH	The Victoria County History

I. THE CAPTAIN SWING PROJECT

BACKGROUND TO THE PERIOD

Agricultural protest was not a new phenomenon. It has its roots in the 16th century when landlords started to create large leasehold farms through enclosure, thus absorbing small farms. Hedge-breaking incidents occurred in certain parts of southern England as the rural proletariat expressed their dissatisfaction with this new development.[1] Likewise, price-fixing riots occurred from the latter part of the 16th century as the lower orders expressed discontent with the price of staple foods and the increase in the export of grain to London.[2]

During the 18th and 19th centuries, localised unrest had occurred during the grain famines of 1795 and 1800; during post-war unemployment in 1816; and during 1822 when threshing machines were attacked in parts of East Anglia. Agricultural labourers first engaged in overt and covert protest from *circa* 1790.[3] One factor in this was the demise of the live-in farm servant and the emergence of the day-wage labourer. In short, farmers, being mindful of financial considerations, moved away from the age-old practice of employing farm labourers on an annual basis, providing accommodation and victuals in favour of paying labourers by the day and leaving it to them to find their accommodation, sustenance, etc. The advantage to the farmer was that he only had to employ labourers when they were needed. During the winter months, when there was less work for the labourers, the farmer was no longer responsible for keeping them.[4] An additional problem was that labourers became landless as cottage gardens and commons were absorbed into farms through enclosure.[5] Accordingly, there was little scope for farm labourers to enjoy a level of self-sufficiency through tending their own small plot of land. This having been said, there was some interest in providing allotments for the labouring classes in certain parts of the country from the last decade of the 18th century.[6]

The Swing Riots occurred between 1830 and 1832 and were described by one early 20th-century historian rather aptly as the *Last Labourers' Revolt*.[7] The fundamental cause of the riots was perceived to be the use of threshing machines by farmers, although other factors, such as wages, the condition of workers, the administration of the poor laws at parish level, and even restrictions on gleaning, were contributory factors to the riots. The threshing machine had been introduced during the Napoleonic Wars to address the labour shortage brought about by able-bodied labourers being recruited into the armed forces. The heavily depleted agricultural work force, many of them aged or young, could not adequately process the harvested grain, and so industry came to the rescue in the form of the threshing machine. The first threshing machines were introduced to English counties during 1800. These were portable machines mounted on wheeled carriages.[8] Threshing by hand was an extremely labour-intensive process and involved beating the grain with a flail, as shown in the following illustration.

Illustration I.a. Hand threshing

The traditional winter occupation for agricultural labourers in cereal-growing areas of the country was hand threshing the harvested corn. This could very easily take three months or more to complete, and provided much needed winter employment at a time when there was little alternative work available, due to adverse weather. It is true that the winter months could be used to perform a certain amount of maintenance work around the farm, but with work on the fields impracticable due to weather conditions, this would not amount to very much. Animal husbandry would be left to the experts, such as cowmen, horsemen, etc. Agricultural labourers, who were engaged to thresh grain in the time-honoured fashion with flail and swingel, were expected to thresh a predetermined quota at each session. Anything threshed in excess of that quota could attract a bonus payment.[9] Therefore, the advent of the threshing machine was seen by at least a proportion of the labouring work force as having the potential to threaten that employment, and render many labourers unemployed at the time of year when alternative employment was scarce.

Farmers found that machines were a more efficient and less labour-intensive way of threshing grain, and were not prepared to revert to the manual methods once peace was restored. As Farmer Spurgeon of Bradwell-juxta-Mare, in Essex put it during a conversation with Arthur Young:

> Last years wheat which was badly done [by hand] at 2s a quarter, was
> done by the machine perfectly well.[10]

It is worth mentioning that Farmer Spurgeon was an early Essex Swing victim as the extract in Illustration I.b shows.[11]

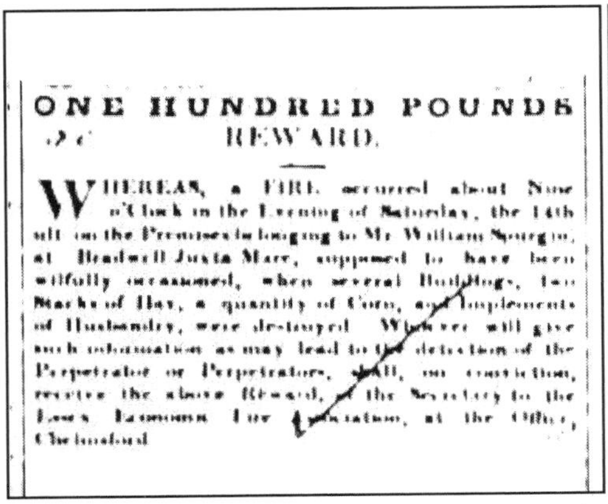

ONE HUNDRED POUNDS
REWARD

WHEREAS a fire occurred about Nine o'clock in the Evening of Saturday the 14th ult on the premises belonging to Mr William Spurgeon at Bradwell Juxta Mare, supposed to have been wilfully occasioned, when several buildings, two stacks of hay, a quantity of Corn and Implements of Husbandry were destroyed. Whoever will give such information as may lead to the detection of the Perpetrator or Perpetrators, shall on conviction, receive the above reward of the Secretary to the Essex Economic Fire Association at the Office Chelmsford

Illustration I.b. Bradwell Reward Notice (left)
(reproduced by permission of Essex County Record Office)
with retyped content (right)

Earlier in the century agricultural rioting had occurred at the end of the Napoleonic Wars in 1816, and again in 1822, although both were limited to the cereal-producing region of East Anglia.[12] This rioting focused upon the threshing machine and, to a lesser extent, innovations, such as the mole plough - a less labour-intensive tool for producing shallow trenches for field drainage.[13] Mechanisation in agriculture was perceived by a large proportion of agricultural labourers as the fundamental cause of winter unemployment, and, therefore, recourse to the parish for relief. The situation in post-war England was exacerbated by the fact that something approaching 350,000 men were demobilised from the armed forces and returned to the labour market, many of them being destined for the countryside.[14] In 1830, however, we know that much of southern England had been affected by concentrated attacks on threshing machines by agricultural labourers.[15]

Poor Law

The English Poor Law was also a cause of a certain degree of dissatisfaction amongst the labouring poor, with overseers and assistant overseers bearing the brunt of the dislike. The office of overseer dates from two pieces of Elizabethan legislation of 1572 and 1594, the latter requiring that all parishes were required to appoint an overseer annually.[16] His role was to raise the finance with which to relieve the poor through a poor rate, and to disburse the monies raised to any of the poor who might apply to him for relief. This relief could be in cash or kind, for example, loaves of bread might be supplied to a family.

In 1819 an Act of Parliament entitled *The Select Vestries Act* was passed. This piece of legislation gave the option for parish vestries to appoint select vestries, comprising between five and twenty parishioners to minister to the needs of the poor.[17] They were required to meet once a fortnight and to scrutinise each application for poor relief. Another element of the Act was the appointment of paid assistant overseers. Again, their role was to carefully scrutinise all applications for poor relief and to take steps to reduce poor law expenditure.[18] Both select vestries and assistant overseers were optional facilities, of which parishes could avail themselves, if desired. Another element of the Act was the facility to relieve claimants who had squandered their wages away, thus being unable to support their families, by way of a parish loan that was repayable within twelve months.[19] Defaulters would be liable to imprisonment in the House of Correction. A typical order is shown below in Illustration I.c.

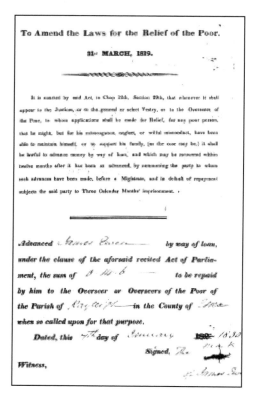

Illustration I.c. Loan document
(reproduced by kind permission of Essex County Record Office)

The measures provided under the Select Vestries Act were all designed to reduce poor law expenditure, especially in relation to the able-bodied poor. This, in turn, was viewed by a proportion of those affected, as an infringement on their perceived rights to receive poor relief when other sources of pay were not available to them.

Why Captain Swing?

The agricultural unrest came to be called *The Swing Riots* because many of the anonymous threatening letters sent to farmers were signed with the pseudonym, 'Captain Swing'. A number of theories have been expounded as to why the words 'Captain Swing' were used. There are grounds for believing that the rank is associated with the leader of the harvest gangs, who were also known as captains. At least one contemporary newspaper suggested that the word 'Swing', in this context, related to the command that the captain of the harvest gang gave to the scythe men each time they commenced a sweep through the harvest field, '*Altogether, swing!*'.[20] Scythe gangs worked in a line across the field and needed to start each harvest run in concert, hence the command. Because of the back-breaking nature of scything, the men would cut the first thirty feet of corn and then walk back to their start line, thirty feet being deemed the distance necessary for them to straighten their backs before the next run. Another theory put forward was that the 'Swing' element alluded to the flexible part of the threshing flail that was known as the swingel. Both theories have their merits, although in reality the true origin of the phrase is not known.

UNMASKING SWING

Hobsbawm and Rudé's work identified 1,475 incidents involving protest during the period 1830 to 1832 in England.[21] By contrast, the FACHRS research team identified a total of 3,283 incidents in England, Scotland, and Wales.[22] These break down as shown below in Tables I.I and I.II, the latter relating to protest crime carried out during the Swing period in urban areas. Map I.i shows the geographical spread of Swing.

TABLE I.I
All Swing Offences

Offence	Total	Offence	Total
Animal maiming	76	Machine-breaking (threshing)	539
Malicious killing of livestock	9	Machine-breaking (other agricultural machinery)	47
Anonymous threatening letters	272	Murder	1
Assaults on poor law officials	25	Poor law riot	19
Attempted incendiarism	54	Racial riot	5
Burglary	16	Rent riot	3
Enclosure riot	3	Rescue of protesters from custody	102
Extortion	2	Robbery	252
Food riot	10	Theft	2
Gleaning riot	1	Tithe riot	69
Highway robbery	3	Verbal threats (to commit incendiarism, etc.)	18
Incendiarism	1,292	Wage riot	284
Incitement	3	Wilful damage (fences, crops, tackle, etc.)	32

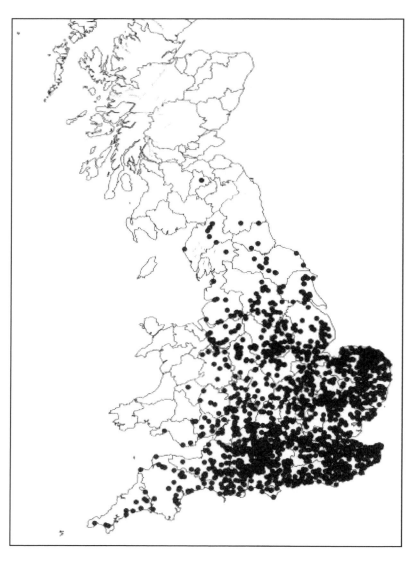

Map I.i. The true extent of Swing

The principal crime committed during this period was incendiarism and attempted incendiarism to farms, with a total of 1,346 offences carried out. Machine breaking of threshing machines and other agricultural machinery and implements totalled 586 offences. Wage riots, the sending of anonymous threatening letters, and robbery were the other main offences to be carried out. Some other interesting offences were revealed in the course of the protest. For example, in late November 1830 rioting agricultural labourers held up and robbed the occupants of coaches at Froxfield in Wiltshire, Reading, and Hungerford in Berkshire.[23] On Christmas Eve 1830, a looker employed by a farmer to guard his stacks, was attacked and bludgeoned to death by incendiaries at Strumpshaw in Norfolk.[24] This was the only murder to have been carried out by Swing rioters. It has not been possible to establish any further information about this crime; therefore it is impossible to tell whether there were other factors that led to the man's untimely demise. Racial rioting occurred in Lincolnshire and Northamptonshire over the employment of Irish labourers during harvest time in 1831 and 1832.[25] The employment of the Irish in preference to local labour was a contentious issue amongst the indigenous labouring poor, who often saw their employment as being to the detriment of local workers.

During November and December 1830 there were thirty-five attacks on non-agricultural machinery. In addition to these there were three incidents of arson and thirteen strikes for more wages, one of which, in Wolverhampton, resulted in the fatal ducking of a strike-breaker. These are detailed in Table I.II below.

TABLE I.ii
Non- agricultural incidents

Offence	Total
Cholera riots	53
Incendiarism to non-agricultural premises	3
Machine-breaking (non-agricultural)	35
Found on enclosed premises	1
General unrest	48
Political riot	28
Seditious meeting	7
Strike	13

The geographical pattern of non-agricultural machine breaking is shown in Map I.ii below. The darker shades indicate counties where there was a higher occurrence of this crime. Paper mills were one of the main targets for protesters.

A secondary feature of the Swing disturbances was that of agricultural wages. This is reflected by the fact that nearly three quarters of all riots during this period were focused upon wage rises, as Fig. I.1 demonstrates.

For the most part these riots occurred during daylight hours, with large groups of men going from farm to farm, or even village to village, assembling at a specific farm and adopting a menacing attitude intended to intimidate the target into raising wages. However, at one Essex farm a more sinister device was employed when Farmer South of West Mersea was awoken at 3 am to find about a dozen farm labourers in his house, two in his bedroom, demanding that he accompany them around the local farms in support of their claim for higher wages. The poor man was so terrified that he was unequal to the task of tying up his boots and had to be assisted by the two labourers. To emphasise their demands a noose was placed around his neck, adding to his terror.[26] After being forced to accompany the rioters to other farms in the adjacent parishes of Little Wigborough and Peldon, he managed to make his escape.

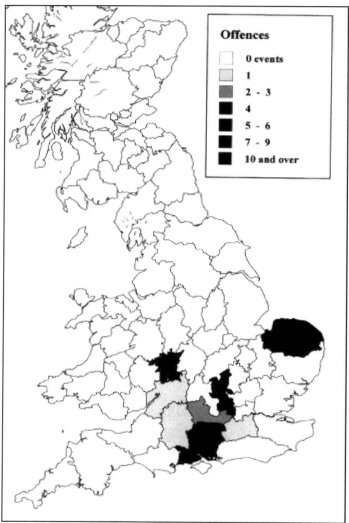

Map I.ii. Attacks on non-agricultural machinery

Only one other instance of a wage riot taking place at night has so far been identified. This occurred in the Cambridgeshire parish of Trumpington. All other identified wage riots occurred either during the day or, in the case of two Kentish riots, during the evening. It could be speculated that the latter followed meetings in the local beershop or inn. It was common for the planning of riots to be carried out in the local beershop, a point that many respondents of *Rural Queries* made, see below.

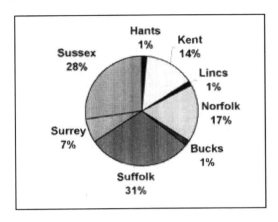

Fig. I.1. Wage riots by county

A proportion of protest against the Anglican clergy was often 'encouraged' by tenant farmers keen to see a reduction in the tithe, blaming their inability to raise wages on tithe demands.[27] Therefore, it is perhaps not surprising to see, that there were sixty-nine tithe-riot incidents during the period. Agricultural labourers made up the bulk of those committed for this form of riot, but as Fig. I.2 shows, glovers, shoemakers and even some farmers were pro-active in this form of protest.

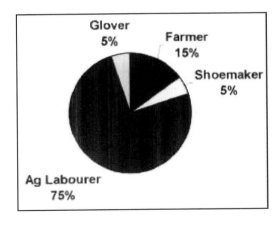

Fig. I.2. Occupational status of tithe rioters

Map I.iii shows the extent of tithe rioting during this period, the shaded spots representing counties where a relatively high level of this form of protest occurred.

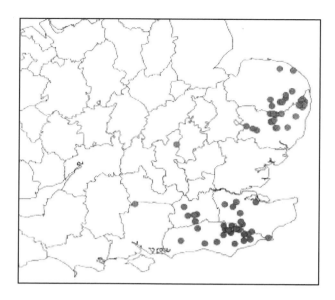

Map I.iii. Tithe riots

There were ten incidents of food rioting, often perpetrated by men as opposed to the traditional women-led riots of previous centuries. The extent of the food riots is shown below in Map I.iv. The spots represent areas where food rioting occurred. The food riot at Helston in Cornwall on 22 February 1831 involved 300 tin miners who prevented a grain ship sailing from the port (see Map I.iv.).[28]

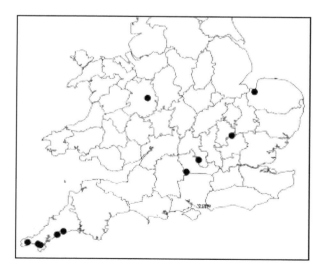

Map I.iv. Food riots

A total of 262 anonymous threatening letters and notices have been identified as having been sent during this period. This category includes a number of instances where threatening slogans were chalked on barn walls along the Dover to London road in Kent. These have been combined and plotted in Map I.v., the white areas indicating counties where farmers received no letters; the shaded areas indicate where letters were received. Farmers in the county of Kent received more letters than any other county. In all, 222 farmers are known to have been the victims of anonymous letters in the main that threatened incendiary attacks (see Table I.III below).

TABLE I.III
Recipients of anonymous threatening letters

Victim	No.
Assistant overseers	1
Miller	2
Magistrates	3
Female	4
Overseers	5
Clergymen	11
Miscellaneous victims	24
Farmer	222

These letters ranged from descriptions of what would befall the farmer if wages, etc., were not raised, to succinct letters, such as that received by Farmer Ashford of Orsett in Essex, which simply read:

What the Poor Lacketh, the flame will catcheth.[29]

One farmer received an anonymous envelope containing burnt linen, which was taken as a threat that all of his possessions would be reduced to ashes if a recent pay demand were not met.

Some letters, such as the one reproduced below, give an indication of the dialectical English that was prevalent amongst farm labourers during this period.[30] The transcript reads:

Mr Brockies

We Sent this to you to let you know
That if yo Do Not give too
Shillins A Day Every thing Shall
Come to Ashes We have Come from
Kent in that intentione And so
We mene to go through Essex
We brought this to your dore Becaus

We don't like to put you to
No exspence
And we ment to Burn the Pashnidge [parsonage] up first[31]

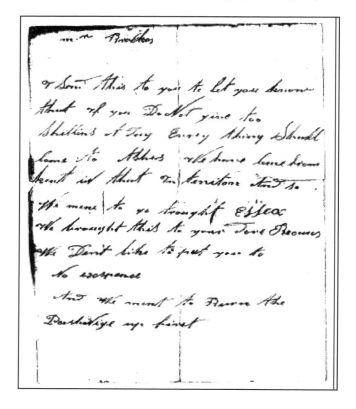

Illustration I.d. Hawkwell Letter
(Reproduced by kind permission of the Essex Record Office)

A letter sent to Reverend Hurlock, of Dedham in Essex, contained two matches, as if to emphasise the threat to him and his property. However, it was strongly believed that this letter was written by local farmers keen to see a reduction in their tithe payments.

There were forty-five occasions when anonymous threatening letters actually preceded incendiary attacks on farms. The remaining two hundred and seventeen letters were not followed up by protest action, so far as is known. The geographical areas where incendiary attacks followed the receipt of anonymous letters is shown in Map I.v., below. It shows that in eleven instances farmers in Kent had their farms fired after receiving threats of this type. However, to place this in perspective, this only accounts for 6% of incendiary attacks in the county. In other counties the figures varied between 4% and 5%. Map I.v shows the counties where incendiarism followed the receipt of an anonymous threatening letter.

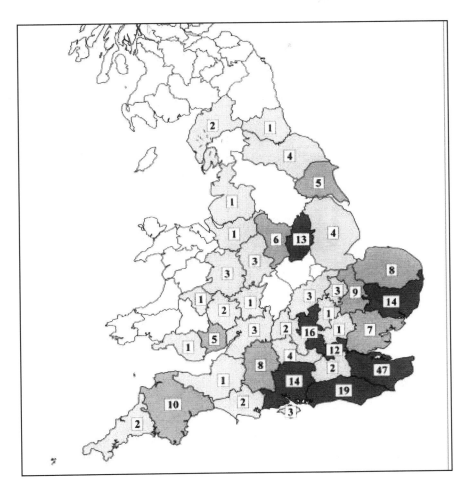

Map I.v. Letters leading to incendiarism

One final word on anonymous letters, the scholars at Eton School sent a letter to their headmaster with a view to him disabling his thrashing machine![32]

Protester Patterns

The project revealed that only 1% of known protesters during the period of Swing were female, with only two women being involved in machine breaking. The first of these was Elizabeth Parker, 22 years of age from Beverstone in Gloucestershire, who gave her occupation as agricultural labourer and who was transported for seven years. The other was Jane Taylor of an unknown Norfolk parish, who was sentenced to three months' imprisonment. As the sentencing trend employed by the courts was to award more severe sentences to ringleaders, it would seem that Elizabeth Parker was one such person. A total of nineteen labourers were indicted for this act of machine breaking, with only three being sentenced to transportation. William Compton was transported for fourteen years and Worthy Mann to seven years. The remainder were either imprisoned or discharged.

Fourteen women, mainly servants, were indicted for incendiarism including 16-year-old Hannah Simmons of Whitchurch in Shropshire. Her act was in response to mistreatment at the hands of her employer. She was sentenced to death but recommended to mercy.[33] In all, eight servants were indicted for acts of incendiarism and one for committing a robbery. There is no indication of the motivation for these acts, with the exception of Elizabeth Moore of Sneinton in Nottinghamshire, who was adjudged insane.

The other offences committed by women protesters were poor law riot, rescue of prisoners, and involvement in a gleaning riot. The latter dates from a judicial decision of 1788 when it was decided that gleaning was not a common law right and that gleaners required permission to enter the harvest field to glean. This judgement led to a number of confrontations between gleaners and farmers.[34] The gleaning riot incident of the Swing era took place at Winfarthing in Norfolk, when agricultural labourer's wife, Susannah Jolly, had a confrontation with overseer of the poor and farmer, John Symonds, during harvest time 1830. Jolly was convicted in December of that year, but the sentence for this misdemeanour is not known. The average age of female protesters was twenty-four years, with the median age being twenty-two years.

Moving on to male offenders, the majority of offenders were agricultural labourers; in fact, that class accounts for 61% of all male protesters. This is hardly surprising as the root cause of the riots was firmly based in agriculture and the effects felt by agricultural labourers. Nevertheless, it is interesting to consider the other occupations that became involved in the Swing protest. Table I.IV below shows the full range of all known non-agricultural-labourer protesters.

Some of the occupations shown, such as artisans associated with rural life, are to be expected. Some, however, are a little out of the ordinary. The straw-plait dealer was a gentleman by the name of Joseph Saville, who travelled East Anglia collecting straw plait for use in the Luton straw-hat trade. On the night of Friday 17 December he was apprehended on the Suffolk/Cambridge/Essex border after some Swing letters were seen to fall from his green gig.[35] When arrested, he was found in possession of a number of threatening letters directed at the Anglican clergy. According to reports in the contemporary press, he was a lay Methodist preacher, or as *The Times* put it, 'more properly called a Ranter'. He was tried and convicted, being sentenced to twelve months' imprisonment, and fined fifty pounds.

In November of the same year another 'ranter' had been apprehended for distributing anonymous threatening letters at Stone in Herefordshire. Henry Williams, a journeyman tailor and ranter was less fortunate than Saville, for he was sentenced to fourteen years' transportation for his crimes. This incident provoked less publicity than the Saville affair. No evidence has come to light to suggest that there was an orchestrated assault on the Anglican clergy by Methodists. On the subject of the clergy, one Anglican curate and schoolmaster was indicted with sending anonymous threatening letters to the Sheriff of Nottingham.[36] He was acquitted.

TABLE I.IV
Non-agricultural-labourer protesters

Occupation	No.	Occupation	No.
Anglican clergyman	1	Miner	1
Apprentice	4	Naval pensioner	1
Army deserter	1	Needle maker	1
Attorney's clerk	1	Occupation not stated	414
Baker	2	Paper maker	3
Beer-house keeper	1	Pargeter	1
Beggar	1	Parish labourer	6
Blacksmith	4	Pauper	6
Boat builder	1	Ploughman	27
Brazier	1	Ranter	1
Bricklayer	6	Razor grinder	1
Butcher	4	Road surveyor	1
Carpenter	11	Saddle maker	1
Carter	3	Sailor	1
Chimney sweep	1	Sawyer	3
Cooper	1	Schoolmaster	2
Cordwainer	1	Servant	10
Farm servant	2	Shepherd	3
Farmer	5	Ship's carpenter	1
Farmer's son	3	Shoemaker	8
Fisherman	1	Shopkeeper	1
Footman	1	Soldier	2
Gardener	1	Spadesman	1
General labourer	17	Stonemason	4
Glazier	1	Straw-plait dealer	1
Glover	2	Tailor	9
Grinder	1	Tanner	2
Groom	3	Thatcher	3
Haybinder	1	Tythingman	6
Hoop maker	1	US citizen	1
Itinerant	1	Vagrant	3
Joiner	1	Watchman	1
Lace worker	1	Waterman	1
Maltster	1	Weaver	2
Mason	1	Weslyan preacher	1
Match seller	4	Wheelwright	2
Miller	2	Yeoman	1
Mill worker	1	Youth	3

The age range of male protesters ran from under sixteen to over eighty years. Those aged between sixteen and thirty-nine years formed the nucleus of protesters, as Fig. I.3. shows.

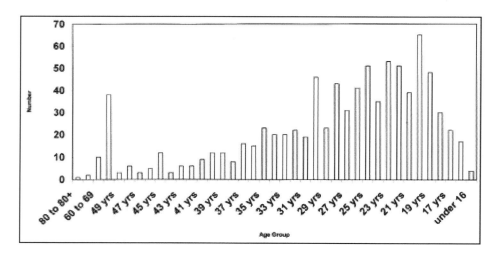

Fig. I.3. Age range of male protesters

How were the protesters dealt with? The majority of offenders were sentenced, on conviction, to a term of imprisonment, either in the county gaol or the local house of correction, for terms ranging from four days to three years. Some sentences included hard labour, one was accompanied by a whipping, and a number included a recognisance to keep the peace for up to two years. The sentencing breakdown is shown in Figs I.4 and I.5.

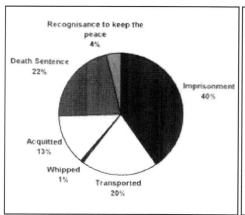 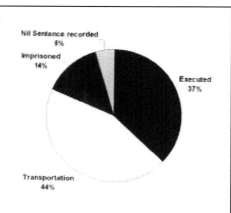

Fig. I.4. Sentencing patterns *Fig. I.5. Capital sentencing patterns (executed and respited)*

Figure I.4 shows the range of sanctions that were applied to protesters, whereas Fig. I.5 indicates the patterns of capital and respited capital sentencing. In the case of the latter, the breakdown includes alternative sentences that were employed when the original capital sentence was respited. In many cases sentence of death was declared by the judge, who would then respite the sentence before the end of the assizes. In other cases appeals for clemency to the Secretary of State for Home Affairs resulted in the death sentence being changed to a lesser punishment. The basic rule of thumb was that sentence of death should only be applied as an exemplary measure designed to deter other potential offenders.[37] If the situation dictated, then the judge was obliged to reduce the sentence of death to a term of transportation, imprisonment or other sanction.

The Victims

The majority of Swing victims were farmers, unsurprisingly, since the main focus of unrest was upon threshing machines and other forms of mechanisation. Nevertheless, other occupations and callings were to be found amongst the victims of protest. The main classes of occupation are to be found below in Table I.V.

TABLE I.V
Occupations of victims

Victim class	Number
Anglican clergyman	88
Female	60
Landed gentry	48
Overseers	36
Justice of the Peace	16
Assistant overseer	13
Miller	13
Member of Parliament	10
Military officers	9
Maltster	7
Paper maker	7
Constable	7
Innkeeper	5
Surveyor of the Roads	4
Work-house official	4
Threshing-machine owner	3
Parish clerk	2
Tithe proprietor	2
Prosecution Association member	1

It is immediately noticeable that the highest numbers of victims within this classification were members of the Anglican clergy. This is attributable to the question of tithes and the perception that they had an adverse effect on wages, although their position as chairman of the parish vestry must also have been a factor. Females form the next highest grouping; the majority of these were farmers although there was one threshing-machine proprietor. We have already seen that a small proportion of women were pro-actively involved in the riots and acts of incendiarism, often as the only means of expressing resentment at their treatment at the hands of employers. The question of women as victims of protest crime is one that will be further investigated, especially with regard to their standing in the parish vestry. Further research needs to be undertaken to establish what proportion of these particular victims had served as overseers in the past.

Turning to the question of overseers and others charged with administering the poor laws, it will be noted that in total fifty-three victims have been identified as overseers, assistant overseers, or officials charged with administering the poor laws. In some cases these people became the targets for attention more for the way in which they administered the measures than by virtue of their position within the vestry. Although a comparatively small number of assistant overseers were victims, the labouring poor particularly disliked the holders of this post.[38] Their role was to reduce poor law expenditure at parish level and to vigorously apply poor law legislation, including the settlement laws. At Brede in Sussex rioting labourers carted their assistant overseer out of the parish in the cart used for removing paupers under the settlement laws.[39] Other parishes in Sussex emulated their Brede counterparts, much to the chagrin of local poor law officials.

The landed gentry were perceived by many agricultural labourers to be culpable in keeping rents up, which in turn kept wage rates down. Accordingly, a proportion of victims came from the landed classes. Their treatment by the protesters was similar to that meted out to clergymen and lay tithe proprietors, and was possibly instigated, either wittingly or otherwise, by farmers pleading inability to raise wages due to high rents. Undoubtedly there were some cases of farmers making use of the situation to encourage a reduction in rent.

To single out Justices of the Peace and Members of Parliament for attention by protesting labourers might, on the face of it, seem a little crass, especially where Justices of the Peace were concerned. In some cases this would have been a case of settling old scores in relation to previous dealings with the law, both criminal and as related to the poor law. The local bench set wage levels at county level, which was another possible reason for focusing activity upon them. Finally, the very fact that protesters could move at will across the countryside and even attack the symbol of law and order, figuratively speaking, was indicative of how confident such protesters were of being able to evade detection. In short, it cocked a snoop at the local law enforcement system.

Perceptions of the causes of the riots

The widespread nature of the Swing Riots was a factor in their inclusion in *Rural Queries* by the Royal Commission into the Poor Laws.[40] Question 53 asked respondents, *'Can you give the Commissioners any information respecting the causes and consequences of the agricultural riots and burnings of 1830 and 1831?'* In all five hundred and twenty-six parishes from forty-six counties responded to the question (see Map I.vi). Of those, only one hundred and forty-two parishes actually suffered protest. In other words, less than three-quarters of respondent parishes could be said to have not directly experienced Swing activity. Nevertheless, those charged with replying to the questionnaire felt qualified to comment on the causes of the riots.

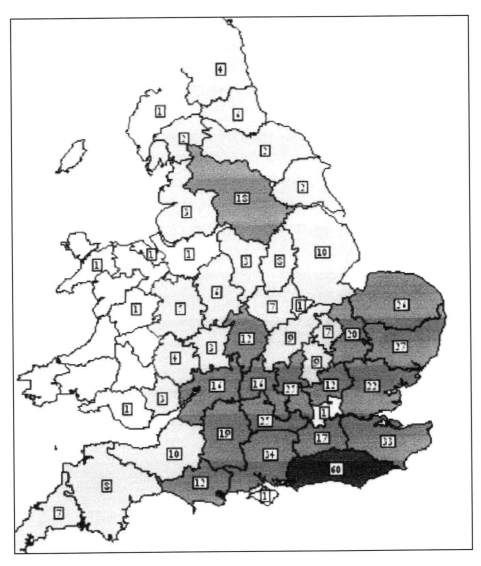

Map I.vi. *Rural Queries* responding counties

The perception of what caused the protest predictably varies from county to county. The most popular answers are shown below in Fig. I.6. Wages are the most popular of the perceived causes, with unemployment coming a close second. After those, seventy respondents blamed beer shops. The Beerhouse Act of 1830 allowed:

> 'A householder assessed to the poor rate, to retail beer from his own
> house on payment of two guineas.'[41]

This legislation was designed to discourage the work force from drinking spirits by making beer more readily available. However, the beer shops were, by their very nature, the resort of the labouring classes and therefore they were able to drink and associate without being overlooked by farmers, vestry members, etc. This in turn meant that the beer shops became ideal locations for labourers planning criminal activity, such as poaching expeditions or acts of protest crime.[42] The empirical evidence of wages riots in Essex has indicated that most of these were planned on licensed premises. The advent of the beer house made planning less likely to be overheard.

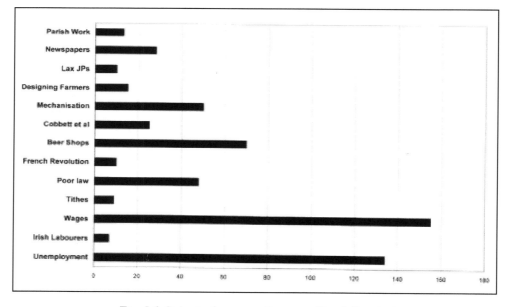

*Fig. I.6. Principal causes of protest (*Rural Queries)

In view of the fact that existing published work on Swing cites the root cause of the disturbances as mechanisation, it is perhaps surprising that only fifty respondents actually cited machine breaking as being the cause of the riots. This does support the findings of the project in that machine breaking only accounted for 18% of protest during this period. Contemporaries viewing the riots with hindsight appear to have concluded that unemployment and wage levels were the real trigger for protest.

The details of all the perceived reasons for the protest are to be found below in Table I.VI.

TABLE I.VI
Perceptions of protest from *Rural Queries*

Cause	No.	Cause	No.
Able-bodied relief	1	Lax JPs	5
Absentee clergymen	1	Malice	5
Agent provocateur	2	Marital differential	1
Association	1	Mechanisation	43
Beer shops	55	Newspapers	21
Cobbett, *et al.*	12	Not the labourers	3
Contagious infatuation	1	Oppression	1
Damage by owners	1	Parish work	12
Designing farmers	6	Pique	3
Discontent	8	Poor farmers	5
Distress	17	Poor law	31
Enclosure	3	Poor supervision	2
Europe	1	Rate in aid of wages	3
France	1	Reform	1
French revolution	4	Revenge	14
Game laws	3	Revenge against overseers	1
Housing	1	Roundsman system	2
Hunger	1	Sedition	1
Idleness	2	Seditious speeches	1
Immigrant workers	2	Speenhamland	3
Indigent labourers	1	Subsistence prices	1
Inflammatory addresses	1	Threshing machines	1
Insurance fraud	1	Tithes	6
Irish labourers	1	Unemployment	130
Kent	1	Wages	139

With one or two exceptions, most of these categories require no explanation. Cobbett, *et al.*, is mentioned by twelve of the respondents. William Cobbett was a political journalist, who was aptly described by one biographer as *The Noblest Agitator*.[43] He was an active champion of the lower classes and, at the time of Swing, made a number of speeches in support of the oppressed farm workers.[44] In addition, he raised a petition on behalf of the oppressed poor, which he sent to the King at Brighton. However, this was rejected, much to Cobbett's annoyance. He published radical comments in his *Two-penny Trash,* a news-sheet published specifically for the poor. He also gave a speech at Battle in Sussex, which prompted incendiary Thomas Goodman of that village, to attribute his actions to the encouragement that he received from Cobbett.[45] How much Cobbett influenced the rioters is open to debate, but certainly a number of respondents looking back to the riots attributed some blame to him.

There were six references to France, the French Revolution and Europe. These allude to a revolution in Belgium as its people strove to break away from Holland, and a revolution in France in July of 1830, when the people rose against a weak king. This was symbolised by Eugene Delacroix's famous painting, *Liberty Leading the People*.[46] There was a perception in England that events on mainland Europe, especially north Europe, could have an impact on unrest in England. Certainly, there is evidence to support this viewpoint as discontent in 1800 and 1848 ably demonstrate.[47]

Six respondents cite designing farmers as being a cause. This rather intriguing nomenclature refers to those farmers who saw an opportunity to encourage landowners to reduce rents as the result of protest activities by their own work force. They would undoubtedly have encouraged their workers by citing high rents as the cause of the low wages that they could pay, in a rather cynical attempt to place pressure on those who set the rent. This classification could also be applied to those farmers who sought a reduction in tithes by sending letters to clergymen that emulated genuine Swing letters.

Marital differential refers to the practice of paying higher wages to married men. The reason for most parishes doing this was to insure against additional pressures being placed upon the poor law system, when whole families were forced to turn to the parish for support. It was a lot cheaper to support single men than families comprising two adults and six or more children.

Turning to those who attributed the riots to the workings of the poor law rate in aid of wages and the Speenhamland System are synonymous. Basically, the system worked like this. A sliding scale, based on the price of the quartern loaf, was established by the parish setting the basic agricultural labourers' wage at three times the cost of the loaf for him, and one and a half times for his wife and each dependent child. Farmers were encouraged to pay this wage rate, but where they failed to do so, the shortfall would be made up out of the poor rate.[48] The 'Roundsman System' referred to a variation on the Speenhamland System whereby labourers claiming relief were sent around to each of the farmers in the parish to see if they could obtain work. They took with them a ticket on which the farmer would either note that he had no work or, if he could offer employment, the wage that he was prepared to pay. This was returned to the overseer who would make up any shortfall out of the rates.[49]

Rural Queries do serve to give us an interesting insight into the way in which the middle (and to a lesser extent landowning) class viewed the causes of Swing. They tend to demonstrate that the period of unrest was not limited to the threshing machine and other forms of mechanisation, and that there were a number of other factors to be considered.

CONCLUSION

The conclusion of the Swing Project is, in many ways, just the beginning. A large amount of data pertaining to unrest in England, Scotland, and Wales has now been placed upon the database and will be progressively analysed over the coming months. Other focused research will have to be undertaken on certain aspects of the data, so that a fuller understanding of the Swing Riots and their wider implications can be achieved.

The Swing Project, which was much more wide-ranging in scope than the Arithmeticke Project, has proved once and for all the worth of collaborative research projects of this type, and of e-mail as the principal mode of communication.[50] It has produced a great deal of information on the incidence of Swing and allied protest during the years 1830 to 1832. For information of the full, known extent of protest crime during this period, see the CD-ROM. The research has enabled the individual researchers to achieve a greater knowledge of social unrest in their own locality, which in itself is of the utmost importance. This is reflected in a number of the essays that are to be found in this volume. Two of these focus upon acts of protest during the Swing era that occurred in industrial and urban settings, respectively. Whilst not rural protest *per se*, they open up the possibilities that the Swing Riots were the catalyst for other, non-agricultural protest across the country. Finally, and most importantly, it has introduced new evidence to the Swing debate, which has to be to the greater historical good. The essays in *Swing Unmasked* have been selected to stimulate thinking on a myriad range of issues associated with popular protest.

NOTES

1   Charlesworth, A, 'The Geography of Land Protest, 1548 to 1860,' in Charlesworth, A, (ed.) *An Atlas of Rural Protest, 1548 to 1900*, (Croom Helm, 1983) p.8 ff.
2   Walter, J, 'The Geography of Food Riots, 1585 to 1649,' in Charlesworth (1983) p. 72.
3   Charlesworth, A, 'The Rise of an Agricultural Proletariat,' in Charlesworth, (1983), p.131.
4   For a more expansive explanation *see:* Armstrong A, *Farmworkers in England and Wales: A Social and Economic History, 1770 to 1980*, (Batsford, 1988).
5   Beckett, J V, 'The Disappearance of the Cottager and Squatter from the English Countryside: the Hammonds re-visited,' in Holderness, B A and Turner, M, (eds) *Land, Labour and Agriculture, 1700 to 1920: Essays for Gordon Mingay*, (Hambledon, 1991) p. 55 ff; Turner, M, *English Parliamentary Enclosure: Its Historical Geography and Economic History*, (Dawson, Kent, 1980); *see also references in:* Mingay G E, (ed.), *The Agrarian History of England and Wales, 1750 to 1850*, (Cambridge, 1989); a useful overview of enclosure from the 16th century forward is: Johnson, A H, *The Disappearance of the Small Landowner*, [1909], (Merlin Press, 1963).
6   Burchardt, J, *The Allotment Movement in England, 1793 to 1873*, (Royal Historical Society, Suffolk, 2002).
7   Hammond, J L and B, *The Village Labourer, 1760 to 1832: A Study of the Government of England Before the Reform Bill*, [1911] (Gloucester, 1987). This description is not necessarily accurate as work on localised rioting by one historian has shown; *see:* Reay, B, 'The Last Rising of the Agricultural Workers: the Battle of Bossenden Wood,' *History Workshop*, (1988) issue 26; and Reay B, *The Last Rising of the Agricultural Labourers: Rural Life and Protest in Nineteenth-century England*, (Oxford, 1990).
8   Collins, E J T, 'The Diffusion of the Threshing Machine in Britain, 1790 to 1880,' *Tools and Tillage*, vol. 2, (1972) p. 17.
9   Hobsbawm, E and Rudé, G, *Captain Swing*, (London, 1969).
10 Peacock, A J, *Bread or Blood: The Agrarian Riots of East Anglia, 1816*, (London, 1964) p. 71.
11 *Chelmsford Chronicle*, 3 September 1830.

[12] Peacock, A J, (1964); Charlesworth, A 'A Comparative Study of the Spread of the Agricultural Disturbances of 1816, 1822, and 1830 in England,' *Journal of Peasant Studies*, 11 (1984); Muskett, P, 'The East Anglian Agrarian Riots of 1822,' *Agricultural History Review*, 32 (1984).

[13] Fussell, G E, *The Farmers Tools: British Farm Implements, Tools, and Machinery, AD 1500 to 1900*, (London, 1952).

[14] Hay, D, 'War, Dearth, and Theft in the 18th century: the record of the English courts,' *Past and Present*, 95 (1982).

[15] Hobsbawm and Rudé (1969).

[16] Nicholls, G, *A History of the English Poor Law, Volume I*, [1854], (Augustus Kelley, New York, 1967), pp. 160, 179.

[17] Nicholls, G [1854] Volume II, p. 181.

[18] Nicholls, G [1854] p. 183.

[19] Nicholls, G [1854] p. 186.

[20] *Kent and Essex Mercury*, 9 November 1830.

[21] Hobsbawm and Rudé (1969), Appendix 1.

[22] The Family & Community Historical Research Society project into the true extent of Captain Swing was tasked with examining newspapers, Home Office papers, court documents, etc., for England, Scotland and Wales to determine the full extent of the Swing Riots.

[23] *Gloucester Journal*, November 1830.

[24] *Nottingham Journal*, a looker was a person engaged to keep a lookout on a specific area, in this case a farmyard.

[25] *Nottingham Journal*; *Lincolnshire, Rutland and Stamford Mercury*; *Doncaster Gazette*.

[26] ERO Quarter Sessions depositions, Q/SBd 6/1.

[27] *Ibid*; Evans, E, *The Contentious Tithe: The Tithe Problem and English Agriculture, 1750 to 1850*, (London, 1976).

[28] *Nottingham Journal*.

[29] ERO, Q/SBd 6/1.

[30] Görlach, M, *English in 19th Century England; An Introduction*, (Cambridge, 1999).

[31] ERO, Q/SBd 6/1/19.

[32] *See:* Batt-Rawden, V, 'Between the Lines' for a transcript of this letter.

[33] Leach, J S and Davies, N, 'Fire in the Farms: When the Shadow of Captain Swing Reached Shropshire' in this volume.

[34] King, P, 'Legal Change, Customary Right, and Social Conflict in Late 18th Century England: the origins of the great gleaning case of 1788,' *Law History Review*, (1992).

[35] *The Times* 23 December 1830, quoting the *Suffolk Herald*.

[36] *See:* Leivers, C, 'The Reverend Swing' in this volume.

[37] *See:* Holland, M, 'Guilty as Charged: the trial of an Essex incendiary,' in Holland, M and Cooper, J (eds.), *Essex Harvest: A Collection of Essays in Memory of Arthur Brown*, (Chelmsford, 2003), for an example of exemplary sentencing during this period; on clemency petitions *see:* Gattrell, V A C, *The Hanging Tree: Execution and the English People, 1770 to 1868*, (Oxford, 1994) pp 197-221, 417 ff. Carter, P, 'Early 19th century Criminal Petitions: an introduction for local historians,' *Local Historian*, 8, (2001).

[38] Mingay, G E, 'Rural War: the life and times of Captain Swing,' in Mingay, G E, (ed.), *The Unquiet Countryside*, (London, 1989).

[39] Mingay, (1989), p. 39.

[40] BPP XXXIV (1834).

[41] Richardson, J, *The Local Historian's Encyclopedia*, (New Barnet, Herts, 1985), p. 270.

42 Jones, D J V, *Crime, Community, and Police in Nineteenth Century Britain*, (London, 1982) pp. 39-40.

43 Green, D, *Great Cobbett: The Noblest Agitator*, (London, 1983).

44 Schweizer, K W and Osborne, J W, *Cobbett in his Times*, (Leicester, 1990), p.122; Dyck, I, *William Cobbett and Rural Popular Culture*, (Cambridge, 1992), pp 152-89.

45 Dyck, (1992) p. 173.

46 This painting can be seen by visiting the following Web site, breitman.homestead.com/Liberty.html

47 Wells, R A E, *Insurrection: the British Experience, 1795 to 1803*, (Gloucester, 1983); Wells, R A E, *Wretched Faces: Famine in Wartime England, 1763 to 1803*, (Gloucester, 1988); Saville, J, *1848: the British State and the Chartist Movement*, (Cambridge, 1990). In more recent times the fuel protest that swept across Britain at the turn of the last century was prompted by a similar series of protests that took place in France over a number of issues that affected the common people.

48 For a copy of the original Speenhamland System see Wiener, J H (ed.), *Great Britain, The Lion at Home: A Documentary History of Domestic Policy, Volume I*, (New York, 1983), pp. 278-79. The scheme was called the Speenhamland System after the village in Berkshire where the justices sat when making the original decision.

49 Lees, L H, *The Solidarities of Strangers: The English Poor Laws and the People, 1700 to 1948*, (Cambridge, 1998), pp. 67, 103-4; *see also:* Boyer, G R, *An Economic History of the English Poor Law, 1750 to 1850*, (Cambridge, 1990).

50 The Arithmeticke Project was the first collaborative project undertaken by FACHRS and was designed to examine the diffusion of Hindu-Arabic numerals in replacing Roman numerals in historical documents. See Wardley, P and White, P, 'The Arithmeticke Project: a collaborative research study of the diffusion of Hindu-Arabic numerals,' in *Family and Community History*, (2003), 6:1 pp. 5-18.

II. SWING RIOTS IN SURREY

Judy Hill and Mary James

During the Napoleonic wars agriculture experienced a boom but this ended with the cessation of hostilities, prices fell and agriculture suffered. Unemployment among farm workers increased; moreover the situation was exacerbated with the demobilisation of approximately 250,000 men from the armed forces who swamped the rural market already gutted with excess labour. 'By 1816 the balmy days of wartime agricultural prosperity were over, to be replaced by some years of rent abatements, arrears and short leases, and the sort of discontent expressed in the south by the labourers disturbances of 1816 and 1830-1.'[1]

In Surrey rural under-employment was the norm except perhaps at the height of the harvest. Parish accounts clearly show full employment was only achieved during the months of August and September. This was recognised in a House of Lords statement:

> Because arable farming is by nature rhythmic in that its needs for labour vary at different times of the year, it was unable to offer stable employment outside planting and harvest times [...] The result was seasonal unemployment and underemployment at low wages.[2]

The burden of unemployment was concentrated in the winter months. 'During the winter months the anxieties of labourers were at their peak. Anything which deprived them of work at that time was likely to be regarded with hostility.'[3] This explains the hostility to the threshing machines that replaced manual threshing, the traditional winter labour for the months November to January. William Cobbett commented that labourers 'know that one threshing machine takes wages from ten men'.[4] A writer from Norwich wrote:

> farmers will upon reflection recognise the expediency of abolishing that labour supplanting engine the threshing machine. That they have always excited a feeling of exasperation among the peasantry [...] by the disuse of threshing machines more valuable property may be saved from destruction the necessitous labourer presented with the mean of employments.[5]

As E L Jones noted 'the conjunction of a growing population with little alternative to agricultural work and the introduction of the threshing machine - much the earliest machine of any importance in English farming - resulted in chronic winter unemployment and distress in southern England during the nineteenth century.'[6]

Surrey farming was generally backward in adopting advances in technical improvements. William Stevenson in 1813 spoke of old-fashioned ploughing methods and the lack of modern farm buildings in Surrey. He also noted that some threshing machines were being used in Surrey but predominately in the Guildford and Godalming area.[7] In Surrey in November 1830 at the time of the rural unrest it was reported in the press:

> there is scarcely a farmer in the neighbourhood employing a machine
> to whom rumour has not served a threatening notice.[8] In the vicinity of
> Colnbrook 'several farmers in the neighbourhood have removed their
> threshing machines from their premises',[9]

and according to G Smallpiece, farmers in the neighbourhoods of Cobham and Guildford had broken their threshing machines before 'the rioting took place to prevent visits of machine-breakers'.[10] On the other hand the *Chronicle's* Chertsey correspondent reported:

> there is not a single instance of a threshing machine ever having been
> used by any gentleman or farmer in the parish.[11]

It must be recognised even in regions like Surrey where the threshing machine was of no serious significance, the threshing machine had become a symbol of the poor agricultural worker's misery and a focal point for dissatisfaction rather than a major cause of it.[12]

AGRICULTURAL DEPRESSION

The rising in Surrey took place against the background of the increasing pauperisation of labourers. This is evident from the increasing demands for poor relief made to the overseers of the poor. After 1827 there was a succession of bad harvests and especially a very severe winter of 1829 to 1830, 'the snow was already on the barn in early October'.[13] The summer of 1830 was wet and cold and the harvest poor. Parishes were finding it near impossible to provide relief for the increase in unemployed able-bodied workers. In 1820s the 'downward pressure on wages was relentless reflecting the cancer of under and unemployment'.[14]

In 1829 a petition was presented to the House of Commons from inhabitants in Middlesex and Surrey 'deeply affected with the prevalence of national distress especially the alarms privations of the industrious classes of the community'.[15] A number of select committees on agriculture met in 1820, 1821, 1822, 1833 and 1836. The loudest representations were made by arable farmers and landowners in the south-east, confirming the continuation of an agricultural depression. The fact that so many select committees were called, clearly indicates that the attempts of farmers to meet the difficulties of the agricultural depression were not successful. In 1833 George Smallpiece reported on Surrey to the Select

Committee on Agriculture 'near Guildford at the time the worst class of labourer were paid 1s a day the best 1d or 2d more. The lack of long-term hiring for jobs, local farmers preferred to hire for the job and would generally not hire for a longer period than the harvest time'.[16] This appears to be a growing trend. In 1794 in Surrey it had been reported, 'it is daily becoming the practice to do as much by the piece as possible'.[17] After 1795, as a result of high wartime food prices and a surplus of labour, farmers were encouraged to a greater extent than before to employ labourers for wages. Farmers were abandoning the practice of boarding their labourers in their own houses and farmers were also less likely to pay in kind. As J P D Dunbabin notes 'the agricultural labourers were therefore no longer shielded from price fluctuations except perhaps through the Poor Law'.[18] The growing dependence on wage labour left the rural agricultural labourer competing for employment in an overcrowded labour market and vulnerable to agricultural depression, technical improvements in farming and higher prices. In the south earnings of agricultural labourers were 'being reduced below subsistence level by the fact that population was growing at a faster rate than the expanding agrarian economy could absorb'.[19] There was a growing disaffection among the poor, as the image of a paternalistic and deferential society was more of myth by 1830.

> The reality was often an oppressed and resentful class of labourers ill
> paid under employed and unable to escape the controlled environment
> of rural life for the anonymity and freedom of the town.[20]

The south of England rural labourer should have been ideal for recruitment for the industrial towns of the north of England, 'the rural labourer's tragedy was that he remained immobile [...] the rural labourers were poor because they were numerous'.[21]

Many factors were suggested at the time as contributing to the increasing hardship endured by the agricultural labourer. In Surrey on 1 September 1830 Henry Drummond of Albury Park wrote to Viscount Melbourne concerning the unrest in the southern counties, pointing out that he did not think the provincial magistrates could:

> put an end to the disaffection which prevails [...] except such as tend to
> the extinction of the public debt or in the meantime to the shifting of
> the pressure of taxation from the lower to the higher classes.[22]

Henry Drummond wrote to William Bray of Shere on 25 September 1830, attributing the high price of cottage rents and:

> the obstruction that is thrown in the way of erecting dwellings and the
> refusal of farmers to let them have small of that very land which the
> farmers say they cannot profitably cultivate,[23]

as another reason for the unrest. It was reported in the *Windsor and Eton Express* 'that the premises of bailiffs and overseers are chiefly attacked or menaced'[24] because large farms required a bailiff and this expense was seen as attributing to a rise in the price of produce.

The article pointed out 'the farmer ought to manage his own land and be with his labourers himself'.[25] It criticised a landlord who took a farm 'for amusement', a reference to gentlemen farmers who were blamed for bringing desolation to the countryside. An editorial in the *Herald* urged a change of policy: 'the reduction of the national taxes of rents and tithes and above all parliamentary reform. These measures and no other than these measures [...] will save our beloved country from a convulsion'.[26] The *Chronicle* also advocated economic remedies demanding the removal of taxes on essential commodities and the repeal of the malt tax.[27] A few weeks earlier the *Herald* on 20 November had offered another solution to the unrest, namely finding jobs for the labourers. 'The great panacea for the present distress of the agricultural poor is to be found in giving them employment and from no other source can permanent benefit arise.'[28]

This sentiment was not mirrored at a meeting between the Lord Lieutenant, Lord Arden, and sixty-three of the magistrates for Surrey who met at the Spread Eagle Inn in Epsom on 20 November 1830. They reported that if the 'late diabolical proceedings of incendiaries' continued and the large meetings of people 'assembled together under pretence of demanding increase in wages and a reduction of rent and tithes they will be prosecuted'.[29] Although sympathy was expressed 'with the sufferings which the circumstances of the times may have imposed on many of the working classes of society',[30] no additional measures were proposed to alleviate the suffering. At the same time it is evident the magistrates were alarmed by the disturbances in the county. The meeting recommended that all magistrates swear in special constables to preserve law and order on the occasion of meetings concerned with wages, rents and tithes. The swearing in of special constables was seen as necessary because, as there was a relatively small number of troops available, local magistrates were forced to depend on various expedients to deal with the problem. Press reporters were refused admittance to the meeting for 'it was hinted that the magistrates might have communications to make among themselves respecting the state of the county, of a character too alarming to make a disclosure prudent'.[31]

UNDER-EMPLOYMENT AND INADEQUATE WAGES

For the labourers it was a rising against unemployment and the abuses of the poor laws that seemed unable to provide sufficient relief. William Cobbett had warned that the agricultural depression with its subsequent under-employment and inadequate wages would cause problems. Thousands of agricultural labourers 'ended up in parish employ, subject to penny-pinching dictatorial vestries'.[32]   William Cobbett wrote of the hardship endured by the agricultural labourer in November 1830. 'The great and general cause is the extreme poverty of the working people; or in other words the starving state in which they are in'.[33] By the mid-1820s William Cobbett began to prophesy a major rural rebellion and by 1828 he was dating it to the winter of 1830/31, insisting that his readers recognise that the unrest was not a recent phenomenon but the result of long standing grievances. I Dyck identified the labourers' grievances as the demands for higher wages, the destruction of threshing machines, an end to hired overseers, direct access to the land, reform of Parliament and the granting of poor relief as a right and not as a privilege.[34] After the poor harvest of 1829 cold, hunger and lack of work formed the lot for the labourers during the winter and early spring of 1829/30 and the expectation of another hard winter was a very grim prospect. Cobbett also identified employment of paupers in parish-sponsored work schemes as degrading and produced a petition against the use of labourers as 'beasts of burden'.[35] In rural Surrey thousands of agricultural labourers became dependent on outwork provided by the parish. There were others, like Cobbett, who recognised the inadequacy of outwork provided in the parishes for a small remuneration. Reverend J Clementin wrote to Sir Robert Peel on 11 November 1830 pointing out those who are compelled:

> work on the highways or other slavish employments during the winter season for half the necessary wages [...] have come to the determination of not submitting to this kind of oppression any longer.[36]

C Collins of Sittingbourne agreed:

> the labourer although entitled to a just return for the sweat of his brow has been in too many cases denied his due and beaten down to the lowest fraction.[37]

A poster distributed in 1830 agreed with these sentiments pointing out to farmers inadequate wages were being paid. 'The labourer is worthy of his hire. I do not call upon you to listen to wild and unreasonable demands but I recommend you at least to follow the example of those farmers who deal justly by their labourers.'[38] Agricultural writer Mr Poulett Scrope echoed this sentiment and stressed 'wages and parish allowance must be immediately raised'.[39] On 1 December 1830 four months after the start of the unrest in Surrey, Henry Drummond of Albury warned Lord Melbourne that:

> the people are quiet now because [...] they have gained their object of a general increase of the means of subsistence either from their employers or from the overseers [...] His Majesty will have been greatly misinformed if he has been advised that the present is a passing or temporary state of things or that any measures will subdue it except such as tend to extinctions of the public debt or in the meantime to the shifting of pressure of taxation from the lower to the higher classes.[40]

He was right. The outbreaks of violence in Surrey would continue spasmodically until the winter of 1832. The initial response of the parishes to increase relief payments with the expectation that it would bring order to the parishes did not happen. In 1830 Nassau Senior argued that wages for the labourer:

> are not a matter of contract but a matter of right that they depended not on the value of the labourer's services, but on the extent of his wants or his expectations.[41]

In 1830 the Government of the Duke of Wellington was not sympathetic to this plea. In fact the Government denied the existence of long-term agricultural distress, only accepting the temporary nature of distress resulting from several bad seasons. On 4 February the Lord Chancellor read to both Houses of Parliament an address from the King:

> His Majesty feels assured that you will concur with him in assigning to
> the effect of unfavourable seasons and to the operation of other causes
> which are beyond the reach of legislative control or remedy'.[42]

On the other hand Nassau Senior in his three lectures on the state of wages and the causes and remedies of the present disturbance ascribed the Swing riots to the maladministration of the poor law system in 1830. This view was later reflected in the Poor Law Report condemned as 'the report with its rigged evidence showing that Swing's violence seems to have arisen from an idea that all the privations arose from the cupidity or fraud of the Poor Law officials'.[43]

In Surrey ratepayers were reluctant to increase the payment of poor relief: 'with labour and other costs pared to the bone attempts were made to reduce or merely contain escalating poor relief expenditure'.[44] Local Surrey landowners and farmers emphasised their own hardships as a result of the post-1815 agricultural depression and the level of taxation that includes the burden of the poor rate and, where appropriate, the payment of tithes. According to Professor Armstrong rents and farm profits absorbed together some 61-66% of the total income from farming, leaving only about a third to be shared among the increasing numbers of labourers.[45] In some Surrey parishes it is possible to trace from the early 1820s the increasing problems of collecting the poor rate. In Bletchingley in October 1823, the assembled vestry threatened that non-payers of rates would be prosecuted.[46] The following year, as a result of a shortfall in rate collection, the clerk recorded in the vestry minutes that 'it would be expedient to borrow the sum of £200 towards defraying the expenses of the parish for the current year'.[47] In Surrey the larger villages and towns experienced the greatest difficulty in collecting the due rates. G E Mingay believes there was a widening gap between rich and poor and he suggests that:

> it arose in part from the greatly increased numbers of poor who in larger
> villages created a burden which made it impossible for the old kind of
> private, personal paternalism to continue.[48]

This is evident in Dorking, a large market town, with a population of 4,711 in 1831.[49] In the winter of 1822/23 so 'severe has been the pressure of the rates throughout the past winter season arising out of numerous hands for whom it has been impossible to find any kind of profitable employment'.[50]

In Dorking by the late 1820s it was reported that in the winter months there were large numbers of men unemployed: 'it was a common occurrence to witness the pitiable spectacle of large groups of unemployed mechanics and other workmen standing involuntarily idle'.[51]

In many parishes, especially the more populous ones, the annually elected overseers of the poor employed paid assistant overseers to administer the poor relief system. It was hoped this paid official would maintain more accurate accounts and increase efficiency in the collection of the rates. One of the key roles of the assistant overseer was the responsibility for inspecting the individual circumstances of claimants, always with the view to 'balancing the books'. They were seen as professional men whose main function was to reduce the parish poor rate and to administer the poor relief efficiently. As a result assistant overseers often found themselves targets of hatred because they stood between the labouring poor, the farmers and the wealthier rural residents.

THE OUTBREAK OF VIOLENCE

The 1830 outbreaks of violence took the form of machine breaking, arson attacks, wage riots and threatening letters, which were used to exert pressure on landowners to raise wages and get rid of threshing machines. The Swing riots were confined to the arable farming areas of the south and east of England, where real wages were at their lowest. In the north of England the position of the labourer was far better. Wage rates were higher and it was common for men to combine agricultural labour with quarrying, fishing, cockle gathering and canal excavation.[52] The disturbances in Surrey were neither so widespread nor were they marked with the same intensity of discontent which characterised the disturbances in Kent and Sussex. At their meeting at the Spread Eagle Inn the magistrates of Surrey had declared:

> the districts of Woking and Blackheath and most of those on the borders
> of Sussex and Hampshire are the chief scenes of discontent and outrage.[53]

It must be remembered this was November 1830 and the disturbances continued into 1832. At the same time it is important not to underestimate the unrest in the county. It can be seen from using Home Office data and newspaper articles there were fifty-eight reported incidents of disturbances in Surrey (Table II.I), between the years 1830 and 1832, considerably more than the twenty-nine incidents cited by Hobsbawm and Rudé.[54] The authors of *Captain Swing* did recognise that research into local records might revise in detail their story and this has proved to be the case. It must also be recognised it is difficult to categorically state the exact number of disturbances as many incidents went unreported. This can be illustrated by the experience of farmer Thompson, who resided near Oxted, in October 1830 and who had all his stock of 'hay, potatoes and other articles totally destroyed'.[55] It was reported at the time:

> it appeared there had been 7 or 8 earlier attempts before incendiaries
> succeeded in their object of burning the outhouses and property they
> contained.[56]

TABLE II.I

Incidents of protest in Surrey, 1830-1832

Month	Date	Day	Parish	Offence	Comment	Premises	Victim	Protester	Year
Aug	03/08	Tues	Caterham	A	HO 52/10 letter from Pinder Simpson *The Times* 18/4/31 10/8/31	Portley Farm - farm buildings	Gower		1830
Oct	22.10	Fri	Oxted	A X 2	23/10/30 *The Times*	Farms; 7 or 8 attempts before on Thompson's farm	Thompson and Ford	Blakey	1830
Nov	4/11	Thur	Easterham nr Godstone	A	*Rochester Gazette* 9/11/30	Stacks of hay and straw	Farmer		1830
Nov	5/11	Fri	Caterham	A	*The Times* 6/11/30 18/11/30 HO 52/10 letter Pinder Simpson CC 9/11/30 *Rochester Gazette* 9/11/30	Caterham Lodge 2 stacks of wheat stacks of barley and oats - 3 barns and threshed quantity of wheat 3 stacks of hay (produce 400 acres)	Simpson Pinder occupier (owned Day Esq)		1830
Nov	11/11	Thur	Byfleet	A	HO 52/10				1830
Nov	11/11	Thur	Cobham	A	HO 52/10				1830
Nov	11/11	Thur	Coombe	A	HO 52/10	Coombe Wood Kingston			1830
Nov	11/11	Thur	Ditton	A	HO 52/10	Farm			1830
Nov	11-12/11	Thur	Englefield Green	A	15 Nov *The Times* from *Windsor Express* HO 52/10 CC 16/11 *Maidstone Journal* 16/11/30	Barn and rick 50 loads of hay damaged	Rt Hon Freemantle William		1830

TABLE II.I (contd)

Month	Date	Day	Parish	Offence	Comment	Premises	Victim	Protester	Year
Nov	11/11	Thur	Merton	A	HO 52/10	Farm			1830
Nov	12/11	Thur	Epsom	L	Assi 94/2070 Threatening letter	To burn outhouses and blow up greenhouses	Charles James and Richard Young nurserymen	Sarah Bird	1830
Nov	13/11	Sat	Abinger	A	16/11/30 CC; VCH p. 429 Vol 1; HO 52/10	Hayrick fire	Mr Elkins		1830
Nov	14/11	Sun	Albury	A	16 Nov *The Times* and CC; 18/11/30 *The Times* 20/11/30 *Political Register*; 3/1/31 and 11/1/31 *The Times*; HO 52/15	15 quarters of wheat destroyed and wagon tilt cut in pieces	James Franks occupier (Owner John Cooke)	James Warner	1830
Nov	14/11	Sun	Albury	S	3/1/1831; 11/1/31 *The Times*; HO 52/15; *Political Register* 20/11/30; *The Times* 16/11/30 and 18/11/30	Mill	James Franks overseer		1830
Nov	14/11	Sun	Capel	A	VCH p. 429 Vol 1	Trouts Farm			1830
Nov	15/11	Mon	Egham	L	15/11 *The Times* reported in *Windsor Express*	Threatening letters to farms with 'machines'			1830
Nov	15/11	Mon	Ockley	A	Assi 94/2070	Stack of hay burnt	Thomas Wenham employer	James Bravery	1830
Nov	16/11	Tues	Egham	A	19/11/30 *The Times*	Egham			1830
Nov	16/11	Tues	Ditton/ Molesey	A	19/11/30 *The Times*	Ditton/Molesey			1830
Nov	12-17/11		Bagshot	A	19/11 *The Times*	Fires nearly every night			1830

TABLE II.I (contd)

l

Month	Date	Day	Parish	Offence	Comment	Premises	Victim	Protester	Year
Nov	19/11	Fri	Chiddingfold	RF	11/12/30 *The Times*	80 men assembled demand rise parish wages	William White gamekeeper and overlooker poor	James Gill plus large mob	1830
Nov	19/11	Fri	Wotton	RT	HO 52/10; HO 44/22	Mr Crawford Magistrate requesting military help	Rev J E Boscowen		1830
Nov	19/11	Fri	Woking	RT	VCH p. 429 Vol 1	Riot			1830
Nov	20/11	Sat	Norwood	A	24/11 *The Times*	Fire	Mr Bennett		1830
Nov	20/11	Sat	Reigate	A	HO 52/10	Barn	Mr Neal		1830
Nov	22/11	Mon	Leigh	R	HO 52/10 Assi 94/2070 FF39	80+ riot		William Wilkins and William Fisher charged	1830
Nov	22/11	Mon	Dorking	RF	HO 52/10; VCH p. 429 Vol 1; CC 27/11/30 *Brighton Gazette* 25/11/30 Assi 94/2070	High Street, Dorking Red Lion Inn riot		James Hubbard William Taylor Samuel Croucher James Penfold William Buckland and James Ireland charged	1830
Nov	23/11	Tues	Guildford area	A	HO 52/15 Letter from Lord Arden	2 farms and 5 fires last 3 weeks			1830
Nov	25/11	Thur	Limpsfield	L	HO 52/10	100 labourers assembled Magistrate dispersed crowd			1830
Nov	25/11	Thur	Egham	A	Hobsbawm and Rudé	Busby Main	Burton		1830

TABLE II.I (contd)

Month	Date	Day	Parish	Offence	Comment	Premises	Victim	Protester	Year
Nov	28/11	Sun	Banstead	A	1/12/30 CC and BH 4/12/30; HO 52/10; The Times 1/12/30; VCH p. 429		Turner		1830
Nov	28/11	Sun	Epsom	A	VCH reports 2 fires p.429 Vol 1; HO 52/10	Haystack			1830
Nov	28/11	Sun	Wimbledon	An attempt	29/11/30 The Times		Mr Hampton farmer		1830
Nov			Chessington	L	Filed Nov no date HO 52/10				1830
Dec	6/12	Mon	Oxshott	A	Hobsbawm and Rudé		Prince Leopold		1830
Dec	12/12	Sun	Cheam	A	Hobsbawm and Rudé Assi 31/26		Tauton William Pyle	Ritchie James	1830
Dec	12/12	Sun	Kingston	L	HO 52/10	Chessington Lodge	Tirry		1830
Dec	18/12		Oxted	A	HO 52/10	Stack of faggots on fire	Mr Palmer		1830
Dec	19/12		Woldingham	A	HO 52/10	Straw stack threshed by machine destroyed	Mr Dartnell		1830
	1830		Kingston	L	SHC Stamp News	Southborough Lodge	Mrs Langley		1830
	1830		Morden	L	Assi 94/2100	Letter threatening to destroy barn and stacks	William Asin	John Longhurst	1830
Sept	22/9	Thur	Limpsfield	A	CC 27/9	12 acres peas, beans and hops destroyed	Benjamin Storr (Steer)		1831
Oct	1/10	Sat	Virginia Water	A	CC 4/10	Clock House	Bowyer		1831
Nov	1/11	Tues	Hook nr Kingston	A	CH and WA 5/11	4 ricks of corn 2 ricks of hay and a shed containing straw	R Blair		1831

TABLE II.1 (contd)

Month	Date	Day	Parish	Offence	Comment	Premises	Victim	Protester	Year
Nov	14/11	Sat	Guildford	A	CC 15/11/31	Rick of oats produce of 22 acres	Daws		1831
Nov	19/11	Sat	Cheam (Lower)	A	CC 22/11/31	Stack of straw and bean haulm	Willis		1831
Nov	22/11	Tue	Albury	A	CC 29/11/31	Rick of oats	Whitburn		1831
Nov	22/11	Tue	Shere	A	CC 29/11	Barley rick	Baker		1831
Nov	23/11	Tue	Bagshot	A	HO 52/20 Letter request pardon if evidence given.	Oat rick burnt			1831
Mar	27/3		Farnham	A and L	HO 52/20	Arson 2 weeks later threatening letter Furze stack fired	belongs to Jack Stevens		1832
Nov	5/11		Pyrford	A	HO 52/10 Lord Arden	2 barns 10 or 11 loads of wheat straw and barley			1832
Nov	5/11		Woking	A	HO 52/20 Lord Arden Mr Maclean Poor Law report 1833 p. 579 Letter (also reference to fires 2 years previous in same parish)	40 loads of hay 15 loads of wheat and straw			1832
Nov	10/11		Crowhurst nr Godstone	A	HO 52/20	'great fire' barns of hay and corn and outbuildings			1832
Dec	19/12		Reigate	F	Assi 94/2134	House break window and demand relief	Assault Thomas Compton guardian poor	John and Joseph Laker	1832

TABLE I (contd)

Month	Date	Day	Parish	Offence	Comment	Premises	Victim	Protester	Year
Winter	1832		Shere	P	Mr Maclean Poor Law report 1833 Appendix A p. 579	Poison given to farm stock 'fat fat hogs died'	Captain Hay farmer		1832
Winter	1832		Chobham	A	Mr Maclean Poor Law report 1833 p. 579	Fire			1832
Winter	1832		Shepperton	A	Mr Maclean Poor Law report 1833 p. 579	Fire			1832
Winter	1832		Egham	A	Mr Maclean Poor Law report 1833 p. 579				1832

Key: A = incendiarism; B = machine breaking; L = anonymous threatening letters; R = ; RF = food riots; RT = tithe meeting riot; S = shooting; P = poison

HO = Home Office National Archives; CC = *County Chronicle*; CH&WA = *County Herald and Weekly Advertiser*; SHC = Surrey History Centre

VCH = Malden, H E, (1967), *Victoria County History of Surrey Vol 1*, London, Dawsons of Pall Mall

Hobsbawm, E J and Rudé, G, (1969), *Captain Swing*, London, Lawrence and Wishart

Of course, these attempts were not fully recorded and often references were made to disturbances without specific details and these incidents were then very difficult to identify clearly. A report on 19 November 1830 claimed that in the area of Bagshot:

> fires have been seen from hence almost every night during the past week. The whole neighbourhood is in great alarm.[57]

As a result fear and alarm became endemic throughout the county although not all landowners or farmers were directly affected. Writing to William Bray of Shere Henry Drummond of Albury observed:

> The rising of the labourers that is taking place throughout the southern counties of England threatens the destruction of all property. They are maddened by oppression [...] they are determined to take the law into their own hands and say they prefer being hanged or shot to continuing as they are.[58]

FIRES ACROSS SURREY

Now a more complete picture of the pattern of disturbances in Surrey has emerged. The first incident in Surrey was a fire at Portley Farm in Caterham on 3 August 1830. Fires continued to be reported throughout November and December that destroyed farm buildings and crops. There were also four incidents of riot, the most serious in Dorking on 22 November 1830. The same month a mill at Albury was attacked and shots were fired. The culprit, James Warner was convicted and hanged in January 1831. Fires continued to break out in the winter of 1831 and to a lesser extent in the winter of 1832, although there were no more reported incidents of riots. During this period of unrest threatening letters were received by some Surrey farmers threatening to destroy their farms. It is most interesting to plot where incidents of unrest occurred (Map II.i). The sparsely populated heath lands in the south-west of the county as, for example, around Blackheath - that covered 1,000 acres - Peasemarsh, Windlesham and Frimley, saw little disturbance, whereas the wealden clay districts, stretching in a thick belt from Albury eastward towards Limpsfield, witnessed much unrest. The soil in this area required drainage and thorough liming, which was expensive and beyond the reach of many farmers. The situation was made worse by the three very wet years 1829, 1830 and 1831 that:

> prevented farmers from getting on the land and caused the discontinuance of manure, excessive cropping and the impoverishment, even the abandonment, of the heavier soils.[59]

Mr Thomas Drewitt reported on the wealden parishes in 1833:

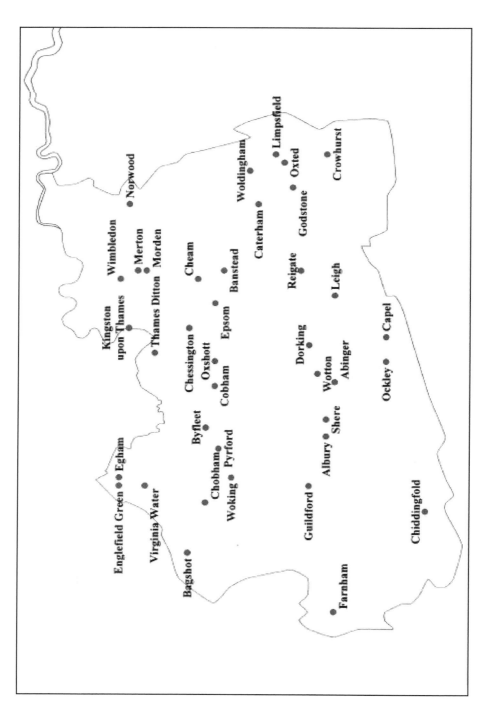

Map. II.i. Swing in Surrey

because they are more difficult of cultivation than the others; that land requires more horse labour to put into any sort of order to produce a crop, but not so much hand labour and the labour of much of the population was thrown away on the roads.[60]

George Smallpiece, Esq., gave evidence to the same committee and when asked which land he would not farm replied: 'I would not have the whole weald to farm if they would give to me'.[61] The other part of the county badly affected by unrest comprised that part of the clay lands that included the area from Woking to Wallington where arable and livestock farming were most common. Here, there had been a decrease in sheep farming as a result of sheep rot. The rot of 1830-31 'which is described as the most disastrous on record swept away two million sheep'.[62] Along with the outbreak of 1879-80,[63] these were the most serious outbreaks of the whole century. Fewer signs of unrest were apparent in the north of the county, where agricultural land was increasingly given over to dairy farming and market gardening and 'where wages were traditionally higher and employment opportunities greater'.[64]

Rick burning and incendiarism, both instruments of vengeance and intimidation, were customary ways of protesting or settling grievances in rural England. According to William Cobbett, arson was principally resorted to where labourers were too weak to force redress through overt means.[65] When a stack was set alight it invariably burnt laterally towards the centre, before erupting into a mighty conflagration. Depending on the size of the stack, it could take considerable time, on average one hour or more for the flames to burst through the stack. It was possible to ignite a number of stacks simultaneously by running fuses made of straw from the central point to each stack. The gap between the time when the stack was lit to the detection of the fire helps to explain why it was so difficult to apprehend the culprits. In fact, the culprits could be miles away or back home when the fire finally burnt through the stack.[66] Landowners may also have been reluctant to come forward with information as was reported in a letter to Melbourne. Insurance officers noted 'most individuals in country parts shrink from the duty of seeking to discover the incendiaries with the necessary determination and perseverance lest by rendering themselves conspicuous they draw their vengeance upon themselves'.[67] It was also suggested the incendiaries had been professionally trained and this is why the authorities were so unsuccessful in apprehending them. Colonel Murray suggested they were not local labourers but men well trained in chemical ignition in France.[68] Once alight and the fire had taken hold, it was extremely difficult to extinguish the flames. The fire fighting equipment was so rudimentary it would take approximately 30-40 minutes to set up the bucket chain and to get the fire engine working. Even when more than one pump was deployed, the chances of extinguishing the flames were slight. This helps to explain why rick burning was one of the most feared of rural crimes. Before 1830 these were usually isolated incidents, unlike the outbreak of violence seen in southern England from November 1830 to 1832.

In Surrey the first fire occurred at Portley Farm on 2/3 August 1830, in the parish of Caterham only six miles from the Kent border. Farm buildings containing corn were destroyed and it was noted that it was the thatch of the barn housing the threshing machine that had been first set alight. There were conflicting rumours that the fire was a reprisal for the employment of Irish labourers or alternatively that it was the Irish labourers themselves who had fired the barn. To add to the mystery the previous occupant of the farm, a former businessman who was said to be highly respected in the neighbourhood, was the only suspect actually brought to trial eight months later. This is an interesting case as it is probable that not all firings in Surrey were committed by disgruntled or unemployed labourers, because the climate of protest gave cover for those who had personal motives or grudges. At the time of the fire this resident farmer at Portley Farm had been insolvent and was about to have his goods seized to pay his debts. He was brought to trial at the Surrey summer assizes of 1831 but was discharged due to lack of evidence.[69] During September and October other fires broke out in and around Godstone and Oxted. In November 1830 there were further fires across Surrey and on 5 November fires at the farm of Pinder Simpson in the parish of Caterham. The fires:

> consumed two stacks of wheat three barns a large building two or three
> stacks of barley and oats and a quantity of threshed wheat in the barns
> making the farmyard a scene of ruin.[70]

It was estimated that the produce of nearly 400 acres of land had been completely destroyed by fire. Fortunately the livestock were saved 'with the exception of a cow which was so scorched' that it had to be slaughtered.[71] The second week of November saw fires near Kingston, Byfleet, Cobham, Englefield Green, Albury, Capel, Abinger, Epsom and Merton. At Englefield Green fire engines attended a fire where a hayrick was burned but a barn was saved in spite of the hose of the fire engine being cut through.[72]

A case of arson that gained particular notoriety took place on 14 November at a flour mill in Albury. The mill contained a large stock of flour and corn that was destroyed in the early hours of the morning and it was reported that a mob stood around and made no effort to save the contents of the mill. When asked to help, some replied: 'why should we, we cannot be worse off than we are'.[73] It is not possible from other reports to verify this account of H E Malden, although in the *Herald* ten years earlier a gang known as the 'Oak Gang' had been involved in sheep stealing in the neighbourhood of Albury and Shere[74] and had committed innumerable burglaries.[75] At the time £300 was raised by subscription and a reward offered for the discovery of the offenders but no one came forward. The gang appeared still to be operating in 1832 when C H Maclean in his report on Surrey noted:

> there is an organized body of men in this parish [...] who are the terror
> of the whole neighbourhood [...]. Those belonging to the gang are
> known and are objects of universal terror.[76]

On 8 January 1831 letters were sent to the Prime Minister from the magistrates of the Guildford Bench and a magistrate from nearby Clandon stating there was evidence that other local people had been involved in the crime. The authorities were anxious to set an example of speedy conviction. Warner was convicted for setting fire to Mr Frank's mill and the execution took place on 10 January 1831, ten days after the trial. It had even been suggested that Warner be hanged on Albury Heath or Newlands Corner in order to 'introduce a salutary effect on the minds of the population'. This did not happen as Lord Melbourne was of the opinion it would not be advisable to make any change in the place of execution.[77]

The facts of the case are not totally clear but what is known is that on 14 November a letter was sent to the Home Secretary stating James Franks became 'odious to the people when he was lately the overseer of the poor'.[78] The mill was set on fire and shots were fired at one of the windows of the mill. James Warner a labourer aged thirty was tried for:

> wilfully and maliciously setting fire to a flour mill at Albury in the occupation of James Franks.[79]

James Warner had been employed by Mr Franks but had left his job. Richard Tidy, another employee, reported at the trial that Mr Franks had accused James Warner of beating his horse and James Warner had told him 'he'll get no good by it; he will get served out for'.[80] William Cobbett reported the event in his *Political Register* and it is interesting to note that, although he supported the cause of the agricultural labourer, he had no time for James Warner. He commented 'a fellow of the most determined atrocity of character'.[81] There seems to have been a great deal of bitterness towards this execution because a note was later found near the work-house in Guildford:

> Warner is murdered Franks, Drummond and Smallpiece shall die [...] I could clear him at the place, you false-swearing villain. We fired the mill. Starving and firing go together.[82]

The same night on which the paper containing the above threats was found, a gun, loaded with slugs, was fired into the bedroom of the master of the work-house at Guildford, which passed through the bedstead and partition, and lodged in the wall of the passage.[83]

Nonetheless Surrey had not seen the end of the unrest. Throughout the month of December fires continued in some parishes including Guildford, Oxted (where a stack of faggots was set on fire), Godstone and at Woldingham, where a stack of straw that reportedly may have been threshed by machine was burned on 19 December.[84] Fires continued to break out at Ockley, Woking, Cobham, Reigate, Epsom, Banstead and Bagshot. The unrest in Surrey continued and there were sporadic outbreaks of arson for the next two years. The *County Chronicle* reported fires throughout the county in 1831. In September 1831 in Limpsfield twelve acres of peas, beans and hops were destroyed and in November there were fires in Guildford, Cheam, Albury and Shere. After an oat rick was burned at a farm in Bagshot in November 1831 a subscription was raised for a reward of one hundred and fifty pounds, but two months later nobody had been arrested and a request was made to grant a pardon for anyone who would give evidence.[85] In 1832 there are fewer recorded cases of arson. In March a stack was fired in Farnham and in November in Pyrford two barns and a large quantity of wheat and barley were destroyed and the same month a 'great fire'[86] in Crowhurst. There were fires also in Woking, Egham, Chobham and Shepperton.[87]

STRANGERS AND REVOLUTIONARY AGENTS AT WORK IN THE COUNTY

During the riots there was a growing suspicion that strangers or revolutionary agents were at work in the county. *The Times* newspaper reported on 23 October 1830 that:

> the employment of threshing machines and also of strangers in that part
> of Surrey (i.e. Oxted) as well as Kent has given rise to much discontent
> among the labourers in these places.[88]

Once the disturbances erupted it was a commonly held view among members of the establishment, both Whig and Tory, that the fires did not originate with the distress of the farm labourers but were being instigated by foreigners. They believed that the unrest was caused either by the 'work of stranger smugglers or foreigners or mysterious gentlemen[89] in gigs driving furiously about the country led by *Captain Swing* scattering fire-balls and devastation'. Both Peel and Lord Grey made this claim that foreigners were the cause of the problem. The Duke of Wellington stated:

> the operations of the conspirators in this country are conducted by
> Englishmen but that the original focus is in Paris.[90]

He traced the financial backing of the Swing rioters to the money of the Paris-based *Société Propagande*. It was also reported:

> that people go about the county on horseback with the appearance of
> gentry making inquiries of the country people about the character of
> their neighbours and informing them that a revolution and war is going
> to break out.[91]

The association of the riots with strangers and foreigners is evident in much of the literature produced at the time. From Egham there were numerous addresses warning against 'the artful and wicked designs of foreigners and strangers'.[92] One read:

> Awake from your trance! The enemies of England are at work actively
> to ruin us. Hordes of Frenchmen are employed doing the deed of
> incendiaries and inciting to acts of tumult [...]. The fires of Normandy
> are revived in Kent are spreading to Sussex and Surrey [...] shall the
> conqueror of the Nile of Trafalgar and Waterloo be tricked by the arts
> and deceits of Frenchmen.[93]

Fears were always heightened when strangers appeared in a neighbourhood. When a labourer named Gasson was robbed in Reigate on 8 October 1830 he reported that the robber told him 'you have been very quiet in these parts but we shall give you a burn before the winter is out and they mentioned the names of several of the principal landowners and farmers in the neighbourhood'.[94]

After two cases of arson in Oxted in October 1830 corn, hay and potatoes were destroyed at two farms. *The Times* reported on the prevailing opinion that an 'organised gang of fellows' was responsible. A man described as a 'wanderer' was taken into custody following the fires. He denied setting the fires, but was said to have had in his possession ammunition, fire-making equipment, a book of instructions on explosives and papers foreseeing revolution.[95] On 23 November 1830 the inhabitants of Staines were in a great state of anxiety and alarm. A man in the street had been stopped and three men had been enquiring after Mr South, a farmer, and informed the man: 'tell Mr South his premises will be on fire in half an hour'.[96] There was a heightened sense of fear across the county at the end of November 1830 as reports circulated that two or three 'gentlemen, well dressed' strangers on horseback were travelling through the county making inquiries as to the names of farmers, whether they used threshing machines, their attitude to the labourers and the wages they paid.[97] Some of the visitors appeared to be very threatening. At Teddington on 10 November 1830 a gentleman on horseback was reported to have said 'he knew that there was somebody of the name of Camphill who had machinery on his farm and he would advise him to take care'.[98] Some descriptions of the 'strangers' were very detailed. Reports from the Kingston fair of November 1830 described a gentleman with a 'cockade in his hat [...] rides a black horse' and another man appeared as his servant riding a black mare 'appears to be about the same age thirty dressed in dark clothes'.[99] Now all rural communities were in a state of constant alert and various sightings of strangers were reported. The son of the owner of Abinger Hall wrote to his father at his London residence:

> people go about the county on horseback with the appearance of gentry making enquiries of the country people about the character of their neighbours and informing them that a revolution and a war is going to break out.[100]

Henry Drummond wrote to Lord Melbourne after James Warner's execution enclosing a statement from a fellow prisoner, Comber, stating that Warner was 'instigated to this deed by a stranger who paid him money'[101] for setting fire to the mill at Albury. The stranger had also paid for several other fires at Tonbridge, Horsham and Stanmore.[102] This was not proved, although Henry Drummond had suggested a plan whereby Comber would try and infiltrate the gang thought responsible by Comber setting fire to one of Drummond's own hay stacks.[103] This plan was not supported by Melbourne who believed it would only encourage false accusations.[104] In the *County Chronicle*, it was reported 'the village of Chobham was thrown into considerable consternation by seven sturdy beggars making their appearance'.[105] They were locked in the work-house overnight but after being questioned were released. The following comment clearly illustrates the unease felt by many:

> it is evident that beggars assume greater boldness than usual knowing that a dread or fear pervades the minds of people [...] at this present

alarming time it would be well for parishes to know that all their
labourers are at home and not leave them unemployed to perambulate
the country.[106]

Many observers were convinced that the incendiaries had no connection with the local
population. In Egham, a householders' meeting declared that the fires in Surrey 'did not
originate in any ill spirit among the inhabitants but had been the work of distant and foreign
incendiaries'.[107] Maurice Bernays, an English tutor living in France at the time of the riots,
wrote to Lord Melbourne confirming he believed there was a connection between the
revolution in France and the riots in England as the means of destruction was identical. He
had also heard: 'a band of incendiaries now under protection in France have declared that
they were told to be sent *au pays du anglais*',[108] although this was never confirmed. One
apparent characteristic of the reports written at the time was to stress the innocence of the
local population. The inference was that outsiders, men from London or foreigners,
instigated the attacks. It seemed more acceptable to attribute these attacks to foreigners or
strangers. It was difficult for farmers to accept their own labourers could have been involved
in burning their crops for it broke the bond between the labourer and his master. Pinder
Simpson wrote to the Home Secretary confirming that he paid his labourers good wages and
that he neither employed strangers in preference to Caterham men nor had he ever had a
threshing machine. He stressed in the letter:

> I have for many years back, constantly employed more of our men than
> my farm required, for the sake of avoiding pauperism and have always
> given full wages, varying from 12s to 15s per week according to their
> abilities.[109]

The Times reported after the fire at Caterham Lodge farm in November 1830 that 'it
is satisfactory to know that labouring people evinced every disposition to arrest the progress
of the flames'.[110] Pinder Simpson, wrote an open letter to 'his brother farmer, workmen and
neighbours'[111] thanking them for their exertions. G Ruthorn, a Bow Street officer, was sent
to Caterham but was unable to identify the offenders. The magistrates of Reigate were not so
convinced that the local people were completely innocent of involvement in the arson attacks
but at the same time they believed outsiders must have instigated them. They wrote to the
Home Secretary on 19 October 1830 confirming an organised group must have come from
London:

> stirring up the labouring classes throughout the county to acts of
> insubordination and that the destruction of farming stock by fire which
> is now becoming so prevalent.[112]

It could be argued that the labourers were driven to protest because they felt landowners and
farmers were not doing enough to relieve their hardship and so the bond was already broken.

Hobsbawm and Rudé commented they identified all these wild rumours of Captain Swing as a Jacobin agent, a papist or a Methodist and rumours of mysterious men travelling through the countryside in gigs stirring up the labourers as 'derived only from imagination'.[113] The poet, John Clare, published a poem in 1830 *The Hue and Cry: A Tale of the Times* and it has been suggested that because of its political content it was published without Clare's name.[114] It satirised the wild rumours of mysterious men riding through the countryside and stirring up discontent.

> *Some said it was Cobbett, some said it was Paine,*
> *Some went into France to Voltaire*
> *And when they got there, why they got back again*
> *To discover that nothing was there.*
> *Some rummaged old sermons, some printed new tracts*
> *And handbills like messengers ran.*
> *Conjectures were many, but few were the facts*
> *As to who was the crooked old man.*[115]

At the same time there were those who were prepared to openly admit:

> A mysterious kind of veil has been thrown over the guilty transactions. They are Frenchmen or fiends that have set fire to English barns and hay ricks in a blaze! What trash! The barns and the agricultural objects are set fire by clownish men who are in a state of starvation who know of no other means of avenging themselves.[116]

At his trial in 1831, William Cobbett had insisted that incendiaries were not strangers but locals, incendiarism 'the most easy mode of protest to perpetrate, the least liable to detection'.[117] This is further illustrated by the fear many landowners had in their labourers' allegiance. Landowners were not totally confident of their labourers' loyalty fearing that labourers might seize weapons and threaten the local population. A letter written in December 1830 to the Home Secretary concerned the '150 to 200 pikes lying in a room at Walton Lodge'[118] and warning 'there are many discontented evil minded persons amongst the lower orders'.[119] This clearly shows that the authorities were not convinced the local inhabitants were totally innocent, nonetheless the Surrey munitions stores were never attacked and as a letter from Winchester reported 'the mob have in no case been armed except with bludgeons, iron bars and scythes'.[120] This also applied to the neighbouring county of Surrey but the fear remained.

ANONYMOUS THREATENING LETTERS

Across the county individuals received threatening letters. On 12 November 1830 it was reported that Sarah Bird, wife of John Bird of Epsom, 'knowingly wilfully and feloniously sent a letter in writing signed certain fictitious signature' to Messrs Young, Nurserymen,

Epsom, Surrey threatening to burn and destroy the outhouses.[121] She demanded, 'Messrs Young unless you rise the pay of the men and boys in your employment in less than five days your greenhouses shall be blown up into thousand pieces'.[122] She was tried and found guilty to be hanged but was later acquitted.[123] On 17 November a coachman's wife near the Rectory of Great Stanmore had refused entry to the persons knocking on her door at 9 o'clock at night and they informed her 'they were incendiaries from Kent and 400 of them were coming that night'.[124] In 1830 at a time when people feared for their lives, Mrs Langley of Kingston received an anonymous letter requesting 'to destroy your machines, second to give your men 15s a week, third to send out £10 by one of your servants down to the gate'.[125] The letter threatened that 'you will see a number of fires this week in this neighbourhood [...] for all they can put round their premises you can not prevent us from setting fire to them or any other premises we think proper to fire'. There were further threats pointing out 'we carry these little things about us that take life away without making any report and will threw fire balls without report also'.[126] A similar letter was sent to Mr Tirry, the occupier of Burnt Stub mansion, Chessington Lodge, Kingston, in December 1830, passed to the Home Office.

> Sir, you will destroy your machines and give your men fifteen shillings
> a week and send out ten pounds.[127]

It continued by threatening the owner that if he did not comply, fire-balls that had been placed around the premises would be set alight. These letters were signed 'the destroyers of machines'. It is evident many farmers and clergymen in various parts of the county received these threatening letters. Reverend Robert Lovett from Staines wrote to Lord Melbourne in December 1830 to draw his attention to the problems of discovering the authors of these anonymous letters. Lord Melbourne assured him if the culprits of the 'infamous productions'[128] were discovered he would give any assistance necessary to bring the offenders to justice.

RIOTS IN SURREY

There were several riots in Surrey but not on the scale of the disturbances experienced in Sussex and Kent. On 19 November labourers in the parishes of Wotton and Ockley assembled in order to prevent the payment of tithes (the 19th being the tithe audit day) to Reverend J E Boscawen, Rector of Wotton.[129] A similar meeting of labourers was held at Woking on 19 November and Mr Drummond, a magistrate, dispersed this meeting. On the same day in the parish of Chiddingfold over eighty men assembled and demanded an increase in parish wages and allowance and William White, overlooker of the poor, was assaulted.[130] On 19 November fearing the outbreak of a riot in the town of Dorking, the Home Secretary directed a squadron of the first regiment of the Life Guards to be sent to Dorking, to be stationed nearby ready to aid the civil powers if need be. On 22 November a mob of forty persons paraded through the town, shouting: 'Down with the tithes, bread or blood'.[131] They were mainly agricultural labourers from surrounding parishes for as the deposition of G Adams states, 'on their way to Dorking they compelled all whom they met to accompany them and threatened those who refused'.[132] The ringleaders of the rioters at Leigh and Horley were William Fisher and William Wilkins, both from Charlwood. William Fisher informed the magistrates at Reigate on 24 November that on the morning of 22 November a man professing to have come from Newdigate brought them a letter in which they were asked by the 'parish men' of Newdigate to meet them at Dorking. It seems they were threatened and coerced that they must go or else they 'must abide by the consequences'.[133] William Wilkins gave similar evidence and also spoke about the hardship of trying to maintain a family:

> We have such large families and such little pay that we can't get along. I worked six weeks for ten shillings and never had a morsel of meat but once. I have a large family of five children.[134]

The local magistrates agreed to hear the labourers' complaints at a meeting at the Red Lion public house in Dorking on 22 November. A number of local tradesmen were present at the meeting including James Penfold, Samuel Croucher, and William Buckland, carpenters who were later tried, found guilty and imprisoned at the 1831 Assizes.[135] *The Times* reported that 'respectable inhabitants were sworn in as special constables while a large mob of labourers assembled in front of the building (the Red Lion) and demanded relief'.[136] It also noted 'great numbers of the agricultural labourers kept arriving from the surrounding country [...] many of them were armed with sticks and bludgeons'.[137] William Crawford, a Dorking magistrate, came out of the meeting and informed the crowd that the meeting had been adjourned for that day. The atmosphere then became truculent and threatening. The mob of eighty or more retaliated by attacking the Red Lion Inn by throwing stones at the windows 'scarcely a single pane of glass being left in the windows where the magistrates were sitting'.[138] Finally, some rioters forced their way into the room where the meeting had taken place and refused to leave until their grievances were redressed. The magistrates were determined 'to enforce the law against all persons guilty of riotous behaviour and to swear in special constables under I Geo IV for the preservation of the peace'.[139] A magistrate read the Riot Act but the mob drowned him out. It was reported four special constables Samuel Bothwell, William Combes, W Barlett and George Dewdney were assaulted by the mob.[140] The troops were called in to restore order and five of the ringleaders were arrested. The mob at once tried to rescue them but without success for a party of Life Guards escorted the men out of town and the mob was gradually dispersed. The five arrested men examined by the magistrates declared they had taken part in the riot because low wages made it impossible to maintain their families. Later six other rioters were arrested and sent to the county gaol.[141] As a result of this disturbance in Dorking the authorities in Guildford, fearful that the rioting might spread there, increased the civil power by swearing in a number of special constables. Unfortunately it was reported, 'the magistrates could place little reliance on them'.[142] The authorities were frightened that the presence of crowds at the fair on 22 November 1830 would provoke disturbances in the town. The Second Surrey Militia in Guildford was placed at the disposal of the civil authorities[143] but no disturbances were reported in the town that day.[144] The local magistrates believed that the presence of the militia 'were the means of obviating riotous assemblies on the day of the fair'.[145]

There were further riots in Surrey and on 26 November about one hundred labourers assembled in Limpsfield and marched to a farmhouse in Oxted to demand an increase in wages. Magistrates met the protesters and they were soon quietly dispersed.[146] At the end of November Lord Arden reported that 'the insurrectionary spilt in the county has been checked by the firm and decided conduct of the magistrates and of Mr Crawford of Dorking in particular'.[147]

In Surrey there is no evidence of a plan for organised rebellion. There is the intractable problem of the uneven local distribution of the unrest. Organisation as in other southern counties was very much on a local scale and Surrey followed the pattern that affected most of south-east England as explained by J P D Dunbabin: 'Riot spread partly by rumour and partly by contagion from individual villages which operated over a radius of at most half a day's journey in each direction. And riots of this kind were all ephemeral to be measured in days rather than weeks'.[148] Why some villages and farms were affected and others not is impossible to answer categorically. It must be recognised 'a village is a subtle complex of past and present where economic and social factors come into play'.[149] Certain landlords and farmers were targeted, fire raising was usually the work of individuals and as the evidence of the subsequent trials shows, many of the people tried were motivated by a private vengeance, for example, James Warner.[150] Rioting seems to have been essentially a local phenomenon, the exceptions being the riots in Woking and Dorking, which were deliberate attempts by a radical group from Horsham to incite riot. *The Times* reported on 22 November 1830 the reply of the Woking labourers to the question about the cause of the meeting, namely, that they had been forced to meet the people from Horsham because they were afraid to disobey. It does appear a radical group based in the town of Horsham made some attempts to agitate both labourers and small farmers in the nearby parishes. Riots in Surrey seem to have been influenced by this group and maybe led by some of these radicals. James Shudi Broadwood, Esq., a large landowner, who owned the Broadwood estates, wrote to Lord Melbourne in December 1830 complaining that 'the ringleaders of the riots at Horsham had not been laid hold of'.[151] It was reported from Horsham that the mob had demanded an increase in wages and a reduction of rent and tithes. The mob wanted to release some of the prisoners confined in the county gaol in Dorking and a man in a smock frock led a group to Dorking. 'Later that day some of the mob moved onto Sussex and joined another assemblage there.'[152]

SUPPRESSION OF THE OUTRAGES

In the autumn of 1830 the Duke of Wellington's ministry seemed hesitant to commit troops to crush the unrest in Kent and Surrey. Political developments on the continent, in France and Belgium, and discontent in some English large industrial towns may have influenced the Government's policy. During the riots the Lord Lieutenant of Surrey and the magistrates kept in constant communication with the Home Secretary. On 5 November 1830 Lord Arden, the Lord Lieutenant of the county wrote to Home Secretary Peel 'it is very unpleasant to communicate events of this kind from which it seems too difficult to devise a remedy'.[153] He was concerned that the Government might not be able to provide military assistance as essential parts of muskets belonging to the local militia had been sent to the Tower of London for safe keeping. On 30 November 1830 it was reported in the *County Chronicle* the King had issued a proclamation that all civil officials would do their utmost to discover, apprehend and bring to trial all perpetrators of the unrest.[154] Lord Grey addressed Parliament and stated he was determined to suppress the outrageous activities of the labourers. 'I declare that it is my determined resolution wherever outrages are perpetuated or excesses committed to suppress them with vigour.'[155] The sixty-three magistrates for Surrey, who met at the Spread Eagle Inn in Epsom, maintained the firm line agreeing that they should 'exert themselves in their respective districts to enforce the laws and put down subordination'.[156] They also confirmed that large meetings of people would be prosecuted.[157] The presence of a military troop served as a deterrent and warning against further disorder. Twice in Surrey in November 1830 the troops were called out: first in Dorking to quell a riot and then in Guildford to prevent riot. At the time the troops were 'providing the only resource capable of policing popular disturbances'.[158] Under the jurisdiction of an Act passed in 1820 (I Geo IV Cap. 37) magistrates could appoint special constables if, on the oath of householders, it was suspected there migjt be or was an outbreak of violence or riot. As a result, by the end of November 1830 associations were being formed across Surrey, including groups at Chobham, Windlesham and Bagshot 'for the purpose of apprehending and prosecuting incendiaries and protecting the persons and properties of the neighbourhood'.[159] In Chobham it was reported between £200 and £300 was raised by subscription to establish an Association in the parish. 'Nearly two hundred of the principal inhabitants and day-labourers cheerfully volunteered their services and were sworn in as special constables.'[160] In Cranley landowners were recommended 'to have all their labourers sworn in as special constables, if they are able to do their duty: and if any refuse to be sworn in to discharge them'.[161] Special constables had also been enlisted in Woking and Wootton where they had been equipped with truncheons, rattles and staves.[162] In November 1830 in Chertsey, 103 special constables had been sworn in and 210 in Epsom.[163] It was hoped this would quell the disturbances. In December 1830 after the riots in Dorking, it was proposed in the town that a 'Dorking Constabulary Association' should be established. Bearing in mind that Dorking was a large market town with a population of 4,711[164] a large force would be needed. A constabulary force was recommended that would be divided into divisions, each division consisting of twenty men with a chief. A meeting of the Lord Lieutenant and several magistrates for Surrey on 2 December 1830 resolved that the Dorking scheme 'be recommended to the several other benches of the county with such alteration or additions as may appear to them expedient [...] it be also recommended that a part of the constabulary force be mounted'.[165] It was hoped as a result the incendiaries would be apprehended and prosecuted, although Henry Drummond of Albury Park did not believe that any 'reliance whatever can be placed upon the special constables who have been sworn in this neighbourhood'.[166] Maybe this was the reason James Shudi Broadwood, a large landowner from Capel, wrote in 1830 to the editor of the *County Chronicle* proposing the establishment of constabulary force in the county.

> I would wish the legislature to compel every occupier of land of the
> annual value or renting of £80 - 100 and upwards who each employ on
> their farms and can command a horse to be mounted special constable
> to furnish himself with a simple uniform (blue coat with red collar
> covering his other usual clothing would be sufficient) his arms to
> consist of a sabre and a pistol.[167]

The scheme was very similar to the scheme adopted in Dorking. In the same way the mounted constables were to be placed in divisions, and occupiers of lands and houses of a rentable value above the annual value of ten pounds, were to be compelled to act as special constables under chief constables. This scheme was not adopted but it is interesting to note there was a growing recognition during the Swing riots of the vulnerability of rural property from attack.

HANDBILLS AND THE PROPAGANDA CAMPAIGN

At the time of the Swing riots printed handbills were circulated throughout the county. One listed the amount of money received by peers from taxes per annum with the explanation:

> Englishmen is it to be wondered at the productive poor are found
> starving in the highways hanging and drowning themselves to get rid of
> a wretched existence while non-productive gentlemen [...] take so much
> from their hard earning.[168]

It is difficult to assess the direct effect of such a poster campaign but T Edward, Esq., of Carshalton, noted in a letter to the Home Secretary that he believed the fires were often started as a result of individual malice but 'it is certain that fires have taken place immediately in concurrence with the extensive circulation of a printed paper giving a false statement of the pensions and appointments of public men'.[169] A propaganda campaign was waged both by those hoping to incite unrest and by the Government encouraging the parishes to remain loyal. Printed handbills of an inflammatory nature were circulated. One handbill encouraged 'Englishmen' to rebel citing the disturbances in relation to the French and Belgium revolutions:

> Remember what the French and the Belgians have done! And what a
> pitiless, helpless and cowardly people we seem. One hour of true
> liberty is worth ages of slavery! Consider is it not more praiseworthy to
> meet an honourable death in defending your rights, than quietly die of
> starvation. Starvation stares while your oppressors are rolling in luxury
> and wealth.[170]

Posters were also circulated, one in October 1830 entitled 'Englishmen Read', which set out the livings of the clergy and income of peers, equating to £4,611,232, 'which will maintain 92,224 families at £50 a year each'. The poster pointed out: 'Englishmen, is it to be wondered at that the productive poor are found starving in the highways hanging and drowning themselves to get rid of a wretched existence' while certain gentlemen like the above were earning large salaries.[171] How effective this poster campaign was is difficult to judge but it is known the authorities took it extremely seriously. For example on 22 December 1830 William Cooper of Horsham was arrested for sticking up handbills in Dorking. He appeared before Mr Arbuthnot, a magistrate, and after making a statement was discharged. In his statement he explained that he distributed the handbills for Mr Steele, a grocer of Horsham. He was instructed to take one hundred handbills and distribute them in Capel, Ockley, Bear Green and Dorking and 'to put some in at every public house at Dorking Capel and Ockley'.[172] The inhabitants of Capel, Ockley and Dorking were cautioned not to be deceived by the handbills and to guard against 'these and any other attempts of designing men, to render them the dupes of misrepresentation which can have no honest purpose or intention'.[173]

In November 1830 the newly installed Whig Government of Lord Grey took more resolute action to suppress the disturbances. In November Lord Melbourne, Home Secretary, issued a proclamation offering a reward of £500 for bringing rioters and incendiaries to justice. Sir Henry Hotham, magistrate for the parish of Chertsey, requested 200 copies for distribution in the 'very large and populous'[174] parish of the king's proclamation offering rewards for the conviction of incendiaries and rioters. On 29 November 1830 a similar poster was distributed in Guildford. The posters pointed out that:

> The king has been pleased to declare that any person who shall discover
> the authors of such outrages shall be entitled to a reward of £50 for
> every such person so convicted and shall also receive His Majesty's
> pardon.

A reward of £500 was offered for persons with knowledge of 'certain wicked incendiaries (who) have destroyed by fire, corn, hay, buildings and other property' (Illustration II.a).[175] The incentive of receiving such large rewards for information did not encourage the local population of Surrey to come forward with information. The Government in turn circulated handbills stating the punishments to be meted out to convicted rioters and incendiaries.[176] In December 1830 M Reid of Thornton Heath made an application for two or three hundred handbills. The handbills were to be circulated in the hundred of Wallington. He believed extracts from various Acts of Parliament setting out the punishments to convicted rioters and incendiaries would act as a deterrent.[177] In 1830 Mr Crawford, a magistrate of Surrey, sent one handbill entitled 'Conversation between two labourers residing in the County of Sussex' to the Home Secretary. The conversation complained that labourers were poorly paid. 'We have been working all day for 8d living on bread and potatoes and as for me I can be no worse of if they won't give us any more wages.'[178] The conversation goes on to complain about indirect taxation, the taxation on sugar, tea, and tobacco, which then 'was given to people who gave nothing in exchange for it, some fine ladies and gentlemen who like to live without work and all the time they make the working class pay the present amount of taxes'.[179] The civil authorities tried to counteract this campaign as they were concerned they would 'excite discontent in the minds of the labouring classes and create dissatisfaction and ill-will towards the Government' (Illustration II.b).[180] The magistrates of Surrey in reply issued their own printed handbills. One handbill stressed that:

> The Magistrates with a view to protect the honest labourer from the mischievous designs of men, known in this case to be strangers to the county and to have no common interest with those whom they would mislead feel themselves called upon in their characters of conservators of public peace and as the true friends of the labourers amongst whom they live to warn them against the objects of these stranger.[181]

Illustration II.a. Poster, Guildford, 1830[175] (© TNA)

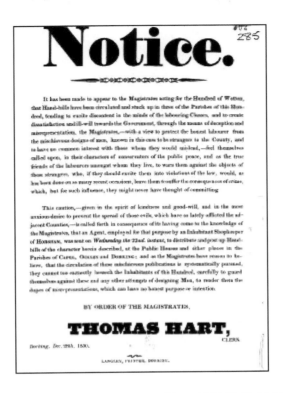

Illustration II.b. Handbill, Dorking, 1830[180] (© TNA)

The government entirely approved of local magistrates producing printed notices to try to counteract the effects of the 'mischievous handbills'[182] and Lord Melbourne wrote to Lord Arden, Lord Lieutenant of the county, in December 1830 giving his support and approval of the campaign.[183]

Another poster circulated in the Egham district and posed the question what was to be gained by burning and destroying the property of gentlemen and farmers as this would only result in ruin for the farmer and unemployment for the labourer.[184] The greatest damage to property was not by machine-breaking or riot but by arson. Hobsbawm and Rudé have estimated the damage liability to individual farmers ranged from between £100 to £800.[185] Farm owners or occupiers who were fully insured would receive compensation, but very few farmers were fully insured. A concern for farmers with the spread of incendiarism was that insurance companies were reluctant to accept new policies or renewed policies. The Sun Fire Insurance Company in October 1830 issued a directive to agents instructing them before accepting new business to enquire if the farmer had been sent any threatening letters or whether there were any disputes between the landlord and the workmen or were threshing machines kept or used on the premises.[186] There is also evidence in Surrey that some farmers were refused insurance cover, for example, Mr Earnshaw's application to insure farm buildings in Godstone was declined.[187] Other farmers were granted insurance but with large premium costs, for example, Mr Marson of Leigh and Horley was granted cover on £2,150 farm buildings and stock, 'but at a premium of 5s per cent'.[188] At the same time tracts were published 'suited to the present times' in the form of dialogues or sermons advising labourers to remain loyal to their employers. These tracts denounced the rioters as evil and included *A Dialogue on rick burning, rioting etc.*[189] in 1830, followed by *A second dialogue on rick-burning, rioting and tithes. A conversation between squire Wilson, Hughes his steward, Thomas the bailiff and Harry Brown a labourer*,[190] in 1831. It ran to twenty pages, sold for 3d a copy and was written in support of the establishment.[191] Other titles in the series included: 'A short address to plain sense on the subject of tithes; Nice pickings; A countryman's remarks on Cobbett's letter to the King; A sermon upon the sinfulness of popular commotion; An address to the misguided poor of the disturbed districts throughout the kingdom; A sermon upon the duty of a Christian subject.'

ARREST AND TRIAL

In Surrey rioters were tried at the Special Assizes. Between 1830 and 1832 the Assizes tried eighteen men for being riotously or tumultuously assembled. Six of these were found guilty and imprisoned for periods of between six to eighteen months and two were imprisoned for three months for disorder and assault. Three men were tried for arson and later acquitted and two for sending threatening letters, who were also acquitted. James Warner was the only man in Surrey to be found guilty and executed.[192] Hobsbawm and Rudé have estimated the total number of prisoners tried was 1,976.[193] Compared with the other counties affected by the riots the number of convictions in Surrey seems insignificant but it must be remembered most acts of arson went undetected and the general sense of fear felt across the county during the years 1830-32 cannot be underestimated.

NOTES

1   Macdonald, S, 'The Progress of the Early Threshing Machines', *The Agricultural History Review,* 23 (1975), 74.
2   House of Lords 58. 1830-31 *Tabular Statement* (227) VIII.321.
3   Horn, P, *The Rural World 1780 - 1850*, (Hutchinson, London, 1980), p. 88.
4   Cobbett, W, Trial King v Cobbett 7th July 1831 Court of the King's Bench Guildhall, (1831).
5   *County Chronicle,* 30 November 1830.
6   Jones, E L, *Season and Prices; the role of the weather in English agricultural history*, (Allen and Unwin, London, 1964) p. 64.
7   Stevenson, W, *A General View of the Agriculture of Surrey 1813*, The Review and Abstract County Reports to the Board of Agriculture (Thomas Wilson and Sons, York, 1818), p. 375.
8   *Windsor and Eton Express,* 15 November 1830.
9   *Ibid.*
10 Smallpiece, G, *Select Committee on Agriculture*, (P.P. 1833 V), p. 613.
11 The *Chronicle,* 13 November 1830.

12 Jones, E L, (1964) p. 64.

13 Hobsbawm and Rudé, *Captain Swing*, (Readers Union Lawrence and Wishart, London, 1969), p. 88.

14 Wells, R, 'Rural Rebels in Southern England in the 1830s' in *Artisans Peasants and Proletarians 1760 -1860,* ed. C Emsley and J Walvin (Croom Helm, London, 1985), p. 129.

15 TNA, Journal of the House of Commons (1829), Vol 85.

16 Smallpiece, G, (1833), p. 610.

17 Malcolm, W J & J, *A General View of the Agriculture of Surrey* (C Macrae, London, 1794), p. 54.

18 Dunbabin, J P D, *Rural Discontent in Nineteenth Century Britain*, (Holmes and Meier Inc, New York 1974), p. 18.

19 Fraser, D, *The Evolution of the British Welfare State*, (Macmillan, London, 1974), p. 57.

20 Royle, E, *Revolutionary Britannia? Reflections on the threat of revolution in Britain 1789 -1848*, (Manchester University Press, Manchester 2000), p. 83.

21 Evans, E J, *The Forging of the Modern State in Early Industrial Britain*, (Longman, London, 1983), p. 138.

22 TNA, HO 52/10, letter 1 September 1830.

23 SHC, Surrey/111/66 E list 46 letter, 25 September.

24 *Windsor and Eton Express,* 13 November 1830.

25 *Ibid.*

26 The *Herald,* 11 December 1830.

27 The *Chronicle*, 30 November 1830.

28 *Herald*, 20 November 1830.

29 TNA, HO 52/10, 20 November 1830.

30 *Ibid.*

31 TNA, *The Times,* 22 November 1830.

32 Wells, R (1985), p. 129.

33 FM, Cobbett, W, *Two Penny Trash*, 1 November 1830.

34 Dyck, I, 'William Cobbett and the rural radical platform', *Social History,* 18 (1985), 2.

35 Cobbett, W, *Petition to the ratepayers of Kensington,* Syndics of the Fitzwilliam Museum, Cambridge.

36 TNA, HO 44/22, 11 November 1830.

37 TNA, HO 44/22, 1 November 1830.

38 TNA, HO 44/23, 1830 Poster.

39 *County Chronicle,* 14 December 1830.

40 TNA, HO 52/10, letter 1 December 1830.

41 Dunkley, P, *The Crisis of the Old Poor Law in England 1795-1834*, (Garland Pub, NY, 1982), p. 99.

42 TNA, The Mirror of Parliament 1830 IV, 4 February, p. 2.

43 Dunkley, pp. 95-8, 106-07, 109-10; Checkland, S G and E, *The Poor Law Report 1834,* (Penguin Books, London, 1974), pp. 121, 123, 408, 410.

44 Wells, R, (1985), p. 130.

45 Armstrong, W A, 'Rural Population Growth Systems of Employment and Incomes' in *The Agrarian History of England and Wales,* ed. G E Mingay, Vol V1, Cambridge, (Cambridge University Press, Cambridge, 1989), pp. 641-721.

46 SHC. Bletchingley Vestry Accounts, P20/2/2, 8 October 1823.

47 Bletchingley, (February 1824).

48 Mingay, G E, *The Agrarian History of England and Wales Vol VI 1750 -1850,* (Cambridge University Press, Cambridge, 1989), p. 964.
49 Brayley, E W, *A History of Surrey,* (Robert Best Ede, Dorking, 1844), Appendix No 2.
50 SHC, DOM/9/3 part 2, 25 March 1823, Dorking Parish Accounts.
51 Bright, J S, *A History of Dorking,* (R J Clark, Dorking, 1884), p. 44.
52 Smallpiece, G (1833), *Report Select Committee on Agriculture,* PP Q12848 -53 North Lancashire.
53 *The Times,* 22 November 1830.
54 Hobsbawm and Rudé, (1969), Appendix 1.
55 *The Times,* 23 October 1830.
56 *Ibid.*
57 *The Times,* 19 November 1830.
58 SHC, Drummond, H, *Letter to William Bray of Shere,* Private papers of Sir Jocelyn Bray (1830).
59 Ernle Lord, *English Farming Past and Present,* (Heineman, London, 1961, 6th edn), p. 322-25.
60 TNA, Drewitt, T, *Select Committee Agricultural Evidence,* Mr Drewitt, St Nicholas Guildford, (1833), p. 478.
61 Smallpiece, G (1833), p. 612.
62 Ernle Lord, (1961 6th edn), p. 325.
63 Chambers, J D and Mingay, G E, *The Agricultural Revolution 1750 - 1880,* (B T Batsford, London, 1966),   p. 128.
64 Hobsbawm and Rudé, (1969), p. 140-60.
65 Wells, R A E, 'Mr William Cobbett, Captain Swing and King William IV', *Agricultural History Review,* 45 (1997), p. 35.
66 Holland, M, Research Swing Riots, FACHRS Conference, (2003).
67 TNA, HO 44/23, 21 December 1830, *Letter from Beaumont, B to Viscount Melbourne.*
68 TNA, HO 44/22, 20 November 1830, *Letter Colonel Murray.*
69 *The Times,* 18 April; 10 August 1831.
70 TNA, HO 52/10, 5 November 1830.
71 *County Chronicle,* 26 October 1830.
72 *The Times,* 15 November 1830.
73 Malden, H E, ed., *A History of the County Surrey Vol 1,* (Dawson, London, reprinted 1967 from 1902 edition), p. 429.
74 *The Herald,* 18 March 1820.
75 TNA, HO 44/1, *Letter from William Bray to Viscount Sidmouth,* 9 February 1820.
76 TNA, The Commissioners Report on the Poor Laws, C H Maclean, Appendix A PP579A.
77 TNA, HO 41/9, letter to G H Sumner, 8 January 1831.
78 TNA, HO 52/10, letter 14 November 1830.
79 *The Times,* 3 January 1831, report, Winter Assizes Kingston, 1 January.
80 *Ibid*, 3 January 1831.
81 FM, Cobbett, W, *Political Register,* 20 November 1830.
82 *The Times,* 10 January 1831.
83 James, M, research, Swing Riots, FACHRS Conference 2003; *The Times,* 11 January 1831.
84 TNA, HO52/10, 19 December 1830.
85 TNA, HO 52/20, 23 November 1831.
86 TNA, HO 52/20, November 1832.
87 Report of Royal Poor Law Commissioners PP, 1834, C H Maclean, Appendix A p. 579A.
88 *The Times,* 23 October 1830.

89 Hammond J L and B, *The Village Labourer 1760 -1832*, (Longmans Green and Co, London, 1920), p. 285.
90 TNA, HO 52/6, Duke of Wellington, 6 December 1830, *Letter to Lord Malmesbury*.
91 TNA, HO 52/10, 11 November 1830.
92 TNA, HO 52/6.
93 *Ibid*.
94 *The Times*, 19 October 1830.
95 *The Times*, 23 October 1830.
96 *The Times*, 23 November 1830.
97 TNA, HO 52/10, 5, 14, 19 and 20 November 1830.
98 TNA, HO 52/10, 10 November 1830.
99 TNA, HO 52/10, 14 November 1830.
100 H E Malden, (1902), p. 429.
101 Drummond H, 16 January 1831, Letter to Lord Melbourne, MP/86/75, Royal Archives, Windsor.
102 *Ibid*.
103 Drummond H, 21 January 1831, Letter to Lord Melbourne, MP/86/76, Royal Archives, Windsor.
104 Melbourne, Lord, 23 January 1831, Letter to Henry Drummond, MP/86/78, Royal Archives, Windsor.
105 *County Chronicle*, 23 November 1830.
106 *Ibid*.
107 *The Times*, 22 November 1830.
108 Bernays, M, 10 January 1831, Letter to Lord Melbourne, MP/86/12, Royal Archives, Windsor.
109 TNA, HO 52/10, Letter 5 November 1830.
110 *The Times*, 6 November 1830.
111 *The Times*, 18 November 1830.
112 TNA, HO52/10, Letter from clerks to the Justice for Reigate to Secretary State for Home Department, 19 October 1830.
113 Hobsbawm and Rudé, (1969), p. 87.
114 Bate J, *John Clare*, (Picador, London, 2003), p. 357.
115 *Ibid*.
116 *Windsor and Eton Express*, 13 November 1830.
117 FM, Cobbett W, Political Register, 22 January 1831.
118 TNA, HO 52/10, Letter 3 December 1830.
119 *Ibid*.
120 TNA, HO 57 (7), Letter 26 November 1830.
121 TNA, ASSI 94/2070 F36, Assizes 1831.
122 *Ibid*.
123 TNA, ASSI 94/2070 FF39, Assizes 1831.
124 TNA, HO 52/10, 17 November 1830.
125 SHC, *Stamp News*, 20 June - 3 July 1984, letter.
126 *Ibid*.
127 TNA, HO 52/10, Letter to Mr Tirry, December 1830.
128 TNA, HO 41/9, Letter to Reverend Robert Lovett, 23 December 1830.
129 TNA, HO 52/10, Letter, 19 November 1830.
130 *The Times*, 11 December 1830.
131 *The Times*, 3 January 1831.
132 TNA, HO 52/10, Deposition of G Adams enclosed in letter from clerk to the Justices of the Hundred of Reigate, 26 November 1830.

[133] TNA, HO 52/10, Deposition of W Fisher, 26 November 1830.

[134] TNA, HO 52/10, Deposition of W Wilkins, 26 November 1830.

[135] TNA, ASSI 94/2070 F36, Lent Assizes 1831.

[136] *The Times,* 3 January 1831.

[137] *The Times,* 27 November 1830.

[138] *Ibid.*

[139] *The Times,* 22 November 1830.

[140] TNA, ASSI 31/36 F325, Assizes 1831.

[141] *The Times,* 27 November 1830.

[142] TNA, HO 52/10, 19 November 1830.

[143] TNA, HO 41/8, 20 November 1830.

[144] TNA, HO 52/10, Letter, 29 November 1830.

[145] TNA, HO 52/10, Letter from magistrates, Guildford, 29 November 1830.

[146] TNA, HO 52/10, Letter, 26 November 1830.

[147] TNA, HO 52/10, 29 November 1830, Lord Ardley to Lord Melbourne.

[148] Dunbabin, J P D, *Rural Discontent in Nineteenth Century Britain,* (Holmes and Meir Publishers Inc, New York, 1974), p. 20.

[149] Hobsbawm and Rudé, (1969), p. 176.

[150] *The Times,* 11 January 1831.

[151] SHC, 6975/1/2, Broadwood Diary entry for 10 December 1830.

[152] *The Times,* 22 November 1830.

[153] TNA, HO 52/10, 5 November 1830.

[154] *County Chronicle,* 30 November 1830.

[155] TNA, The Mirror Of Parliament, 1830, IV p.311, 22 November 1830.

[156] *County Chronicle,* 23 November 1830.

[157] TNA, HO 52/10, 20 November 1830.

[158] Eastwood D, *Governing Rural England,* (Clarendon Press, Oxford , 1994), p. 190.

[159] *County Chronicle,* 30 November 1830.

[160] *Ibid.*

[161] *Ibid.*

[162] SHC, QS2/1/50 -51, Quarter Session 1831, Order book Epiphany Session.

[163] *Ibid.*

[164] Brayley E W, (1844).

[165] TNA, HO 52/10, The Regulations of the Dorking Constabulary, 2 December 1830.

[166] TNA, HO 52/10, Letter, Albury Park, 1 December 1830.

[167] SHC, 2185/212, Copy letter from J Shudi Broadwood to editor of *County Chronicle* (watermarked 1829 probably sent 1830).

[168] TNA, HO 48/28, October 1830.

[169] TNA, HO 44/22, 11 November 1830.

[170] TNA, HO 44/22, Handbill 'Englishmen'.

[171] TNA, HO 48/28, Poster 'Englishmen Read', October 1830.

[172] TNA, HO 52/10, 28 December 1830.

[173] *Ibid.*

[174] TNA, HO 50/10, 26 November 1830, Sir Henry Hotham.

[175] SHC, Poster, Guildford, 29 November 1830.

[176] TNA, HO 50/10, 9 December 1830, Application for hand bills, M. Reid, Hundred of Wallington.

[177] *Ibid.*

[178] TNA, HO 52/10, Enclosed in a letter of Mr Crawford, 28 December 1830.

179 *Ibid.*
180 SHC, Handbill 1830, Notice by order of the magistrates Dorking, 28 December, Langley Printer, Dorking.
181 TNA, HO 52/10, 28 December 1830.
182 TNA, HO 41/9, Letter to Lord Arden, 30 December 1830.
183 *Ibid.*
184 *Windsor and Eton Express,* 27 November 1830.
185 Hobsbawm and Rudé, (1969), p. 224.
186 Sun Fire Insurance *Minute Book,* MS 11,935, (8th October 1830), Guildhall Library, London.
187 Hand in Hand Insurance Co, MS 8666/34, (November 1830), Guildhall Library, London.
188 *Ibid.*
189 SHC, 2185/1413, 1830, *Dialogue on rick-burning, Rioting etc London,* C J G and F Rivington.
190 SHC, 2185/14/14, 1831, *A second dialogue on rick-burning rioting and tithes London,* C J G and F Rivington.
191 *Ibid.*
192 TNA, ASSI 94/2070, 1830; ASSI 94/2100, 1831; ASSI 94/2134, 1832, Assize Records.
193 Hobsbawm and Rudé, (1969), p. 262.

III. FIRE THE FARMS
When the shadow of Captain Swing reached Shropshire

James S Leach and Norman Davies

When the first research was carried out to ascertain if Swing riots took place within Shropshire, the answer appeared to be 'no'. The sources traditionally used by local historians proved unrewarding, and even the knowledgeable staff at Shropshire Records and Research Centre could not help. It was, therefore, very satisfying to slowly find fragments of information, each in turn leading to another. However, such a compilation is inadequate, unless it is possible to uncover the motives of those involved in actions and what influenced them, and to ascertain any link with activities in other parts of the country.

By far the majority of arson attacks in the rural areas of Shropshire were carried out within a few miles of Whitchurch, a market town just south of the border with Cheshire. These fires all occurred during the period 1830-32 but, since they were geographically well distant from Swing activity in southern counties of England, it was necessary to confirm that they were of the same basis.

Shropshire, situated almost equidistant between the south coast and Scottish border, is England's largest inland county, but only became generally known late in the 20th century. Even today many residents of the United Kingdom cannot describe where it is situated without reference to a map, many in the south considering it 'up north' and those north of Manchester, frequently thinking of it as part of southern England. It is a diverse county, having virtually every type of terrain except for a coastline, and its border with Wales is reflected in the language and place names on the western side.

Not only is the topography diverse but, by the late 18th century, industry was well established within the county. Shropshire had, in many ways, become a microcosm of England, a major farming area with large pockets of industry paying workers a higher rate. In the east, Coalbrookdale and other parts of the Severn Gorge had a population employed in metal industries, mineral extraction and pottery. It is suggested by Hobsbawm and Rudé that, due to the availability of high wages in the north, Swing had little influence there, or near London.[1] The presence of industry and demand for farm produce forced up the pay of agricultural workers employed within the vicinity; other parts of Shropshire were similarly affected.

On the western border of Shropshire and extending down to the southern hills, the pastoral activity concentrated on sheep. Cereal production in Shropshire was, at that time, in small pockets, except for the Severn Valley and the eastern plain, which matches land of a similar character in adjacent Staffordshire. In the area of Whitchurch the Cheshire Plain merges into the flat lands of north Shropshire, an area that then extends south and south-east towards Shrewsbury and Wellington, after which it becomes more undulating. Although at the beginning of the 19th century the northern area was predominantly pastureland, a not insignificant amount of cereals appears also to have been grown. The presence of the latest machinery, and also traditional winnowing equipment, confirms that enough cereals were grown to make the investment worthwhile in the area between Shrewsbury and Whitchurch. Advertisements in the weekly *Shrewsbury Chronicle* of farm sales during the early part of 1831, give an indication of mechanisation at that time. It is interesting that, although threshing machines were a relatively new invention, they appear in quite a number of sales (Appendix III.A), a surprisingly high number, when related to the total in use in Shropshire during the early 1880's (Appendix III.B).

It is a suggestion of Dorothy Sylvester that this could be the result of high bread prices during the Napoleonic Wars with France.[2] Even some of the higher parts of south and east Shropshire, such as Clee Hills and Longmynds, were ploughed, which was not to be seen again until the outbreak of war in 1939. Not only was it the variety of soils that influenced where crops were grown, the proximity of Shropshire to the Welsh mountains produces colder, wetter conditions than farmers experience to the south and east of Britain. Statistics from the 1930s show a temperature range between summer and winter of twenty-four degrees, and an average winter cooler than in Shetland.[3] In another way Shropshire reflected the way of life of the country at large. Nationally the enforcement of law and detention of troublemakers was, until the mid-1830s, left to the parish watch. The Peel Metropolitan Police Act (1829) set up the first organised body, which consisted of one thousand men, and commenced its duties on 29 September 1829. The Municipal Corporations Act (1835) called upon boroughs to establish similar law enforcement forces, and in 1839 authority was issued to JPs to follow suit in the counties. In Shrewsbury the new reform council held its first meeting on New Years' Day, 1836, appointing a committee to report on the present state of constables and the night watch. But it was only at the second meeting of the council that a watch committee was elected, as ordered by the Reform Act. At the meeting of 5 February the watch committee reported that they had appointed four constables to act as police officers and nine to be night watchmen. That only made a difference to the county town, and it was not until 1835/36 that similar changes were implemented in Shropshire's other market towns, thus leaving the rural districts unprotected, against criminals and troublemakers travelling out from the now protected towns. But as early as January 1831, at the Shropshire Quarter Sessions, an opinion was offered to the court:

> that the formation of a Constabulary Force throughout the County of
> Salop with a view of the peace and security of property should be
> adopted, and that this court strongly recommends the magistrates in

their respective districts to take immediate steps with a view to its
organisation.[4]

It is likely that this suggestion was prompted by concern about the agrarian riots reported as
sweeping across the more southern areas of Britain. That added to worries engendered by
rioting miners and other industrial workers, these already having disrupted production at
sites in the county.

The notable difference between violent protest by industrial workers and those in the
agricultural community was group size and therefore the magistrates needed to focus on a
suitable response. Industrial employees tended to work, live and protest together and in
relatively large numbers. The rural employee was almost always one of a small workforce,
living in at the farm, or with his family in a tied cottage. His protest therefore had to be on a
more individual basis, if possible in a manner that would avoid the perpetrator being
identified. When violent protest occurred, the usual response by magistrates was to call out
the militia or yeomanry. In the early 19th century this was often a form of class warfare,
landowners using their powers as magistrates to call out the yeomanry against those
protesting about food prices and workhouse legislation. The Shropshire Yeomanry were
called to act against striking colliers and ironworkers at Ironbridge during 1820 and 1821,
violence on the slag heaps to be known as Cinderloo, a name adopted from the Peterloo
Massacre of August 1819 in Manchester.[5]

This then was Shropshire, seemingly immune from the agrarian troubles experienced
in the more southern counties of England. However, it became apparent when studying the
contemporary newspapers that readers must have been aware of what was going on
elsewhere. The *Shrewsbury Chronicle*, the leading local newspaper, which was published
first in 1772, and its competitor *Eddowes Salopian Journal* (est. 1794) each published news
of national and international events. Fortunately excellent copies of both publications are
available at Shropshire Record and Research Centre. On the first day of October 1830 the
former paper reported, 'Outrages in Kent', recording attacks on property to some degree
following the pattern of those carried out by 'the followers of Captain Rock in Ireland'. This
was followed by further reports in the *Shrewsbury Chronicle*, on 8 and 22 October, which
reported continuing and increasing trouble in Kent. These troubles included stack burning
and the quote that 'There is nothing of a political nature in the tumults their objective is the
machine', going on to mention a 'Paddy M'kew motive'. It was now serious enough for
magistrates in Kent to offer a reward of five hundred pounds. The same newspaper, during
the following three weeks, reported outbreaks of violence in Middlesex, Sussex and Kent,
the *Salopian Journal* printing similar reports. At the beginning of December both
newspapers reported trouble much closer to home in Wiltshire, Herefordshire and
Worcestershire, but there did not appear to be any sense of a threat of similar troubles within
Shropshire. That however was to happen very suddenly, and the residents of Whitchurch in
north Shropshire, which at the time had a population of about 2,000, reacted with
commendable speed, suggesting that they were probably anticipating such events.

On the night of Tuesday 14 December 1830, a fire broke out at the farm of William
Heath, situated at Yocking's Gate just over a mile east of Whitchurch town centre. This

caused considerable damage, destroying a barn, a hayrick and killing three cows and a calf. A tragic after-affect was the death of the farmer's wife, said to be due to the trauma of the events. A few hours later on the Wednesday morning a fire nearly destroyed the Swan Inn, a timber-framed property on the High Street in the very centre of the town. The *Shrewsbury Chronicle* of 17 December reported that later, on the Wednesday, inhabitants of Whitchurch had met at the Town Hall to discuss how to protect local property. It went on to say that one hundred special constables had been sworn in and a nightly watch established to operate a patrol throughout the winter months. It is possible that this was an initial response, that being the number of able-bodied men attending the meeting, because a later and more comprehensive report, thought to be compiled by a member of the fire brigade gives the total recruitment as eight hundred, going on to specify how they were employed. A nightly watch of twelve inhabitants was established, to which a further two were later added, who would act as sentinels on the tower of the parish church.[6]

The special constables who were resident within the town were divided into ten divisions each of twenty, these groups were identified by a letter of the alphabet, then placed under the control of a leader at whose home they met when an emergency occurred. Similar arrangements were made for the rural area around Whitchurch, the entire parish being divided into districts and a leader appointed for each. The fire engines were organised to be as effective as possible. Although it is unknown how many were available it is clear from reports that some of the small communities around Whitchurch had their own machines in addition to those based in the town. A number of directors were allotted to each fire engine; their names displayed in the watch room so that they could then be called out when a fire alarm was raised. This was usually done from the top of the church tower, where a plan had been installed with farms and landmarks clearly marked, enabling unambiguous directions to be given if flames were seen.[7]

Special constables and members of the watch did not have to wait long before the effectiveness of their system was tested. On 14 December, at between one and two o'clock in the morning, those on the church tower saw a light to the south in the area between Prees Heath and the village of Tilstock. Fire engines were sent and it was found that a barn was well alight, burning to such an extent that it and its contents were lost. It was the property of a Mr Nunnerley. He and his family were asleep and unaware of the fire although the house was immediately adjacent to the farm buildings.[8] The early arrival of the fire fighters helped save the house and possibly also avoided loss of life. The fact that the site, known as Pickstock, was close to the London Turnpike helped to reduce the journey time.

Then there was a trouble-free period, and local spirits must have risen when, before the end of the year, an arrest was made. The *Salopian Journal* reported on 29 December that John Dumoir, a traveller aged 28, had pleaded guilty to setting fire to William Heath's farm and also stables at the Swan Inn. He had been committed to the county gaol, having admitted after sentence to previously firing ricks in Essex, Sussex and Cambridge. Any feeling of relief in Whitchurch was misplaced. Dumoir appeared at the County Assize the following spring and there was found not guilty, but detained for his own protection. He was '[...] proved to be a vagrant and of low intelligence' reported the *Shrewsbury Chronicle* on 25 March.

Threatening letters, written to farmers and landowners, had been a feature of Swing activity in other parts of England. The publishers of *Eddowes Salopian Journal* seemed to anticipate similar messages being delivered in Shropshire when, on 22 December 1830, they published a review of the law covering them. The following is an extract, which was headed 'Threatening Letters'.

> By the 4th Geo.IV. c54s3 it is enacted that if any person shall knowingly and willfully send or deliver any letter or writing, with or without any name or signature subscribed thereto, or with fictional name or signature, threatening to kill or murder any of His Majesty's subjects or to burn or destroy his or their houses, out houses, barns, stacks of corn or grain, hay or straw, or demanding any chattel, money or valuable security, and shall be convicted thereof, such persons shall be liable to be transported beyond the seas for life.

It is not known what prompted the publishers to produce the warning. Possibly they had become aware of letters in circulation, or even received some, which they had declined to print. It may have been to warn troublemakers of the punishment awaiting them, or to remind magistrates of their powers, this being before the Municipal Corporations Act. Whatever the reason, the following week, and subsequent to the three fires at Whitchurch, they again focused on the power of the law. The following is an extract of 30 December.

Law Regarding Burning and Destruction of Machinery

> By the act of 7 & 8 Geo.IV, it is enacted as follows:- Sec. 2. That if any person shall unlawfully and maliciously set fire to any church or chapel or to any chapel for religious worship of persons dissenting from the united church of England and Ireland, duly registered or recorded or shall unlawfully and maliciously set fire to any house, stable, coach house, outhouse, warehouse, office, shop, mill, malthouse, hop-oast, barn or granary or to any building or erection used in carrying on any trade or manufacture or any branch thereof, whether the same or any of them respectively shall then be in the possession of the offender, or in the possession of any persons with intent thereby to injure or defraud any person, every such offender shall be guilty of felony; and be convicted thereof, shall suffer death as a felon.

> Sec. 8. That if any person riotously or tumultuously assembled together, to the disturbance of the peace, shall, unlawfully and with force, demolish, pull down or destroy, any church or chapel or any house, stable, coach house, outhouse, warehouse, office, shop, mill, malt house, hop-oast, barn or granary or any machinery, whether fixed or moveable, prepared for or employed in any manufacture of any

branch thereof, or any steam engine or other engine for sinking, draining or working any mine, building or erection used in conducting the business of any mine, or any bridge, wagon-way or trunk for conveying minerals from any mine, every such offender shall be guilty of felony, and be convicted thereof shall suffer death as a felon.

Sec. 17. That if any person all unlawfully and maliciously set fire to any stack of corn, grain, pulse, straw, hay or wood, any such offender shall be guilty of felony and being convicted shall suffer death as a felon.

A report in the *Salopian Journal* dated 12 January 1831 indicates that the county's first arson attack of the year was on Wednesday 11 January at 11.30 pm. That was not, however, in the Whitchurch area, but twenty-eight miles south in the village of Cressage. A robbery took place at the Turnpike Gate situated on the Shrewsbury to Worcester road. The elderly woman who kept the tollhouse was attacked, bound and gagged and then robbed of sixteen pounds and some matches were taken. Immediately afterwards the outbuildings of a farm opposite, owned by Mr. Langley, were set on fire. On 9 February the same newspaper reported that a tinker called William Jones and another named Clee, had been remanded in custody for committing the offences. No further reference has been found to the incident or to what happened to those charged. There must be some doubt about any connection between the Cressage events and Swing attacks. It must also be possible that the robbery was a cover for the firing of the buildings, but it seems illogical to draw attention to a robbery by lighting a beacon!

The first issue of the *Shrewsbury Chronicle* for 1831 carried a letter to the editor. The writer suggested that the use of machinery for making Captain Swing's coat is a contradiction to his campaign to keep the use of machinery out of agriculture. By coincidence at about 2.20 am on that morning, 7 January, there was another fire in the Whitchurch area. This was again south of the town, about a half mile from William Heath's farm, and adjacent to the London Turnpike. In this instance, a stack of corn owned by a Mr Moss was destroyed. Two waggoners, who were passing through the town, alerted the watch, they having seen a light at the buildings as they moved north on the turnpike. *The Narrative of the Fires* states that the watch on the tower could not identify any problem in the direction of Heath Lane, and there was a general opinion the waggoners were incorrect. Two parties of watch had gone out and reported all was quiet, then a few minutes later the alarm was raised by a farmer's servant, who confirmed there was a fire and gave the position. The record goes on to say that the fire engines arrived on the spot eleven minutes after being called, thus limiting the damage. It also became obvious why the fire had been difficult to see from Whitchurch, as the incendiary device had been placed in a hollow running up inside of the stack, some intervening buildings adding to the concealment.

The next few months were to prove a period of considerable concern for the residents of the parish of Whitchurch. At 7 am on the morning of 8 January, just as the watch were signing the report, which was always kept of the night's activity, they were called to a fire. Again the site was at Heath Lane, only about 300 yards from Moss's stack yard, where a wooden barn belonging to Mr G T Whitfield was alight. The barn, its contents and two adjacent cottages were totally destroyed.

Four days later on Wednesday 12 January, again at 7 am, a small part of the thatched roof of a cottage at Tilstock was damaged by fire. Referred to in contemporary reports as 'Parry's Cottage', the fire engine attended, but the fire had been extinguished before its arrival.[9] This, however, was to be a busy day. At about 6 pm the fire fighters were called again to the property of Mr G T Whitfield, this time to a barn near Edgeley, on the other side of the Turnpike. The response to the call must have been extremely fast; only a very limited part of the roof was destroyed before the fire was extinguished and, since the building was empty, the cost of the damage small.

From then until the end of the month all was quiet in the Whitchurch area, although there were three fires in other parts of the county. A brief report in the *Shrewsbury Chronicle* mentions on 21 January a fire near Market Drayton; this was probably accidental or very insignificant since no other record has been found. This was followed in the early hours of Sunday 23 January by a fire on the northern edge of the county town. The target was a stack of hay belonging to Cyrus Gittins, apparently a smallholder of Old Heath, as well as having other quite extensive business interests in the centre of Shrewsbury, two miles away. This was reported in both the *Shrewsbury Chronicle* and the *Salopian Journal*, the latter also containing a long letter explaining the incident as seen by a special constable, who was on duty at the time. Apparently the arsonist was never caught and the reason for the attack therefore not revealed. There is no known connection between this fire and Swing activity, it is possible however that Gittins had an interest in farm machinery and that could have prompted the attack. He was in partnership, as an ironmonger, with a man named Cartwright at an address on Pride Hill in the heart of the town. In addition, they ran an iron and brass foundry, manufactured nails and followed the trades of whitesmith and bell hanger. In an individual capacity, Gittins was also an agent for Sun Assurance.[10]

Two other fires were reported in the Shropshire area by the local press before the end of January; these were near to the east and south-east edge of the county. One was on the evening of Friday 21 January, on a farm at Swindon adjacent to the Shropshire/Staffordshire border, about seven miles from Wolverhampton. At 8.30 pm a wheat-rick was fired, then three hours later a rick of barley set alight at a neighbouring farm. A point of interest is that colliers were suspected, someone having reported having seen a man dressed as a miner in the vicinity. This illustrates the entrenched fear of industrial workers' violence. This suspicion was unfounded, however, as the *Shrewsbury Chronicle* reported on 28 January that four servants who lived at the farm had admitted the offence and had been committed to Stafford gaol to appear at the next assizes.

The other fire was on the night of Thursday 27 January when passengers on the Wonder coach witnessed the spectacle of a burning clover stack of 60-80 tons at Manor House Farm, about two miles from Shifnal. It was proved later to have been started maliciously, but the culprit or the reason, were never discovered.

On 2 February the fires started again in the Whitchurch area, when at about a quarter to three in the morning the watchman on the church tower raised the alarm. The flames he had seen were at Dearnford Hall, the home of a tenant farmer named Huxley, and came from a burning stack. This is all reported in the booklet, *Narratives of the Fires*, which goes on to say the night was intensely cold with deep snow covering the ground. But although the conditions must have been difficult the fire engine was out in three minutes and, after struggling to get to the site over frozen rutted snow, the fire was extinguished.

It is interesting that the same source mentions that at this time several unrecorded circumstances threw strong suspicion onto a man named Lea, who was later convicted for this series of fires. The suspicions were strong enough for him to be questioned by a man named Clements, an intelligence officer from Marlborough Street Office [*sic*] who was in the county assisting with the efforts to apprehend the arsonist. The questioning may have frightened Lea and any accomplice he had, because for the rest of the month there were no more incidents. Confidence returned to Whitchurch, and on 28 February the committee in charge of the watch passed the following resolution: ' [...] that the watch be discontinued after the 14th day of March next ensuing, should no circumstances take place in the mean time which render the further continuance of the watch necessary'.[11]

The disbandment was not to happen, because at three o'clock on the morning of 10 March a disastrous fire occurred at the farm of Mr Nunnerley, who had already been targeted on 14 December. The earlier loss of a barn was insignificant when compared with the cost of the second attack. Both Shropshire newspapers, and *Narrative of the Fires*, carry details of the extent of the damage. Even the rapid arrival of the engines could not help and it is possible the fire had been alight for some time before it was seen. All the outbuildings and their contents were destroyed, with the exception of a cow-house, which was attached to the family house. The roof of the house was set alight in several places, the domestic property only being saved thanks to the efforts of a neighbour's staff. Two female servants, who worked for a Mr Kennerley of Heath Cottage, brought a small fire engine belonging to their employer, keeping the fire under control to an extent until the watch arrived. This reveals two factors. Firstly, not only the small villages and hamlets had their own community fire fighting equipment, but also that individual householders had taken steps to be able to protect their property, and that of neighbours; and secondly, in an emergency the community worked together. The contemporary *Narrative of the Fires*, which records the history of the Whitchurch fires, gives credit on page nine to the unstinted effort made by 'The greatest number of those who came forward to give their assistance at the fires was necessarily composed of the working classes [...] who had been working hard during the day and who in many instances have a large family depending for support upon their scanty earnings [...] the loss of a night's rest, and the risk of incurring sickness is a very serious thing'.

Twenty days elapsed before the next fire. It was started at nine o'clock on 30 March in stacks the property of a Mr Bradbury, and just a mile from Whitchurch alongside the road from Ash. A fair had been held that day at Market Drayton and a group of people, including some women and a boy, were using the route to return to Whitchurch, when they saw a man with a lantern and candle at the stacks. The man ran away and one woman chased and caught his coat, but then fell and he escaped. The presence of the group meant the alarm was raised with minimum delay and they are also reported as setting to and pulling the burning parts away to save the bulk. The proximity of the town also meant the speedy arrival of other helpers with the engine, lines were quickly formed and buckets of water passed from a pond and brook to the pumps. As a result most of the hay was saved.

The fear raised by the on-going arson attacks must have been unsettling for other communities, particularly those within relatively easy reach of Whitchurch. Wem, just ten miles to the south, had suffered major fires during the preceding centuries, on one occasion the town being virtually destroyed, and was rightly aware of a possible threat.

Wem formed its own town watch, keeping a nightly log of any untoward activity. It had its first fire engine in 1794, and in 1831 a new appliance was purchased, the money being raised by the church wardens.[12] This expenditure was possibly encouraged by the perceived threat to the area. However, the town was left unharmed, but the engine was at the ready and it went to the next fire in the parish of Whitchurch on 4 April. The huge column of flames could be seen by watchers in Wem and much of the surrounding countryside, as well as from the church at Whitchurch. As a result, the inhabitants of Wem sent their appliance, accompanied by a number of helpers.

Certainly as much help as possible was required to try and contain the fire, which was again at Dearnford Hall, the home and farm of Mr Huxley, who had been targeted on 2 February. The Hall was owned by Samuel Benyon, a successful lawyer with a practice in London and who had married the heiress of the property, his Shropshire home was Ash Hall about two miles distant. On the first occasion (see p.68) the tenant had lost just one stack; this time the damage was extensive, including a range of buildings, together with a large quantity of grain. It proved impossible to save the wooden and thatched structures, the heat being so intense that lead in the casement widows of the house started to melt. Efforts were therefore concentrated on saving Dearnford Hall and stacks in adjacent fields. Even a cottage on the opposite side of the road was put at risk, a strong wind carrying the flames in that direction, but when hope was about to be given up the wind moderated. This must have been an extremely frightening incident for the rural community over an extensive area. Many of the inhabitants of the village of Prees, some four miles away, helped fight the fire but their appliance was not needed.[13]

On the same evening, probably at almost the same time as the Dearnford Hall fire, there was another blaze in part of Twemlow's Fox Cover. A plantation of fir trees and heath covering half an acre of ground, owned by Sir Rowland Hill, were destroyed. Reports are vague, possibly because of the scale of the other fire and the fact that no buildings were involved.

Another influence of Swing had also shown itself in Whitchurch - the anonymous threatening letter. During March two men had appeared at the Shropshire Assizes for 'writing and sending a letter to William Churton, of Whitchurch, threatening to kill and murder him, and also to burn and destroy his property'. The two found guilty were Thomas Cook, aged nineteen an attorney's clerk, and Thomas Salusbury Richardson, a tailor aged forty-seven. There appeared no single or specific reason for the letters; a mix of discontent with general conditions and politics has to be assumed the motivation. William Churton, the recipient, is shown in the 1828 *Salop Directory* as an auctioneer with premises in Whitchurch High Street. Thomas Cook's punishment was the most severe, transportation to New South Wales. Richardson, although older and also believed to be the motivator, escaped with two years' imprisonment, asking the court for mercy as he had a wife and nine children to support.[14]

The summer months were relatively trouble free, possibly because of the longer days and shorter nights. But it is also possible that this was because the arsonists were kept busy with farming activity, and as a result receiving their maximum pay and feeling more content with life. Just one fire is known to have occurred during the summer months, at Aston Green about eight miles north-east of Whitchurch, and well outside the parish. On 11 July the wheelwright's shop was destroyed at about nine o'clock in the evening, the flames being visible from the town. No reason for the fire was discovered, and although the shop would have had a hearth, arson must also be considered a possibility.

After a prolonged trouble-free period, it must have been a shock for Whitchurch residents to be wakened with the dreaded shout of 'Fire', at about three o'clock in the morning of 13 September. The signs of a fire were clearly to be seen, and, as previously, they were to the south in the area of Prees Heath.[15] The engines were said to have been, 'immediately got in readiness', this possibly a little slower than earlier in the year when such an event could be expected at any time. The author of *The Narrative of the Fires [...] of Whitchurch* is given as a clergyman, but it would seem he was also a member of the watch, since he writes of his initial view of this conflagration in the first person. The scene must have been frightening, particularly since it was only revealed to the helpers as they topped a slight rise near the flames. They then saw not one fire but three, all stack-yards but owned by different farmers, Mr Nunnerley had suffered an attack for the third time, a stack was well alight and he was attempting to save another, his efforts being successful. The farm buildings of Mr Darlington at Twemlow's Hall had already been destroyed, and the fire was spreading rapidly from stack to stack. The fire engines were sited to be most effective and a line of workers, which included women, worked hard to pass water to the pumps. Even worse was the fire at the Twemlow's property of Mr Booth. Here the farm buildings were already in ruins and seventeen stacks were ablaze. The engines from Prees and Tilstock were already tackling the fire, attended by inhabitants from those and other villages. Although a considerable amount of damage was caused at each of the three farms, the loss was reduced by the efforts of the fire fighters, the worst being at Mr Booth's, which totalled £2,500 (Appendix III.C). Although the general public did not know it at the time, this was the culmination of the troubles. A fire at a Whitchurch inn, The Lord Hill, on 6 October undoubtedly caused great concern, but was discovered to be due to carelessness.

In the early hours of the morning, while the fires were still burning, a group of men went to look for James Lea at the house of his employer, George Whitfield, already having been looking for him at the actual sites. It would have been reasonable to expect both Lea and Grindley to have been at the fires since, like most other able bodied men, they were members of the watch! The search for Lea appears to have been prompted initially by suspicion, he having been a suspect at the beginning of the year. They found him in the yard, accompanied by another workman. They then proceeded to search the bedroom he shared with Joseph Grindley. The bed had not been slept in, and a jacket lying on the corner was wet. It was later pointed out in court that there had been no rain the previous day, but rain had fallen between 11 and 12 o'clock during the fires. The group of five included a

Whitchurch attorney, George Harper, who, with the others, took Lea into custody.[16] He appeared before magistrates the day after the fire and in October was committed to the county gaol, charged with offences of maliciously setting fire to stacks of grain, corn and hay.

Lea subsequently made a number of statements and these implicated others in the series of fires. When Lea first appeared before the magistrates, Grindley appeared as a witness for the defence. It was only when Lea made a further statement at his own request, on 3 November in gaol, that he made specific allegations regarding the involvement of Grindley. As a result, John Williams, a constable of Whitchurch, apprehended Joseph Grindley at Burslem in Staffordshire on 5 November, at which time he said he had been in Manchester and Liverpool. He was examined at Whitchurch two days later. When Lea's statement was read to him, he declined to say anything then, but agreed to do so if his father was brought to the lock-up house.

Grindley's own view of the fires was dictated to George Harper, a local attorney, who wrote it down as Grindley's father held the inkstand. A further statement was made by Lea on the same day, 7 November, then Grindley made another on the ninth and yet another was given to Mr Harper by Lea on 19 December. A further development was the committal to the county gaol of Samuel Grindley, reported in the *Shrewsbury Chronicle* dated 30 December 1831.

These long and ponderous statements contained admissions of personal involvement, but also accusations about the involvement of other individuals, resulting in further arrests. The statements also referred to discussions between these individuals and suggest that the reasons for the fires included envy, politics and opposition to the local aristocracy. The *Shrewsbury Chronicle* dated 16 March has, on page four, the Calendar of Prisoners for the forthcoming Shropshire Assizes, the list includes not only Lea and Grindley but also the latter's father, Samuel, who was charged with setting fire to a fox covert owned by Sir Rowland Hill. William Balls was to appear charged with 'Setting fire to divers stacks of corn, grain, hay and to certain barns, granaries, and buildings at Whitchurch'. The most surprising name was that of Richard Whitfield, brother of George Whitfield and employer of both Grindley and Lea. He faced charges for sending letters to Mr J Lee, Sir R C Hill, the Earl of Kilmorney, Rev. J Justice, and the Rev. E Nevile, threatening to murder them and destroy their property; also for setting fire at Whitchurch to the barn of Geo. Whitfield.

These individuals had all been in detention or under observation from early November 1831, but there were two more fires in the same area between then and the end of that year. One was on 3 December at cottages owned by Lady Bridgwater and situated alongside Heath Lane, the Turnpike road. There seemed to be no explanation for this, and the newspapers failed to report it in detail. The other was at the farm of John Forgham at Whixall, in the parish of Prees on 11 November, and appears to have been a copycat fire, started by an unhappy kitchen maid in the hope that she would be dismissed from her job of seven years. It was admitted, by her employer that he had beaten her, but only with a small whip. He denied any inappropriate behaviour with her, although admitted his wife may have called him a dirty villain. The girl, Hannah Simmons, pleaded not guilty to arson, which had destroyed two barn floors, four bays, a stable, a cow-house, a cart-house and a granary, plus a very large amount of various cereals and straw. Hannah Simmons and all the individuals involved in the other fires appeared before Mr Justice Littledale at the Shropshire Spring Assizes, the cases reported in the *Shrewsbury Chronicle* published 23 March 1832. The assize jury, members of the local aristocracy and major landowners, including Sir Rowland Hill, and Lord Clive as foreman, took only a few minutes to reach a verdict of guilty on Hannah. The judge considered the matter and then ordered that sentence of death be recorded against her, but her life be spared.

The same jury also found James Lea and Joseph Grindley guilty without any delay, and proceeded to sentence them to death and they were duly executed at Shrewsbury Gaol on Saturday 31 March 1832. Richard Whitfield was also found guilty, after the jury consulted for a few minutes in the box. The judge said he could not permit the prisoner to escape without the severest punishment available for such offences, and he was to be 'Transported for the period of his Natural Life'. The fate of William Balls and Samuel Grindley has been difficult to ascertain, no newspaper reports having been found of their trials. However, it is possible that Grindley received what, for the period, may be considered a relatively light sentence. An entry in the 1841 census returns shows that Samuel Grindley, aged sixty, an agricultural labourer was living at an address in Tilstock Lane with his wife Martha (59) and a daughter Sarah (20).

A brief look at the individuals involved in the Whitchurch fires, their business and activities may help the reader form conclusions. James Lea was aged thirty-two when he died and, although he lived at his employer's farm, he was married. Joseph Grindley was only twenty when executed; his father had a cottage at Prees Heath, which has now been converted into a much larger property. Both were employed as labourers by George Whitfield, a farmer of reasonable substance and apparently respectable; his brother Richard (age 40) was referred to as a farmer and maltster when he appeared at Shropshire Assizes. Whitchurch had strong business connections with Manchester, in the 1928 *Salop Directory* its principle trade said to be shoe making for that city and also malting. Another extremely strong connection with Manchester for many generations was the supply of Shropshire damsons, sold as a dye for the cloth industry. The statements by Lea and Grindley confirm that both of the Whitfields were business visitors to Manchester, and Grindley, when arrested, admitted having been there as well as Liverpool. It is quite possible that the Whitchurch troubles were partly the result of meeting industrial activists in the city area.

A Manchester connection may also resolve the question of how the expertise to assemble the fire-raising materials was obtained. James Lea, in his statement made on 7 November, stated that the first fires started by Grindley, during December 1830 and January 1831, were lit only with matches. However, from 10 March, when he fired Nunnerley's buildings he had found a better way, allowing him to light them and have time to escape. It may be coincidence, but George Whitfield is known to have visited Manchester on 8 January, his own property being damaged by fire after his departure, a greater insight into this is contained in the statement by Lea on 28 March 1832 (Appendix III.D). Grindley threw some of the fire-balls away after Lea had been arrested, and these were found by Samuel Higginson who lived in Heath Lane.[17] When examined by Thomas Blunt, a chemist from

Shrewsbury, he declared that they 'were composed with a great deal of chemical knowledge. The properties of the ingredients must be known, and they must be carefully arranged'.[18]

So what conclusions can be drawn from this examination of a turbulent period in Shropshire rural history? It is reasonable to believe that the majority of fires mentioned were encouraged by the reports of Swing activity in other parts of the country. However, the reason for the individual targets could be very much more diverse than wishing to destroy the latest machinery and maintain employment. The statements made by Lea and Grindley and later read out in court, are much too long for reproduction. In addition to their own discussions, they also record comments by others, critical of wealthy landowning aristocracy. In particular, Richard Whitfield appears to have been a prime mover. Lea, in his statement of 7 November, quotes a conversation involving also George Whitfield and Grindley, in which Richard declares his intention of going to America, but before he went he would shoot 'Bob Hill'. Then going on to say he would also shoot 'old Lee of Redbrook'. The reference to 'Bob Hill' was probably a comment about Robert Chambre Hill, who lived at Prees Hall and was a nephew of Sir Rowland Hill, whose home was Hawkstone Park.

In his statement of 19 December, Lea relates a long tirade made by Richard Whitfield against Sir Rowland Hill, ending with 'I wish someone would kindle him a fire that it might follow him up to London'.[19] A discussion followed involving Grindley, who received a guinea from Whitfield in anticipation of creating a fire on Lord Hill's land. This animosity against the Hill family was fuelled by the recently held elections, at which he took the Parliamentary seat. The seat was to be contested by Squire 'Jack' Mytton standing as a 'Reform' or Whig candidate, who had considerable estates to the north-west of Shrewsbury. He stood down as Parliamentary candidate when he failed to get the necessary backing from sponsors. His support for the Reform Bill was encouraging to the tenant farmers and workers. However, wealthy voters were very much against him both because of his liberal views, and also the extrovert, madcap style of life he pursued. Sir Rowland Hill was, it seems, a rather more remote figure, already owning a huge 16,554 acres of Shropshire. There were, in addition, the acres owned by Robert and the other branch of the family, Lord Berwick at Attingham Park. Nearly one fifth of the county was owned by just seven peers, and by far the largest amount of land in north Shropshire appears to have been under the control of the Bridgewater estate.[20] The focus of control by the aristocracy had brought to the fore uncertainty and fear of further financial pressure on tenant farmers, when they were still feeling the effect of a series of bad years. The statements also indicate that some of the targets for the attacks were known to have voted for Lord Hill, such information being public knowledge at that time.

The statements by Lea and Grindley as reproduced have had names deleted in many places, the reason is not apparent but presumably to protect some individuals from publicity.[21] However James Lea made a final confession on 28 March 1832, just three days before he was hanged, and it does not seem to have been previously published (Appendix III.D). This implicates both George and Richard Whitfield in the planning, if not the execution of the fires, also Mr Kennerley and William Botts. Since Lea's fate was sealed, it would seem reasonable to believe that this is as near the truth as anyone is now likely to get, and the fires in the Whitchurch area were the result of scheming by a group of political activists. Few, if any, of these farmers would at that time hold the franchise, which was limited to freeholders of property worth forty shillings a year or more. They were therefore anxious to see some move towards a system giving them the opportunity to influence their own futures. To this end, they encouraged their young employees, who had an instinctive dislike of the obvious disparity of wealth in the area, to carry out the attacks. This is probably a theme to be found in the other areas where Swing activity was more pronounced, the result of those having access to newspapers and then taking advantage of what appeared to be an increasing amount of rural revolt.

And today, nearly two hundred years after the period of Swing attacks, what can be seen in the Shropshire landscape? The major farms named in the contemporary reports are still to be found, including Dearnford Hall, which was attacked twice (Illustrations III.a and III.b). This is an impressive house in the grand manner built of stone and brick towards the end of the 17th century, the windows are of Regency style and altered from the casements described at the time of the second fire.[22] That was possibly as the result of heat damage at the time of the arson attack on 4 April 1831. Other features have been tailored to meet changing fashion but nothing has been spoilt. The exact site of timber and thatch buildings destroyed by arson is difficult to establish. The contemporary description (see page 70) placed them near both the house and the road, and that could mean at least one of the existing two-storey buildings has been extensively repaired, if not rebuilt.

The most destructive fire, at The Twemlows, resulted in the total rebuilding of the farm buildings. This is well illustrated in the photograph from the air (Illustration III.c), but the residential part of the complex has survived although no longer occupied by those farming the fields around. Other farms, including George Whitfield's, and that of Mr. Bradbury on the Ash road, are also still there. The parish church, St. Alkmunds, stands externally unchanged since it was built in 1712, the tower rising high above the town, making it obvious why it was used for the watch (Illustration III.d). Virtually nothing is to be found of the homes of Grindley and Lea, the former now absorbed into a newer and larger farmhouse, and Lea's cottage seems to have been demolished; the site now just a meadow. All this is set around the surviving Prees Heath, bisected by two trunk roads and for a time a large wartime airfield; much of it would still be recognised by the firewatchers of 1830-31.

NOTES

1   Hobsbawm, E and Rude, G, *Captain Swing*, (Lawrence & Wishart, 1969. rpt pb. Phoenix 2001), p. 174-5.
2   Sylvester, D, *The Rural Landscape of the Welsh Borderland,* (Macmillan, London 1969), p. 319.
3   Watts, W W, *Shropshire - The Geography of the County* (Wilding of Shrewsbury 1939), p. 59.
4   SRRC, Salop Quarter Sessions, Abstract of Orders Vol. 3. p. 284, in printed form.
5   Trinder, B, *The Industrial Revolution in Shropshire*, (Phillimore, Chichester 1973 rpt 81 & 2000), p. 213.
6   Evans, Rev. J, *Narrative of the Fires.. in.. Whitchurch in 1830 and 1831*, (Newling, Whitchurch 1832), p. 6.

7   *Ibid*, p. 7; p. 6.
8   *Ibid,* p. 7.
9   *Ibid,* p. 10.
10 *The Salop Directory*, 1828. Pub. Tibnam & Co. Booksellers, Wyle Cop, Shrewsbury.
11 Evans (1832), p. 12.
12 Woodward, I, *The History of Wem and its Neighbourhood*, (Wildings, Shrewsbury 1952 rpt 1976), p. 73.
13 Evans (1832), p. 11.
14 Hobbs, J L, 'Thomas Cooke of Whitchurch,' *Shropshire Magazine*, (August, 1955), pp. 20-21.
15 Evans (1832), p. 16.
16 *Ibid,* p. 21.
17 *Ibid,* p. 25.
18 *Ibid,* p. 24.
19 *Ibid,* p. 37.
20 Baugh, G C, (ed.), VCH Shropshire. Vol.III. p. 311.
21 Evans (1832), pp. 23-40.
22 Moran, M and Barton, J, *Dearnford Hall*, (Logaston Press, 2003), p. 5.

OTHER SOURCES

Shrewsbury Chronicle, 1830 to 1832, SRRC
Eddowes Salopian Journal, 1830 to 1832, SRRC

Local verbal sources and other assistance

Sincere thanks, to Mrs Joan M. Barton, for providing guidance and invaluable information, both personal and from the archives of the Whitchurch History and Archaeological Group. Mr John Matthews, for use of the aerial photograph of Twemlows Farm. Shropshire Record and Research Centre, now renamed Shropshire Archives, the staff as always giving guidance with considerable patience.

To Dr Trevor Hill and Mrs Margaret Hill, our appreciation for their guidance, which enabled us to carry out and present this study.

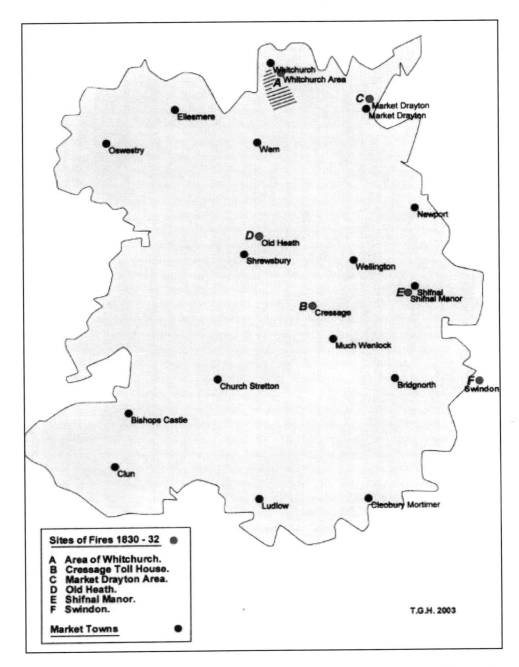

Map III.i. Incendiary events in Shropshire 1830-32, which may have been influenced by Swing activity (*original base-map created by* GenMap UK *v. 2.0)*

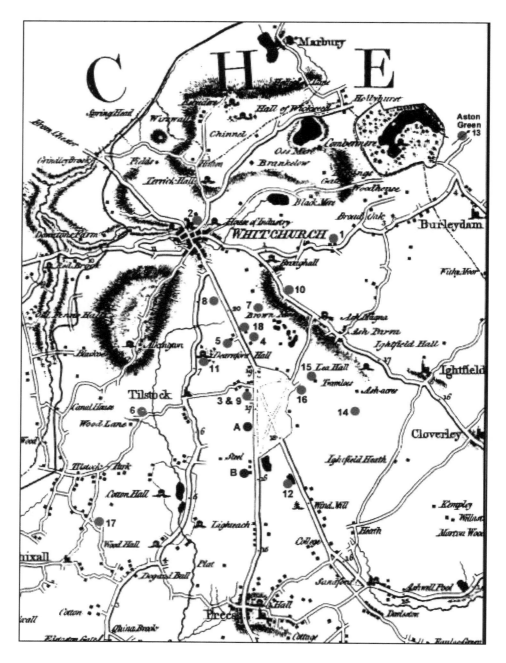

Map III.ii. Points of incendiary incidents 1830-32 in the parish of Whitchurch
*(Map based upon Baugh's Map 1808 annotated by T G Hill 2003
Original map copyright Shropshire Archives)*

References for Map III.ii

The presentation is to illustrate the points in the Whitchurch area where incendiary
incidents occurred during the period 1830-31
Numerical references are listed in chronological order

1830

1.	Heaths stackyard, Yockings Gate	14 December
2.	Swan Inn, Blue Gates, Whitchurch	15 December
3.	Nunnerley's barn, Prees heath	21 December

1831

4.	Moss's stackyard, off Heath Lane	7 January
5.	G Whtifield's house, barn and Down's cottage, adjacent to Heath Lane	8 January
6.	Parry's cottage, Tilstock Park	12 January
7.	G Whitfield's barn at Edgeley	12 January
8.	Huxley's stack on Dearnford Hall farmland	2 February
9.	Nunnerley's building, the same site as no. 3 above	10 March
10.	Bradbury's stackyard, on the Ash road	30 March
11.	Huxley's buildings, adjacent to Dearnford Hall	4 April
12.	Twemlows fox cover, alongside the London Turnpike	4 April
13.	Wheelwright's shop at Aston Green on Whitchurch to Nantwich road	11 July
14.	Booth's stackyard, The Twemlows	13 September
15.	Darlington's stackyard and buildings	13 September
16.	Nunnerley's stackyard, situated away from his farmhouse	13 September
17.	John Forgham's farm. Hannah Simmons arson attack, site approximate	11 November
18.	Lady Bridgewater's cottages	3 December

The following are the sites of the homes of Lea and Grindley,
sentenced to death for the fires.

A.	Cottage of Samuel Grindley, father of Joseph, and also accused of involvement in the attacks
B.	Home of James Lea, where he lived with this wife

Norman Davies

Illustration III.a. Dearnford Hall, 2003

Norman Davies

Illustration III.b. Dearnford Hall Farm buildings, rebuilt after the fires

John Matthews

Illustration III.c. Twemlows Farm, *ca* 1960
*The farm buildings at the rear of the house were rebuilt after the fire
and are an example of a model farm,* ca *1850*

Illustration III.d. St Alkmund's Church
The tower was used for fire watch

Norman Davies

APPENDIX III.A: Extracts from the *Shrewsbury Chronicle*

The following are extracts from the *Shrewsbury Chronicle* published during the early part of 1831. These give an indication of the extent to which mechanisation, and in particular threshing machines, had become part of agricultural activity, even by this early date. For estimate of total county usage see Appendix III.B.

Typical of the advertisements are the following; -

February 18th
At Monkmoor - one mile from Shrewsbury - on 23rd day of February 1831.
Live stock, farming implements, grain, hay, Dairy and Brewing vessels and other effects.
The comprehensive list - which goes into considerable detail includes a *Winnowing Machine* as well as other harvesting equipment.
                    (Monkmoor is now a residential suburb of Shrewsbury)

A second advertisement in the same issue reads-

To be sold by Mr .White at Upton Magna on Wednesday and Thursday, 2nd and 3rd Days of March 1831.
The whole of Livestock, Implements, HOUSEHOLD FURNITURE &c the property of Miss Martha Nevett who is giving up farming
The long list includes - [...] *a capital 4-horse Threshing Machine by Stephen and an excellent Winnowing machine* [...]
                    (Upton Magna, still a small farming village but now also a dormitory for
                    nearby Shrewsbury and Telford)

March 4th
A Sale by Mr Broome at Harnage Grange for Mr Shuker, who is retiring from business.
The lengthy list of sale items includes - *A new portable threshing machine of 4 horse power.*
        (Harnage Grange, very large and prosperous farm near Cressage, recently the home of the High
                    Sheriff of Shropshire)

March 11th
To be sold at Bayston near Shrewsbury by Daniel Bright on Wednesday and Thursday 23rd and 24th days of March 1831 for Mrs Wood who is retiring from the business.
The equipment listed is very considerable and includes -*Threshing Machine (4-horse power) with Winnowing attachment also a separate Winnowing Fan.*
                    (Bayston, now Bayston Hill, 2 miles south of Shrewsbury town centre,
                    a mixed farming area)

And in the same edition, in the north of the county -
Creamore Farm near Wem to be sold by Churton and Sons on Monday, Tuesday, Wednesday and Thursday 28th, 29th, 30th and 31st days of March 1831. The farm, contents, stock and equipment run to several column inches including - *an Excellent Threshing Machine* as well as [...] *Winnowing Machine.*
                    (Creamore is within seven miles of the parts of Whitchurch parish
                    in which most of the fires occurred).

APPENDIX III.B: Adoption of Farm Machinery, 1772-1880

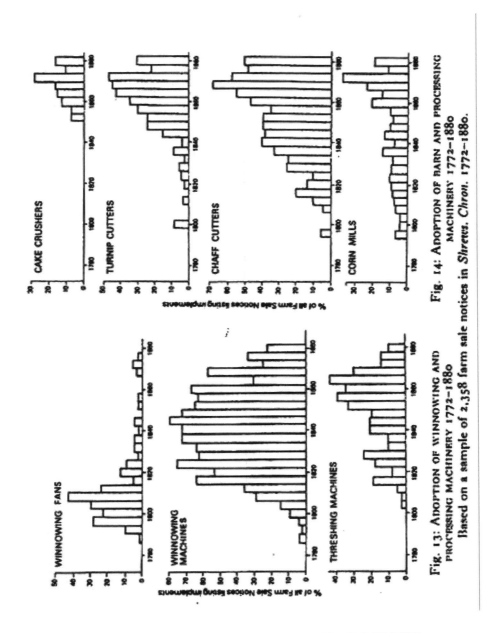

from G C Baugh, VCH - Agriculture Shropshire *Vol. IV (1989)*

APPENDIX III.C: Valuation of Property Destroyed in the Fires, 1830-31

The following is an indication of the monetary cost of the fires in the Whitchurch area, and is from *A Narrative of the Fires which occurred in the Parish of Whitchurch, in the Years 1830-31*

Valuation of property destroyed in the fires as far as could be ascertained

		£	s	d
1.	Heath's Barn and Cowhouse, 3 Cows 10 tons of Hay	150	0	0
2.	Swan Inn buildings, rebuilding cost.	348	0	0
3.	Nunnerley's barn, containing straw and hay.	200	0	0
4.	Moss's stack of corn.	70	0	0
5.	Whitfields's barn and Downe's cottage	260	0	0
6.	Parry's cottage.	70	0	0
7.	Whitfield's barn near Edgeley.	No cost recorded		
8.	Huxley's stack, Dearnford Hall.	No cost recorded		
9.	Nunnerley's buildings, 5 cows, 2 horses, 10 pigs, 1 cow and 2 pigs injured, house damaged.	400	0	0
10.	Bradbury's tacks and eight tons of hay.	36	0	0
11.	Huxley's building, Tilstock.	600	0	0
12.	Twemlows fox cover, fir trees and heath on an acre and half of ground destroyed.	30	0	0
13.	Darlington's 2 barns and other buildings containing wheat, barley, oats and peas. 1 large stack of wheat, 1 of oats, and a considerable quantity of straw.	800	0	0
14.	Booth's 2 barns, 2 ranges of buildings, a stable, waggon house and other farm buildings containing a large quantity of wheat, barley, muncorn, oats and peas, 4 stacks of wheat, 5 of barley, 5 of hay, 1 of oats, 2 of straw, 2 waggons, 1 cart, a thrashing machine and winnowing machine plus various other implements of husbandry, 37 geese and 1 calf.	2,500	0	0
15.	Nunnerley's stack of hay.	25	0	0
16.	Lord Hill Inn stables	No cost recorded		
17.	Lady Bridgewater's cottages	No cost recorded		
		5,453	0	0

APPENDIX III.D: Last Confession of James Lea

**A copy of the last confession of James Lea dictated in Shrewsbury Gaol
from an original in the possession of Mr R J Nunnerley,
of Mile Bank Farm, Whitchurch by J McCarter in 1938.
Kindly provided by Mrs Joan Barton.**
The following is reproduced with spelling, name and format as per Mrs Barton's copy.

James Lea saith as follows -

The first Beginning that there was anything about firing was through Geo Whitfield of Heath Lane he persuaded us to burn the barn of Mr. Nunnerly's of Prees heath in Tilstock Lane he had spits against Mr. Nunnerley through cutting the hedges in the arson (sic) land.
2.   The next that was done was persuaded by Dicky Whitfield and Geo Whitfield for the purpose of alarming the County all was persuaded to be done by the two Whitfields only the buildings of Mrs Brown of Prees Heath and that was Mr. Kennerley's will it should be burn downand the Plantations and the other property of Sir Rowland Hill was burnt through the Whitfields - Richard - George and john but chiefly John on account of his being ill used as to the wooden hall farm. George Used to keep mee up after the family wear gone to bed and used to plan how every fire was to be dun.
Yong William Botts wrote some letters for mrs brown and put them into the post office himself George used to wish places to be burnt most when mr Lee of redbrook as enny thing to do with. Samuel Grindley ad nothing to do with the fires that one of Mr Kennerley talked to me about Mrs brown property being burnt down, it was at the masters in the Plantation coming from the House there was only George and me Mr. Kennerley and the Geo^e Rich^d and John Whitfield wanted to persuad me to set fire to the Twemlows after the Election that was the first under Sir Rowland.   Thirs is no one Except John and Geo^e Richd Whitfield and Mr. Kennerley and Yong Willm Botts that know anything about these fires, they give me no money. But plenty the used to perposed me that I should never want for anything me or my family there was one place they wanted me to Burn Down that was Mrs Lees of Redbruk Flint but we would not go there. he george Whitfield always used to want us to Burn those stacks down - Grindley was not present at these Conversations but he did all the fiers I don't know that he knew anything about Whitfields he always went to do the fiers he cannot say who caused the fiers he suspected theer was some one George was afrade to trust Grindley never kindled a fier I never dust go he Grindley genrealy went by him self he went by him self always except to the Twemlows and then I went with him. But not near, I do not know that Yong Willm Botts used to go with Grindley to set them on fire or not, it is true that Richd Whitfield was at the fier at heath Lane and george knew it was to be burnt when he went to Manchester he had the Hemp taken out of thestacks the day before. No one taught us how to make the bulbs Grindley always made them he told me was the first.
Simpson the boy knew nothing about the fires not one of the servants at the house knew anything about our Conversations - they thought I took great liberties - That is the truth about it I thought never to have toud I had made an oath never to tell I made it to George

Whitfield it was about the time mrs. Browns property was burnt if it had not been for Mr. Kennerley the whitfields are a very bad family.

I do not know that any one had any thing to do with these two fires except the witfields without it was Darlington of Prees and I do not now for certain that he had.

I used to Talk to Grindley wat was to be done he used to be very willing to go and do them after the fire at Nunnerleys Barn.

I was with Grindley the night Twemlows was set on fire I knew when I went out they were to be set on fire.

It was a day after the swan Building was burnt that George Whitfield began talking about fiering, he had nothing to do with that and the other fire that I know of this was one night we were sitting together that he began talking about it.

My wife never knew anything about it and I took an oath particularly not to tell her George Whitfields said I must not tell.

I have talked to Mr Kennerley several times but he never Mentioned any other fier than Mrs. Browns there was no one present when I took the oath not to tell but george and me.

The account I give was correct except about the Whitfields and old Grindley.

Wllm Botts knew all about it and was eager to have them done as I was he wanted to have a piece of Building of Mrs Browns Burnt Down but he said she would not build it up again but throw the land to Moss it is where Botts father lives.

I never did much amiss Except firing and I should not have done that except I had been persuad

Mr Kennerley is a very spiteful man.

My master would have Persuaded me to shoot Sir Robert Hill as he came to Market but I never hive any heed to him or I might have done it he said the Great Men would go on in the way the were in till the were shot as the were in Ireland I think he said.

My wife has persuaded me to tell But I did not take any heed of what she said.

The Mark of

X

James Lea

The foregoing statement was voluntarily
Made in our presence and the same being
Read over to him he said it was true and
Made his mark to it this 28th March 1832.

    Joshua T Dale
    H.R.Griffiths

IV. BURN UP THE *PASHNIDGE* - THE SWING RIOTS IN ESSEX

Michael Holland

Essex is situated on the eastern side of England to the south of Suffolk and west of Cambridgeshire, Hertfordshire, and Middlesex. Kent is to the south across the Thames, see Map IV.i for location.

Up until the early 20th century there was very little industry in the county, its main economy being based on farming, although malm clay deposits, especially in the southern part of the county were used for brick and tile production. Cereals were extensively grown in the county during the 18th and 19th centuries; dairy production took place in the south-west corner; market gardens proliferated on the border with Middlesex. The marshland fringes along the southern and eastern sides were used extensively for sheep grazing.

Essex was no stranger to protest crime. Subsistence rioting had occurred at various points of the 18th century; incendiarism had occurred during the famine of 1800; and north Essex had been affected by the Bread or Blood Riots of 1816.[1] Between November 1828 and March 1829, eight acts of incendiarism were carried out in the parish of Witham in mid Essex. In addition, an anonymous letter was sent to a Witham farmer, threatening to fire his farm. The threat was not followed by direct action.[2] In fact, between 1783 and the start of 1830 there were 282 protest incidents across the county. This averages out to 6.1 per annum. In the peak years of 1800, 1816 and 1822 there were forty-six, twenty, and fourteen protest incidents, respectively.

Turning to the Swing Riots in Essex, according to Hobsbawm and Rudé:

> The Essex riots were preceded by a fire at Rayleigh, near Southend, on 5th November.[3]

This essay will seek to prove that assertion incorrect and to catalogue the full extent of protest crime in Essex between 1830 and 1832. For this period there were ninety-four Swing offences committed, which break down as follows: 1830 - sixty-three, 1831 - twenty-one and 1832 - ten incidents.

Map IV.i. Location of the county of Essex

PRELIMINARIES

On Monday 29 March 1830 an incident occurred where dire threats were made towards the surveyor of the highways for the parish of Childerditch, in south Essex, by four unemployed agricultural labourers. Childerditch made use of the Roundsman Scheme whereby claimants were required to go round to each farmer in the parish to seek employment before relief would be afforded them. These labourers had been instructed to do the rounds of the parish by the overseer in search of work. The surveyor of the highways had indicated to them that a certain farmer might provide work for them. When this turned out not to be the case, four labourers turned on the surveyor and made a series of intimidatory comments. The latter threatened the labourers with arrest if they did not desist. Later that day they encountered the overseer again and, on this occasion being armed with cudgels, threatened to:

> Knock your head as flat as a bull's turd.[4]

Another of the labourers bemoaned the fact that he no longer had his old bayonet, as he would have liked to have run the surveyor through with it. This incident serves to illustrate the strength of feeling that existed in parts of Essex towards vestry members. It could be said to have been one of many 'straws in the wind'!

INCENDIARISM

On Monday 26 April an act of incendiarism was carried out on a farm at Layer-de-la-Haye in the occupancy of Mr Pearson. All buildings, with the exception of the house, were destroyed, together with grain stacks, newly threshed grain, two calves, two bullocks, and three horses.[5] A number of farming implements were also destroyed, although reports make no mention of a threshing machine. The newspaper reports on the fire commented that:

> Incendiarism is suspected but not by a parishioner as the victim is
> highly thought of.[6]

Needless to say, the incendiary was never caught, nor, for that matter, was anybody suspected of the offence.

At about 9 pm on Saturday 14 August 1830 an incendiary attack occurred at Melon Hall at Bradwell-juxta-Mare on the Dengie Peninsular, which is situated on the North Sea coast. The farm was in the occupancy of Mr Spurgeon, a keen advocate of the threshing machine, since the French Wars. The fire started in the empty ox barn and then spread to three further barns, all of which were destroyed. In addition two stacks of hay, one stack of grey pease [*sic*], a waggon and the threshing machine were all destroyed.[7] The insurers, the Essex Economic Fire Association, offered a reward of one hundred pounds for information leading to the apprehension of those responsible.[8]

According to the 1831 census, 69% of the population on the Dengie peninsular were agricultural workers, which in turn meant that winter manual threshing work was central to their personal economy.[9] It is highly likely that Mr Spurgeon's threshing machine would have been hired out to farmers in the surrounding area and so mid-August was doubtless selected by the incendiaries to have maximum impact on the harvest. It would also virtually ensure that farmers would have to revert to hand threshing to the benefit of the labourers.

On the morning of Saturday 11 September 1830 a fire broke out on Mr Robert Feedham's premises at Great Holland, in north-east Essex. The fire destroyed a double barn containing corn, a cowshed, a stable, farming implements, waggons and carts. Again, incendiarism was said to be the cause.[10] It is likely that Feedham's use of a threshing machine was the prime factor for, in December 1830, rioters smashed his machine. During the middle part of September 1830 an incendiary attack was carried out on a farm in Broxted in north-west Essex; no further details are known of this incident.[11] Another incendiary attack took place in mid September in south-west Essex at a village called Stondon Massey. Nothing further is known about this incident.[12] During the night of Thursday 4 November 1830 another incendiary fire occurred at Beauchamp Roding in west Essex, in the occupancy of a Mr Walden.[13]

AN OUTRAGEOUS CRIME

In addition to the acts of incendiarism that were committed in Essex between April and 5 November 1830 there were two incidents of animal maiming. This crime covered a range of attacks on animals and livestock, ranging from the cutting of manes and tail hair to render the animal less saleable, to mutilation.[14] During the early part of July 1830 an animal was maimed in Aythorpe Roding in west Essex, the property of Robert Tabrum. A 13-year-old labourer, Charles Knight, was indicted for this offence and sentenced to a term of imprisonment. The exact details of the offence are not known.[15] On Wednesday 13 October 1830 a farm labourer severed the ear from a lamb on a farm owned by Thomas Rose. The offender, Joshua Griggs, was indicted and, on conviction, was sentenced to be transported for seven years at Chelmsford Quarter Sessions. He was a recidivist, hence the sentence.[16] No reason was ever given for this atrocious act and it must be assumed that it was out of sheer spite against farmer Rose.

On 5 November 1830 an arson attack occurred at Hogg's Farm in Rayleigh in the occupancy of farmer and overseer of the poor, John Sach. This was the incident referred to by Hobsbawm and Rudé as the start of the Swing disturbances in Essex. The locations of Swing incidents in Essex are shown in Map IV.ii below. Shortly after the Rayleigh fire two men were apprehended on suspicion of incendiarism. One was a labourer, who had been born and bred in Rayleigh. The other originally came from Kent, having moved to Rayleigh on his discharge from the Royal Navy in 1815. This fire will be discussed in greater detail below.

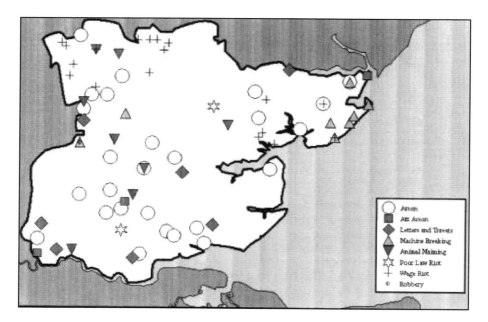

Map IV.ii. Incidents in Essex, 1830-32

There were three further incidents in Essex during November, a poor law riot with a slightly different slant and two more acts of incendiarism. On 24 November there was an act of incendiarism at Thaxted, and then on 30 November an attack in Brightlingsea. Not much is known about either incident, probably because the local newspapers were dominated by the arrest of the incendiaries for the Rayleigh fire.

RIOTS

The offence of riot can be misleading. In the context of this essay the word is restricted to overt acts of protest. However, the newspapers and court records of 18th and 19th century Essex (and elsewhere in England) frequently used the word 'riot' to describe anything from a tumultuous assembly of farm labourers bent on improving their lot, to a fight in a local hostelry over the price of beer. The legal definition of riot is:

> A tumultuous disturbance of the peace, by three persons or more assembling together of their own authority, with an intent, mutually to assist each other against any who shall oppose them, in the execution of some enterprise of a private nature, and afterwards actually executing the same in a violent and turbulent manner, to the terror of the people, whether the act intended were of itself lawful or unlawful.[17]

At the time of Swing, the normal procedure adopted by the authorities was for a Justice of the Peace to attend the scene, supported either by parish and special constables or the military, and to order the rioters to disperse by reading the Riot Act. Basically, this took the form of an instruction to the rioters to disperse within the hour or face the prospect of being arrested for felony, which could lead, on conviction, to a capital sentence. It also authorised armed force to be used if conditions dictated.

Starting with the poor law riot, this occurred during the evening of Monday 22 November 1830 at Great Coggeshall, when a group of farm labourers, together with a few local farmers, congregated outside the houses of the two parish overseers to protest about the rating of some parish cottages inhabited by farm labourers. Technically, it was well within the law for cottages to be rated for the purposes of underwriting the relief of the poor under legislation enacted in 1819.[18] However, in reality, such a move was likely to cause at least some resentment, or a riot. Such was the case at Great Coggeshall.

As the mob approached the houses of the two overseers a drum was beaten, a form of 'rough music' to demonstrate dissatisfaction with the situation and, indeed, the overseers who implemented the rating.[19] At Mr Kirkham's house, the mob smashed the windows and made threats that they were going to drag him out and tear him limb from limb. At Mr Patterson's house they contented themselves with smashing the windows.[20] Order was eventually restored and the ringleaders were committed for trial. They were subsequently bound over by a sympathetic magistrate to keep the peace in their own recognisance of ten pounds each .[21]

The bulk of Swing unrest in Essex commenced in December 1830, with wage riots predominating. These occurred mainly in the north-west of the county, although four occurred in the north-east as Map IV.ii shows. In fact, most of the protest occurred in the northern half of Essex. There was a cluster of machine-breaking incidents on the north-east coast of Essex. The southern half of the county suffered incendiarism, anonymous threatening letters, and threats to commit incendiarism, all directed at farmers.

The wage riots normally took the following form. A group of labourers would arrange to visit the farms in a parish collectively, with the object of intimidating each farmer to raise the wages to a predetermined level. As they moved from farm to farm they would encourage (or coerce) labourers at work at that farm to down tools and join them, thus achieving a snowball effect. The testimony of George Barker of Clavering is typical of what many labourers experienced as they went about their work.

> I went to the [saw] pit to work on Saturday morning the others, namely
> George Matthews, James Westwood, James Joslin, Robert Newland,
> James Wright and several others came up to me and said that I should
> not work. They took me along against my will. We went to other farms
> where they took other labourers against their will.[22]

Wage riots that occurred before the Swing period were invariably planned in a local inn or hostelry on the night before the riot. There is every reason to suppose that Swing wage (and other) riots would have been planned in the local beer shop.[23]

The first wage riots in Essex occurred over a three-day period commencing on 2 December and ending on 5 December 1830 at the villages of Ridgewell, Birdbrook and Stambourne. According to the rector of Stambourne, Reverend James Hopkins, a crowd of about fifty labourers from Ridgewell toured the local farms in the three parishes demanding a rise in wages. No arrests were made, despite a number of special constables having been sworn in, therefore the identity of the ringleaders is not known.

On Monday 6 December a series of wage riots occurred, where approximately one hundred and fifty farm labourers:

> Tumultuously and riotously assembled in the parish of St Michaels near
> Colchester and compelled certain farmers by intimidation to sign a
> certain piece of paper, for the purposes of obtaining an advance in
> wages.[24]

Their demand was for two shillings a day and beer until Lady Day.[25] Armed with heavy bludgeons they coerced 'peacefully disposed labourers' to join the mob, forcing them to leave their work. The rioters visited six farmers in the parishes of St Michael's and Mile End, Colchester, each being required to sign the piece of paper acceding to their demands. The note read:

> I wish to have 2s a day and beer to Lady Day. This is all I wish, but I
> will have it by fair or foul means.[26]

One of the Colchester magistrates, Sir George Smyth, went to Mile End in response to the riot and ordered the rioters to disperse.[27] This they did, but then a short time later re-assembled and, as a result, the ringleaders were arrested.

The nine ringleaders were tried before Mr Justice Taunton at Chelmsford Assizes on 18 December 1830. The two men, Hardwick and Wright, who had been identified as the prime ringleaders, received twelve months' imprisonment with hard labour; their lieutenants nine months, six months, and three months' imprisonment, based upon their level of involvement. They were relatively lucky, for in his pre-trial address Mr Justice Taunton had said:

> Persons tumultuously assembling and extorting money, victuals, or other articles by threats or violence are liable to the death penalty.[28]

The average wages of farm labourers in the area of Colchester was between nine and ten shillings per week. It depended upon the industry of the individual labourer and the generosity of the employer. Had the rioters been successful, the weekly wage would have risen to twelve shillings in cash and a further one shilling in beer, making a gross wage of thirteen shillings.[29]

Other wage riots occurred in Essex as the following Table IV.I shows. With the exception of Little Wigborough, Peldon and West Mersea all of the riots occurred during normal working hours. In the case of these riots, which were committed by the same group of men, the offence occurred in the early hours of the morning in somewhat bizarre circumstances.

TABLE IV.I
Wage riots in Essex

Date	Day	Parish	Date	Day	Parish
10/12/30	Fri	Arkesden	10/12/30	Fri	Henham
2 to 5/12/30		Birdbrook	10/12/30	Fri	Henham
11/12/30	Sat	Clavering	10/12/30	Fri	Little Wigborough
6/12/30	Mon	Colchester	10/12/30	Fri	Peldon
6/12/30	Mon	Colchester	01/12/30	Wed	Ridgewell
6/12/30	Mon	Colchester	7/12/30	Tue	Saffron Walden area
06/12/30	Mon	Colchester	2 to 5/12/30		Stambourne
07/12/30	Tue	Elmdon	06/12/30	Mon	Steeple Bumpstead
14/12/30	Tue	Finchingfield	10/12/30	Fri	Steeple Bumpstead
14/12/30	Tue	Finchingfield	10/12/30	Fri	Steeple Bumpstead
7/12/30	Tue	Great Clacton	06/12/30	Mon	Tendring
12/30		Helions Bumpstead	07/12/30	Tue	Wenden Lofts
			10/12/30	Fri	West Mersea

Mr South, a farmer of West Mersea, an island on the River Colne, was awoken at 3 am by a commotion. On investigating he found that a number of farm labourers had entered his house, presumably by making a forced entry. Furthermore, one of the labourers, William Lappage, was on his stairs and another, William Warner was actually in his bedroom. They ordered him to get dressed and demanded that he accompany them around the local farms in support of their claim for higher wages. The poor man was so terrified that he was unequal to the task of tying up his boots and had to be assisted by the two labourers. To emphasise their demands, a noose was placed around his neck, adding to his terror.[30] South later estimated that there were one hundred and fifty rioters present.

He was forced to accompany the rioters to other farms in adjacent parishes. At Peldon they visited the premises of Mr Charles Wiffen. He refused to come out to speak with them, addressing them from his upstairs bedroom window, possibly unaware of South's predicament. They demanded that he pay the labourers 2s 3d (11.25p) per day plus beer. Wiffen's response was that the farmers could not afford such a sum. Either during these negotiations or whilst the mob was *en route* to nearby Little Wigborough their hostage managed to make his escape and report his ordeal to a magistrate.

Only three of the estimated one hundred and fifty rioters were actually brought to trial over this incident, possibly because in the dark only they could be identified.[31] Accordingly, William Lappage, William Warner, and William Smith were sentenced to a term of imprisonment for their actions that night. Wages for agricultural labourers in the area were not raised as a result of the action. The same applied to other areas where the work force rioted for better wages. Did they really believe that collective action like this would lead to better wages? The answer might be in a letter that was circulating amongst labourers at the time. It read:

> Samuel Whitbread, Labourer
> Stapleford Tawney, Near Romford, Essex
>
> To the hard working (but ill used) labourers of Stapleford Tawney, Stanford Rivers, and other parishes.
>
> Countrymen
>
> The time is now come when the poor labourer is determined to have more of those comforts that he produces, than he has at present. In the counties of Kent, Surrey, Sussex, Hampshire, Berkshire, Wilts, Lincolnshire, and Norfolk, the labourers all have struck for higher wages, they say they wont starve upon 8 or 10s a week any longer. They go to the farm houses after they have got together as many labourers as they can, perhaps 200 or 300 men from 5 or 6 different parishes and make the farmers promise to give them 14s a week in Winter and 15s in summer, and now the men have 14s instead of 10s. They don't mind the farmer bouncing and blustering. They said that they would have it now and they have got it. The men in Kent and Sussex that first struck began to plan the thing on Sunday and went about it on Monday. If Essex rises, it will make ten Counties and I know this, that it is the fault

of the labourers themselves if they have 10s a week instead of 14s, which the brave men of Kent, Sussex and the other Counties are getting. This is good news, my boys, make good use of it.
I am,

A Poor Man's Friend[32]

Whilst there is no evidence to link this letter that was circulating south-west Essex with events further north, it could be surmised that at least part of its contents was widely known across Essex. Furthermore, it is possible, taking account of the way in which news of protest spread from parish to parish amongst the labourers, that this letter underwrote the demands presented in north Essex. It is worthy of note that no wage riots took place in the area of Romford during the period.

MACHINE-BREAKING

The threshing machine was perceived by many to have been the root cause of the Swing Riots.[33] In Essex fifteen machine-breaking incidents took place between 4 and 13 December 1830, as Table IV.II below shows. With the exception of Great Dunmow, where a mole plough was destroyed, all of the attacks were on threshing machines owned or operated by the victims. It took a great deal of effort to smash one of these machines and so the rioters were invariably armed with sledge-hammers, pickaxes and crow-bars, and similar implements and tools.

TABLE IV.II
Machine-breaking in Essex

Date	Day	Parish	Victim	Protester
04/12/1830	Sat	Great Holland	SKEEL	WEBB John
05/12/1830	Sun	Ramsey	PALMER O	
05/12/1830	Sun	Great Holland	FEEDHAM	BAKER Henry
05/12/1830	Sun	Great Holland	SCOTT	DUNNETT Charles
06/12/1830	Mon	Sheering	BEALE	
07/12/1830	Tue	Great Clacton	MOSS George	TILLETT John
07/12/1830	Tue	Great Clacton	CAUVILL	CROSS
07/12/1830	Tue	Great Clacton	WELHAM John	EADE Stephen
07/12/1830	Tue	Great Clacton	LAKE	WEDD
07/12/1830	Tue	Ramsey	CAMPION	
08/12/1830	Wed	Walton-le-Soken	WILSON	PHILIPS
08/12/1830	Wed	Little Clacton	CAUVILL	DURRELL
08/12/1830	Wed	Kirby-le-Soken	BAKER	PHIPPS
09/12/1830	Thu	Great Dunmow	WARD John	PAYNE Charles
13/12/1830	Mon	Great Clacton	SMITH	BLOOMFIELD

Source: Contemporary newspapers and ERO, Depositions, Q/SBd 6/1

Table IV.II shows the day, date, parish, victim and, where known, the ringleader of the rioters. Machine-breaking riots followed a similar pattern to wage riots, with planning being carried out the night before and the snowball effect of gathering labourers as the rioters moved towards their target farm. In many cases labourers were coerced or intimidated into joining the riot.[34] Some rioters used the threat of destroying threshing machines as a bargaining tool for higher wages, as the following deposition shows:

> Samuel Baker, farmer of Kirby-le-Soken on his oath saith, on Thursday morning 8th December 1830 a large mob of labourers, about 200 strong threatened to break threshing machines in the parish of Kirby if they did not get more wages.[35]

Farmer Samuel Wilson of Walton-le-Soken describes the moment that a mob arrived at his farm to destroy his machine:

> Samuel Wilson of Walton-le-Soken on his oath saith on Wednesday 8th December 1830 a number of persons consisting of nearly 300 collected together and in a riotous and tumultuous manner proceeded to the informant's premises in Walton. Amongst them was John Philips who was the first person to come through the gate with a large hammer in his hand. He called to the mob to halt! After the gate was opened, he and others went to the cart lodge where the threshing machine was lodged, drew it out and smashed it.[36]

With a mob of that size resistance would have been pointless and the only thing that the victim could do was to let the rioters accomplish what they came to do and hope that they would then leave.

Threshing machines were not the only pieces of agricultural equipment to receive the attention of machine breakers. A mole plough, which was used to dig drainage channels in fields, was destroyed at Great Dunmow.[37] The victim's deposition read as follows:

> James Hockley, farmer of Great Dunmow on his oath saith, On 10th December having some suspicion that some person would injure or destroy the mole plough on my premises, I went to the field at 8.30 p.m. Before I came up to the plough, I could distinguish three men. I called out, 'What the devil are you doing here? What business do you have here?' I perceived that Charles Payne and John Porter, labourers, both of High Easter, were standing by the plough together with a third man whose name I did not know. Charles Payne said, 'We have come to cut this plough to pieces. I know it shall not work here anymore.' I ordered them to go off my premises. They went away. The next morning, I again went to the field with John Ward, the owner of the plough. We found it broken and totally unfit for use.[38]

As with wage riots, the authorities sought to prosecute the leaders of machine-breaking riots, allowing the rank and file and those caught up in the riots or coerced into joining to go unpunished. From the employers' viewpoint, those labourers who claimed to have been coerced into joining a riot but declined to give evidence, would find their short term employment prospects problematic. Those who did give evidence would have been assured employment, but may well have been ostracised by their peers.

In total, fifty-six agricultural labourers were prosecuted for machine-breaking, eight of these had committed offences at more than one farm and seven were transported for a period of seven years. The other multiple offender, William Bloomfield, 32 years of Great Clacton, was ordered to be transported for life. The probable reason for this was that at the Lent assizes of 1820 William Bloomfield had been indicted with stealing rabbits, but discharged by proclamation.[39] This meant that either the grand jury felt that there was insufficient evidence to convict or, that the prosecutor had failed to attend court.[40] A further fifteen protesters were transported to Australia for seven years, six received terms of imprisonment, ranging from three to twelve months with hard labour. The remainder were discharged or required to enter into a recognisance to be of good behaviour. These were lesser offenders who had, in all probability, been caught up in the fervour of the riot.

Before we move on to other offences, the final word on machine-breaking must come from a poem written by a Little Clacton machine-breaker.[41]

It was on the eighth of last December
Which many of us well remember
When Little Clacton Mob did rise
Which put the people in surprise.
They rose up in the dead of night,
Which put the people in a fright;
For higher wages was there [sic] scheme,
Likewise to break the Lodge machine.
Then in the morn we went straightway,
And broke it up without delay:
And thus we did begin our mob,
But soon it proved a fatal job.
For that same night, mark what I say,
They took three married men away;
From wives and children and from home;
And God knows whither the'll return.
I being press'd to join the throng'
For they took all both old and young:
My adversary standing by,
And marked what ere I did or say
A freind [sic] of mine did come,
And said to me you'd better run;
For ther's a warrant out for you
And what he said, I found was true,
The night was cold, the snow was sleaing,
My wife and children all were weeping,

When I from them was forc'd away
For there I dare no longer stay
I being put in such a fright;
I left my home that very night;
And at a friend's house near by,
Three nights and days there did I lie.
Then when I heard they had searched for me.
Thinks now I must further flee;
Then off to London I did go,
My heart was filled with grief and woe.
I did awhile in London dwell,
And hoped all things would end quite well.
In hopes that I should get off clear,
If I could stay a half a year.
And as I had got a situation,
I very soon should left that station;
But by some means it got about,
And very soon they found me out.
And on the morn of New Year's Day,
From London I was forc'd away;
The Essex Runner came so bold,
And took me off to Springfield Gaol.

Then soon for trial I did stand,
The first thing was hold up your hand
Guilty or not, the chairman cry'd

Guilty my lord I soon replied.
Then they were all in consultation,
And talking about transportation;
My adversary looked at me,
No doubt he wished me cross the sea.
But so the chairman sentenced me,
One year in Springfield Gaol to lie.
Nine months to be kept at hard labour
The same he said unto my neighbour.
The last three month's locked in my cell,
In solitary lonely dwell;
I hope the Lord will be my friend,
And give me patience to the end.
Now when in prison I did lie,
And often wished for liberty;
Our living, work, and bed was hard,
And from all comforts we were bar'd.
We work'd all weathers, wet or dry,
And were debarred from liberty;
Kept close all day until the bell,
Did ring to take us to our cell.
Then soon our keeper's came around,
To see if we were safe and sound;
With keys in hand they walk so hard,

And quickly were our doors bar'd.
All night the watchman goes his round,
And lightly treads the hollow ground;
The time of night to us he told,
And gently cries out all is well.
Then in the morn the bell does ring,
And quickly up the turnkeys spring;
Unbolt, unlock, and out we go,
And for our bread stands in a row.
Then to the treading mill we run,
Until the clergyman does come;
And then to chapel we prepare,
To hear him read and say the prayers.

Now to conclude and make an end,
I don't wish any to offend;
No doubt some folks will me blame,
But 'tis the truth, and can't be shamed.
But as I have reached my house again,
I hope, I hope there to remain;
Others may rise and they may scheme
I'll mob no more nor break machines
But, as the school boy's copy say,
A void alluring company.

THREATS

Moving on to anonymous threatening letters, seven were sent to farmers and the clergy in Essex between 3 December 1830 and 20 January 1831, as Table IV.III shows.

TABLE IV.III
Anonymous threatening letters

Date	Day	Parish	Victim	Protester
03/12/1830	Fri	Orsett	ASHFORD	FLETCHER Meyrich
10/12/1830	Fri	Hawkwell	BROCKIES	SHEPPARD John
14/12/1830	Tue	Dedham	HURLOCK Rev	Unknown
18/12/1830	Sat	Barking	Multiple recipients	Unknown
20/01/1831	Thu	Great Hallingbury	BOURCHIER Rev	CASS Thomas
08/01/1831	Fri	Danbury	HILTON	BANNISTER Francis
08/01/1831	Fri	Danbury	BANNISTER	BANNISTER Francis

Source: Contemporary newspapers and ERO, Depositions, Q/SBd 6/1

It is highly likely that other letters were received by farmers, landowners and the clergy during this period and that the recipients simply destroyed them. It will be seen from

Table IV.III that there were multiple recipients in Barking. Who exactly received letters during this period in Barking is simply not known, for the matter was reported in the newspapers, more or less in passing.[42]

The anonymous threatening letter was an oft-used device adopted by protesters who wished to intimidate farmers and the like into acceding to their wishes, which were often a rise in wages, a reduction of living costs, and, in one Essex instance, a reduction in the tithe payment. None of the Essex anonymous letters were followed up by direct action; in fact, across the entire country fires followed very few threatening letters.[43] In Essex for the period 1783 to 1841, only five out of forty-one anonymous threatening letters sent to farmers and the like, were followed by incendiary attacks.[44]

It has been estimated that across the country during the 1830s only 25% of the adult labouring population could be considered to be literate.[45] In 1838-39, 46% of the population of Essex was shown to be illiterate.[46] This figure is based on the ability to write their name in the marriage register. The evidence would point to the fact that, in any given rural parish, a very small number of labourers would be capable of writing a structured letter.

Therefore, in many cases where a farmer received an anonymous threatening letter, the process of identifying the writer would be relatively easy. An example of this is the letter that was received by Farmer Ashford of Orsett on 3 December 1830. It read simply, and it must be said, menacingly:

What the Poor Lacketh, the flame will catcheth.[47]

Suspicion immediately focussed upon Meyrich Fletcher, one of Ashford's labourers, who, it was subsequently revealed, had purchased a piece of writing paper from the village shop identical to the one on which the letter was written. In fact, Mary Layzell, who ran the shop with her husband, deposed to that effect.[48]

In view of these two pieces of evidence, Fletcher was arrested and examined regarding this matter. He was adamant that he was innocent, stating:

I never wrote or sent the writing above described.[49]

His denial was not accepted, especially as he was neither able to produce the writing paper or account for its use. Accordingly, he was charged with

Threatening to burn and destroy the house, outhouse, barns, stacks of corn and grain the property of Thomas Ashford.[50]

He was committed for trial at the next quarter sessions, where the grand jury, after examining the prosecution evidence, found 'No True Bill'. Accordingly, he was discharged. In other words, they considered that the evidence was not strong enough to secure a conviction against Fletcher. Why they should come to this decision is difficult to comprehend, especially in light of the disturbances going on throughout the country.

One week after the Orsett letter, Colonel Kesterman's bailiff at Parsonage Farm in Hawkwell (near to Rayleigh), received a letter demanding that the workers be paid a higher wage as follows:

> Mr Brockies
> We Sent this to you to let you know
> That if yo Do Not give too
> Shillins A Day Every thing Shall
> Come to Ashes We have Come from
> Kent in that intentione And so
> We mene to go through Essex
> We brought this to your dore Becaus
> We don't like to put you to
> No exspence
> And we ment to Burn the Pashnidge up first[51]

The letter was left in the farmyard close to the house, and was found by Mr Brockies' five-year-old daughter. As in the case against Meyrich Fletcher, suspicion quickly fell upon literate farm labourer John Shepherd who worked at Parsonage Farm, and a warrant was issued for his arrest. Shepherd was aged about twenty years, was married with one or two children. In the late 1820s he had applied for parish aid to pay for the funeral of a daughter, but this was refused on the grounds that he owned a cottage, which he rented out in nearby Rettendon.[52]

Shepherd was duly arrested by the two Hawkwell parish constables and examined before Justice Lodwick of Rochford Hall. He admitted writing the note but insisted that he did not write it for any evil intention or motive. In fact, he claimed that he wrote it for a bit of fun.[53] Shepherd was committed to Chelmsford Gaol pending his trial at the next quarter sessions.

On Friday 14 January 1831, Shepherd appeared at the Chelmsford quarter sessions on four indictments, namely:

1. Did wilfully, maliciously, and feloniously deliver a certain writing without any signature, directed to Daniel Brockies, threatening to destroy the houses, outhouses and co the property of Jeremiah Kesterman Esq. Of which the prosecutor as bailiff to Mr Kesterman had charge and care, and that the prisoner delivered the said letter with the intent and view to extort money from the said Daniel Brockies with menaces and without reasonable cause;
2. Did send the letter aforementioned with the intention of demanding money;
3. Did deliver the said letter, but without demanding money;
4. Did send the said letter but without demanding money.[54]

A barrister, Mr Knox, represented Shepherd, which was unusual for someone in his station of life. Mr Knox raised a number of objections to the indictments, which were overruled by the court. Shepherd pleaded not guilty.

The first person to give evidence for the prosecution was Daniel Brockies, who stated that he was handed the letter by his wife at about 8 am. He went on to describe the premises. Cross-examined by Mr Knox, he informed the court that Shepherd lived next door to him under the same roof. He said that he had worked for him for five or six years and was employed by him at the time that the letter was written. He said that when he first read the letter he thought that it was a serious threat. Then, when he realised who had written it, he thought that it was done:

> More for an increase in wages than anything else.

He added that he could not swear that he did not say to Mr Harris (the rector of the parish) that Shepherd did it in a *frotie*.[55]

The parish constables then gave evidence of Shepherd's arrest and what had been said to them. John Coe said that Shepherd's response was:

> I wrote the letter and I am very sorry for it. I did it because I thought
> that I could get a trifle a day more by it: it is a bad job.[56]

Robert Ashby, the Rochford constable who had assisted Coe in the arrest, added that Shepherd had said that he had no intention of doing any burning.

Reverend Harris was called by Mr Knox to provide a character witness for Shepherd, which he stated that he was unable to do because he knew nothing of him personally. He did, however, offer to read some testimonials from other people. The court would not permit this. Parish Constable Coe said that he knew nothing amiss of him. After a short deliberation he was found guilty and sentenced to six months' imprisonment with hard labour. The chairman of the bench informed him that, had it not been for his previous good character, he would have had little hesitation in sentencing him to transportation.[57]

With regard to the two letters sent at Danbury by Francis Bannister in January 1831, the grand jury returned a verdict of No True Bill, and so Bannister was discharged. Little is known about the people responsible for the other letters sent in Essex, although the Great Hallingbury letter was sent to the rector of the parish telling him that if the parish overseer was not removed from office, the rector's barns would be burned. Thomas Cass of Great Hallingbury was convicted of this offence and sentenced to eighteen months' imprisonment with hard labour.[58] His reason was that he felt that the overseer was failing in his job and not relieving the poor in a satisfactory way.[59] The letter to Hurlock at Dedham has all the hallmarks of a local farmer dissatisfied with the tithe demanded by Hurlock.

INCENDIARISM

We now turn to acts of incendiarism, and attempted incendiarism, in Essex at the time of Swing. This was the most devastating offence that could be inflicted upon the farmer. It not only had the potential for rendering the farmer homeless and possibly ruining him, but could also affect the livelihood of local farm labourers, by rendering them unemployed. Whilst many farmers were insured, and those that were not could claim reparation from the hundred in which the farm was situated, there would have been a short-term period when there was no money for wages, etc. Table IV.IV below details all known acts of incendiarism, and attempted incendiarism, in Essex during this period.

TABLE IV.IV
Incendiarism and attempted incendiarism in Essex

Month	Date	Day	Time	Parish
Jan	02/01/31	Sun	Night	Basildon
Nov	04/11/30	Thu	Night	Beauchamp Roothing
Dec	23/12/31	Fri	Eve	Billericay
Dec	16/12/31	Fri	Night	Birchanger
Sep	03/09/31	Sat	Night	Boreham
Jan	31/01/32	Tue	Night	Bowers Gifford
Aug	14/08/30	Sat	Night	Bradwell-juxta-Mare
Nov	30/11/30	Tue	Night	Brightlingsea
Dec	11/12/31	Sun	Night	Brightlingsea
Sep	??/09/30		Night	Broxted
Feb	19/02/32	Sun	Night	Elsenham
Dec	07/12/30	Tue	Night	Great Chesterford
Sep	11/09/30	Sat	Night	Great Holland
Apr	02/04/32	Mon	Aft	Great Waltham
Apr	02/04/32	Mon	Night	Great Waltham
Dec	14/12/30	Tue	Night	Horndon-on-the-Hill
Apr	26/04/30	Mon	Night	Layer-de-la-Haye
Nov	05/11/31	Sat	Night	Leigh
Dec	14/12/30	Tue	Eve	Leytonstone
Dec	07/12/30	Tue	Night	Ramsey
Nov	05/11/30	Fri	Night	Rayleigh
Nov	22/11/31	Tue	Night	Shenfield
Jan	13/01/32	Fri	Night	South Weald
Mar	29/03/32	Thu	Night	Stapleford Tawney
Oct	??/10/30			Stondon Massey
Dec	10/12/31	Sat	Night	Tendring
Nov	24/11/30	Wed	Night	Thaxted
Jul	18/07/31	Mon	Night	West Bergholt
Feb	05/02/31	Sat	Eve	Writtle
Mar	08/03/31	Tue	Night	Writtle
Jan	28/01/31	Sat	Eve	Writtle
Mar	24/03/31	Thu	Aft	Writtle

TABLE IV.IV (contd)
Attempted incendiarism

Month	Date	Day	Time	Parish
Mar	16/03/31	Wed	Night	Harwich
Jan	13/01/31	Thu	Night	Mountnessing
Nov	13/11/32	Tue	Night	West Ham

Source: Contemporary newspapers and ERO, Depositions, Q/SBd 6/1

Where the day of week is known this is included in the table; most attacks took place at night, although there were six exceptions to this rule. Afternoon attacks would only occur when no one was about the stack yard to raise the alarm and thwart the attack. Most incendiaries preferred to work under cover of darkness to mask their activities and to prevent detection and arrest.

Some comment on the characteristics of farm fires might be prudent at this point. Stacks of corn, hay, straw, etc., were raised off the ground to permit air to circulate and prevent the contents of the stack from composting down and suffering spontaneous combustion. They were thatched to protect them from the elements. Incendiary attacks on stacks invariably required the wall of the stack being ruptured, the straw (or whatever) being pulled out to act as a crude fuse. Once lit, the flames would burn laterally into the stack before erupting in a mighty conflagration, as the newspapers of the day were wont to describe it, two or three hours after the fire had first been lit.

The actual act of lighting the fire could be a problem. Matches were expensive and probably beyond the income of a farm labourer. They were also unreliable. It was not until 1833 that the matches that we know today were first invented.[60] So, how else could ignition be achieved? A tinderbox could be used but trying to strike a strip of metal against a piece of flint out in the open at night could prove problematic, especially in adverse weather conditions. Methods that were used by Essex incendiaries include using a carefully masked lantern and using the lighted candle within to start a fire.[61] Another method was to light the tinder before leaving home, wrap the smouldering material in a rag, and introduce it to the side of the stack.[62] Whatever method employed, the result would be an inferno that would very easily communicate itself to other stacks and farm buildings, and that would be very difficult to control. The fire-fighting facilities that were available during this period were extremely basic. The best that could normally be hoped for would be for the fire to be contained to minimise collateral damage.[63]

All but two of the Essex incendiary attacks resulted in no one being arrested and tried for the crime. Arrests were made following many of the incendiary attacks, but only two went as far as the assizes. These were the incendiary attack at Rayleigh, cited by Hobsbawm and Rudé as being the first Swing offence in Essex, and the Writtle fires. Labourers were arrested, examined and released following the attacks at Basildon and Writtle, but nobody was brought to book. Accordingly, we have but two people who went on trial for this capital offence.

Taking Writtle first, the four fires that occurred in 1831, a sixteen-year-old labourer, Charles Atkins was arrested following his behaviour at the scene of the fire that occurred on

28 January. Basically, his demeanour led the authorities to believe that he had been responsible for a number of fires in the locality. However, once arrested and examined by the magistrates, it became apparent that he was not responsible. Therefore he was released without charge.[64] Following the fire on 8 March brothers George and Samuel Lines, Samuel Beamer, and William Quinn were arrested, Quinn having been found in possession of a key to the premises and a flint and knife. They were examined and committed for trial.[65] The evidence pointed to the fact that the Writtle incendiaries had been caught and no doubt they would have been put on trial for their lives, had it not been for a fourth fire. This occurred on 24 March and a sailor, William Jennings, was apprehended. A search revealed that he was in possession of a tinderbox and matches, and a quantity of plate that had been stolen in a burglary at Althorne.[66] On being examined he admitted being responsible for the other three attacks. It would appear that his motive was a form of protest against farmers, although his primary objective was burglary. He was convicted and executed for his crimes.[67]

Turning to the Rayleigh fire, this incendiary attack occurred on the night of 5 November 1830 at Hogg's Farm, close to the centre of Rayleigh. It was in the occupancy of John Sach, farmer and overseer of the poor for the parish. The fire was discovered at 1.15 am by a labourer on his way home from loading the kilns at the local brick-fields. The alarm was raised and fire-fighting operations commenced. The chronology of events is detailed below.[68]

- ❖ 11.45 pm   (approximate) Probable time fire lit
- ❖ 1.15 am   Fire discovered - alarm raised
- ❖ 1.20 am   Victim at scene; general alarm raised by church bell; fire fighting commenced by bucket chain
- ❖ 1.35 am   Messenger sent for engine at Rochford
- ❖ 2.05 am   Fire engine leaves for the fire - travelling time half an hour
- ❖ 2.35 am   Fire engine at scene
- ❖ 3 am   Bucket chain organised; engine starts to work
- ❖ 6 am   Fire contained - no risk to house; stacks and barn beyond redemption
- ❖ 8 am   Fire engine returned to Rochford

As was common with all fires (both deliberate and accidental), most of the local populace would turn out either to assist at the fire or enjoy the spectacle. Many farm labourers treated fires as an opportunity to partake of quantities of ale, which was supplied to those assisting in fighting the fire. Fire fighting is thirsty work and ale was the only refreshment available to allow body fluids to be maintained. Amongst those who turned out was a labourer named James Ewen. He had worked for Sach in the past and had also come into contact with him in his capacity as overseer of the poor. Sach had relieved Ewen on three occasions by way of loan, a method reserved for claimants who either made themselves unemployed or squandered their wages on ale or the like.[69]

Ewen's behaviour at the fire attracted suspicion. He allegedly made a number of comments to total strangers concerning his responsibility for the fire, and the fact that Sach had underpaid him. He is even said to have attempted to recruit two strangers on an expedition to fire the churchwarden's farm the following night. He said of the fire:

> They served them so in Kent and so we will here, if you are a trump.[70]

He and another Rayleigh labourer were arrested, examined, and committed for trial at the next assizes. His co-defendant made application to see a magistrate on arrival at Chelmsford Gaol and subsequently turned King's evidence.[71] He gave incriminating evidence against Ewen from the perspective of an accessory to incendiarism.[72] James Ewen was convicted and sentenced to hang. Despite strenuous attempts at clemency, he was executed on the morning of 24 December and buried on 26 December 1830, the entry in the parish burial book being annotated with the words:

> Hanged for incendiarism - suffered the extreme penalty of the law.[73]

It is noteworthy that following the sentencing of James Ewen, protest crime in Essex slowed considerably, having peaked on 11 December, as Fig. IV.1 shows. You will see that once the trial started on 17 December, protest crime fell away. It was not until January 1831 that there was a brief rise in protest activity, before dropping away again. Judges were required to use capital sentencing carefully. The criterion for applying sentence of death to a convicted offender was that it must have had an exemplary effect on those who might seek to emulate him or her.[74] The evidence would suggest that sentence to, and the execution of, James Ewen, had a salutary effect on protesters in Essex at this time.

On 14 December there were acts of incendiarism at Leytonstone and Horndon-on-the-Hill. At the latter the newspapers reported that:

> The peasantry worked with indefatigable zeal, by whom much property
> was saved. They were heard to declare that if it was wilfully caused and
> the person known, they would cast him into the flames.[75]

Whether this was a case of journalistic licence or a truthful statement on the part of the labourers is difficult to tell. The use of the word 'peasantry' might point to the former.

The New Year saw another incendiary attack, this time at Basildon (about ten miles from Rayleigh), on the premises of Mr Raynham. The fire was discovered in the early hours of 2 January. The fire destroyed much of the farm, including a number of pigs. It was noted in the press that:

> After the fire had somewhat abated several labourers were seen
> devouring the carcasses of pigs that had perished in the fire.[76]

Such behaviour was by no means unprecedented by labourers whose basic diet consisted of bread. They could not be criticised for a piece of opportunism. Joseph Such was arrested on suspicion of incendiarism and examined. His arrest came about on the strength of some hearsay evidence given by a Rayleigh labourer, who worked for the churchwarden, Mr Brewitt. Such stated that he had passed the farm on his way home from a club, but had seen nothing of the fire. For want of further evidence, he was discharged.[77] Nothing has been found that would identify the club referred to by Such.[78]

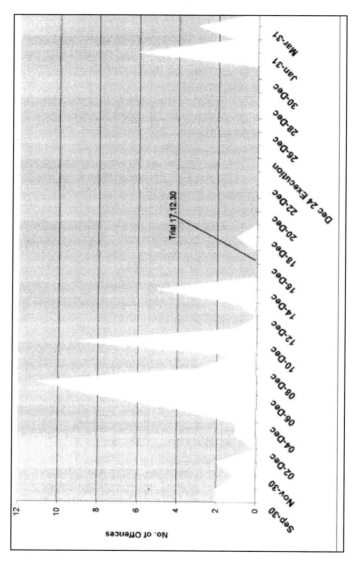

Fig. IV.1. Essex Swing incidents September 1830–March 1831

There were a further eighteen acts of incendiarism; two attempts to commit incendiarism; three anonymous threatening letters; and six animal maiming incidents. There were no further wage riots or machine breaking incidents. In fact, for the next fifty years incendiarism was to be the principle means of protest in Essex.[79] It would seem that attacks on farm mechanisation ended with Ewen's conviction. There were two further wage riots in Essex post Swing. These were at Lawford in 1836 and South Weald in 1839.[80] One final note on incendiarism, on 5 November 1831 an attack occurred on a farm in the occupancy of Samuel Fairchild at Leigh, about five miles south of Rayleigh. No one was ever arrested for this fire.[81]

PROTESTERS AND THEIR *RAISON D'ETRE*

What inspired men to turn to protest crime in order to express dissatisfaction with their situation in life? This is not easy to answer. According to the 1831 census there were 38,234 agricultural labourers in Essex. It is known that one hundred and sixty-eight agricultural labourers, one thatcher, one hay binder, and a sailor were indicted for acts of protest during the whole period of Swing. It is also known that there were twenty-five wage riots and fifteen machine-breaking riots. The number of people indicted for involvement in these riots is seventy-seven and fifty-six, respectively. This averages out to just over three people per riot. However, those indicted were the ringleaders. The evidence shows that machine-breaking and wage riots attracted large groups of men, albeit some of them under duress.

A conservative average for involvement in each type of riot would lead us to conclude that about thirty agricultural labourers were involved in each incident. This gives us a figure of just under four thousand labourers being involved in overt acts of protest. This in turn reveals that about 4% of agricultural labourers turned to acts of protest as an expression of dissatisfaction. This does not mean that the remaining 96% were totally satisfied with their working conditions. There were a number of ways in which a labourer could covertly take his revenge on his employer. The most common method was to be less industrious, so that each task took longer to fulfil and resulted in the employer actually paying more for each job to be done. Other ways included theft of small amounts of produce, pieces from a saddle for home shoe repairs, etc.

It must be assumed that labourers who took more drastic action had reached the point where they could no longer tolerate the pay and conditions without some form of violent response. It must have been extremely difficult for labourers to eke out an existence on starvation pay in the knowledge that their employer was enjoying a far better lifestyle as a result of their industry. There is another factor to all of this - ale.

Returning to the case of James Ewen, the Rayleigh incendiary. There is evidence that shows he was drinking in the local beershop with his co-defendant on the night of the fire.[82] Furthermore, he made remarks to his co-defendant, which would be consistent with a man getting progressively intoxicated, one of which was:

I have threatened him many a time but this is the settler now.[83]

It therefore seems probable that Ewen, having moaned and complained about his employer during the course of the evening, decided to turn words into action and set fire to the farm. As stated above, wage and machine-breaking attacks were frequently pre-planned in the local hostelry. Little research has been performed on the relationship between the Beerhouse Act of 1830 and protest, which identifies a possible gap in existing knowledge.

RESPONSES TO PROTEST

From the end of November 1830 ten letters were sent to Viscount Melbourne, Secretary of State for the Home Department, from members of the magistracy in Essex expressing concern over the level of protest crime in the county.[84] For example, the magistrates in Billericay sent the following:

> I, John Staples Holland, clerk, magistrate of Billericay in the County of Essex crave your indulgence in permitting us to allow a reward to be payable for information that would help to convict the Rayleigh arsonist. I appreciate that I reside outside that hundred, but feel that it is in the interests of us all to ensure that this matter is dealt with in an exemplary manner.[85]

By the time that this letter had been received at the Home Office, Ewen and Richardson were already in custody, so the reward could only have been used to possibly persuade other witnesses to come forward.

On 30 November 1830 the three Rochford magistrates, Justices Barrington, Lodwick and Wayne, wrote the following to the Home Office:

> Rochford Hall
>
> November 30, 1830
>
> My Lord,
> In times like the present when no man's property can be considered safe from the depredations committed upon machinery or from the still more mischievous work of incendiaries it behoves the local magistracy to be on the alert and to question as far as may be in their powers the views and intentions of persons particularly strangers.
>
> As magistrates for the County of Essex we beg to state to your Lordship from an authority which may be relied upon that there have been and are persons travelling about this part of the county with a view of making enquiries as to the employment of machines by the agriculturists and they take down in writing the information which they may obtain.
>
> It is not our wish to trespass unnecessarily upon the subject, but if it appears to us that the only mode of preventing an extension to this mischief is by putting the law in force to such an extent as the

magistrates can fairly act - And we beg therefore to enquire of your Lordship whether we should be justified in taking into custody and causing any strangers to be searched who we may learn from good authority have been making enquiries and noting down answers respecting the employment of machinery by the land holders.

> J. Lodwick
> G. Wayne
> J. Barrington[86]

What exactly prompted this letter is difficult to say. There were a number of reports prevalent at this time concerning men in closed gigs travelling about the countryside, making notes about the use of threshing machines. These always seemed to be second- or third-hand reports. The only positive event was the detention of the Ranter, Joseph Saville on the Suffolk/Essex/Cambridgeshire border, although this incident occurred in mid December 1830.[87]

Justice Barrington convened a meeting at the Kings Head Inn at Rochford, of local farmers, with the intention of swearing them in as special constables to counter the perceived threat to farms in the neighbourhood. This was in response to a directive from Viscount Melbourne calling upon magistrates across the country to:

> Act with vigour and reject out of hand any suggestions that concessions
> can be made to the disaffected.[88]

Some discussion took place concerning the plight of the labouring poor, and then the farmers concluded that the root cause of the riots was the threshing machines and the impact that they had on the labourers. They concluded by advising Barrington to do as they intended, put his threshing machine away and pay his labourers a living wage. Barrington responded:

> Threshing machines are entitled to the protection of the law as any
> other form of property. To surrender to blackmail in such a case is to
> connive at, or rather assist, in the establishment of tyranny of the most
> oppressive character.[89]

The farmers were not convinced, and the meeting broke up a short time later with only one special constable having been sworn in.

Other parts of the county fared better. In the Ongar Petty Sessional Division the Justices enrolled one hundred and nineteen special constables at three sittings on 11, 18 and 24 December 1830, from a range of occupations and all levels of the social strata, from agricultural labourer to peer of the realm.[90] At Saffron Walden, the Lord Lieutenant, Lord Braybrooke, was instrumental in attesting three hundred and fifty-one specials for operations against rioting labourers.[91] At Chelmsford five hundred special constables were sworn in for the duration of the Swing Riots. The norm was for specials to be sworn in for a specific period of time but the following applied at this time.

> As it appears impossible to calculate [how long] the present feverish spirit might remain, it was at last concluded that the words 'until discharged by competent authority' would itself furnish a terminor to their services.[92]

One of the duties of the Chelmsford specials was to provide crowd-control cover at the gaol on the morning of James Ewen's execution. Troops were used to protect the actual scaffold, but the special constables were needed as secondary cover against rioting or even a rescue attempt.

The operational structure of the Chelmsford special constables appears to have left nothing to chance as the following shows.

> 14th December 1830
> Numbers of Special Constables sworn in within six miles of Chelmsford amounts to 100 mounted Special Constables and 400 foot Special Constables. Staves are to be supplied to each parish.
> Recommended:
> 1. That mounted Special Constables be nominated to provide communications between the magistrates and the groups.[93]
> 2. Named persons in each parish to supply waggons that can be used to transport Special Constables.
> 3. Mr Archer [clerk to the justices] to collect the names of all those sworn in as Special Constables.
> 4. Pattern staves to be sent to each parish where staves have not been provided.
> 5. Special Constables in each parish to nominate a leader.
>
> 17th December 1830
> Resolved that a card or mark be provided to distinguish Special Constables on duty.[94]

In the Tendring Petty Sessional Division the magistracy were at pains to make abundantly clear what their intentions were should rioting break out, as the following poster demonstrates. They were also prepared to use the mounted special constabulary, in the same way as cavalry or yeomanry regiments might be used, to deal with mobs if they refused to disperse following the reading of the Riot Act. This does serve to show the strength of feeling of the landed classes in this part of Essex. Whereas farmers in Rochford preferred to adopt a conciliatory and pragmatic approach to the needs of the labouring poor, those in Tendring displayed a much firmer approach.

Petty Sessions,[95]
MANNINGTREE,
December 7, 1830.

The Magistrates of the HUNDRED OF TENDRING hav-ing received Information of ILLEGAL ASSEMBLIES of the LABOURERS, have deemed it expedient to swear in SPECIAL CONSTABLES in every Parish and the Magistrates recommend that the Special Constables so sworn, will select one Person in each Parish through whom Orders may be communicated. Should any Out-rage occur, information is to be forwarded by a Horse-man to the Chief Constable of the Division, and a Noti-fication to be given to a Constable of each Parish through which the Horseman will pass, and such Constable to assemble all those of his Parish.

In the preservation of the public Peace, it is expected many of the Residents in the Hundred will unite, who may not form part of the Constabulary Force; especially to them, the Magistrates earnestly inculcate the necessity of Order and a uniform system of Action in unison with the Chief Constables, to whom the Magistrates' instructions will be regularly communicated.

It is hoped that the Remonstrances of the well-disposed may have had due effect on the misguided Populace, but should any in future assemble and commit Outrage, the Constables will use all possible exertions to procure the aid of contiguous Parishes.

The Mounted Force, of which the Magistrates doubt not a large Body will be formed, will not advance, except in cases of immediate necessity, beyond that on foot, and on coming up to the Multitude they will require them to select three or four Individuals to state their grievances to the Magistrates, and then to disperse; but should they unfortunately refuse to comply, and commit any Acts of Violence, the Ringleaders must be secured, in order that they may be dealt with according to Law.

The Chief Constables will assure the misled People that the Magistrates are always ready to redress every Grievance in their power, and that acts of Outrage and Tumult neces-sarily tend to augment the Distress of which they complain, and of which all Classes in a greater or less degree now participate.

The Magistrates most earnestly recommend to the whole of the Constabulary Force, the strictest observance of good Order and Sobriety.

THOMAS NUNN,   **H. R. SOMERS SMITH.**

The use of special constables to augment the parish constables meant that, at no time during the Swing riots in Essex, did any magistrate consider it necessary to request military assistance to put down the disturbances. Whilst there is no doubt at all that the disturbances in Essex proved less violent and prolonged than in some other parts of the country, the perception at the time was of protest activity that threatened the stability of the county.

PERCEIVED CAUSES OF PROTEST

One outcome of the Swing riots nationally was an idea that the current poor law system that had been operating, with enhancements, since 1601 had come to the end of its useful life and needed to be reformed as a matter of urgency.[96] A Royal Commission was set up and, in order to solicit opinions from vestries across the country, a questionnaire was sent out to all rural parishes enquiring about the administration of the poor laws at parish level.[97] The final question asked for opinions on the causes of the Swing riots.[98]

In Essex twenty-two parishes responded to the question, although only eight of those had actually experienced the Swing riots at first hand. Unemployment and low wages were most often cited as being root causes of the protest in Essex. The breakdown is as follows:

Braintree Contagious Infatuation; wages; unemployment

Chelmsford Poor housing; enclosure; wages

Great Coggeshall Threshing machines; rating cottages; wages

Epping Unemployment

Finchingfield Unemployment; poor laws

Gestingthorpe Kent

Harlow Distress; unemployment

Great Henny Wages; idleness

Ingatestone Unemployment

Lawford Distress; beer shops; unemployment; threshing machines; wages

Little Waltham Poverty; unemployment; poor laws

Prittlewell Evil disposed persons

Rayleigh Unemployment

Rochford Threshing machines; winter unemployment; wages

Sible Heddingham Unemployment; wages

Stansted Mountfitchet Poor Law; unemployment

Stondon Massey Unemployment; wages

Thaxted Wages; unemployment

Thorpe-le-Soken Beershops; tithes; rent; threshing machines; designing farmers

West Ham Wages

Wickham Bishops Unemployment

Witham Unemployment; wages

Most of the answers are self-explanatory. Gestingthorpe's reference to Kent means emulating the rioters in Kent and the encouragement to protest brought about by the initially paternalistic and weak sentencing patterns employed by Kent magistrates. Thorpe-le-Soken's reference to 'designing farmers' means those cases where farmers encouraged their work force to protest in a cynical attempt to force down rents or tithe payments.[99] Farmers often cited these as the main reason that they were unable to offer their workers a pay rise.

The respondents at Braintree cited 'contagious infatuation' as a principle cause. This referred to the practice adopted by some parishes of putting labourers, who applied to the overseer for relief, to work on the parish roads.[100] By putting a number of disaffected men together and permitting them access to people using the roads, such as carriers, meant that news of disturbances elsewhere could readily be transmitted to them.[101]

It must be remembered that the various respondents were viewing the disturbances with hindsight three years after they had first broken out, and that much had happened at parish level since the riots. However, the overall impression is that *Rural Queries* is a useful resource in evaluating the probable causes of the disturbances.

CONCLUSION

The Swing riots in Essex peaked during December 1830 in the run up to James Ewen's trial and execution. Protest during 1831 still occurred, but seemed to lack the fervour of the previous year. As already discussed, no further machine breaking occurred in Essex after 13 December 1830. In fact, all post-1830 protest involved covert acts of incendiarism, animal maiming, and the transmission of anonymous threatening letters. There were twenty-one acts of protest in 1831 and ten during 1832, the final act being an attempted incendiarism at West Ham in November of that year.

When compared to other counties, Essex did not fare too badly in the Swing riots. Nevertheless, many farmers were intimidated by the rising and made initial concessions in order to reduce the risk of protest activity on their farms. As time went on, however, farmers reverted to the practices that they had in place prior to the start of the riots. Once the initial furore of December 1830 had died down, many farmers reverted to mechanised farming for purely economic reasons.

Acts of protest against farms and farmers continued after 1832, but not with the same intensity as during the Swing period, until the mid-1840s. During this period the number of incendiary attacks over the three-year period of 1843 to 1845 surpassed the Swing level. In 1844 alone there were sixty incendiary attacks on farms, three less acts of protest than 1830. Nevertheless, despite the fact that farmers and landowners continued to feel the wrath of agricultural labourers as farms were fired, it somehow lacked the intensity of the Swing riots.

I set out in this essay to demonstrate that Hobsbawm and Rudé's assertion that Swing in Essex commenced on 5 November 1830 was flawed. The evidence of incidents before this date, especially the attack on Mr Spurgeon of Bradwell-juxta-Mare and, more specifically, his threshing machine during August 1830, point to the fact that there was a burgeoning protest movement gathering pace across Essex. This was to manifest itself as the farming proceeded into the threshing season, when the machines would be used progressively to process the harvested corn. The incendiary attack at Rayleigh on 5 November was, however the first positive link with the disturbances in Kent, when Ewen is said to have commented:

'They served them so in Kent and so we will here, if you are a trump'[102]

By the same token, the Rayleigh fire, which received extensive press coverage, was the first occasion during the Swing period when an incendiary was actually arrested and, more importantly, convicted with a Swing crime. There is no doubt that Essex Swing started before the accepted 5 November 1830.

NOTES

1   Peacock, A J, *Bread or Blood: The Agrarian Riots in East Anglia, 1816*, (London, 1964); Dunbabin, J P D, (ed.), *Rural Discontent in 19th Century Britain*, (New York, 1974).

2   Gyford, J, *Men of Bad Character: The Witham Fires of the 1820s*, (Chelmsford, 1991).

3   Hobsbawm, E and Rudé, G, *Captain Swing*, (London, 1985), p. 122.

4   ERO, Deposition by Cornelius Squier, Q/SBb 499/18.

5   *Chelmsford Chronicle*, 30 April 1830.

6   *Ibid*, 30 April 1830.

7   *Ibid*, 20 August 1830.

8   *Ibid*, 3 September 1830.

9   ERO, Census Returns for the Dengie Hundred, Q/Cr 2/8/1.

10 *Chelmsford Chronicle*, 17 September 1830.

11 *Rochester Gazette*, 21 September 1830.

12 BPP, XXXIV (1834), *Rural Queries* answer to Question 53 *To what do you attribute the recent spate of agricultural rioting*, submitted by Reverend John Oldham of Stondon Massey.

13 *Bury Post*, 10 November 1830 - whilst most Essex Swing incidents were reported in the county's newspapers, occasionally they were to be found amongst reports in other counties. During previous years of protest activity in Essex, the newspaper editors adopted a circumspect approach to reporting incendiary attacks. Their main reason for this strategy was for fear of emulation. It must be assumed that the Beauchamp Roding fire was one such occasion.

14 For information on this crime see Archer, J E, 'A Fiendish Outrage: a study of animal maiming in East Anglia, 1830 to 1870', in *Agricultural History Review*, (1985), 33:2 pp 147-57.

15 *Kent and Essex Mercury*, 3 August 1830.

16 ERO, Deposition of Thomas Rose, Q/SBd 6/1.

17 Vincent, V H, *The Police Code and General Manual of the Criminal Law*, (London, 1901), p. 153.

18 Theobald, W, *A Practical Treatise on the Poor Laws as altered by the Poor Law Amendment Act and Other Recent Statutes*, (London, 1836), pp. 24, 506.

19 For further information on the use of Rough Music, see Thompson, E P, *Customs in Common*, (London, 1991), p. 467 ff.

20 ERO, Deposition of John Kirkham, Q/SBd 6/1.

21 *Chelmsford Chronicle*, 24 December 1830.

22 ERO, Deposition of George Barker, labourer of Clavering, made on 11 December 1830, Q/SBd 6/1.

23 Jones, D J V, *Crime, Protest, Community, and Police in 19th Century Britain*, (Routledge Kegan Paul, 1982), p. 34. The discussion in this book focuses upon arson and the beer shop, but the principals are the same. The main thrust of the argument was that the beer shops were places where the labouring poor could congregate unsupervised. Therefore crime or protest planning could be conducted without fear that the authorities would intervene. See also Jones, D J V, 'Rural Crime and protest in the Victorian Era', in Mingay, G E, (ed.) *The Unquiet Countryside*, (Routledge, 1989), p. 116. For a brief overview of the Beer Bill see Smart, W, *Economic Annals of the Nineteenth Century: 1821 to 1830, Volume II*, ([1910]) Augustus Kelley, New York, 1964), p. 541. There are indications that a wage riot in Steeple, Essex in June 1800 had been planned at a local annual fair.

24 *Cambridge Chronicle*, report of Essex Assizes, 18 December 1830.

25 Lady Day fell on 25 March and was one of two customary dates for the payment of rents, the other being Michaelmas, 29 September.

26 *Cambridge Chronicle*, 18 December 1830.

27 There is no reference to the Riot Act actually being read on this occasion.

28 *Cambridge Chronicle*, 18 December 1830.

29 These calculations are based on the average wage for the area taken from BPP XXX to XXXIV (1834).

30 ERO, Quarter Sessions, Deposition by Daniel South of West Mersea, Q/SBd 6/1.

31 ERO, Quarter Sessions bundles, bills of indictment, Q/SBb 502/3/1.

32 TNA, letters to the Secretary of State for Home Affairs, 1830, HO 52/7.

33 See discussion in the Introduction.

34 See the testimony of George Barker of Clavering above.

35 ERO, Deposition of Samuel Baker, Q/SBd 6/1.

36 ERO, Deposition of Samuel Wilson, Q/SBd 6/1.

37 For more detailed information on mole ploughs and their use in Essex see, Fussell, G E, *The Farmers Tools: British Farm Implements, Tools, and Machinery, AD 1500 to 1900*, (London, 1952), p. 31 ff.

38 ERO, Deposition made by James Hockley of Great Dunmow on 14 December 1830, Q/SBd 6/1.

39 ERO, Recidivists appearing at the Epiphany Sessions on 4 January 1831, Q/SBb 502/98.

40 See Beattie, J M, *Crime and the Courts in England, 1660 to 1800*, (Oxford, 1986), pp. 318, 400.

41 Poem by convicted machine breaker Benjamin Gardener Hackshall, of Little Clacton, Essex, describing a riot that happened at Little Clacton on 8 December 1830 and his time in gaol.

42 *Kent and Essex Mercury*, 28 December 1830.

43 See discussion in Introduction above.

44 *Chelmsford Chronicle, Chelmsford Gazette, Essex Herald, Ipswich Journal*, and *Kent and Essex Mercury*, 1783 to 1851.

45 Vincent, D, *Literacy and Popular Culture: England 1750 to 1914*, (Cambridge, 1993), p. 21.

46 Hobsbawm and Rudé, (1985), p. 42.

47 ERO, Deposition by Farmer Ashford, Q/SBd 6/1, sadly the letter is no longer extant.

48 ERO, Deposition by Mary Layzell, Q/SBd 6/1.

49 ERO, Examination of Meyrich Fletcher, Q/SBd 6/1.

50 ERO, Indictment against Meyrich Fletcher, Q/SBd 6/1.

51 ERO, The case against John Shepherd of Hawkwell, Q/SBd 6/1/9. The use of language in this letter is discussed in the Introduction above.

52 ERO, Hawkwell Overseers Minutes, D/P 217/8/1.

53 ERO, Examination of John Shepherd, Q/SBd 6/1.

54 *Chelmsford Chronicle,* report of the case against Shepherd, 14 January 1831.

55 This would appear to be a dialectal corruption of the word *Fret,* meaning to become distressed with discontent according to the Oxford English Dictionary. It could also be a corruption of *Frout,* which, according to Partridge, E, *The Penguin Dictionary of Historical Slang,* (London, 1982), means, angry, annoyed, or vexed.

56 ERO, Sworn evidence by John Coe, *Chelmsford Chronicle,* 14 January 1831.

57 Under the Black Act of 1715 the sending of anonymous threatening letters was a capital offence. Fortunately for Shepherd, this had been repealed in 1823.

58 ERO, Entry of Calendars for 1831, Q/SMc 5.

59 *Chelmsford Chronicle,* 18 February 1831.

60 Hubbard, H G, *The Rushlight,* Vol. 1: 1, (November 1934).

61 TNA, Clemency Papers, Rex versus James Cook, HO 17/108 vol. 36 (1829).

62 ERO, Deposition of Thomas Fletcher of Halstead in 22 January 1838 in the case of Rex versus Abraham Rayner, Q/SBd 13/3/38.

63 For a fuller explanation of the fire-fighting facilities at the time of Swing see, Holland, M, 'Guilty as Charged: the trial of an Essex Swing incendiary' in Holland, M and Cooper, J, *Essex Harvest: A Collection of Essays in Memory of Arthur Brown,* (Chelmsford, 2003), pp 101-2.

64 *Chelmsford Chronicle,* 11 February 1831.

65 *Ibid,* 11 March 1831.

66 *Ibid,* 25 March 1831.

67 *Ibid,* 22 July 1831.

68 The chronology is based upon calculations on the time that it would take for the fire to become apparent and the timings for summonsing the fire engine from the Hundred town. The assistance of Senior Divisional Officer Robert Fossett of Essex Fire and Rescue Service and Mr Hugh Gilmore, LVI, MRCVS, is acknowledged regarding these calculations.

69 For more detail on this see the Poor Law section in the Introduction above.

70 TNA, Clemency Papers Rex versus Ewen, HO 17/40.

71 ERO, Petty Sessional Minutes for Chelmsford referring to the interview with Richardson, P/C M1/13. For a discussion of the process of turning King's Evidence see, King, P, *Crime, Justice, and Discretion in England, 1740 to 1820,* (Oxford, 2003), pp. 49, 226; Langbein, J H, *The Origins of Adversary Criminal Trial,* (Oxford, 2003), p. 203 ff.

72 For a more detailed appraisal of the case see Holland (2003), pp. 99-115; see also Woodgate, T, 'A Motive of Private Malice Combined with General Malice', *Essex Journal,* (1993).

73 ERO, Rayleigh Burial Book, D/P 332/1/12.

74 Gatrell, V A C, *The Hanging Tree: Execution and the English People, 1770 to 1868,* (Oxford, 1994), p. 511.

75 *Chelmsford Chronicle,* 17 December 1830.

76 *Kent and Essex Mercury,* 4 January 1831.

77 *Ibid,* 1 February 1831.

78 For further reading on labourers' clubs see Thompson, E P, *The Making of the English Working Class,* (London, 1988).

79 The year 1884 marked the point at which farm labourers appeared to abandon incendiarism as a means of improving pay and conditions. 1884 was the year that the Parliamentary Reform Act was passed. This enfranchised agricultural labourers.

80 *Chelmsford Chronicle*, report on wage riot at Lawford 15 July 1836; ERO, Process Book of Indictments concerning John Bigsby, and Thomas Hammond of South Weald, Q/SPb 22.

81 *Chelmsford Chronicle*, 18 November 1831.

82 Holland, (2003), p. 107.

83 *Chelmsford Chronicle*, report of the trial of James Ewen, 17 December 1830.

84 To place this into perspective magistrates in all of the counties affected by Swing were writing to the Home Office, many of them requesting that troops be deployed in their counties to deal with what many saw as revolution and insurrection.

85 TNA, Letters to the Home Office, HO 52/7. According to Maureen Scollan, Department of History at the Open University, Justice Holland would have been entitled to act in the Rayleigh area if he had desired, but was enquiring about the reward probably out of courtesy.

86 TNA, Letter from the Rochford Magistracy to the Home Office, HO 52/7.

87 *The Times*, 28 December 1830.

88 Ziegler, P, *Melbourne: A Biography of William Lamb, Second Viscount Melbourne*, (London, 1987), p. 136.

89 *Kent and Essex Mercury*, report of the special petty sessions at the King's Head, Rochford, 28 December 1830.

90 I would like to thank Mr Peter Hall-Garrett, Department of History, University of Essex for permitting me to access his research files on Ongar Special Constabulary.

91 I would like to thank Mrs Jacqueline Cooper for granting me access to her research papers on the special constabulary in Uttlesford and Clavering Hundreds.

92 ERO, Petty Sessional Minutes for the Chelmsford Division, 10 December 1830, P/C M1.

93 Mounted specials were not a new idea. They had been used very effectively in north Essex during the Bread or Blood Riots of 1816.

94 ERO, P/C M1 for 14 and 17 December 1830.

95 ERO, Tendring Magistrates' printed notice, 1830, Q/App 1 reproduced by kind permission of Essex Record Office.

96 Brundage, A, *The Making of the New Poor Law, 1832 to 1839*, (London, 1978).

97 Across the country an average of 10% of rural parishes returned answers to *Rural Queries*. In Essex fifty parishes responded to at least some of the questions posed.

98 BPP *Rural Queries* XXXIV (1834).

99 Evans, E J, *The Contentious Tithe: The Tithe Problem and English Agriculture, 1750 to 1850*, (London, 1976).

100 Many parishes that did not suffer any form of protest used this method to occupy unemployed labourers.

101 See Charlesworth, A, *Social Protest in a Rural Society: The Spatial Diffusion of the Captain Swing Disturbances, 1830 to 1831*, (Liverpool, 1979).

102 See the Rayleigh fire above.

V. SWING IN DERBYSHIRE

Clive Leivers

It is generally recognised that the expansion of industry in the north of England, with the consequent increased competition for labour, led to higher wages and better conditions for the agricultural labourer in that part of the nation. John Marshall has suggested that the River Trent can be regarded as 'the dividing line between two main areas of influence', and that north and west of the Trent the agricultural labourer was 'spared the hopelessness which rotted village life in the southern counties' [1]

This suggestion may be over-simplistic on the evidence from the research done by FACHRS members, although it is certainly the case that the counties with most incidents were in the south and west of the country. But, for example, Nottinghamshire had more incidents than Leicestershire or Northamptonshire, although one has to consider the depth and extent of the research carried out when making such comparisons.

What is undoubtedly the case is that the counties north of the Trent were subject to rural disaffection during the Swing years; this essay studies the situation in one of the Midland counties - Derbyshire - on the basis of the evidence of the recent FACHRS research.

In the 1830s agriculture still played a major role in the Derbyshire economy. Even twenty years later, 22% of the county's workforce were employed in agriculture (the comparative figure for England and Wales as a whole was 24%), and only the textile industry was a bigger employer, with a third of the labour force.[2] However, the situation varied across the county. At the beginning of the nineteenth century, Farey, in his survey for the Board of Agriculture, gave the county average of 'agriculturalists' (the farmers and agricultural labourers) as 1 in 5 of the population; in Appletree hundred, the proportion was just below 1 in 3; Repton and Gresley hundred showed just above this proportion, whilst the more industrialised Scarsdale hundred was just on the county average.[3] In 1851, 50% of employees in the Ashbourne registration district were engaged in agriculture.[4]

So to some extent the county provides a reflection of the national division between the predominantly agricultural and industrial areas and, as will be seen, the pattern of protest broadly reflected that division. Map V.i shows the distribution of the reported incidents in the county.

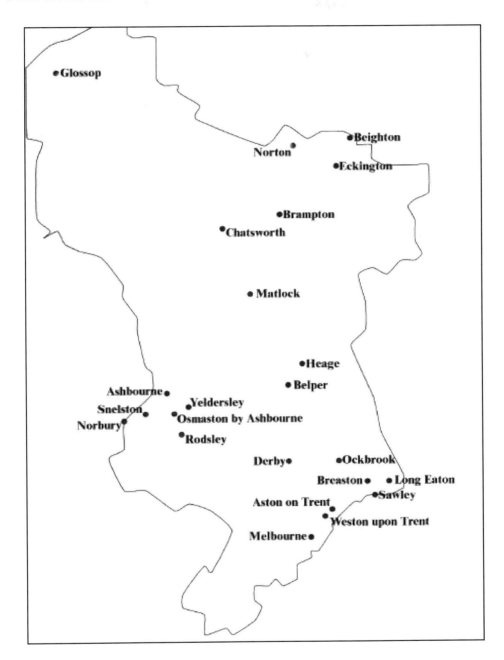

Map V.i. Incidents of Swing in Derbyshire

At the beginning of 1830 a petition was drawn up by the county worthies for presentation to the Government, headed by the Duke of Wellington, drawing attention to the 'extreme depression of the Agricultural interest'. This was placed in the county town and ten other locations, mainly in the northern part of the county, for the collection of signatures; within a week nearly 1,700 people had signed. The petition was forwarded to the Duke on 1 February and the text gives a good indication of the concerns of the county. Having expressed 'constitutional and respectful sentiments', which it was hoped would be 'satisfactory to His Majesty's Government' the memorial pointed to 'rents greatly reduced [...] tenants ruined [...] labourers unemployed [...] farms thrown out of cultivation [...] and sales of produce [...] at a price infinitely below the cost of production'. As a result, the county was unable to maintain its demand for manufactured goods, or to contribute its usual share of national taxation. The petitioners respectfully and earnestly prayed for some measures to relieve the prospect of ruin 'in which many of us are, and all of us fear to be, involved'.[5]

There was little evidence of action by the central Government, but individual landowners acknowledged the difficulties faced by their tenantry. In April 1830 Lord Melbourne 'returned 20% upon all his farms' in the parish of Melbourne 'in consideration of the present depressed state of the agricultural interests'. Two months later, Earl Stanhope, 'being convinced of the pressure under which farmers are labouring', returned 15% to his tenants at Dale Abbey and Stanton by Dale. In Nottinghamshire, Lord Middleton at Wollaton returned 20% and Earl Manvers 10% 'in consideration of the almost unprecedented depression of the agricultural interest'.[6] The editorial of the *Derby Mercury* on 14 July 1830 praised 'the instances of the liberal conduct of landlords to their industrious tenantry' and urged others to follow the reported examples.

Throughout the year that newspaper had carried reports of protests in other parts of the country - violent action against reductions in parish relief, arson attacks and the destruction of threshing machines. At the end of November the situation of the county's labouring population was considered to be enviable in comparison to their fellows in the 'disturbed districts of the country' but, within a week (on 1 December 1830), came the first report of an incident on the Derbyshire borders at Ellaston (Staffordshire), where a stackyard was fired and ten guineas offered for the 'discovery of the wretch who perpetrated this malicious outrage'.[7] A week later the first incidents within the county were reported.

In the same area as the Ellaston fire, Henry Coxon, a twenty-year-old labourer, was arrested for sending letters to the overseers of the three adjoining parishes of Rodsley, Yeldersley and Osmaston, threatening to burn their stacks of hay and corn. One newspaper reported that others in the village of Osmaston had also received threatening letters, which called for a rise in labouring wages. The handwriting was recognised as that of a former inhabitant of the village, and Coxon was arrested when he arrived in Osmaston on a 'good horse much jaded', and asked whether wages had indeed been increased. The letters had been signed 'by a friend of the people' and bore a London postmark. This perhaps suggests that Coxon had accomplices outside the county and had been inspired to send threats to his native village. His naïve enquiries on his return to Osmaston scarcely suggest a deeply cunning conspirator.

However, the *Derby and Chesterfield Reporter* concluded that there was little reason to fear a general uprising among the labourers, who were regarded as peaceably inclined; the editorial did warn against paying credence to rumour and the hoaxes, which were apparently prevalent among the inhabitants of Derby.[8]

The first actual arson attack in the county was carried out on 5 December 1830 at the farm of John Hopkins at Long Eaton, 'no doubt [...] the work of an incendiary'; a reward of six hundred pounds was subsequently offered. The local inhabitants were reported to have expressed 'universal indignation' against the perpetrator, with 'surprise on every countenance' that such an outrage could have occurred. In the same issue, a Nottingham newspaper carried a report of a further arson attack a few miles from Long Eaton, at Breaston. A ten-pound reward was offered and a local labourer was arrested, who had been in dispute with Harriman, the farmer concerned. It is rather surprising that no report of this incident was carried in the Derbyshire newspapers; there was no later report of any action against the arrested man.[9]

The Lord Lieutenant, the Duke of Devonshire (to whom, according to the *Nottingham Review* a letter had been sent threatening to burn down Chatsworth House), consulted the justices about the state of the county; their 'concurrent testimony [...] from every quarter' was that 'there does not exist any particular distress among the lower orders of the people', who were 'well affected and peaceable' and ready to 'afford their assistance for the suppression of tumult from whatever quarter it may proceed'.[10] Consequently, the *Derby Mercury* was anxious to reassure its readers that the Long Eaton incident was the only such instance in the county.

> Not only is there not the least appearance of a disposition to riot anywhere, but in these districts of the county a manly spirit to oppose violence and suppress tumult pervades all classes of the community. It is not less conspicuous among the labourers in agriculture and trade, than among the substantial householders and the higher classes of the people.[11]

However, this newspaper also warned against the spread of false rumours: a threatening letter was falsely said to have been received by the incumbent at Spondon; a reported meeting of labourers at Mickleover was, in fact, one man applying for an advance of wages. (The *Reporter* did, however, acknowledge that this individual had managed 'by great exertion' to assemble fourteen or fifteen of his fellow labourers, but they were easily persuaded to disperse.) The newspaper acknowledged the risk, 'in the present excitable temper of the public mind', of opening 'our columns to paragraphs having an inflammatory tendency', in the desire to give 'early intelligence' to its readers.[12]

The commendable spirit referred to was evidenced by the establishment of night watches in the villages between Nottingham and Derby, probably in response to the arson in Long Eaton. In the village of Spondon 'the whole of the respectable householders [...] have unanimously agreed to patrol the village in turn during the long winter nights. Six of them to be nightly on duty. 50 special constables have been sworn in and a subscription raised for the defraying of all incidental expenses'.[13]

Constables were appointed at Aston and Weston-upon-Trent, and many men in the county town 'not merely of the higher and middling classes but [also] well disposed persons of the humblest rank' enrolled as special constables. This was despite the view that wages remained 'adequate to the wants of the work-people', with the result that 'no spirit of insubordination had manifested itself'.

George Lamb, writing from the Home Office to the land agent at Melbourne on 15 December 1830, encouraged the establishment of a watch on the estate - 'My Lord (Melbourne) highly approves of it being established'. No money was to be spared in making the watch effective, with Melbourne prepared to 'contribute as much as necessary' and Lamb offering '£5 to begin with'.[14]

The example set in South Derbyshire was soon followed in Scarsdale hundred to the north-east of the county. A 'great number' of special constables were sworn in at Chesterfield and 'almost all the towns and villages [...] had arranged themselves into a Constabulary force'.[15]

Despite another arson attack at Sawley (near to Long Eaton) on the 20 December, at the end of the year the judgement of the *Mercury* was that 'the whole county remains perfectly peaceable', which, in comparison to the situation in the southern counties, was a valid enough conclusion. There was, however, clearly a good deal of apprehension abroad about an increase in the number of protest actions.

The anxieties were shown by the *Mercury* report of 12 January 1831, concerning a fire at the farm of William Mason at Belper. This was said to have 'originated no doubt by accident, but an erroneous account is going the rounds of the newspapers'. The *Courier* confirmed the accidental nature of the fire, a judgment reached by assembled magistrates the morning afterwards.

The same issue of the *Mercury* also reported the trial at Quarter Sessions of Henry Coxon. He had pleaded guilty to the sending of threatening letters and was sentenced to transportation for life. There was no indication of motive given in the press account or in the Quarter Session order books. The last mention of the unfortunate Coxon came a month later when he was transferred from the county gaol to a hulk at Woolwich awaiting transportation.[16]

A week later, the influence of the Swing incidents in other parts of the country was shown by the reports of a strike by cotton spinners at Glossop in the north-west of the county. One hundred and sixty men were reported to have marched on the factory of Thornton and Ridgway at Hayfield, to persuade the workmen there to join the strike for increased pay. The slogans shouted were 'Four and two pence or Swing'; 'Four and two pence or shoot' (several pistols were allegedly fired); and 'Four and two pence or blood'! About ten ringleaders were arrested and bound over to appear at Derby assizes.[17]

Despite the earlier statement that the Belper fire was accidental, a servant of the farmer was suspected of starting the fire, but was released after examination. By the end of January 1831, two further arson attacks had been reported in the county - at Ockbrook and Weston-on-Trent (two men had been pursued by the watchers at Weston but had escaped).

The *Nottingham and Newark Mercury* reported that the farmer at Ockbrook and other neighbours had recently received letters from Swing and that two men had been 'strictly examined' by magistrates, but released. The following week the paper retracted the report about the receipt of threatening letters.[18]

Yet another fire was reported in early February at Aston Upon Trent, an arrest was made, but the suspect was released without charge, and a week later the newspaper carried a reward advertisement for information about the incident.[19]

This spate of attacks in the Trent valley then died down and the next incidents were reported from the north-east of the county. On 19 February, the *Courier* carried an account of an abortive arson attack at Brampton on the outskirts of Chesterfield, when a firearm was discharged into a fold yard and a quantity of burning wadding discovered near a stack of stubble. It was not until 13 April that the next incident was reported in the *Derby Mercury*, which quoted a report in the *Sheffield Iris* of an arson attack on a grinding mill at Beighton on the county border with Yorkshire. The *Courier* amplified this report by adding that Staniforth, the mill owner, had received a threatening letter before the mill was fired. (Farey had listed Staniforth among those farmers in the county who owned 'thrashing-mills', the spread of which he reported as considerable in the county). A fortnight earlier, a Mr Osborne of Norton Woodseats, a few miles from Beighton, had received letters, signed Swing, threatening his life.[20]

In July 1831, protests returned to the Ashbourne area, which had seen the first incidents in the county. Two large haystacks belonging to Thomas Hartshorn at Hanging Bridge were destroyed during the night of 4 July, 'no doubt the work of an incendiary, threatening words being previously written on the adjacent building and a quantity of deal shavings having been discovered'. The three following editions of the paper carried a reward notice (three hundred pounds), but to no effect. The *Courier* surmised that the cause had been resentment about the employment of Irishmen. The same motive was attributed by the *Mercury* to an incident the following day, 5 July, when two acres of turnips belonging to an Ashbourne publican were pulled up 'and left in regular rows'! This was thought to be in protest at the employment of Irishmen to get in the publican's hay harvest.[21]

The next two incidents were reported only in the *Courier*. At the end of August 1831 a stack of hay was fired in Matlock, supposedly 'the act of an incendiary', and early the following month a considerable amount of cart gearing was destroyed in stables at Norbury - a further occurrence in the Ashbourne area. It was reported that two large bludgeons had been left on the premises 'with which the villains no doubt intended to defend themselves'.[22]

Three months later the *Derby Mercury* contained extensive accounts of rioting in the county town over the rejection of the Reform Bill by the House of Lords. On Saturday 8 October 'a large body of persons assembled in the Corn Market'. Shops and houses were attacked in the town, including the property of William Bemrose, the Tory opponent of Reform, who was also the proprietor and editor of the *Derbyshire Courier*. The rioters then marched to Markeaton Hall, the home of Francis Munday, lately MP for the county and to Chaddesden Hall, home of H S Wilmot; windows were broken at both properties. Returning to Derby, 'as the mob advanced towards the gaol, shots were fired and a man named Garner killed'. On the following evening, a crowd estimated at 1,500 assembled in the Market Place and proceeded to smash gaslights and stone houses. Their leader was subsequently alleged to have been a man aged around twenty, employed at a silk mill. These actions were not aimed solely at the opponents of Reform; of the thirty-six residents, who claimed damages from the Corporation, six voted for Whig candidates in the election of 1835 as compared to seven Tories. There were grocers, victuallers and hosiers among the victims, as well as an alderman, the corporation chaplain, the clerk to the magistrates and the clerk to the Lord Lieutenant. On the following Monday another crowd assembled, the Riot Act was read, carbines were fired by the troops supporting the magistrates, and another man killed. Despite all the agitation in Derby the *Mercury* was pleased to report that there were no disturbances in other parts of the county. Sixteen people, aged between seventeen and thirty-four, and including one woman, were subsequently brought to trial at the assizes, accused of riot and breaking into the gaol. Most were acquitted, but two men, aged thirty-one and seventeen, were found guilty of rioting and received sentences of seven years' transportation.[23]

Only two more reports of sporadic arson attacks were carried in the *Mercury*. In December 1831 a hayrick was fired in Derby; the paper considered it 'difficult to imagine the motive of the perpetrator', since the stack belonged to a 'kind and humane master'. Then, at the end of January 1832, there was another mill fire in the north-east of the county, with the destruction of a corn mill in Eckington. Both these incidents were also reported in the *Courier,* together with an account of a malicious stack fire at Heage in November 1831, and the destruction by fire of a barn in Derby in February 1832, 'no doubt the act of an incendiary'.[24]

These relatively isolated incidents then seem to have come to an end. There were no such incidents reported for the rest of 1832 and so all the events in Derbyshire took place in a period of some fifteen months between November 1830 and February 1832. The outbreaks were sporadic and it is difficult to assign motives. Apart from the Reform rioters and the Glossop strikers, the incidents seem to have involved only one person; there were no gangs of labourers threatening parsons, farmers or poor law officials, or breaking threshing machines. Indeed, the only 'classic' Swing incident in the county - the protest directed against Poor Law officials in the Ashbourne area - resulted in the only person brought before the courts (again with the exception of the Reform rioters and the Glossop strikers). It is tempting to conclude that the other incidents were inspired by personal grievance, although the cluster of protests in the Trent valley and around Ashbourne does perhaps suggest that the less favourable conditions of the agricultural labourers in those areas was an underlying cause of disquiet.

What does emerge from the Derbyshire experience, is an indication of the influence of press reporting. The extensive coverage of the events in the southern and eastern counties of England, undoubtedly raised the level of concern among the 'respectable inhabitants', and the tactics of the rioters were copied in the Derbyshire incidents. The fame of 'Captain Swing' was certainly evident in one of the battle cries of the Glossop weavers - 'Four and twopence or Swing'.

NOTES

1   Marshall, J D, 'Nottinghamshire Labourers in the Early Nineteenth Century', *Transactions of the Thoroton Society,* 64 (1960), p. 58.
2   Smith, A D, *The Derbyshire Economy in 1851*, (Derbyshire County Council, Matlock, 1997), p. 29.
3   Farey, J, *General View of the Agriculture of Derbyshire Vol 3,* (London, 1817), p. 537.
4   Smith, (1997), p. 28.
5   *Derby Mercury,* 13 January 1830; 27 January 1830; 10 February 1830.
6   *Ibid,* 28 April 1839; 18 June 1830; 23 June 1830.
7   *Derby and Chesterfield Reporter,* 25 November 1830; *Derby Mercury,* 1 December 1830.
8   *Derby Mercury,* 8 December 1830; *Derby and Chesterfield Reporter,* 2 December 1830.
9   *Nottingham and Newark Mercury,* 11 December 1830; *Derby Mercury,* 8 December 1830.
10 *Derby Mercury,* 15 December 1830; *Nottingham Review,* 17 December 1830.
11 *Derby Mercury,* 15 December 1830.
12 *Ibid,* 15 December 1830; *Derby & Chesterfield Reporter,* 16 December 1830.
13 *Ibid,* 8 December 1830.
14 Usher, H, 'More Light on Captain Swing', *Derbyshire Miscellany*, (Spring 1989), p. 36.
15 *Derby Mercury,* 15, 22, 29 December 1830
16 *Ibid,* 12 January 1831; *Derbyshire Courier,* 8 January 1831; Derbyshire Records Office, Quarter Sessions Order Books O/SO 1/29.
17 *Ibid,* 19 January 1831.
18 *Nottingham and Newark Mercury,* 22, 29 January 1831; *Derby Mercury,* 19, 26 January 1831.
19 *Derby Mercury,* 2, 9 February 1831.
20 *Ibid,* 13 April 1831; *Derbyshire Courier,* 19 February 1831 and 30 April 1831; Farey, Vol 2, (1815), p 49.
21 *Derbyshire Courier,* 9 July 1831; *Derby Mercury,* 6, 13, 20, 27 July 1831.
22 *Ibid,* 27 August and 3 September 1831.
23 *Derby Mercury,* 12, 19 October 1831; *Derbyshire Courier,* 14 January 1832; Wigley, J, 'Derby and Derbyshire during the Great Reform Bill Crisis 1830-32', *Derbyshire Archaeological Journal,* 101 (1981), pp 143-46.
24 *Derby Mercury,* 7 December 1831 and 25 January 1832; *Derbyshire Courier,* 19 November and 10 December 1831; 14, 21 January 1832; 11 February 1832.

VI. 'DOWN WITH MACHINERY!'
An investigation into the Wycombe Paper-mill Riots of 1830

Vanessa Worship

Illustration VI.a. High Street, Wycombe, showing the Guild Hall and the Red Lion Inn
(Sparkes, I G, High Wycombe As It Was (Hendon Publishing Co Ltd, Nelson, 1975)

INTRODUCTION

An important aspect of an investigation into widespread social unrest is the need to focus on the local as well as the global picture. The purpose of this essay is to gain a deeper understanding of the effects of the whole Swing movement by studying the impact of one incident of protest on the local community of High Wycombe. Paper mills had been operating in the Wye Valley, Buckinghamshire since the 15th century, employing local people and utilising the chalk streams of the Chiltern Hills to produce fine quality paper. Some machinery had already been introduced into the mills before 1830, but in that year several mill owners were in the process of installing new machinery, which it was thought would severely affect employment levels in the industry. Inevitably, news of the Swing disturbances in neighbouring counties encouraged the paper-makers of Wycombe to express their discontent. They set out to destroy the new machines, believing them to be the equivalent of the farm workers' threshing machines. Unfortunately, the Wycombe men were unaware of the vital distinction in law between agricultural machinery and industrial machinery. The destruction of the latter was a capital offence and therefore punishable by the death penalty.

BACKGROUND

The Swing movement had gathered pace as it swept across southern England throughout the summer and autumn of 1830. According to Hobsbawm and Rudé's 1969 account, the first incident of arson was at Orpington, Kent on 1 June, and the first threshing machine was destroyed at Lower Hardres, near Canterbury on 28 August.[1] However, recent research carried out by members of the Family & Community Historical Research Society found that, in fact, the earliest recorded incident of machine-breaking was on 10 April at Orpington. The first case reported in the *Bucks Gazette* was in early September. This was a riot at Otmoor, near Bicester, Oxfordshire, where villagers were protesting about losing their rights to common land.[2] Meanwhile, Swing incidents were spreading rapidly throughout Kent and into Surrey. During the early part of November there were also several serious riots across the counties of Sussex, Hampshire, Wiltshire and Berkshire.

Most of the Swing protests were aimed at farmers and involved setting fire to haystacks and destroying threshing machines. However, there were also some incidents where manufacturing machinery was the target. At Hungerford in Berkshire on 22 November, Richard Gibbons' iron foundry was attacked, resulting in the destruction of his entire stock of wrought iron and all the machinery. At Fordingbridge in Hampshire on 23 and 24 November, a sacking factory was the target, and in Southampton a sawmill was damaged with the loss of seven thousand pounds' worth of circular saws. Also on 24 November at Wilton, near Salisbury, John Brasher's woollen cloth manufactory was attacked and five engines destroyed 'in order to make more work for the poor people'.[3]

In Buckinghamshire, several incidents occurred in the immediate period leading up to the dramatic events that are the main focus of this essay. By 11 November at least six Buckinghamshire residents, including two paper manufacturers, had received threatening letters. Mr Richard Plaistowe of Loudwater Mill near Wycombe, was one of the recipients. He had been in the process of installing machinery worth two thousand pounds, but on receipt of the letter, he decided to suspend further work.[4] In addition to threatening letters, there were arson attacks on two successive days, 16 and 17 November, at farms in Nash and Wavendon.[5] On 17 November, a large group of gentry and gentlemen of the south of the county attended a meeting at the Windmill Inn at Salt Hill, chaired by the Marquis of

Chandos, the Lord Lieutenant of Buckinghamshire. Among other measures, the meeting resolved that 'in order to put a stop to the Horrid Attempts of some Diabolical Miscreants to injure Property and produce Confusion in this Country', special constables should be sworn in to suppress any disturbances (see Illustration VI.b). The report of the meeting and its conclusions was published in local and national newspapers as well as in the *Farmers' Journal*.

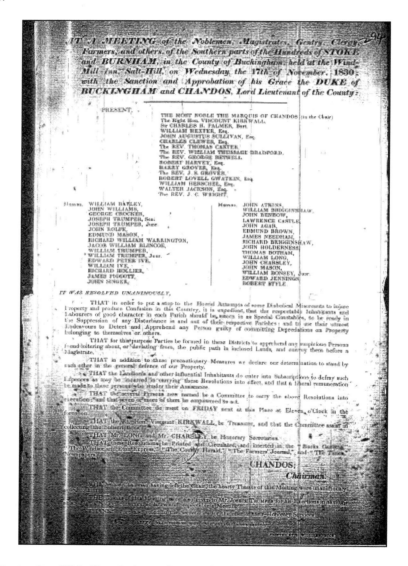

Illustration VI.b. Resolutions of a meeting held at the Windmill Inn, Salt Hill 17 November 1830. *(TNA, HO52/6)*

Further threatening letters were received over the course of the next week in Wycombe and Marlow, and the general feeling of unease in the county intensified. On 22 November, the Bucks Yeomanry were mobilised, although it emerged later that they were being sent to Winchester to assist in quelling the disturbances there, thus causing consternation among Buckinghamshire residents, who hoped that they would not be needed in their own county in their absence.[6] In response to the call of the Lord Lieutenant's meeting, the magistrates of Wycombe themselves called a meeting of the principal inhabitants of the neighbourhood, to be held in the Guild Hall of the borough of Chepping Wycombe (the old name for High Wycombe) on Friday 26 November at 12 noon, in order to prevent incendiary attacks and to 'preserve the Public Peace' (see Illustration VI.c).

Illustration VI.c. Announcement of a meeting to be held on 26 November 1830 at the Guild Hall, Chepping Wycombe. *(TNA, HO52/6)*

A TASTE OF THINGS TO COME

Just as it is today, Friday was market day in Wycombe and consequently, the town was very busy on the morning of 26 November 1830. According to the *Bucks Gazette*, on Wednesday 24 November a number of paper-makers had announced that a meeting of the trade would be held on the Rye, an open area about half a mile from the town centre, on the forthcoming Friday, the same day as the magistrates' meeting (see Map VI.i). The paper-makers invited 'all who were oppressed' to attend, and stated that if the machinery were not removed from the mills, it was their intention 'utterly to destroy it'.[7] A typical placard seen in the Midlands at the time proclaimed 'Down with machinery - a free trade in corn'. Thus the scene was set for confrontation.

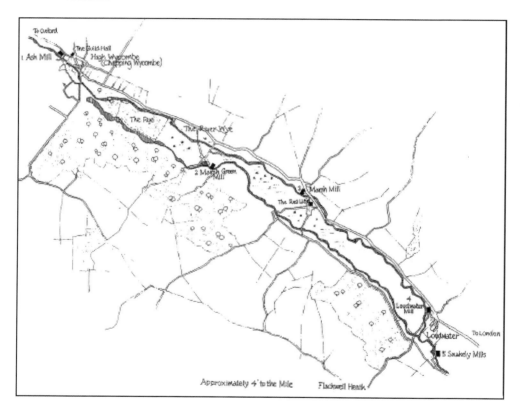

Map VI.i. Map showing the five mills on the River Wye where machinery was destroyed

The *Bucks Gazette* reported that the Reverend George Scobell, chairman of the magistrates' meeting, had just commenced his opening address that Friday morning, when an 'immense multitude' entered the hall. Lord Carrington tried to reason with them, but they refused to listen and shouted at him: 'Pay your election bills'. The chairman was then removed from his seat and replaced by a man the *Gazette* described as 'a loquacious itinerant barber', who complained of the general distress and promptly closed the meeting. At this point, the crowd began to demolish chairs and tables and smash the windows, after which they marched off towards West Wycombe, to Ash Mill, a paper mill owned by Messrs John and Joseph Lane (see Map VI.i). Many of them allegedly carried large hammers and were intent on demolishing machinery. The Lanes had recently installed a new machine, which had a cylinder armed with knives for grinding the rags, a process previously done by hand. As luck would have it, men of the Newport Pagnell troop of the Bucks Yeomanry were riding through Wycombe at this time, on their way back from Hounslow, and were directed to Ash Mill to deal with the protesters. This incensed the mob and the Riot Act was read, but to no avail. The rioting continued, until a wise gentleman persuaded Dr Scobell that perhaps the best way to pacify the crowd would be for himself and the troops to withdraw. This they did and surprisingly the mob dispersed, although it was noted that some went on their way complaining bitterly and vowing to have their revenge.[8]

The town was thus left in a state of uneasy calm. Many of the shops closed early that Friday afternoon, and fifty special constables were sworn in as a precautionary measure in case of further trouble. But, in the words of the *Gazette's* reporter, the quiet weekend was only 'the prelude of a melancholy catastrophe'. As early as five o'clock on the morning of Monday 29 November, a horn sounded on Flackwell Heath, about two miles south east of Wycombe, and, before dawn, a large crowd of men had gathered. They were armed with sledge-hammers, crow-bars and pickaxes, and set off towards the scene of their humiliation on the previous Friday, Lanes' Mill.[9]

A DAY OF RIOTING

News of the impending trouble prompted the magistrates to send off appeals for military assistance to Windsor and to the Marquis of Chandos. By nine o'clock in the morning, the angry crowd had reached Ash Mill and, finding the door locked, they attempted to break in. Two shots were fired from inside the building, one of which hit William Bryant, a paper-maker from Flackwell Heath, in the arm. This incensed the crowd and they began breaking windows and smashing down the door. As they were about to enter the mill, four gallons of vitriol were thrown at them and several men were badly burned. The rest carried on undeterred and proceeded to demolish the hated new machine. Within fifteen minutes they had achieved their task, but they left all the old machinery intact. According to the newspaper report, the person responsible for the vitriol attack was then thrown into the stream and was lucky to escape with his life.[10]

Their work at Lanes' mill completed, the crowd then marched back through the town, gathering more supporters on the way and levying contributions on the shopkeepers as they went. The crowd was estimated to be four-hundred strong at this time. Zachary Allnutt's mill at Marsh Green was to be the next target along the River Wye and here another machine was destroyed. Moving further downstream to John Hay's mill, the rioters were met by the mill owner himself, who appealed to them and promised that he would cease to operate his machinery until some agreement was reached between the masters and the paper-makers. He told them he employed fifty-three men and, if they damaged his property, these men would be thrown out of work. It was all in vain. In spite of Mr Hay's pleas and being threatened by one of his workers wielding a red-hot poker, the rioters proceeded to demolish the machinery. At this point, the Reverend Mr Vincent read the Riot Act, but the crowd ignored him and continued on their way along the Wye Valley. A slight diversion at this point took the men to the farm of Mr Richard Lansdale, where they destroyed a threshing machine for good measure.[11]

According to the *Bucks Gazette*, the protesters then adjourned to the Red Lion public house at Marsh, where they 'plentifully regaled themselves with beer' before carrying on to the mill of Mr Richard Plaistowe at Loudwater. Since receiving a threatening letter, Mr Plaistowe had issued a notice that his machine was not to be used but, nevertheless, it too was destroyed by the revived mob. At this point, the High Sheriff of Buckinghamshire, Colonel Vyse, arrived along with several other gentlemen. They were immediately attacked by a shower of stones, the Colonel being cut in the face by a piece of flint. A doctor from Burnham, on horseback and armed with a sword, rode over two females and was thrown from his horse, but recovered his seat and made his escape. According to the report, by this point some of the protesters were tiring and several were also in a state of intoxication. Nevertheless, they carried on to Snakely Mill at Loudwater (see Illustration VI.d), where they were destined to meet their Waterloo.[12]

Illustration VI.d. Snakely Mill, Loudwater
(Mead, A, Days of Glory: The Story of Glory Mill, Wooburn Green, Bucks
(published privately, 1999)

A volunteer force of thirty special constables from Beaconsfield, armed with whatever weapons they could find, were waiting at Glory Mill. They had been told to expect a mob of three hundred people and were advised to proceed upstream to meet the rioters, which they did 'most cheerfully', according to the newspaper report. A party of huntsmen, who had been at Wooburn Green when they heard of the disturbances, soon joined them. The hunting gentlemen rode at the head of the special constables across King's Mead towards Snakely Mill. They wasted no time in attacking the mob. Prisoners were taken and many injuries inflicted on both sides. The rioters threw brickbats and stones, and attacked the constables and huntsmen with hammers and iron bars. During the fighting, Mr Davis' machine was destroyed, and only then did the mob finally begin to disperse.[13]

According to the *Bucks Gazette*, twenty-nine men were taken into custody that day, one of whom was thought to be the leader. He was described as an athletic man, but a total stranger to the Wycombe neighbourhood. Ten of the prisoners were taken to the Red Lion hotel in Wycombe, where they were examined by the magistrates and committed for trial. They were taken away to Aylesbury gaol at about three o'clock, and apparently the parting of the men from their wives and families was 'heart-rending in the extreme'. The remaining prisoners were taken to Beaconsfield, and sent on to Aylesbury gaol the following morning. The cost of the damage was estimated at about twelve thousand pounds, although this was later proved to be greatly exaggerated.[14]

A number of people were badly injured in the riots. In addition to those hurt in the morning at Lanes' mill, a second man was shot in the chest, one man had his eye put out and several others were trampled by horses in the confusion. Women and children were among the casualties and one woman suffered broken ribs. This is the only indication that women also took part in the protest. A special constable from Eton wrote a damning letter to the *Bucks Gazette*, complaining that the local people had done nothing to prevent the riot. He alleged that farmers at Wooburn were sitting by their firesides while their neighbours' property was being destroyed, and yet other men had travelled up to ten miles to protect them. When tackled, the farmers said that they saw the destruction of machinery as a benefit to them, because it would mean the manufacturers would have to employ more hands and thereby the poor rates would be reduced. The constable hoped that the newspaper would expose such 'heartless selfishness' and shame the farmers into better conduct.[15]

When news of the number of prisoners taken at Wycombe reached Aylesbury, there was much concern. The gaol there was already full as a result of the numbers arrested over the weekend for widespread arson attacks and agricultural machine-breaking incidents in other parts of the county. A letter from two surgeons of Aylesbury to the High Sheriff of Buckinghamshire dated 4 December, stated that, on inspecting the gaol, they found it 'unprecedentedly crowded', containing some two hundred and forty prisoners. They expressed their concern that there was a serious risk of disease breaking out, as 'febrile disorders of a typhoid character are now very prevalent in the neighbourhood'.[16]

In the wake of the riots, another meeting was held in Wycombe on 3 December (see Illustration VI.e), at which the gentlemen of the town discussed a plan for preserving the peace and 'protecting all Classes from the great evils arising from the want of employ for the

Labouring Poor'. They formed a Mounted Constabulary Association, and agreed to meet at least once a week for drill practice and sword exercises.[17]

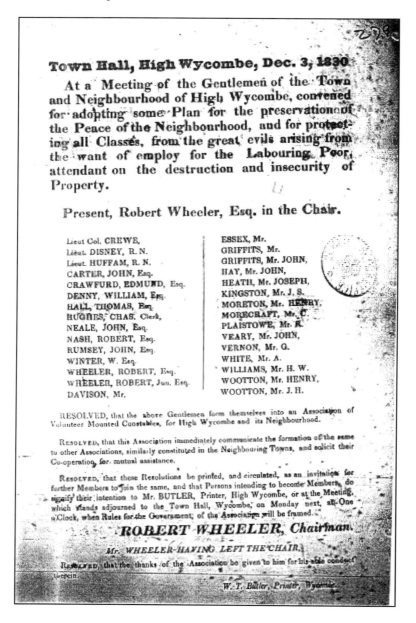

Illustration VI.e. Resolutions of a meeting held at High Wycombe, 3 December 1830
(TNA HO52/6)

In the week following the Wycombe riots, a further fourteen men were arrested and charged with riotous assembly and destruction of paper-making machinery. Another was arrested on 15 December, four more on 21 December, and one on 31 December, bringing the total number charged to forty-nine. Various statements were taken about the events of the day, including one from Richard Hailey, high constable of the second division of Desborough hundred. He stated that one Thomas Blizzard had been 'at the head' of the mob and was 'one of the most active and determined' at Hay's mill. At Plaistowe's mill, Hailey said that Blizzard appeared to be the leader 'giving the word of command and heading the rioters'. Richard Hailey's statement was later to play a crucial part in the evidence presented at the trial of the Wycombe paper rioters.[18]

Thomas Blizzard was a married man from Little Marlow, with two young children. At the time of the riot he was a roundsman, receiving one shilling a day in poor relief and one shilling and sixpence a week as a farm labourer.[19] Blizzard later described himself as a ploughman by trade, and it remains something of a mystery why he should have taken such a leading role in the destruction of paper-making machinery when he was not a paper-maker himself.

A WEEK OF TRIALS

In early December, the Government set up Special Commissions in order to deal with the trials of the large numbers of 'Swing' rioters in the worst affected counties, including Buckinghamshire. Following the Special Commissions at Winchester, Salisbury, Reading and Abingdon, the session at Aylesbury began on Monday 10 January 1831.[20]

The *Bucks Gazette* reported that large numbers of people were pouring into the town from all parts of the country, and were having difficulty finding lodgings. The proceedings began at 1.30 pm, and the judges promptly disappeared to hear divine service before commencing their painful duty. At half past three the grand jury were sworn in. In his opening address, Sir James Allen Park spoke at some length about the present state of unrest in the country. He commented on how the Government had publicised the consequences of such behaviour, so that 'no man could say he was deluded by ignorance into the commission of offences without being aware of the penalties'. He referred to the three different types of case on the calendar, namely, general riot, destruction of machinery, and demolition of property in manufactories. Of these, only the latter was a capital offence, but he was sorry to see that a large number of prisoners were charged with having committed that offence at Chepping Wycombe.[21]

The first page of the Calendar of the Prisoners is shown in Illustration VI.f, and gives the names of some of the paper-mill rioters who were to stand trial before the Special Commission. On Tuesday morning, the judge compared that document unfavourably with that of the Berkshire Special Commission. He pointed out that there was a deficiency in the Buckinghamshire calendar, in that the occupations of the accused had not been recorded.[22] [The *Bucks Gazette* had earlier commented that the commitments of many of the prisoners had been recorded with 'indecent haste' and had prophetically pointed out that 'the legality of the commitments may one day be called into question'.][23]

BUCKS.

A

CALENDAR OF THE PRISONERS,

In His Majesty's Gaol at Aylesbury,

FOR FELONIES & MISDEMEANOURS,

Who are to take their Trials at the Session of Oyer and Terminer and Special Gaol Delivery, to be holden at AYLESBURY, on MONDAY the TENTH Day of JANUARY, 1831, before THE HONOURABLE SIR JAMES ALLAN PARK, KNIGHT, one of the Judges of His Majesty's Court of Common Pleas; THE HONOURABLE SIR WILLIAM BOLLAND, KNIGHT, one of the Barons of His Majesty's Court of Exchequer; and THE HONOURABLE SIR JOHN PATTESON, KNIGHT, one of the Judges of His Majesty's Court of King's Bench.

Richard William Howard Howard Vyse, Esquire, Sheriff.

No.
1. JOSEPH FOWLER, aged 27, Committed 27th November 1830, by The Rev. Charles Robert Ashfield, William Rickford Esq. John Lee, Esq., LL. D. and Robert Ledgate Esq. charged on the oath of Richard Ballad and others; with having on the 20th November last, at the Parish of Waddesdon, in the said County, unlawfully, maliciously, and feloniously broken and destroyed a thrashing-machine, of the value of five pounds, of the goods of James Briggs.

2. ROBERT HOPCRAFT, aged 23,
3. EDMUND JARVIS, aged 32,
4. JOHN EVANS, aged 28,
5. JOSEPH RIDGWAY, aged 30, } Committed 30th November 1830, by The Rev. Charles Robert Ashfield and The Rev. Alexander Lockhart, charged on the oath of John Ross and others, with having on the 29th November instant, riotously and unlawfully assembled with other persons to the number of fifty, at the Parish of Waddesdon, in the said County, and unlawfully, maliciously, and feloniously broken and destroyed a certain machine called a winnowing-machine, of the value of ten pounds, of the goods of Richard Howe.

6. JOSEPH HOLLAND, aged 27,
7. ISAAC DAVIS, aged 10,
8. GEORGE HILLSDEN, aged 21, } Committed 29th November 1830, by The Rev. Alexander Lockhart and The Rev. Charles Robert Ashfield, charged on the oath of James Collegridge and another, with having on the 29th November instant, riotously and unlawfully assembled with other persons to the number of thirty, at the Parish of Waddesdon, in the said County, and unlawfully, maliciously, and feloniously broken and destroyed a certain machine called a chaff-cutting-machine, the property of William Rickford Esq.

9. PURCELL CORNELIUS TURNER, aged 40,
10. STACEY JARVIS, aged 24,
11. JOHN NORMAN, aged 20,
12. THOMAS SCOTT, aged 18,
13. FRANCIS TACK, aged 35,
14. JOHN COPCUTT, aged 19,
15. ELIJAH COWELL, aged 19, } Committed 29th November 1830, by Robert Ledgate Esq. and The Rev. Charles Robert Ashfield, charged by the oath of Richard Ballad, with having on the 20th day of November last, at the Parish of Waddesdon, within the said County of Bucks, unlawfully, maliciously, and feloniously broken and destroyed a certain thrashing-machine, of the value of five pounds, of the goods of the said Richard Ballad.

16. THOMAS HUGHES, alias WILLIAM HUGHES, aged 38, Committed 29th November 1830, by The Rev. William Massage Bradford and John Augustus Sullivan Esq. charged on the oath of John Frith, with having at the Parish of Beaconsfield, unlawfully assaulted and beaten the said John Frith, contrary to the form of the statute in such case made; and that he also in the presence of the Magistrates, behaved in a riotous manner and threatened the lives of the Magistrates, and attempted to rescue certain prisoners who were committed for a riot, and went in charge of the said John Frith and the civil power.

17. JOHN REYNOLDS, aged 29,
18. JOHN WALKER, aged 21,
19. JOSEPH PRIEST, aged 36,
20. JAMES BARTON, aged 39,
21. ROBERT CAREY, alias JOHN DELL, aged 23,
22. ALFRED SALTER, aged 19,
23. THOMAS FISHER, aged 36,
24. RICHARD WEEDON, aged 41,
25. JOHN SAWNEY, aged 54,
26. JOHN EAST, aged 21,
27. WILLIAM NIBBS, aged 21,
28. JAMES STRETTON, aged 19,
29. EDMUND BARTON, aged 24,
30. JAMES STONE, aged 30, } Committed 29th November 1830, by John Augustus Sullivan Esq. and The Rev. William Massage Bradford, charged at the oaths of William Lacey and others, with having on the 29th November last, unlawfully, riotously, and tumultuously assembled together, to the disturbance of the public peace, at the mill and in the premises of Mr. William Robert Davis, at the Parish of Chepping Wycombe, in the said County, and feloniously were present aiding, abetting, and assisting divers persons to us yet unknown, with the feloniously and unlawfully destroying certain machinery used in the manufacture of paper in the said mill, used in carrying on the trade or manufacture of a paper-maker, at the mill and on the premises of the said William Robert Davis, at the Parish of Chepping Wycombe aforesaid, in the County of Bucks aforesaid, against the form of the statute in that case made.

Illustration VI.f. Calendar of the Prisoners in His Majesty's Gaol
at Aylesbury, 10 January 1831
(CBS, D/LE/H12/12/29)

In the first case, ten men were accused of riotous assembly and destruction of machinery at Lanes' Mill. Several witnesses were called to give accounts of what they had seen on the day. It emerged that Thomas Blizzard, Richard Weedon, William Smith, David Lunnon and William Shrimpton, had all been seen breaking the machine, but none of the witnesses had observed any personal violence. Thomas Bowles and William Bryant had been active before the mob broke into the mill, but they had not been seen inside, Bowles having been injured with the vitriol and Bryant shot in the arm. John Walduck had been encouraging the mob outside but had not been seen inside the mill, although he had stayed with the mob. Mr Lane testified that the machine destroyed had been worth three hundred pounds. Mr Bodkin, the defence lawyer, tried to assert that there was some doubt as to whether there had been a riot prior to the machine breaking and, if there had not, then in that case the prisoners should be liable to transportation, rather than the death penalty. However, the judge said there was no question in his mind that there had been a riotous assembly. The prisoners were asked if they had anything to say in their defence, but they all remained silent. Several people appeared as character witnesses, one of whom was a paper manufacturer, and he told the court that the lowest wages in the industry, which men like the accused could earn, were from ten to fifteen shillings per week. The jury took a short time to decide that all of the accused, with the exception of the two injured men, Bowles and Bryant, were guilty as charged.[24]

The next case was that of four men charged with breaking the threshing machine of Mr Richard Lansdale. Few details of this trial were given in the *Bucks Gazette*, apart from the fact that Blizzard pleaded guilty. The rest were found guilty, but Sarney was recommended for mercy because of his good character and the fact that he did not appear to have been very active. No other cases against the Wycombe rioters were heard that day. On Wednesday 12 January, the court heard of the events at Davis' mill. Twenty-four prisoners were placed at the bar for having 'unlawfully, riotously and tumultuously assembled together' and 'feloniously destroyed certain machinery' used for manufacturing paper. The case for the prosecution was put by Mr Gurney, who stated that it was an 'awful spectacle' to see so many accused of a capital offence. Yet the number charged was small compared to the numbers who had actually taken part on the day. Several gentlemen and special constables had tried to protect the mill from the mob and they were attacked 'in a most brutal and desperate manner'. While some of the mob had succeeded in breaking into the mill and destroying the machine, others had continued attacking the civil authorities and the prosecution asserted that, whichever group the men were in, their crime was the same. The first witness was Mr Davis, who stated that the machine destroyed had been worth eight hundred pounds. He identified several of the accused as having taken part in its destruction, but he gave Arthur Wright a good character, saying he had known him since childhood. Several other witnesses related the facts of the case and identified various prisoners. John Sarney had been seen striking at Mr Charsley, the coroner, with an iron bar while he was on his knees but a special constable had prevented the blow. The same witness took a hammer from one of the rioters and Sarney threatened to 'knock his brains' out if he didn't give it up, but he did not strike him. Many other witnesses were called to give evidence on the events of the day.[25]

Mr Bodkin then put the case for the defence. Again, no witnesses were called but several people spoke as character witnesses for the prisoners. Mr Bodkin asserted that there was no evidence against some of the men, who had been taken into custody before the machine was broken, and Mr Justice Park said that he intended to direct the jury to acquit them on those grounds. He then summed up the case. He pointed out that Mr Davis had pleaded with the men not to destroy his machine and said that he would not use it again. The judge commented that while such behaviour was natural, such 'timid compliances' only encouraged further outrages. On the other hand, he praised the Sheriff, who had shown great firmness, which had the effect of dispersing the mob. The jury took only a few minutes to come to the conclusion that eight of the prisoners should be acquitted, but the remainder were guilty as charged.[26]

Proceedings on the following day, 13 January, began with the trial of fourteen men accused of demolishing machinery at Zachary Allnutt's mill. The men all pleaded guilty. Four further cases of paper-mill rioters were heard in quick succession and in all, twenty-three men pleaded guilty to the offences. What had caused this dramatic turn of events? The answer is to be found in the Home Office correspondence at The National Archives. A series of confidential letters from Mr George Maule to J M Phillips Esq., at the Home Office, shows that moves were being taken behind the scenes to cut short the proceedings of the Special Commission at Aylesbury. On 11 January, Mr Maule had written that an overture had been made to Mr Gurney, the prosecuting counsel, on behalf of the prisoners accused of destroying machinery at the High Wycombe paper mills, 'that they may be allowed to plead guilty upon condition of having their lives spared'. He added that Mr Gurney considered the paper-mill cases as worse than any cases in Berkshire. The letter had been sent by express and requested a reply by the following morning (see Illustration VI.g.). The second letter, dated 12 January, contained brief details of the trials of that day and stated that on the following day the remaining prisoners would all plead guilty on the understanding that their lives would be spared. Mr Maule had apparently spoken with the Duke of Buckingham, who 'seemed perfectly satisfied'. Mr Maule said that he expected proceedings to draw to a close the following evening.[27] The final letter, dated 13 January, related that twenty-three prisoners had, at their own request, pleaded guilty and thus the proceedings would finally close on Saturday 15 January.[28]

In the courtroom on 13 January, Mr Gurney begged that the court would allow judgement of death to be recorded only. Mr Justice Park stated that he presumed their counsel had advised the prisoners. If they had been tried, he said, many of them probably would have suffered. The prerogative of mercy was vested solely in the Crown. It was not for the court to decide the terms to which their sentence would be commuted. Sentence of death was recorded and the twenty-three prisoners dismissed. The remainder of that day and all of the next was taken up with other cases of agricultural disturbances.[29]

There is evidence that some people considered the Wycombe rioters to have been wrongly advised by their defence counsel to plead guilty on 13 January. A petition letter from Robert Wheeler of Wycombe, dated 28 January, expressed the opinion that 'some of the men [...] are thought by many of our respectable neighbours to have lost the advantage a trial might have given them, either to have obtained an acquittal or by evidence or character to have established a more favourable consideration'. John Hay of Wycombe Marsh, one of the paper-mill owners whose property was damaged in the riots, wrote to Lord Melbourne on 29 January. He said that the men had 'from some inexplicable cause [been] induced to plead guilty, ignorant no doubt of the consequences but in the hope of a mild punishment'. He asserted that if the other three cases had been heard, his own and those of Mr Plaistowe and Mr Allnutt, then 'a very different light would have been thrown on the conduct of several individuals, and a very different fate would have been the result'.[30]

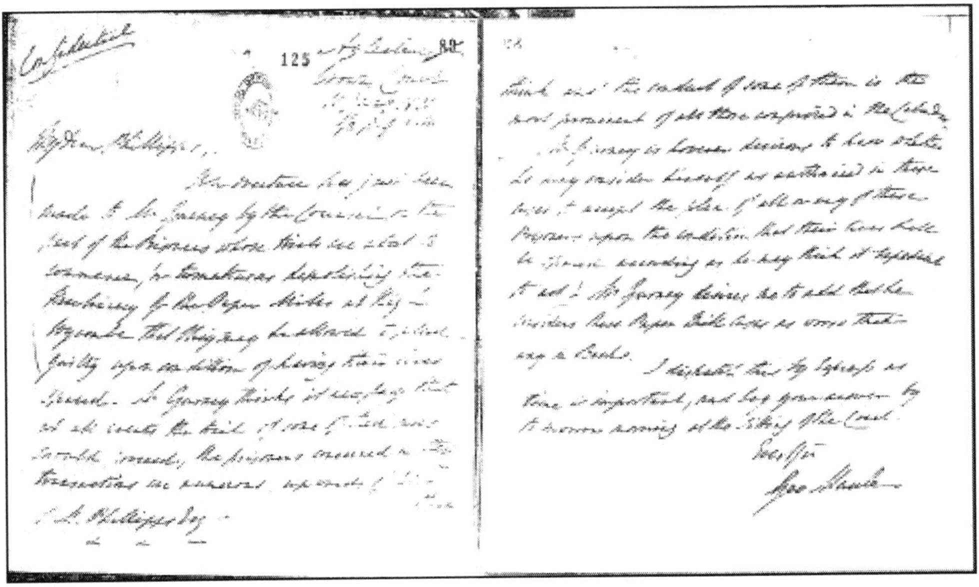

Illustration VI.g. Letter from George Maule to the Home Office dated 11 January 1831.
(TNA, HO 40/17/fo125-6)

The morning of Saturday 15 January was the climax of the week of trials. The court was packed to hear the sentences passed on the prisoners found guilty of breaking machinery in the Wycombe paper mills. All but two of the paper-mill rioters stood in the dock. Mr Justice Park stated how painful it was to see so many before him, for all of whom the law permitted the death sentence. The Court had determined to recommend these prisoners 'to the King's royal consideration and mercy'. Their lives would certainly be spared but upon what terms he could not say. The prisoners were then taken away. Finally, Thomas Blizzard and John Sarney were placed at the bar to receive their sentences. The judges donned the traditional black caps and Mr Justice Park gave an address almost as long as that with which he had started the proceedings at the beginning of the week. The *Bucks Gazette* reported that throughout his speech, the judge was 'deeply affected and wept repeatedly'. Blizzard had been selected, he said, because he was 'the head and front of every engagement that took place'. Also, it had been noted that no one had come forward to give a character reference for him. As for John

Sarney, the judge stated that he was guilty of 'extreme wickedness'. He had been chosen because of his conduct at Davis' mill where he exhibited 'gross personal violence' and the fact that he took a more active part at each mill than almost anyone else. The judge said that they were therefore considered to be 'two fit subjects for capital punishment'. The dreaded death sentence was passed and as the two men were led away, their distress was apparent to everyone on the court. Sarney trembled excessively and Blizzard 'groped about the dock completely doubled up'. Mr Justice Park then closed the Special Commission at Aylesbury, leaving the people of Buckinghamshire in a state of shock.[31]

AFTERMATH

No sooner had the sentences been passed, than a petition was organised pleading for the two men's lives to be spared. An editorial in the *Bucks Gazette* stated that 'the good people of Bucks, we know, revolt at the idea of the spectacle of those men paying the forfeit of their lives'. The article also pointed out that, contrary to the judges' assumption, the men involved in the paper-mill riots were completely ignorant of the important distinction between the riotous breaking of a threshing machine and the riotous breaking of a paper-making machine. 'Need we plead the ignorance of these men?' the editor asked. Quoting from the *Morning Herald* he said it had been pointed out that indeed many legal gentlemen in the area were unaware that the paper-mill rioters were committing a capital offence. He asked that 'some allowance be made for the ignorance and folly of a mob of some inflamed workmen', who were not hardened criminals.[32]

A separate petition was raised by six paper-mill owners and Richard Lansdale, the farmer, whose threshing machine had been destroyed (see Illustration VI.h). This was sent to Lord Melbourne, Secretary of State for the Home Department, on 20 January 1831. Three of the signatories to this petition were also victims of the rioters: W R Davis, Richard Plaistowe and John Hay. They stated that, 'in common with a very large proportion of the subjects of this realm, we deprecate the frequent punishment of Death inflicted for offences which it is hoped might be atoned for by a visitation less severe'.[33]

On 24 January, with only five days to go before the scheduled execution, the reprieve finally came for the two Wycombe men, Thomas Blizzard and John Sarney. The editor of the *Bucks Gazette* launched into a long diatribe, expressing the view that the Government should do something about the 'deplorable ignorance of the peasantry', which had been exposed by the trials of the Swing rioters. He stated that, unlike their counterparts in manufacturing towns, agricultural labourers did not have access to knowledge, because of the fact that they were spread over a wide area and therefore unable to benefit from 'social intercourse'. He went on to speculate on the role that newspapers might play in educating the poor, if only they were allowed. The editor asserted that:

> Had newspapers been in general circulation among the agricultural
> labourers, there might have been rioting, but there would not have been
> so much destruction of machinery. The consequences of the offence
> would have been known immediately [...].

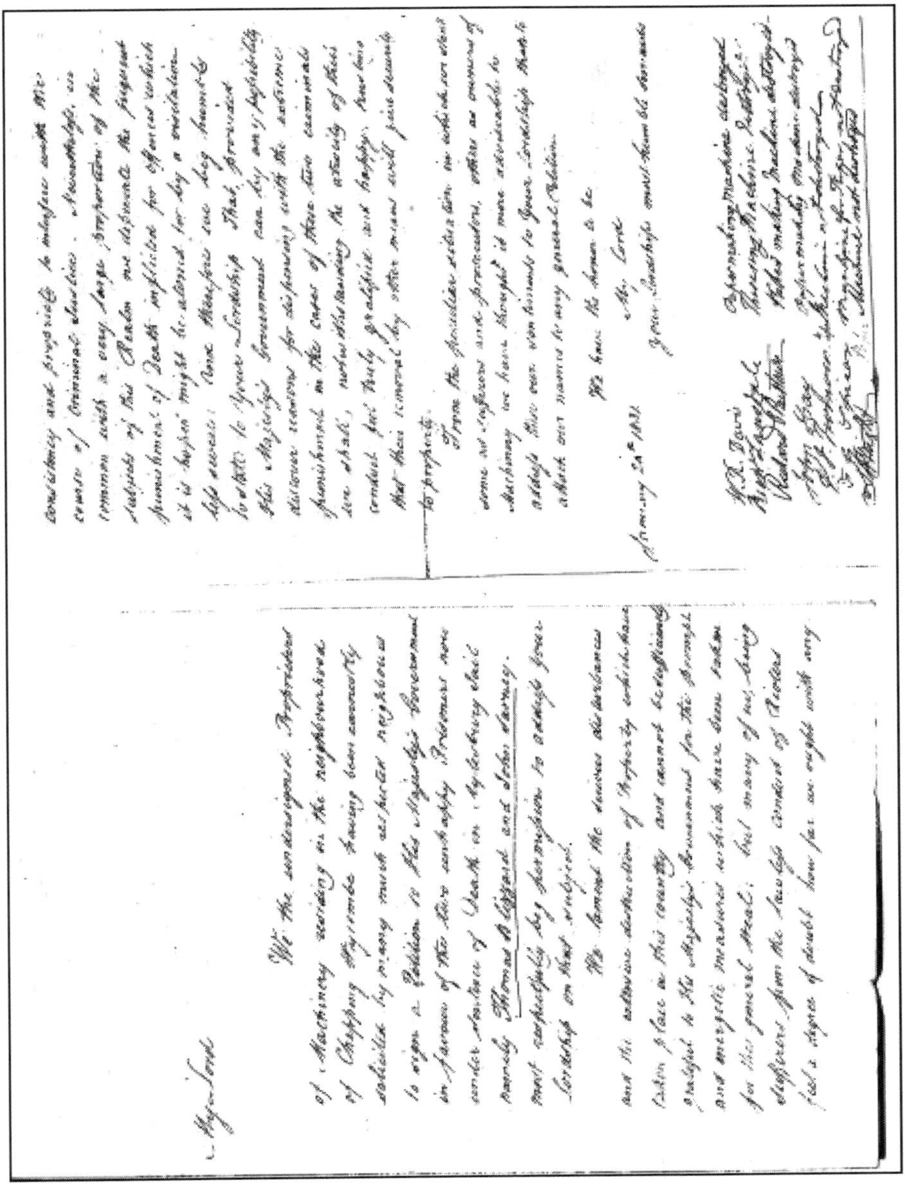

Illustration VI.h. Petition signed by Wycombe paper manufacturers on behalf of Blizzard and Sarney
(TNA, HO 17/46 Part 2)

He speculated that perhaps the rioters would then have been more cautious, knowing that their actions could result in the death penalty. However, the editor also pointed out that men are bound to resort to lawless acts when their 'means of subsistence' are so low that they are reduced to a state of 'lingering starvation'. He asserted that the forthcoming parliamentary session must include a plan of reform. For a start, he advocated a reduction in taxation to boost manufacturing and commerce and increase the national wealth. And, if after that, the labourer was still 'pining in adversity', he suggested that perhaps emigration could offer a solution to the problem. But if such an experimental measure were to be considered, it should only be done as part of a complete revision of the poor laws. Thus, the *Bucks Gazette* anticipated the forthcoming reforms of the new Whig government.[34]

As to the fate of the two prisoners so dramatically reprieved from the death sentence, Thomas Blizzard was transported for life, along with Richard Weedon. John Sarney was also sentenced to be transported for life, but in fact remained in England on board the prison hulk, *Hardy*, for several years. The remaining paper-mill rioters, who had the death sentence recorded against them, had their sentences commuted as follows: twenty-six men were to be transported for seven years; two were sentenced to hard labour, one for eighteen months, one for two years; twelve men received prison sentences, one for eighteen months, the rest for one year. Three of the men, who were sentenced to transportation, were not actually transported. John Sarney was eventually given a pardon in June 1836, after numerous petitions and a letter from Edmund Collins, farmer and overseer of Chepping Wycombe, offering to employ him upon his release. William Hancock was transferred to another prison hulk and pardoned in August 1835. Robert Carey died on board the prison hulk, *York*, in April 1831.[35]

The twenty-six men who were to be transported, were transferred to the *Proteus,* and left Portsmouth bound for Van Diemen's Land, later re-named Tasmania, on 14 April 1831. The ultimate fate of some of the men is shown in Table VI.I. The sources show that only one convict, James Barton, ever came back to England. He returned to his wife and family in Wycombe Marsh and died in 1866.[36] One, Stephen Atkins, was joined by his wife and child and, after his release, spent the remainder of his days in Victoria. Five others also left Tasmania for Victoria, while twelve remained in Tasmania for the rest of their lives. The fate of seven others is not known. Nevertheless, we can safely assume that only two of the transported paper-mill rioters ever saw their families again - an outcome which none of them could have possibly foreseen on that fateful November day when they set out in such high spirits to march from Flackwell Heath to Wycombe.[37]

THE WYCOMBE PAPER-MILL RIOTS IN CONTEXT

It is now necessary to consider the Wycombe paper-mill riots in the context of the Swing movement as a whole. Firstly, we shall look at how those in authority were prepared to deal with the crisis. The wave of protest that swept across the south of England and beyond throughout 1830 was to be described by J L and Barbara Hammond some eighty years later as 'the last labourers' revolt'. The south of England was said to be 'in a state bordering on insurrection' and the Duke of Buckingham wrote from Hampshire to the Duke of Wellington that 'this part of the country is wholly in the hands of the rebels'. According to the Hammonds, in the early days of the rising there was some sympathy for the labourers. Some concessions were made. For example, in Hampshire, Henry Hunt, acting as an intermediary between the farmers and the mob, obtained a promise of a substantial increase in wages for the labourers. But such conciliatory measures were to be short-lived. The authorities soon became alarmed both at the speed with which the trouble spread and the fact that there were so few troops available to deal with it. Landowners began to fear that their kind would be swept away, as they had been in France, unless the rebels were suppressed. A circular from Lord Melbourne on 24 November urged the authorities to use 'firmness and vigour' in dealing with the disturbances and assured them of 'immunity for illegal acts done in the discharge of their duties'.[38]

There is evidence of some understanding of the plight of the poor labourers in Buckinghamshire, as evidenced by the tone of the editorials in the *Bucks Gazette*, but it is clear that most of those in authority in the Wycombe area were not prepared to tolerate riotous behaviour in their community. The meetings held at Salt Hill and in the Wycombe Guild Hall are indicative that the threats of violent action were being taken seriously and that the authorities were prepared to use whatever force they deemed necessary in order to keep the peace.

Next we need to consider how the Wycombe paper-mill riots fit in to the pattern of Swing riot incidents across the country. According to Hobsbawm and Rudé, there were between twenty and twenty-five cases of industrial machine breaking, the most widespread and costly being the Wycombe paper-mill riots. The total damage done by the Swing rioters was estimated at more than one hundred thousand pounds, while the damage at Wycombe amounted to £3,265. The events at Wycombe are comparable to other incidents involving industrial machine breaking. The pattern of events was similar to that at Fordingbridge in Hampshire on 23 and 24 November, where a mob of three hundred labourers destroyed all the threshing machines in the area before marching into the town, demanding money and beer prior to breaking machinery in two factories.[39] Other similar attacks took place in Norfolk at around the same time, notably at the paper mills at Taverham and Lyng. Earlier in the month, paper machinery had also been destroyed at Colthorp in Berkshire.[40]

Who were the rioters? According to Hobsbawm and Rudé, those who were charged were mostly 'peasants' or 'country labourers' in almost every county. They went on to say that this was not the case in Buckinghamshire where, apart from a few craftsmen, the offenders were almost evenly divided between labourers and paper-makers. However, this would appear to be rather a sweeping statement and should be treated with caution because, as stated earlier, the Aylesbury magistrates did not record occupations on the Calendar of Prisoners. The only source for evidence of Buckinghamshire rioters' occupations comes from the prison hulk records, which by definition relate only to those who were transported, not to those who were charged. Also, many more took part in the riots than were charged, so it is impossible to ascertain who the majority of the rioters were.[41] My own research for the Family and Community Historical Research Society's project showed that out of one hundred and sixty-six men charged in Buckinghamshire, fourteen were agricultural labourers, six were ploughmen, seven were labourers, four agricultural labourers/paper-makers, two paper-makers and nine had other occupations. The occupations of the remaining one hundred and twenty-four accused men were not known. Thus, the number of known paper-makers who took part was quite small, but the actual number could have been much higher.

TABLE VI.1
The Wycombe paper-mill rioters

Name	Age	Native place	Final sentence	Pardoned	Fate (where known)
Stephen Atkins	27	High Wycombe	transportation for 7 years	3/2/1836	family migrated to Victoria, died 1879
David Barton	23	Loudwater	transportation for 7 years		died 1885 Tasmania
Edmund Barton	24		18 months hard labour		
James Barton	28	Wycombe Marsh	transportation for 7 years	26/8/1835	returned to England, died 1866
Thomas Blizzard	30	Little Marlow	transportation for life	6/4/1838	died 1843 Tasmania
Thomas Bowles	34	Flackwell Heath	transportation for 7 years	3/2/1836	died 1872 Tasmania
Joseph Briant	23	High Wycombe	transportation for 7 years	3/2/1836	died 1858 Victoria
William Briant (1)	47	High Wycombe	transportation for 7 years	3/2/1836	
William Briant (2)	23	Wooburn	transportation for 7 years	3/2/1836	
John Butler	21	High Wycombe	transportation for 7 years	3/2/1836	died 1858 Tasmania
William Butler	51	Little Marlow	transportation for 7 years	3/2/1836	died 1860 Tasmania
Robert Carey	25		transportation for 7 years		died on prison hulk York 17/4/1831
Robert Carey (alias John Dell)	23		discharged		
John Crutch	18	Flackwell Heath	transportation for 7 years	3/2/1836	died 1879 Victoria
John Dafter	51	Chepping Wycombe	12 months imprisonment		
John Dandridge	45	Wooburn	transportation for 7 years	3/2/1836	
John East	21	Hertford	transportation for 7 years	3/2/1836	died 1/11/1857 Tasmania
Thomas Fisher	26	Beaconsfield	transportation for 7 years		died 1870 Victoria (?)
Benjamin Francis	40		12 months imprisonment		
John Gibson	34		discharged		
James Hall	37		12 months imprisonment		
William Hancock	36	Wooburn	transportation for 7 years	8/8/1835	on prison hulks until 1835
Moses Holt	21	Maidstone	transportation for 7 years		left Tasmania for Victoria 1840
David Lunnon	26		18 months imprisonment		
James Miles	18	Chilworth, Surrey	transportation for 7 years		died 1851 Tasmania
John Moody	26	Little Marlow	transportation for 7 years		died December 1831 Tasmania

TABLE VI.1 (contd)

Name	Age	Native place	Final sentence	Pardoned	Fate (where known)
William Moody	22		12 months imprisonment		
William Nibbs	21	Little Marlow	transportation for 7 years	5/4/1836	died 1884 Tasmania
Joseph Priest	36	Wycombe Marsh	transportation for 7 years	3/2/1836	
John Reynolds	29		12 months imprisonment		
William Russell	20		12 months imprisonment		
Arthur Salter	19	High Wycombe	transportation for 7 years	3/2/1836	died 1891 Victoria
John Sarney	54	Flackwell Heath	transportation for life	15/6/1836	on prison hulks until 1836, died 1840
William Shrimpton	63		2 years hard labour		
John Smith alias Budd	27	High Wycombe	transportation for 7 years		
William Smith	30		12 months imprisonment		
James Stone	29		acquitted		
Henry Stratford	44		12 months imprisonment		
James Stretton	19		discharged		
Samuel Summerfield	20	Henley, Herts	transportation for 7 years	3/2/1836	died 1864 Tasmania
John Walduck	21	Kingston-Upon-Thames	transportation for 7 years	3/2/1836	died 1886 Tasmania
Henry Walker	22	Wycombe Marsh	transportation for 7 years	3/2/1836	
John Walker	37		discharged		
William Walker	25		12 months imprisonment		
John Watts	20		12 months imprisonment		
James Webb	29		12 months imprisonment		
Richard Weedon	41	Chepping Wycombe	transportation for life		
Edmund Wingrove	24	Lane End	transportation for 7 years	3/2/1836	died 1847 Tasmania
Arthur Wright	18		12 months imprisonment		

Sources: *Bucks Gazette*, Nov 1830 to Jan 1831
CBS, Unclassified documents from Swing Riots box
Chambers, J, 1991
Geoffrey Sharman Tasmania GenWeb Web site, 30/11/03
FreeBMD Web site, 30/11/03

In Buckinghamshire, as in many counties, there was a tendency to blame 'strangers' for instigating the Swing riots. These illusive people were often described in the newspapers in such terms as 'a respectable-dressed man', who was seen in Wiltshire, 'two gentlemanly-looking men' in Bedfordshire and 'two well-dressed men in a green gig' in Oxfordshire. These examples indicate an unwillingness to believe that local people were capable of such anti-social behaviour without being encouraged by some suspicious outsider. Thus, the *Bucks Gazette* reported that the ringleader of the Wycombe paper-mill riots was 'an athletic man' and a 'total stranger' to the town.[42]

There were Special Commissions to deal with the trials in five counties, including Buckinghamshire. The first ones were held in Hampshire and Wiltshire, and the judges there were noted for their severity in sentencing a total of one hundred and fifty-three men to death. In the event, three men were executed in Hampshire and one in Wiltshire. *The Times* noted that the Berkshire Commission was 'a merciful contrast to that at Winchester' as a different team of judges was presiding and this more lenient pattern continued at Aylesbury.[43] However, as before, two men were chosen to suffer the death penalty, to serve as examples to the other prisoners. As we have seen, nonetheless, Blizzard and Sarney were more fortunate than their fellow rioters in Hampshire and Wiltshire, as they were eventually reprieved. Across the whole country, the total number of Swing rioters executed was nineteen; the total number transported was 481, while 644 were imprisoned. As stated earlier, twenty-six of the Wycombe paper-mill rioters were transported to Van Diemen's Land and seventeen were imprisoned.[44]

What was the local effect of taking so many able-bodied men out of their communities, many of them leaving their families behind? According to Hobsbawm and Rudé, one in three married men who were transported, left their wives and children living 'on the parish'. One such was Mary Blizzard, the wife of Thomas, who appears in the Little Marlow Overseers' account book in the 1830s and 1840s. In the quarter up to Lady Day, 25 March 1835, she received a total of £3 2s 6d in poor relief.[45] Mary must have had a constant struggle to make ends meet and in December 1841, an inventory shows that household goods worth £2 12s 0d were seized from her in payments of rent arrears.[46]

CONCLUSION

Finally, it is necessary to consider what, if anything, was achieved by the Wycombe paper-mill riots in particular, and the Swing Riots in general. Hobsbawm and Rudé's conclusion was that there was no direct evidence of a causal link between the Swing riots and reform of the poor laws in 1834, merely a 'probability' that the riots were one factor among many.[47] In the compilation of the Poor Law Report, one of the questions asked of parish officials throughout the country was, 'Can you give the Commissioners any information respecting the causes of the agricultural riots and burning of 1830 and 1831?'[48] In Buckinghamshire, a majority of those asked, considered that wage levels were a major factor (22%), the second most common answer was unemployment (18%), while one of the factors in third place was the poor law (12%). However, only a limited number of parishes were involved in the survey and Wycombe was not one of them.[49] It remains a matter for speculation whether the new

Whig government of 1830 would have acted so swiftly to commission the Report on the Poor Laws had the Swing movement not happened.

Hobsbawm and Rudé stated that in the immediate aftermath of the Swing movement there was some improvement in wages and conditions. They quoted a Norfolk man as saying that 'If we had never had any fires our wages would not have been more than 10s a week; now they are 11s'. However, they also expressed some doubt as to whether the effects were lasting.[50] Jacqueline Cooper, in her recent history of Saffron Walden, concluded that wages increased temporarily, but that ultimately the outcome of the riots was a great disappointment to the poor. She also pointed out that despite the execution of three young men found guilty of arson in 1829, this crime became more widespread in the region after the Swing riots than it had been before.[51] In other parts of the country too, there were sporadic incidents of arson and rioting in the years following the Swing riots.

As to the local effects of the Wycombe riots, one historian has expressed the view that the riots 'only accelerated change by forcing some paper-makers into bankruptcy, leaving the trade in the hands of those who could afford to buy and protect new machinery'.[52] In fact, only one paper-maker actually went bankrupt, and that was Zachary Allnutt. In 1839, both Plaistowe and Lane were still trading; their names can be seen listed in Robson's *Directory* for that year.[53] The controversial machinery was gradually reintroduced, but the numbers of people employed in the industry would seem to indicate that the paper-making trade continued to thrive in Wycombe in the aftermath of the events of 1830. In 1798, there had been seventy-five paper-makers in the parish of Chepping Wycombe, and by 1851 this had risen to 190.[54] Unfortunately, there are no figures available for the 1820s and 1830s. The Wycombe paper industry continued well into the 20th century, although sadly, today, paper is no longer made along the Wye Valley.

It is hard to say with any certainty what was achieved by the Swing riots, but there is little doubt in my mind that the events of 1830 gave the upper classes what in modern parlance would be termed a 'wake-up call'. Those who governed the country were made to realise that something must be done to alleviate the conditions of the labouring classes. The passing of the 1832 Reform Act, the 1833 Factory Act and the 1834 Poor Law Amendment Act, all within four years of the 'last labourers' revolt', are indicative of the importance of all the Swing protesters, including the Wycombe paper-mill rioters, in arousing political conscience and should not be underestimated.

NOTES

1   Hobsbawm, E J and Rudé, G, *Captain Swing*, (Lawrence and Wishart Ltd, 1969), p 98.
2   *Bucks Gazette*, 11 September 1830.
3   Hobsbawm and Rudé (1969), pp 138, 121, 125.
4   Chambers, J, *Buckinghamshire Machine Breakers: The Story of the 1830 Riots*, (Jill Chambers, Letchworth, 1991), p 15.
5   *Bucks Gazette*, 20 November 1830.
6   Chambers (1991), p 17.

7   *Bucks Gazette*, 4 December 1830.
8   *Ibid*, 4 December 1830.
9   *Ibid*, 4 December 1830.
10 *Ibid*, 4 December 1830.
11 *Ibid*, 4 December 1830.
12 *Ibid*, 4 December 1830.
13 *Ibid*, 11 December 1830.
14 *Ibid*, 4 December 1830.
15 *Ibid*, 4 December 1830.
16 TNA, Home Office Counties Correspondence, HO 52/6/281-3.
17 TNA, HO52/6/279.
18 CBS, unclassified document from the 'Swing' box.
19 Hammond, J L and Barbara, *The Village Labourer 1760-1832*, (Longmans Green & Co., 1920), p. 283.
20 *Bucks Gazette*, 8 January 1831.
21 *Ibid*, 15 January 1831.
22 *Ibid*, 15 January 1831.
23 *Ibid*, 4 December 1830.
24 *Ibid*, 15 January 1831.
25 *Ibid*, 15 January 1831.
26 *Ibid*, 15 January 1831.
27 TNA, Home Office Disturbances Correspondence, HO 40/27/fo127.
28 *Ibid*, HO 40/27/fo129.
29 *Bucks Gazette*, 15 January 1831.
30 TNA, Clemency Petitions, HO 17/50.
31 *Bucks Gazette*, 22 January 1831.
32 *Ibid*, 22 January 1831.
33 TNA, HO 17/46 Part 2.
34 *Bucks Gazette*, 29 January 1831.
35 Chambers (1991), pp 104-93.
36 FreeBMD Web site, 30 November 2003.
37 Chambers (1991), pp. 104-93.
38 Hammond and Hammond (1920), p. 242-3.
39 Hobsbawm and Rudé (1969), p 121.
40 *Ibid* (1969) p 198.
41 *Ibid* (1969) pp 242-43.
42 *Ibid* (1969) pp 239-40.
43 *The Times*, 1 January 1831.
44 Hobsbawm and Rudé (1969), pp 259-60, 308-9.
45 CBS, Little Marlow Overseers Account Book 1833-48, PR141/12/3.
46 CBS, Inventory of goods seized from Mary Blizzard, PR240/10/5/41/2.
47 Hobsbawm and Rudé (1969), p 297.
48 BPP XXXIV Royal Commission into the Poor Laws (1834).
49 CBS, Report on the Poor Laws 1834, L.000:36 appendix.
50 Hobsbawm and Rudé (1969), p 298.
51 Cooper, Jacqueline, *The Well-ordered Town: A Story of Saffron Walden, Essex, 1792-1862* (Cooper Publications, 2000), p 135-6.
52 Rattue, James, *High Wycombe Past*, (Phillimore and Co Ltd., Chichester, 2002), p 19.

53 Robson's *Directory*, 1839.
54 Ashford, L J, *History of High Wycombe from its Origins to 1880*, (Routledge and Kegan Paul Ltd, 1960), p.212; Thorpe, David, *Bucks in 1851 - The Evidence of the Population Census*, (Bucks Archaeological Society, undated), para 86-7.

VII. BETWEEN THE LINES

Valerie Batt-Rawden

My brief for the FACHRS Swing Riots project was to research available local papers for Berkshire and to extract details of rioting and destruction of machines and property between the dates 1830 to 1832, in order to compare them with those obtained by Hobsbawm and Rudé. During the course of this research it became obvious that Berkshire could not be examined in isolation from the wider picture. Each local paper reported incidents from as far apart as Carlisle, Ely, Gosport, Isles of Sheppey and Thanet, Nottinghamshire and Hampshire. Although the worst damage was inflicted in the rural areas by supposedly illiterate agricultural labourers, the research shows that towns were also affected by threatening 'Swing' letters, demands for higher wages and by others either rioting in sympathy or with their own 'axe to grind', and that some of the ring leaders were far from illiterate.

Once the widespread riots had been contained, and with a Government more aligned to the need for reform, especially of the Poor Law, questionnaires were sent to all parishes involved and various reasons were given for the causes.[1] Those that were returned were simplified and localised, as was to be expected, and are borne out by the examples from the newspaper research given below. It was this simplicity that prompted further research in order to find an answer to the question 'Why did the Swing Riots spread so widely and last so long?'

The title 'Swing Riots' can only be seen as an umbrella term for what was, in effect, a series of incidents, but with common cause, which spread nationally. Reading between the lines shows them to be perpetrated not merely by groups of rampaging and illiterate rioters but by desperate individuals, whose lives, and those of their families, were inexorably changed as a result. E-mail contact has made it possible for information and references to be exchanged with other researchers, in Gloucestershire, Wiltshire and Hampshire, more quickly than is usually the case, in order to follow the stories of some of those individuals linked to Berkshire families of the present day.

From the distance of over two centuries it is possible to see the complexity and multiplicity of the causes for the longevity, spread and ferocity of the Swing riots compared to others. England had suffered a number of riots, especially during the 18th century.[2] The reasons were the same - the poverty of the lower orders, who did not have a voice. Most were small and quickly repressed, although the Gordon Riots of 1780 in London did a hundred thousand pounds' worth of damage, ten times that of the French Revolution, and The Riot Act became law after the Catholic Jacobite rebellion in 1714, which opposed the new Hanoverian King George I. Twelve Luddites were hanged in York in 1812, for the capital offence of breaking machinery.[3] Those hanged during the Swing riots were convicted of the same offences under the same law. However, there were national and international events, which appear to have had a direct bearing on the spread and duration of the Swing riots, viz:

❖ The 'Industrial Revolution', which escalated the drift from agriculture to industry in the 18th century.[4]

❖ The 'French Revolution' 1789 destabilised Europe and a series of bad harvests resulted in the Corn Law of 1815, which prohibited the import of corn until the price reached eighty shillings a quarter. This effectively raised the price of bread, the staple food of the labourers. The Government was seriously divided on the issue.[5]

❖ The end of the Napoleonic wars (1815) had brought in an influx of returning soldiers with few expectations of employment or parish relief and the threshing machine had reduced the need for winter labour. In East Anglia a poor harvest and a hard winter brought the labourers to starvation level in the spring of 1816 and riots broke out throughout Suffolk, Norfolk and Essex. Rioters demanded higher wages.[6] Their battle cry was 'bread or blood for breakfast'. There were a number of fairly violent incidents involving machine breaking, which were badly organised and quickly suppressed. These riots showed similarities to the Swing riots under consideration.

❖ The Enclosures from 1760, which were intended to improve agriculture, exacerbated the problems of cottagers without land and reduced their ability to provide for their families.[7]

❖ In Berkshire, the Speenhamland System (1795), although a philanthropic endeavour to address the inequality of financial assistance for paupers, in practise worsened the problems. With the sharp rise in the cost of bread, corn prices and growing local hardships, it did not try to fix wages but to supplement agricultural wages through the Poor Law allowances to vary with the price of bread and size of labourer's family. Since this had to be claimed through the labourer's parish, it impeded the movement of labour. It did not differentiate between pauper and poor. As a result, it appeared to increase indolence and numbers of children.[8]

NEWSPAPER RESEARCH

Berkshire in 1830 was one of the largest, mainly agricultural, counties in England, sharing borders with other rural counties of Hertfordshire, Surrey, Hampshire, Oxfordshire and Wiltshire. It had no large industries. Reading was an important market town with a slaughter-house, which only closed in the late 20th century. It held the county gaol and it was an important river crossing with a malting industry, still in existence. Newbury had become important because of sheep and wool, and Windsor, although it boasted breweries, was important because of Windsor Castle, home of the King. Assizes were held in Reading and Abingdon.[9]

Most of the Berkshire incidents were in the Hampshire/Wiltshire border area during November/December 1830 and are reported in *Windsor and Eton Express, Reading Mercury, Berkshire Chronicle* and *Bucks and Windsor Herald*. The originals are not available and there were difficulties in finding the details of events in the microfilms of the large broadsheets. They were often hidden in long-winded reports covering several columns. The incidents were frequently duplicated in one or more of the papers and found under several headings (shown in italics below).

The first Berkshire incident was reported in the *Windsor and Eton Express* on 13 November 1830, although the first had occurred in Kent in early spring. The first mention of these in the *Windsor and Eton Express* was on 6 November 1830:

> The cry for bread and labour is loud, machines are daily being
> destroyed (from *Kent and Essex Mercury*)

It was dissatisfaction over the heavy tithes paid by farmers, which took up most of the earlier editorial reporting. In fact, the early Swing riots were not mentioned and 'The State of the Country' appeared to be calm.

The authorities may have hoped that the unrest would die out over the summer and not re-emerge. There would have been employment during the spring sowing and harvest, which was still labour intensive, and there is no doubt that many people would travel great distances to find work during the latter season, which was allowed under the Settlement Laws of 1662.[10] An example was the exodus to the hop fields of Kent as well as potato picking north of the River Thames. This would have the effect of spreading information and unrest and, once the harvest was over and the families had returned to their own homes, with little hope of winter employment, it would flare up once more. It is conceivable that those who had successfully organised the early riots might even have travelled with them as advisors.

The *Windsor and Eton Express* reports indicated that there was a great deal of local sympathy for the labourers' cause, but The Riot Act (1715) had given local magistrates powers to deal with destructive mobs, which could not be ignored, and also:

> The Government of the Duke [of Wellington] took active measures for
> their [the Swing Riots] suppression, and before its resignation in

November 1830, had increased the military forces in the disturbed districts, offered rewards for the conviction of incendiaries and issued special commissions for the trial of the leading rioters. *(Wellington 1889)*

Each incident was dealt with at local level and local people were sworn in, in haste, as special constables on many occasions and:

> [...] Justice and justices of the peace, sheriff, under sheriff, mayor, bailiff and other head-officer [...] every high or petty constable [...] and other peace officer

were authorised by The Riot Act (1715) to disperse:

> any persons to the number of twelve or more, being unlawfully, riotously, and tumultuously assembled together, to the disturbance of the publick [*sic*] peace

by going 'among the said rioters, or as near to them as he can safely come' and:

> shall openly and with a loud voice make or cause to be made proclamation in these words or like in effect:

> Our Sovereign Lord The King chargeth and commandeth all persons, being assembled, immediately to disperse themselves and peaceably to depart to their habitations or to their lawful business, upon the pains contained in the Act made in the first year of King George the First for preventing tumults and riotous assemblies. God Save The King. (*Riot Act 1715*)

They were given one hour to disperse before their presence ceased to be a misdemeanour and became a felony, ultimately punishable by death. As well as disturbing the peace, the act adjudged a felony to include demolishing or pulling down 'or begin to pull down any church or chapel [...] dwelling house, barn, stable, or other outhouse'.[11]
Only once, in the *Windsor and Eton Express* reports, was it noted that a reading had taken place, so perhaps many dispersed before this could be done.

> Saturday 26 November at Brimpton. The Rev. C Cove swore in his parishioners as specials and met the rioters and read the riot act [...] after a fight the ringleaders and 10 rioters were chained and taken to Reading Gaol.

It took some courage to face the rioters and, in some cases, the Yeomanry, a volunteer cavalry force (1794-1908), were called in, as they were best equipped to respond most speedily; especially as so many incidents took place in the heart of the country some distance from a town.

There was also a King's proclamation to 'anyone who catches a rioter':

> £50 for each rioter apprehended and convicted and £50 and pardon for anyone who reports a ringleader or perpetrator. (Berkshire Chronicle *and* Bucks and Windsor Herald *26 November 1830*)

Under the same legislation any accomplice to an incendiary who turned King's evidence was entitled to a reward and a free pardon.

There were many reports of letters and threats being delivered by 'gentlemen' on horse-back and some on 'big bay' horses leading the incitement to riot. This description is so often central to romantic fiction, and maybe these reports were just that, in order to explain the reason for well-organised attacks. It did not seem possible that it could be the work of 'illiterate labourers'. On the other hand, there might have been some substance in these reports. The Duke of Wellington, Prime Minister at the time, in a letter to Lord Malmsbury (London 6 December 1830), was thought to believe that:

> We have in this country unfortunately a very numerous class of men, well educated, who have no means of subsistence, and who have no employment. These are the gentlemen who go about in gigs. You will ask how are these men subsisted. How are the gigs, etc., paid for? I answer that I know that the Societe Propagande at Paris had at its command very large means from subscriptions all over Europe, but particularly from the Revolutionary Bankers in France. A part of this means is, I think now applied to the purpose of corrupting and disturbing this country.[12]

However correct was his belief:

> it was evident from the adroitness and careful preparation with which these outrages were committed that others besides the 'smock frocks' were at the bottom of the conspiracy. 'They all wear smock frocks [*see Illustration Vii.a*] now', says Lord Ellenborough in his diary (vol. ii) 'but their language is better than their dress'.[13]

But was there any truth behind the stated opinions of Wellington and Lord Ellenborough? Were the incidents in Kent in the spring of 1830 - thirteen in January, twenty-two in February, fifteen in March and seventeen in April - merely co-incidental to the civil unrest in France at the same time?

Illustration VII.a. Man wearing a smock frock

Charles X was deposed in favour of Louis Philippe, 'Citizen King' in the 'July Revolution' and escaped to England.[14] The first riot that is attributed to 'Swing' occurred in the parish of Lower Hardres, Kent, on Saturday 18 August 1830, where a threshing machine was smashed. Is it not feasible that other *émigrés* escaped with Charles, landing in Kent? Were they the reported 'gentleman in gigs', some of whom were observed to speak in a foreign language, who were suspected of financing and co-ordinating the unrest? If so, they would certainly have had first-hand knowledge of the effectiveness of organised rioting. A selection of events from newspapers relating to incidents follows.

Editorial
> 20 November There was a meeting at the Town Hall attended by 400/500 people. Windsor and Neighbourhood desire to create an association to stop incendiaries.

Agricultural Distress
> On 22nd November editorial opinion thought that work should be found for the agricultural labourers, 'however petty'. 'We deeply lament to see that the horrid system of firing ricks, which has long devastated Kent and Sussex, has reached our county'.

The Alarming State of Berkshire
> 19 November in Henley, several farmers destroyed threshing machines in fear of reprisals yet no threatening letter had been received.

> On 25th November it was reported that Abingdon, Wallingford, Newbury, Lambourne, Nettlebed, and Benson had suffered more machine breakers. 'Yesterday, Bath coach stopped between Newbury

and Hungerford, the harness was cut and the paintwork damaged. Money was demanded from passengers. The coachman withstood demands and proceeded.'

'Wallingford, 4 rioters, Lambourne, 10 rioters were taken to the House of Correction for threatening to break machines.' 'Eastbury, 1 threatened to fire the town. Committed for trial.' 'Special Constables sworn in at Eton, Salt Hill, Burnham, Beaconsfield, Maidenhead, Winkfield, Egham, Chertsey, and Staines.'

Court Procedures

On 23 November at Aston Tirrold, ringleaders were charged with assault and being unlawfully assembled with 100 persons for riot. One was imprisoned with hard labour and five were discharged at 20/- each [each in his own cognisance].[15] At Eastbury, ringleaders were charged with assault. Eleven were given prison sentences from three to nine months. Twenty-two were designated imprisonment with hard labour. Two were sentenced at Reading to 18 months.

26 November 1830 at Abingdon [Assizes] those caught were charged with assault on a constable, rescuing prisoners, riot and common assault. Three were committed to prison; for his part in riots at Kintbury, Smith, alias Winterbourne, was executed. This conviction was also reported in the *Editorial.*

Friday 7 January. Abingdon Assizes The prisoners thanked the court very respectfully at the conclusion, [of the trial] and quitted the dock with every symptom of gratitude for the leniency of the sentence. *(Windsor and Eton Express)*

There were, however, some events, which at the time were deadly serious, but now make us smile.

Reported in a London Journal

An individual 'with moustachios' entered an experimental chemist in the Strand asking for 'any preparation that would produce instantaneous light by contaction'. The chemist offered his invention, the 'Promethean', for which he had obtained a patent. The invention, if attached to a small bomb, and fired from a rifle or cross bow, would, upon coming in close union with ammunition wagons, set them on fire instantly.

The man produced an arrow filled with combustible material, to which they fitted one of the bulbs to the beard of the arrow, and this was demonstrated successfully. The individual purchased 700 of these bulbs. A man answering to the description was seen lurking about a farm at Battle. He returned to London some time later minus his moustachios! The chemist reported this to the police because he felt he was guilty. The 'invention unconsciously sold by the chemist has been the cause of so much destruction of property'. (*Windsor and Eton Express* 18 December 1830)

Maybe from the following report it can be deduced that the man with 'moustachios' was also at work in Holyport.

Mr Winkworth's rick yard, at Holyport, was watched by a man who heard a report (less than a pistol shot) and a hiss, and saw flames issue from a straw house in the rick yard and spread to 4 barns. His ricks were of wheat, peas, barley and oats. Eight ricks out of 18 were preserved by engines from Maidenhead. Had they all been destroyed the value would have been £5,000. He had received a threatening letter, labourers of the area not suspected. (*Reading Mercury*)

To someone born in Windsor those incidents, which occurred in and around that town were most interesting and showed that not all were serious, although probably seemed to be so at the time.

The following reports were put together from different local publications of 20 November 1830, with a different slant on the same case:

The Mayor remarked that 'during a great part of this week Mr "Swing" appears to have been amusing himself'.

Several threatening letters signed 'Swing' had been circulating throughout Windsor. One threatened the Castle, saying that there should be a more efficient guard. It was taken seriously and put on alert. 'Six additional "centinals" [*sic*] were placed on duty'. One letter was received by the mayor, Mr Bannister, which should have been sent to the butcher, Mr Adams. One was sent to Mr Wright the assistant overseer as follows, in a threatening tone but respectful none the less!

Sir, I understand you are a hard hearted and oppressive overseer, this is to inform you, unless you alter your present proceedings, you will have much cause to regret the same. I am, Sir, yours etc SWING.

The Postmaster noted that all the letters had been written in the same hand and in order to catch the perpetrator an individual was stationed in a house opposite the post office to catch the 'poster of letters' by a sign from the postmaster, who was waiting at the letterbox. Threatening letters were sent as usual, but not at the post office, even though watch was kept for two or three nights. A 'who done it'. Was there some collusion somewhere?

Newspaper reports state that most letters were written by the labourers themselves, except in one case, where a Methodist lay preacher was found to have several copies in his possession.[16] However, the above letter was one of at least thirteen written to an assistant overseer, who was particularly hated by the agricultural labourers because he was paid to reduce the level of poor relief under the Select Vestries Act (1819).

3 December 1830. A message was received at the *Windsor Herald* office that rioters were at Wooburn. Eton boys and inhabitants were sworn in as constables, and set off for Salt Hill armed with cudgels. Post-chaises were provided to take them. Some arrived at Burnham, but there were disagreements and they would not move until all had assembled. They adjourned to a local pub until the rest arrived. They got to Wooburn after rioters had been dispersed by a detachment of foot guards and marched to Beaconsfield. Out of the one hundred and fifty from Eton only sixty remained. All the others had gone home.

A threatening letter to Dr Keate was sent to the *Windsor Herald* office at 38 High Street on 3 December, and notes were sent requesting townspeople to attend a meeting at the White Hart Inn. Many turned up and found it to be a hoax. Some made jokes as follows:

Hairdresser - work of a blockhead.
Shoemaker - last time he would answer such a request.
Printer - would not be pressed.
Bookbinder - would not be bound to wait.
Watchmaker - was wound up to the highest degree at the joke.
Tailor - called it superfine.

The Dr Keate referred to above was headmaster of Eton College at the time and the 'threatening letter' is no doubt the one sent to him by the Eton boys themselves; after the example of the Swing letters, which had been circulating for several months. It and Dr Keate's answer are reproduced below.

THRESHING OR THRASHING?

'Dr Keate, Dr Keate
There's distress in your beat
So the sufferers assert, great and small
And it's plain to be seen
That your *thrashing machine*
Must be at the bottom of all.

Now I you advise
Dr Keate, if you're wise
And would keep your tail from harm,
To desist while you can,
And adopt a new plan
Of grand *fundamental reform!*'
Signed **SWING**

**To which the facetious Doctor is
represented as having replied thus:**

Dr Swing, Mr Swing
It's not a true thing
what your sufferers assert, great
and small
And you, Sir, at once,
Are convicted a dunce
And must go to the bottom of all
Some though, perhaps
Have deserved my hard raps,
And you, Sir, shall soon understand
But this cannot apply
To my system, for I
Do the whole of my thrashing *by hand*
And whilst some masters may pay
But a shilling a day
To labourers tilling the sod
It is very well known
That on *grounds* of my own
I have handsomely paid - *by the rod*.

(contributed by Cynthia Coultas from *Bristol Gazette and Public Advertiser* 6 January 1831)

BETWEEN THE LINES

It is obvious that the national research undertaken by the FACHRS has been justified and the figures show that the incidents of machine-breaking, rick-burning and other damage, were greater in number than were reported in Hobsbawm and Rudé. The use of e-mail to report data gathered from the local newspapers and other sources, has also facilitated interaction between members of the research team working on this project, and has allowed a closer look between the lines at the effects of Swing upon the lives of participants.

As a member of the Berkshire Family History Society's Discussion Group, which keeps in contact by e-mail, it was possible to put out a general enquiry for information from any member whose ancestors had been involved in the riots. Three answers were received.

Reply No 1. From John T. Fowle
Fulwar Craven Fowle Vicar of Kintbury 1795 - 1840

The following is a bit of family history and as such may not be of interest to all. Fulwar was my 4th great-grandfather.

Fulwar Craven Fowle was the vicar of Kintbury Church as well as Magistrate during the period when the Swing riots or Bread riots took place in 1830.

In mid-November 1830 several villages in the Kennet Valley banded together and on Sunday the 21st the Mob was breaking machines. At 4 o'clock in the morning they came to Fulwar and he agreed that some machines should be brought from Barton Court and these were smashed. Also each parson was to contribute two pounds and Fulwar did this. There were further negotiations at Hungerford on an increase in daily pay. Fulwar, although obviously sympathetic to the idea of better pay for labourers, was not necessarily popular because as magistrate he had to administer the gaming laws, and the harshness of these was one of the subjects of the men's protests.

On 22 November Mr Dundas asked for military assistance. Hearing that the Kintbury mob was planning to attack the town of Newbury, he arranged with Lord Craven to meet his party of horsemen, with fifty grenadiers who had reported to him, on the London-Bath road. The rioters fled and some seventy were rounded up, including the leaders, Norris, Oakley, Darling, and Smith alias Captain Winterbourne.

Some of the local gentry thought Fulwar's tactics were too soft. He received a letter of mild reproof from the Home Office. He immediately replied and, with support from his parishioners and a letter to the Secretary of State for the Home Department by Mr. Dundas, the matter was clarified A commission was set up in Reading to try the rioters 'with the utmost severity'. Fulwar visited the ringleaders at Reading but, in the end, many Kintbury men were transported. Only three were left for execution, of these, two were later spared, and only Smith alias Winterbourne was executed.[17] His body was returned to Kintbury and he was buried in the Kintbury churchyard with Rev. Fulwar Craven Fowle officiating.[18]

The conviction of the men mentioned was reported in the *Windsor and Eton Express* under Court Procedures (see above).

Interestingly, another report states that the Vicar of Kintbury was given '£2.00 for every man arrested'. Perhaps this compensated for the two pounds paid out for each threshing machine destroyed.[19]

Fulwar Fowle's story is a good example of the sympathy of those in authority at the time and their attitude to the causes and the rioters themselves. The low level of violence and gentlemanly bearing of those convicted was remarked upon on more than one occasion during the course of this research. That Winterbourne was buried in consecrated ground, although a convicted and executed 'felon', was unusual in the extreme. It indicates that rioting for such a reason was not seen as a crime by the vicar or his parishioner who petitioned for mercy.

Both Mr Charles Dundas MP and Fulwar Fowle, in his capacity as Magistrate, had been instrumental in establishing the Speenhamland System.

At the Pelican Inn, Speenhamland on 6 May 1795 at ten o'clock in the morning a General Meeting, chaired by Mr Charles Dundas MP was convened to which the Sheriff and all the Berkshire Magistrates had been invited; although there were only nineteen present. The end result was the declaration that 'farmers and other agricultural employers of the county were 'earnestly recommended' to increase the pay of their labourers in proportion to the present price of provisions: but if they did not or could not do so, the Magistrates undertook to give relief to all 'poor and industrious men and their families' by 'an allowance from the poor rates' on a sliding scale according to the current price of bread'. (*The Kintbury Family* by Margaret Sawtell née Fowle)

Although this was a Berkshire initiative, it is obvious that other agricultural counties followed a similar system, with the resultant feeling of desperation - that the labourers were left with stark choices, to riot or starve.

Reply No 2. From Ray West
William Watts

One of my ancestors (William Watts), was transported to Tasmania on the *Eliza*? After being convicted of feloniously destroying a threshing machine, the property of John Fosbury of Highclere. Originally he was received aboard the hulk 'York' at Portsmouth on 11 January 1831.

William Watts (a sawyer) was born 1807 in West Hannay, Berkshire and was convicted of theft of five pounds from Thomas Evans of Burghclere on 23 November 1830; also riotously assembled with one hundred others.

William Watts was on the list, by Geoffrey Sharman, of those former Swing rioters living in Van Dieman's Land (Tasmania) before 1856. He appeared with coded details, which have been translated as follows:

Born 1806, trial in Hampshire, transported to Tasmania on *Eliza*, died 1833 in Tasmania. Died in Hobart Hospital and was buried in Trinity churchyard, Hobart.

From the Winchester Court proceedings:

William Watts, Ag Lab, was charged with three incidents on 29 November 1830. Destroying a threshing machine of John Fosbury on 23 November 1830, there is no confirmation that he robbed Thomas Evans, Farmer on the same day.

Robbery Burghclere Transportation for 7 years	Wed 23 Nov 1830 am Special Commission	Thomas Evans Farmer	
Machine-breaking Highclere Transportation for 7 years	Wed 23 Nov 1830 Special commission	John Fosbury Farmer	
Machine-breaking Burghclere Transportation for 7 years	Wed 23 Nov 1830 Special Commission	Riotous assembly	

From a photocopied transcript of the Special Commission of Assize proceedings in Winchester in December 1830 it is possible to follow the conviction of William Watts for his part in the destruction of machinery he was 'Attainted of Felony' and:

[...] transported beyond the seas, to such colony as his Majesty may direct, for the term of seven years.

It is obvious that every man had a very fair trial and although many were sentenced to death few had the sentence carried out. The presiding judge, Baron Vaughan, preferred to make an example 'of those who have most guiltily offended'.

Joseph Mason was transported with his brother Robert, and both Mason men are mentioned by Hobsbawm and Rudé as two of the ringleaders. Robert Mason had sentence of death recorded against him, as did the 'prisoner Winkworth' to whom the judge said:

You were tried twice, and though you were in one case very properly
acquitted, yet it must not be forgotten that you were a tithing-man and
as such it was your duty to preserve the peace.[20]

Of Joseph, Baron Vaughan said:

The prisoner J. Mason, who stands before me, is a man moving in a
better condition of life [...] not acting under pressure of distress [...] you
have taken a very conspicuous part, and have been a leader [...]. He
must be cut off from all communication with society, and be
transported for life.

In his diary, a photocopy of which is in the Berkshire Record Office, Joseph mentions
his lack of education. This is dispelled somewhat by the above remarks, and he gives a
graphic and fluently colourful description of life as a transportee to Australia. He refers to
his first sight of the rocky islands at the approach to Australia as 'Islands of Desolation'.
They had 'no cooked victuals' only 'dry biscuit as the wind and waves put out the fire [...]
the southern winter is so cold'.

After eighteen weeks' journey, they sight Sydney lighthouse on 25 June and, until
landfall on 11 July, he remarks that he enjoyed the company of his brother and 131 other
countrymen:

men of honest principle surrounded by persons I had been told
possessed every vice without a single virtue. (*Joseph Mason, assigned
convict. 1831-1837*)

This is proof, no doubt, that some labourers were intelligent enough to promote
dissent without the help of 'gentlemen on bay horses'. He does not mention the Swing riots
other than in passing, but it appears that the rioters were treated more leniently than other
felons who were sent to Van Diemens Land under terrible conditions. They were licensed to
a particular master and, apart from working very hard, it was possibly not much worse than
in England, at least for Joseph. It seems that pardon was arranged some six years later and
his family and friends sent money for his return ticket. It is perhaps significant that it would
have come at the very start of the new Queen's reign. For many, this would have come too
late, having either perished, as had William Watts, or had already married or settled as the
new Australians.[21]

Reply No 3. From Mike Horder
John Stingemore

One of my ancestors, John Stingemore was involved in the 1830 Battle
of Pythouse near Tisbury Wilts.

John Stingemore does not appear in Jill Chamber's books *Wiltshire Machine Breakers:
Volume I The Riots and Trials* and *Volume II The Rioters* but, in Vol. II, p. 265, is a quote

taken from the Salisbury Infirmary Minutes, in which a Thomas StingeMAN is one of five men:

> discharged from the Gaol and sent here with wounds upon the heads, hands.

No other similar name is mentioned amongst those transported or otherwise. However, in the 1851 Wiltshire census transcript, there are entries as head of households for a Thomas Stingimore (labourer 65) and a John Stingimore (labourer age 42). It looks as though they may have been involved in the riots but not punished other than by being taken to Fisherton Anger Gaol.

The Pythouse battle that the correspondent referred to was described in a newspaper account reproduced on the Web site having been taken from the above book (Vol. I pp 67-8). This gives a full account of the damage, which was inflicted on persons and property at Pythouse Farm and the action taken by the property owner and others to calm the situation. However, it appears that the Yeomanry had other ideas and one man was shot and several injured, especially among the Yeomanry. It could be taken as descriptive of many of the events that took place throughout the country, not only in Wiltshire. The owner of Pythouse, Mr Bennet, was himself a victim of a thrown stone; although such violence appeared to be rare.[22]

The thread of history continued, by following up a chance remark to a local historian friend from Ascot, Berkshire, at the start of the Swing riot research, when yet another man was mentioned as involved, from yet another county.

Benjamin Timbrell, ancestor of Charles Timbrell of North Ascot, was also on Geoffrey Sharman's list as follows:

> b - 1803 Quenington Gls [*Gloucestershire*]; m ENG [*England*] ch [*with children*]; de. [*deported*] 1836 d [*died*] 1838 VIC [*Victoria*] EGLSO2 [*Sailed on the Eliza after trial in Gloucestershire*]

> 'Benjamin Timbrill' was arrested for destroying a threshing machine belonging to J. Preater [*Procter*] of Eastleach Martin on 27 Nov 1830 and tried in Gloucester Assizes in Jan 1831. He was transported for 7 years to VDL [*Tasmania*] and sailed on Eliza II on 6 Feb 1831. According to Geoffrey Sharman of Tasmania he left VDL in 1836 and died in Victoria in 1838. He was baptised in Quenington on 2 Jan 1803. In various documents his age is given in 1831 as 25/26 and 28.[23]

Pardons were granted in general in 1835, but to lifers or those committed to fourteen years, conditional pardon was granted in 1837. He is known to have had a wife, Sylvia, and one child who were 'on the Parish'.[24] His plight must have been desperate to risk the fate that befell him and knowing that his family would have possibly been supported by parish relief or the Poor Law (1834), but Benjamin obviously stayed after his pardon was granted, as many did. It would be interesting to follow his movements after his removal to Victoria. Many men took up with another woman in Australia, even though they still had a wife and family in England.

If it is possible to imagine oneself in the shoes of both rioters and victims of destroyed threshing machines, burned ricks and threatening letters, it is easy to see how serious were the Swing riots. The more vocal of the rioting labourers fanned the discontent, showing how desperate was their cause. Many of them were sober family men, engendering much sympathy, but were willing to bear the retribution, which they knew would come their way.

CONCLUSION

The Swing Project has been successful in showing an increase in the numbers of events over those stated by Hobsbawm and Rudé, but it has also raised more questions. Why were these riots more successful and widespread? Most previous riots had been localised, disorganised and quickly suppressed. As a result of Swing, six hundred men were imprisoned, five hundred sentenced to transportation and nineteen were executed, which was lenient when equated with the twelve Luddites hanged at York in 1812.[25]

If the newspaper reports were to be taken on their own it would be easy to simplify the rioting labourers as undisciplined, rampaging mobs, burning, extorting money and destroying property, aided and abetted by gentlemen on 'bay horses' with nothing else to do but have fun. The research above shows a different story. It shows desperation among Britain's agricultural labourers, brought to the point where the alternatives were riot or starve. The causes were accumulating before 1830, certainly during the 18th century, when Britain was changing from an agrarian to an industrial economy. In Berkshire, the Speenhamland System, although philanthropic in intent, had the effect of creating greater hardship. Along with the enclosures, Corn Laws, high tithes and unsatisfactory parish relief, there was a climate ripe for dissent. However, there had been riots for centuries, why then did the Swing riots succeed where others had failed?

In the main, the rioters' plight engendered considerable sympathy. The leniency of the Magistrate after the first flurries of rioting in Kent in the spring of 1830, was assumed, by the rioters in Lower Hardres, to be support for their cause. As a result, rioting escalated and spread through Essex and Surrey, and into Berkshire and other rural counties. Add to this the perceived support and financial backing of the 'gentlemen in gigs'. There were also those who were assisting in the acceleration of the Swing Riots for their own reasons, in order, no doubt, to embarrass and impress the Government with the need for reform. There were also reports that the 'mobs' were joined by artisans and craftsmen in country towns, who were affected equally by the economic climate. An example is the attack on the paper mills in High Wycombe and machinery damaged (*Windsor and Eton Express*). Also, the ringleaders of Swing riots were shown to be more educated and organised than just 'illiterate labourers'.

It appeared also, from the reports of the Winchester Assizes and Berkshire newspapers, that some judges were sympathetic and, although there were many sentenced to death, only a few were actually hanged. They were transported instead, and there were many more who were acquitted. Sympathy was maintained by the demeanour of the convicted men.

> These men with no rights, no land, no work for years on end maintained their moral values and standards of decent and even courteous behaviour. (*Kintbury Family History*)

Public opinion was aroused, and there were petitions begging for mercy for convicted men. A letter was written requesting that the wife of a transportee should accompany her husband and asking for financial help.[26] It was, however, refused, but the public were obviously kept up to date by very comprehensive newspaper reporting and full editorial comments. This fact became obvious during this research. Thus the problems were public knowledge, no longer would the lower orders suffer in silence.

POSTSCRIPT

Although Parliament had been occupied with reform for many years, the intransigence of Prime Minister Wellington (1828-1830) had delayed any real progress. The Anglican Church was more concerned with the souls of the poor and their places in a church, than for the provision of bread for the labourer. However, Wellington's resignation on 2 November 1830, as a result of a disastrous King's Speech, and his: 'determination to repress all disturbances in England by force',[27] which showed no understanding or consideration for the causes underlying such disturbances, cleared the way for a Whig Parliament bent on reform, especially the Poor Law. The questionnaire sent to all parishes asked the following question:

> Can you suggest any reasons for the recent spate of agricultural rioting?

In Berkshire, low wages were the main reason given. There were many reports of promises made by landowners to increase wages, which often did not come about or were reduced later. Some even practised job-sharing for a shared wage. Wellington's remark to the Duke of Buckingham (4 December 1830) showed his attitude, and also the inefficiency of the vestries, which were bound to administer the Poor Relief:

> I concur in your reflections upon incautious promises to raise wages to twelve shillings a week. Those who would suffer most from such a generous measure would be the labouring classes themselves. We shall do no good with the poor and poor laws 'till the gentlemen of the country and the clergy will themselves attend parish vestries'.[28]

During the time scale considered, 1830-1832, there were other riots, which are referred to in other essays, but one struggle worthy of note is one, which not only stemmed from Swing, but can be seen as a catalyst for change and reform.

In November 1830, landowners in Dorset promised wages of nine shillings a week, which were barely enough to maintain subsistence, but, when wages were later reduced to six shillings a week, a group of agricultural workers in Tolpuddle, Dorset, gathered together to form a Trade Union Friendly Society in order to support others like themselves. Trade Unions were deemed legal in 1832, but more likely in the industrial north. Unfortunately, one man betrayed the others and, in 1833, they were transported for the crime of swearing an oath of allegiance, under an obscure Navy Mutiny Act of 1797. However, the strength of public opinion brought them a pardon after one year of transportation. The Tolpuddle Martyrs cleared the way for trade unions, which gave a voice to the working man.[29]

Although it would be several decades before the labourers themselves would benefit, there were many changes, which showed that poverty was a consideration. The Reform Bill and the Fuel Allotment became law in 1832, this latter alleviated the plight of the cottager after enclosures.[30] The Laws of Settlement were modified in 1834 to allow labourers to seek work elsewhere. The Poor Law Amendment Act came into being in 1834 (*Notes on British History* pp. 745-56). This, however, did not solve the labourers' problems, although it did differentiate between pauper and poor. The Tithe Commutation Act in 1838 assisted landowners. Both landowners and parishes subsidised the emigration of whole families rather than pay a living wage. The building of work-houses, to which paupers were committed, was intended as a threat to those who were thought too lazy to work, but instead caused the break up of families and a shadow of fear, which stretched into the 20th century.

NOTES

[1] BPP XXXIV (1833), Question 53. *Rural Queries for Berkshire*
[2] Briggs, Asa, 'Bread and food riots common in 18c' p.97, and 'Gordon riots 1700' p.98 in *England in the Age of Improvement*.
[3] Edwards, W M A, *Notes on British History, 1783-1901* (Rivingtons, London, 1948), p. 721.
[4] Briggs, *England in the Age of Improvement*.
[5] Corn Laws repealed 1846.
[6] Peacock, A J, *Bread or Blood*. Courtesy Bridget Andrews, Library Project Manager, Museum of English Rural Life, University of Reading.
[7] Briggs, *England in the Age of Improvement*, p. 37.
[8] The involvement of Fulwar Fowle and Charles Dundas in the Speenlandham Declaration is from The Kintbury Family by Margaret Sawtell née Fowle and is quoted as minuted in the Berkshire Sessions Order Book (not validated by author); Briggs, *England in The Age of Improvement*, p. 53.
[9] Moule's *English Counties in 19c*, (London 1836).
[10] The Settlement Laws (1662), which made birth or residence a qualification for Parish Relief and inhibited travel to find work, were modified in 1834 as part of the Poor Law Amendment Act of the same year.
[11] The Riot Act was ordered to be openly read at every quarter-session, and at every leet or law-day (I Geo I c2 Ch5). At least one conviction was overturned because 'God Save The King' was omitted. It was repealed in 1973 and superseded in 1986 by Public Order Act.
[12] Wellington dispatches, 2nd series, vol vii. p. 373 from *Wellington* (London 1889) p. 264.
[13] Greville Diary, 1st series, vol 2, Nov 22, *Wellington*, p. 265.
'Smock frocks' was a familiar descriptive term for farm labourers. This refers to the uniform

wearing of smocks, a long linen/cotton or coarse long sleeved, woven over-shirt. The patterns of the smocking usually denoted the county in which the wearer lived and worked. Thus it was easier to return an insolvent labourer to the parish of his birth, which was liable to pay his parish relief, or provide a place in a work-house.

14   *Notes on British History*, p 741. The Whig Government in 1830 gained confidence by the return to constitutional government in France.

15   In his own cognisance. Bound to pay the fine without another standing bail.

16   Methodist Lay preacher found with 'Swing' letters on the Suffolk/Cambridge/Essex borders. Reported in *Windsor and Eton Express* December 1830.

17   A petition for mercy was presented to the court and Darling and Oakley were reprieved from hanging. (*Kintbury Family History*)

18   Chambers, Jill, *Berkshire Machine Breakers*. Photograph of Winterbourne's headstone in Kintbury Churchyard. William Smith alias Winterbourne buried 12 January 1831 (Kintbury Parish Records, p. 72); Speenhamland System and other family information *Kintbury Family History* by Margaret Sawtell née Fowle and George Sawtell.

19   Oakley remarked at his trial that 'Old Fowle has £2.00 for every man he commits to Jail, in that way he keeps out of the work-house' Chambers, *Machine Breakers*, p. 42, also referred to in *Kintbury Family History*.

20   Tithing-man, Parish Constable, unpaid, appointed by manor court until 17th/18th century then appointed by Parish Vestry or JP (*Family Tree Magazine*, February 2004 Vol 2 No 4, p. 55). Powell, Sue, *Rural Crime Dictionary* definition - tithing (man) 'ten householders living near together and collectively responsible for each other's behaviour'.

21   David Kent and Norma Townsend, *Joseph Mason, Assigned Convict. 1831-1837*, BRO T/B 8, written by Joseph Mason of Wherwell, Hants on his return from a sentence of transportation. (BRO D/EWD/21).

22   The present house, built in 1725, on the site of the Elizabethan house, and occupied by the Bennet family for over 700 years, is now luxury apartments.

23   Main references From John Loosley:
Gloucester Journal 27 Nov 1830 and 8 Jan 1831; Glos Record Office Ref. Q/Gc 5/4 and Q/SG 2 *Transportees from Gloucestershire to Australia 1783-1842*, ed. Irene Wyatt; Information from Kaye Purnell in NSW, e-mail: kayepur@ozemail.co.au.

24   From Timbrell family research undertaken by Ruth and Charles Timbrell of Ascot. Further information on Benjamin Timbrell and family in Chambers, J, *Gloucestershire Machine Breakers*, Letchworth, 2002 *passim*.

25   Briggs, *England in the Age of Improvement, passim*.

26   Chambers, *Berkshire Machine Breakers*, p. 392.

27   *Notes on British History*, p. 746.

28   *Wellington* (1889), p. 263.

29   Swing and Tolpuddle Martyrs, The Tolpuddle Museum Web site www.tolpuddlemartyrs.org.uk.

30   Burchardt, Jeremy, *The Allotment Movement in England, 1793-1873* (Royal Historical Society, 2002), pp. 52-3. An Act of Parliament sponsored by a private member but backed by the government, required trustees of fuel allotments to let them to the poor as conventional allotments. The Act was passed in 1832.
A fuel allotment is defined as a, 'portion of land made over in trust to the poor collectively under some enclosure awards to compensate for lost rights of fuel gathering' (Burchardt, p. 52).

OTHER SOURCES

Reading Mercury and *Berkshire Chronicle* and *Bucks and Windsor Herald* are available on microfilm
    at Berkshire Records Office.
Windsor and Eton Express available on microfilm at Slough Library.
Kent, David and Townsend, Norma, *Joseph Mason, Assigned Convict. 1831-1837,* Berkshire Record
    Office, Reading. References from Noel Gimmett and Marion Cougens, Special Commission
    Assizes at Winchester December 1830
Pauline White used Jill Chambers *Wiltshire Machine Breakers Vol I The Riots and Trials* and *Vol II
    The Rioters;* 1851 Wiltshire census transcript; www.cha.org.uk/houseinfo;
    www users.chariot.net.au/-ramacs/the machine breakers.htm.

APPENDIX VII.A BPP XXXIV (1833) Question 53. *Rural Queries for Berkshire*

Bradfield Putting unemployed labourers to work on the roads,
idleness, wages
Bray Discontent
Burghfield Low wages and restricted earnings
Coleshill Low wages; harsh conditions; animosity between labourers
and farmers
Cookham Distress
Drayton The mild punishment of the Kent rioters
Great Farringdon Unemployment and low wages
East Hendred Contagion
Hurley Spite
Kintbury Threshing machines; contagion; wages
Lambourne Low wages; threshing machines; seditious preachers;
France; political feeling
Letcombe Regis Low wages; beer shops
Long Wittenham Poor Laws
Milton Low wages and labourers working with smugglers and
receiving cheap spirits
Shottesbrook Unemployment
Shrivenham Low wages and mischievous men
St Mary's Reading Low wages
Speen Insurrection in France and Belgium; low wages; threshing
machines
Sutton Wick the influence of newspapers; ranters
Uffington Emulation of Sussex and Hants labourers; wages
Ufton Nevett Beer shops
Wargrave Unemployment and poor wages (7s to 8s a week),
beershops, seditious publications
Wasing Ill disposed persons; beer shops; wages
Winkfield Evil minded persons influencing labourers

ACKNOWLEDGEMENTS

Thanks are due to the following researchers for their valuable help in supplying information about the individuals mentioned in *Between the Lines* without which this study would not have been possible.

1. John Fowle for his copies of the pages of the Fowle Family History and other documents.
2. Noel Gimmett FACHRS (Hampshire) for notes on William Watts and a copy of the transcript of The Special Commission of Assizes Winchester in December 1830 (transcribed by Noel Gimmett and Marion Cougens).
3. Pauline White FACHRS (Wiltshire) for her research on John Stingemore.
4. John Loosley FACHRS (Gloucestershire) for his notes on Benjamin Timbrill; Ruth Timbrell for information on the wife and child of Benjamin Timbrill from her family history research.
5. Jill Chambers for advice on newspaper and other sources.

VIII. THE LIFE AND DEATH OF RICHARD NOCKOLDS HAND-LOOM WEAVER OF NORWICH

Stella Evans

Richard Nockolds was unique in Norfolk. In a county with a very high incidence of Swing offences, he was the only person to be executed for such an offence. He was a hand-loom weaver who turned to violence during the disturbances, which occurred in Norwich in the winter of 1829-1830. He was also a member of a local radical 'band'. This case study looks at how the last eighteen months of his life were affected by both private and public concerns, and at the conflicting attitudes of the 'operatives' and the magistrates in Norwich in 1830.

One of the more interesting aspects of doing research through using newspapers is the number of human-interest stories that emerge. Stories that show aspects of the living, breathing people who we, as social historians, are searching for amongst the dusty documents at our local record offices, libraries and museums. In reading the Norfolk papers for 1829-1832 I found the same sensational moralistic tone that is common to some Victorian novels and the modern popular press. Despite, or because of, this tone newspaper reports can give us an insight into the day-to-day lives of a wide range of individual people; their attitudes to events in their own lives, and their attitudes to each other. Attitudes that help us to piece together and examine the reasons for the private acts of an individual who influenced, and was influenced by, the public events of recorded history.

While searching for reports of Swing incidents in the Norfolk papers for the FACHRS project, three stories in particular attracted my attention: first, the case of the farmer who left his threshing machine by the highway to be broken up for firewood, because 'it was not worth a groat';[1] secondly, the case of a group of rioters who were given, what amounted to, a suspended sentence 'so that they might not lose their harvest work';[2] and the third was a story that developed in the Norwich papers over a period of months and contained this graphic description:

> In consequence of disclosures made by Nockolds the apprehension of seven men has taken place during the week. A number of others are implicated. The apprehensions made appear to have spread alarm

amongst them, as upon being enquired after several have absconded. When the officer entrusted with the warrant against one man went to his house he rushed upstairs and attempted to make off by jumping out of the window, precautions, however had been taken against such a plan of escape, and the fellow dropped into the arms of a constable who was stationed at the back part of the premises.[3]

This essay will look at the background events that affected these men, at the 'disclosures' made by Nockolds at his trial, and that of some of his associates, and draw conclusions about their activities and concerns; concerns that reflect significant support in urban areas for the plight of rural workers. Richard Nockolds was unique in Norfolk. He was the only person who was hanged for committing a Swing offence. The other thing that made him unusual was that he was not an agricultural labourer, but a hand-loom weaver from Norwich.

In the medieval and early modern periods, and for much of the 18th century, Norwich had been second only to London in size and commercial importance but, in the early 19th century Norwich was, like other traditional cloth centres, such as Gloucester and Hereford, losing its trade to the steam mills of the equally traditional centre round Halifax. By the 19th century the size of the city was growing fast, but other cities in the midlands and north were growing faster.[4] As the 19th century progressed, and the textile manufacturers in the West Riding took over the production of the simpler fabric, the Norwich cloth trade came to rely more and more on the weaving of 'stuffs' for the fashion market,[5] and the weaving of that essential item of women's clothing, the shawl.[6] The production of silk cloth continued in Norwich until the 1950s.[7]

In 1830 Norwich had a population of approximately 36,000, of whom over 3,000 were weavers. That was nearly one tenth of the citizens, a large enough proportion of the population to form a separate community. A separate entity within which, if it was not possible to be acquainted with everyone who formed part of that community, it would have been possible to recognise a fellow weaver by certain characteristics of dress and physical appearance, and probably to know them by reputation.

Weavers and weaving are so much a part of the history of Norwich, that it is still possible to see the high lofts and big windows of the weavers' three-storey cottages in various parts of the city (Illustration VIII.a).

These lofts were designed to accommodate the draw looms on which the local worsted damask cloth was made. Looms that required the employment of a 'drawboy', who sat above the loom and pulled up groups of threads in a pre-arranged sequence (Illustration VIII.b).

Other Norfolk weavers specialised in the production of bombazine, a combination cloth of silk and worsted that was often dyed black for mourning wear. This cloth could be woven on a simpler loom, which could be housed in a room with a lower ceiling.

The Norwich wool merchants bought their yarn from as far apart as Blythburgh in Suffolk,[8] and Kidderminster.[9] The manufacturers did try to keep up with the times by setting up weaving sheds containing several looms. But it was not until 1836 that the first steam-driven weaving and spinning mills began to operate.[10] This was fifty years after the introduction of powered mills in Yorkshire, and serves as a reminder that the Industrial Revolution affected the lives of several generations. The trading methods in the early 19th century, like weaving itself, had become established over the centuries. The manufacturer, or his agent, issued a ticket to the operative. This ticket was, in effect, an order for work to be undertaken. It entitled the weaver to buy yarn from the wool merchant and to sell back the finished cloth, with the expectation of further orders. A possible third member of the trading set-up was the carrier. These men acted as merchants' agents in the villages within a radius of twenty miles of Norwich. The carriers, probably correctly, were suspected by the weavers of being profiteers, of buying the yarn cheaply, of having it woven at 'under the price', and passing on some of the reduced cost to the wool merchants. Another grievance against the carriers was that they took work away from the city. There is no direct evidence whether one of Nockolds associates, Josiah Davidson, was a village weaver or an agricultural labourer, possibly both. Either way he lived at Swanton Abbott, a large village lying about ten miles north of Norwich, on the Worsted Road, where the local public house is still called 'The Weavers Arms'. As he seems to have been frequently in Norwich, like *Silas Marner*, he probably acted as his own carrier.[11] He would have walked the ten miles into Norwich with his own cloth. Then he would have rested at his brother's house, in St Augustine's, before returning with his yarn.

Illustration VIII.a. Weavers' 'cottages', with high lofts, Magdeline Street, Norwich

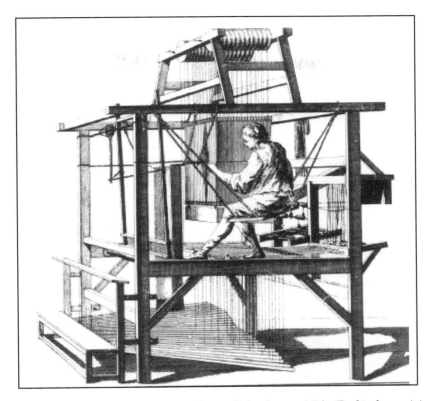

Illustration VIII.b. Setting up a Draw loom (Priestley, p. 14)[4]; *(By kind permision of Norfolk Museums and Archaeological Service)*

In the 1830s the weavers were a force within the city and had their own organisation, The Norwich Weavers Society.[12] These 'operatives' were, of course, hand-loom weavers. They were self-employed craftsmen, who worked their own looms in their own homes, bought their own materials and hired their own help. Weavers were of both sexes. In 1849 one female weaver could, by working late into the night, earn enough to keep her children at school. Her wages were about 18s (90p) a week when she was in work, but she paid a girl 3s (15p) a week to 'do her ends'. Although these earnings were greatly reduced when averaged out over a year, the girl still had to be paid when there was no work, so that she would be available whenever she was needed. Candles, of course, had to be paid for, for working at night. This weaver also had the help of her little boy, who probably worked unpaid. She was lucky in that her husband was a carpenter in fairly regular employment.[13] In 1830, John Duffield received £1 0s 0½d for a piece of '28 bombazine', on reduced wages, and his expenses, including yarn, were reckoned at 7s 3¾d (37p), he asserted that his wife was as good a weaver as himself for course work, but that she could not take the work for fear of reprisals.[14] A piece of bombazine would have taken about two weeks to weave. At this rate, many weavers had to apply for poor relief.[15] In the standard book on 19th century Norwich, J K Edwards' essay about the industrial development of the city points out that:

> By no means all the whole of the working people of Norwich were involved in the change or in the distress, just the weavers. But these formed such a large and vulnerable section of the city's workforce [...] as to give the period all the starkness of a tragedy.[16]

The first newspaper reports of distress and disturbance among the Norwich operatives were a week before Christmas in the notoriously cold winter of 1829/30. This was a time of year when trade in the cloth industry was always slack, and in 1829 the cold winter followed a wet summer.[17] As a consequence, food prices were rising, and local philanthropists were issuing blankets and coal to the poor. On Friday 18 December, the weavers' committee published a handbill. After stating that a few of the masters opposed them 'more from obstinacy than of great necessity of being compelled to reduce their wages', they asked the 'Payers of the Poors' Rate' to support their cause and 'by weekly subscription on our behalf enable us to obtain those rights which the ignorant and avaricious are endeavouring to wrest from us'. This is the language of men steeped in the tradition of Tom Paine, men who were proud of their independence, men who were used to radical argument. Many of the weavers were freemen of the city who had fallen on bad times, but their use of language was regarded by the authorities as revolutionary. Such petitions were not unusual in the 18th and 19th centuries, as they were one way for people, who did not possess the vote, to make their voice heard. On this occasion the petition ended by saying 'A deputation will call on you on every Monday morning to receive your subscriptions'. The distribution of this handbill resulted in an emergency meeting of the magistrates, who issued a warning against 'co-operation'. On the Monday the city remained quiet. During the evening the weavers held a meeting at Raneleigh Gardens. It broke up quietly and, on the Tuesday, a further handbill was published. This was addressed to 'The Governor, Deputy Governor and Guardians of the Poor in this city'. It proposed the immediate raising of a sum equal to twice the yearly poor rate, to be used in the manufacture of 'bombazines, etc.', so that 'every weaver, now unemployed and belonging to this city, might be employed at the full rated wages'. Thereby in the course of a very short period it would nearly cause the cessation of the poor rate.[18]

That evening there was a violent incident in St Augustine's. Ten or twelve men, 'their faces covered with black crepe and coloured handkerchiefs', broke into the premises of Mr William Springhall. They forced their way to his attic and cut the work from his eight looms. There was no point in weavers breaking the machinery of their employment, the cloth was easier to destroy, and commercially much more valuable. In the course of the tumult, Springhall was shot in the abdomen, and 'left weltering in his blood'. The *Norfolk Chronicle* reported that he was on the way to recovery, and started talking of the 'villainy of small and secret bands'.[19]

Later, Richard Nockolds admitted to being one of this raiding party, but not to having fired the shot. At this time his wife would have been eight months pregnant with their youngest child. The baptism of William Nockolds, the youngest of six children, in January

1830, is recorded in the parish records of St James with Pockthorpe, where Richard himself had been born in 1796.[20] Pockthorpe, at that time, was an area of rapidly built speculative housing. It is situated outside the city walls to the east of the city. Here, in 1830, rows of ten to fifteen back-to-back houses had already declined, since they had been erected after the Napoleonic wars. 'This decline had made the condition of the labouring poor bad, and that of the hand loom weavers worse.'[21] In 1844-45 the reports of the Health of Towns Commissioners commented:

> Here is a concentration of all the evils that can afflict the manufacturer, want of employment and its consequent poverty, crowded and badly constructed habitations, filth, want of sewerage and drainage, an impure air, and want of water.[22]

The fact that, in this area, many of the back alleys to later Victorian terraces still have name plates that describe them as lanes, can show the modern observer the narrowness of these 'courts'. Richard Nockolds' cottage was described as being 'opposite the barrack gate'. This would have been near to a half-demolished row of one-up-one-down cottages, built in 1795, that still stand in Barrack Street (Illustration VIII.c).

Illustration VIII.c. Cottages, Barrack Street, Norwich *ca* 1796

As the loom would have taken up the whole of one room, the weavers' families must have lived and slept in the other. Evidence given by witnesses at the trial of Hardy and John Shepherd illustrate further the cramped living conditions in the poorer areas in Norwich.

Hardy Shepherd ran a small general provisions shop in his cottage, and the witnesses describe him at work on his loom at the back of the shop, and his brother coming downstairs from work on another loom in the upper room.[23]

Over the Christmas period, in 1829, relations between the masters and the operatives in the city did not improve. The *Norfolk Chronicle* for 2 January 1830 reported daily meetings at Raneleigh Gardens. Mr Gurney attended one of these meetings. He was a member of the large Quaker banking family, and he sympathised with 'the distressed poor'. He 'conveyed' to the paper the weavers' committee's denial that 'a system of intimidation' was being used 'to prevent those willing to take work at the proposed reduced rate to do so'. Average earnings for the weavers were now as low as 10s (50p) a week before expenses. The same newspaper carries reports of hearsay allegations that work was being cut from looms and of food being taken from the houses of weavers who were working for this rate. This edition of the newspaper also carried the first reports of Swing riots in Kent.[24]

A fortnight later, events in Norwich began to escalate. The Relief Committee of the Court of Guardians decided to install sixty looms in the work-house in order to provide work for the paupers. The weavers, however, saw this as just another way to keep wages low. When walking home through the oldest part of the city after this meeting one of the committee members, Mr Willett, was recognised by some of the weavers, who 'commenced hooting and hustling him'. Colonel Harvey, a seventy-six-year-old retired army officer was passing, and 'considered it his duty, as a magistrate of the city, to interpose his authority'. This resulted in stones being thrown at both gentlemen, they took refuge in the Free School Building and the gates of the Cathedral Close were closed. The Mayor was notified, and when he arrived, he read the Riot Act. Two people were arrested, but the newspapers only report the fate of one of them, John Burrows. Despite two attempts by the weavers to rescue him, he was tried on the following day for assault on Col Harvey, and was sentenced to three months' imprisonment.[25]

At midday, while John Burrows was being tried at the Guildhall, some of the municipal looms were being transported down St George's. Blocking the route to the work-house was a 'riotous multitude'. A troop of the 7th Dragoon Guards was called to the scene, and once again the Riot Act was read. Despite this, the looms were seized and thrown over the bridge, into the River Wensum. Once they had achieved their object of destroying the looms, the crowd dispersed and the expected attack on the work-house did not materialise.[26]

In his 'confession', which he gave to the prison chaplain after he was condemned, Richard Nockolds admitted to being 'among the foremost' of the people involved in this action, and it was on the following day that the first of two incidents occurred in which he confessed to making use of oil of vitriol. Mr Wright, 'one of our most considerable manufacturers', was attacked outside his own home. The attacker, presumably Richard Nockolds, ran up to him and threw the contents of a bottle of vitriol in his face. Mr Wright ran after his attacker, and 'drawing a pistol from his pocket, he discharged the contents at the person', 'the shot, however, did not take effect'. The papers at this time reported that, although his face was badly burnt, Mr Wright did not lose the sight of his right eye.[27] Later reports, after the execution of Richard Nockolds, said that he had been blinded.[28] The fact that people on both sides of the dispute felt it necessary to carry loaded firearms, is an indication of the atmosphere of fear and distrust prevailing in the city at the time.

The other incident in which vitriol was used occurred a fortnight later, on 25 January 1830. This was an attack on a carrier and shopkeeper, who acted as a manufacturer's agent in Tasburgh, some eight miles south of Norwich. Charlie Green was suspected of getting yarn woven at 'under the price', and of selling 'the articles, when made, to the manufacturer of whom he bought the yarn'. Green was about a mile outside the city when he was set upon by five or six men, one of whom poured vitriol into his ear. His cart was taken, his horse was set loose, and weaving materials and other goods strewn about the lanes. A year later, John and Hardy Shepherd were arrested for this crime, it was alleged that some of the yarn that was taken during the robbery was found in their possession. Although the trustworthiness of the identification of the yarn was disputed in court, they were both found 'Guilty'.[29] They were under sentence of death in Norwich Castle on 2 April 1831; on 6 April a respite was received until 23 April. After this their sentence was commuted to transportation, life for Hardy and seven years for John. The keeper's Journal for the County Gaol has an entry dated 6 June 1831, which reads 'Two Shepherds sent to Portsmouth',[30] and on 12 July 1831 the *Norfolk Chronicle* reported that 'they returned to this city as free men'.[31]

At the end of January 1830, the local newspapers were reporting that there was a gradual thaw and that the city was quiet and, at the end of March, in a series of meetings, the master manufacturers agreed to 'advance wages by $1\frac{1}{2}$d of the 3d per dozen recently taken off'.[32] This meant that the weavers were still earning less than one shilling (5p) for every dozen skeins of yarn that they used. During the summer any disturbances in the streets were attributed by the papers to the election that followed the death of George IV, and to pressure for electoral reform. When William Cobbett visited the city in March, the *Norfolk Chronicle* printed his lectures in full.[33] An entry fee of one shilling was probably more than many of the weavers could afford, but the reports of Richard Nockolds' confession said that 'his mind was injured by the writings of Carlile and Cobbett and other inflammatory writers';[34] 'Carlile' was Richard Carlile, a disciple of Thomas Paine and radical bookseller in London, who was imprisoned for publishing books and pamphlets 'calculated to excite sedition and rebellion'.[35]

A picture of Richard Nockolds' 'band' of radicals can be gleaned from various local newspapers. The *Bury Post* reported that he was:

> the head of an extensive body of men who gave him the title of 'Counsellor' and one of the Shepherds that of 'Attorney'.[36]

The two Norwich papers, in identical reports, apparently a press release by the Prison Chaplain, averred that 'two of the more violent of the guilty' were known significantly by the title 'Executioners'. These two had been given funds to help them emigrate, and money was being collected to help Nockolds and his family to follow. This statement, or confession, describes Nockolds as having 'established a Sunday reading room in the house of one of his associates'. Members paid a penny each week so that he could buy 'papers suited to his taste'. They met at the time of church service on Sunday morning, and again in the evening.

The statement goes on to deplore his 'studious contempt of all the decencies of the divine Sabbath'.[37] A few years later, in 1834, Charles Dickens, writing under the pseudonym Timothy Sparkes, was to denounce the hypocrisy of men who wished to deny the poor any recreation on the only day of the week on which they were not employed in heavy labour.[38]

All through the summer of 1830 reports were reaching Norwich of the Swing disturbances in Kent, Sussex and Hampshire. It is only necessary to read the Parliamentary reports in the local press to realise that these events were widely known and discussed. By the beginning of November the weavers were again noticeably restless. The speeches of Col Harvey and Sheriff Bignold were shouted down in Common Hall, and the meeting had to adjourn to St Andrew's Hall, from the Guildhall, in order to accommodate the large crowd. The first instances of riot and arson by agricultural workers in Norfolk had been reported in October, and by the end of November they were occurring almost daily, and in every part of the county. This continued throughout December and into the New Year. On Saturday 8 January 1831, Richard Nockolds met Josiah Davidson at the house of Josiah's brother, Robert. It was Robert's evidence during the trial that convicted his brother and Richard. Robert did not go to the authorities himself but, once he had been arrested, he agreed to give evidence for the prosecution, in order to save his own life.

In his evidence, Robert said that when they had met at his house the talk, not unnaturally, turned to the troubles of the agricultural workers. Richard asked Josiah if there had been any fires out his way (Swanton Abbott). When Josiah answered in the negative he took out of his pocket a ball of cotton, with a tail about half a yard long. He laid it on the hearth and set light to it. He then said 'that would set the stacks agoing'. Josiah offered Richard 5s (25p) to come and fire some stacks in Swanton Abbott, and said that he could get a further 2s 6d (12½d) from his brother David. Robert told them not to take any money from David 'as he was too bad off', and Richard replied that he did not do it for money.

On the Sunday morning, Richard Nockolds and Robert Davidson set out for Swanton Abbott. Robert admitted that he carried a pistol with him, but said that Nockolds had given it to him. At Scottow they met Aaron Cooke, and Richard asked him the way to North Walsham. That evening at Swanton Abbott, Nockolds dropped some pieces of paper outside three farms. When he was subsequently asked where they had been printed, he said that they were not printed. They then visited three other farms and left fire-balls burning in the stack yards. They reached Norwich again about four o'clock the next morning. On Monday morning, the three threatening letters were picked up at Swanton, one of them by a little girl who took it to her schoolmaster. All three hand-written letters were produced in court. They read:

> £500 reward will be of no use
> I have done it alone and can keep my own counsel
> I will surprise you more than this be foure you are one year older
> Keep that in mind

On the outside was written 'The Truth'.

The jury were asked to compare the three letters with torn pages in a copybook that had been found in Richard Nockolds' house. The *Bury Post* reported that 'During the whole of the time of the trial, Nockolds gave the minutest attention to the evidence, and at the close of each case for the prosecution he addressed the jury pointing out the discrepancies in the evidence as given by the accomplice and those who were called to corroborate him'. He pointed out that there was no evidence that he could write, nor any sample of his handwriting. He denied all knowledge of the copybook, saying that one of his children could have brought it into the house, most probably by his eldest son, who worked for Robert Davidson. He reminded the jury that he had been found not guilty of another arson attack on the same evidence the day before, and that Robert Davidson had admitted to giving evidence in order to save his own skin.[39] The *Norfolk Chronicle* reported that:

> When the Learned Judge first put on the black cap a suppressed shriek
> was heard in the gallery. Nockolds turned round and said 'If my wife is
> in court let her be taken out; I thought she had gone,' and after he had
> received sentence he kissed his hand to those behind him and jumped
> down.[40]

A fortnight after the trial, the local newspapers were full of Richard Nockolds' confession, execution and funeral. His confession in both the Norwich papers reads like a press release by the Prison Chaplain in which he 'devoutly prayed for mercy from God' and 'showed an affectionate anxiety that his children should avoid the errors that had brought him to his untimely end'.[41] The *Bury Post*, however, tells a different story: 'The Chaplain, [...] commenced reading the Burial Service immediately on leaving the Castle door, but, at the request of the culprit, no prayers were read on the scaffold.'[42] The editor of the *Norwich Mercury* was obviously among the magistrates at the castle entrance. He reported that:

> As he entered the court, he said in a most undisturbed manner 'Which
> way?' [...] he walked firmly forward and on passing the above
> gentlemen he said bowing 'I wish you a good morning, gentlemen'. He
> hesitated when he first saw the gallows, but recovering himself, walked
> firmly down the castle bridge.[43]

Both papers remarked on the size and silence of the crowd that had gathered in the cattle market. The reporter for the *Norfolk Chronicle* obviously visited the cottage in Pockthorpe where:

> The body of Nockolds [...] was exhibited every day till the internment
> [...] at one penny each, and we understand that a considerable sum of
> money has been raised in this way for the widow, from the immense
> number of persons whose curiosity led them to view the corpse.

The same man seems to have been among the spectators on Thursday afternoon, when the funeral took place at St. James' Church. There were a dozen pallbearers, while his wife and children were supported by his parents, his brothers and 'several other relations all respectably dressed'. Once again the streets were crowded.[44]

Why was Richard Nockolds executed? One interpretation of these events highlights the difference between early 19th century attitudes to the nature of guilt, the proof of guilt, and the appropriateness of any sentence pronounced or carried out, and early 21st century thinking on the veracity and significance of witness statements. Although there were several people involved in the attack on Charlie Green, only Richard Nockolds was eventually punished for that crime. Again, it is apparent from the newspaper reports that Robert Davidson, who carried the gun to Swanton Abbot, was, probably, the person who had shot Mr Springhall, but at no time was he prosecuted for this. Turning King's evidence apparently exonerated him from prosecution for any other crimes. Nockolds' young companion, Josiah Davidson, who had collapsed under interrogation, and the two Shepherd brothers, were all reprieved, while David Davidson and Richard Hunt, who appeared in the dock with him, were found not guilty. It was only after he was condemned that Nockolds confessed to the attacks on Mr Wright and Charlie Green. This same confession, which was published after his death, said that robberies in Worsted and Westwick had also been traced to him, as had several other fires, but at no time were these assertions tested in court. It seems very probable that the authorities felt the need for a scapegoat, that Richard Nockolds was chosen to be an 'example' that had incurred the full force of the law, an example that would deter other people who might contemplate similar crimes. Indeed, it would appear that he was fully aware that in committing arson he was risking his own life, and by his insistence on the innocence of the Shepherd brothers, was prepared to take the blame for other crimes, if it would save the life of his friends. When pronouncing the sentence the judge is reported as saying:

> The crime which you have been found guilty of, is pronounced by the law to be a capital felony, and one which of late has been unhappily prevalent in the country. We have had youths of seventeen and eighteen brought before us for committing the like offence, but you are a person arrived at maturer years and ought to know the dreadful consequences attending the commission of such crimes. You are found leaving your wife and children, and going without any apparent malice against the parties, though fully bent on mischief. [...] You were not an agricultural labourer, and driven to the extremities that some of them have been, but residing in Norwich and following the employment of a weaver. You therefore committed this act for the purpose of exciting general confusion and alarm throughout the country. Arson is a heinous crime and greatly aggravated in this case; it therefore becomes my painful duty to pronounce upon you the sentence of death.'[45]

This sentence, and the precise reporting of it in the newspapers, was aimed at two audiences, it was meant to convey the dread of retribution to contemporaries, and the memory of it into subsequent generations. The death sentence for arson and machine breaking, as provided for in the Parliamentary Act V Geo. III, ch. 29, was expected to be exemplary, and intended to deter others from similar actions.

There is also some evidence that Richard Nockolds was a popular hero, if not within Norwich as a whole, at least within the community of weavers. The demonstrations at Common Hall, and the stoning of the successful candidates after the election, showed considerable popular dissent within the city, while the radicals had made no secret of their activities. Indeed, the local press opined that: 'with so little caution did he and his accomplices conduct themselves, and to so many did they confide their secrets, that had the proper enquiry been pursued with tact and energy, the guilty parties must have been brought to justice', and that 'the neighbourhood would have been spared many of the atrocious crimes that have lately been committed'.[46] The bravado exhibited by, and the flamboyant character of Richard Nockolds himself, the unusual silence at his execution, the exhibition of the body, the size of the fund raised for his family, and the large turnout at his funeral, all suggest that he was well known; certainly the newspaper reports would have engendered much excitement and interest.

These reports help historical researchers look into the minutiae of individual lives and give an insight into the human condition at a given period; they enable us to examine the moral dilemmas that faced our ancestors. Not only giving some understanding of how the various layers of society saw their contemporaries and interacted with them, but also why they were prepared to actively support each others' cause. As in all historical study, this case has suggested several layers of concern. This particular human interest story reveals a significant degree of empathy and support between urban and rural workers, and has highlighted the attitudes of both the radicals and the authorities, of the operatives, the manufacturers and the magistrates in Norwich. The Judge's assumption that, had Richard Nockolds been an agricultural labourer, his crime would have been understandable, possibly forgivable, Mr Gurney's support for the weavers, and Colonel Harvey's opposition, all reflect differing social attitudes of the period. These were conflicting attitudes that led to escalating political demonstration and disturbance. The sensational style of the newspaper reports, and the reported contents of Richard Nockolds' confession, are strong indicators of the fears of the authorities that the riots and demonstrations were part of a nationwide conspiracy, that machine breaking in both the countryside and the growing industrial towns might be the fore-runner of revolution. The events reported in the Norwich papers may be used to contribute to the debate about the reasons why revolution did not develop in Britain at that time. Also about the effect that events, such as execution, emigration, and electoral reform, had on the revolutionary zeal of the radicals. The execution of Richard Nockolds had no apparent effect on the frequency of stack fires in Norfolk, they continued on a regular basis during the early 1830s, and *The Times* was reporting arson as a form of protest in Norfolk as late as the 1840s.[47]

I would like to add two postscripts.

The wife of Robert Davidson, the prosecution witness, was later arrested for making 'the balls for firing stacks, etc.'[48] Also, amongst the medieval graffiti that adorns the chapel at Norwich Castle, and which was used as the condemned cell during the 19th century, can be seen this monogram (Illustration VIII.d).

Illustration VIII.d. Copy of graffiti at Norwich Castle

Notes

1.   *Bury Post*, 12 January 1831.
2.   *Ibid*, 25 July 1832. This practice was not uncommon, and was as much concerned with the self-interest of the landowners as with the welfare of the agricultural labourers. General editor.
3.   *Norfolk Chronicle*, 9 April 1831.
4.   Priestley, U, *The Fabric of Stuffs*, CEAS, (University of East Anglia, Norwich, 1990), p. 14.
5.   *Ibid*, p. 39.
6.   Clabburn, P, *Shawls*, (Shire Publications Ltd, Aylesbury, 1981), p. 11.
7.   Priestley (1990), p. 42.
8.   Mackley, A, *The Poaching Priors of Blytheburgh*, (The Blytheborough Soc., 2002), p. 24.
9.   *Norfolk Chronicle*, 2 April 1831.
10.   Priestley (1990), p. 41.
11.   Eliot, G, *Silas Marner* (London, 1861).
12.   Edwards, J K, Industrial Development, in, Barringer, C, (ed.), *Norwich in the Nineteenth Century*, (Gliddon Books, Norwich, 1984), p. 149.
13.   Pound, J, Poverty and Public Health in Norwich 1845-1880, in, Barringer, C, (ed.), (1984), p. 54.
14.   *Norfolk Chronicle*, 2 January 1830.
15.   Edwards, J K, Industrial Development, in, Barringer, C, (ed.), (1984), p. 146.
16.   *Ibid*, p. 143.
17.   Pound, (1984), p. 54.
18.   *Norfolk Chronicle*, 26 December 1829.
19.   *Ibid.*
20.   Nockles, K, [family database 2003].
21.   Pound, (1984), p. 47.
22.   *Ibid*, p. 49.
23.   *Norfolk Chronicle*, 2 April 1831.
24.   *Ibid*, 21 January 1830.
25.   *Ibid*, 16 January 1830; letter to J J Colman, 16 January 1830, NRO Col/2/113.
26.   *Norfolk Chronicle*, 16 January 1830.
27.   *Ibid*, 16 January 1830.
28.   *Ibid*, 16 April 1831; *Norwich Mercury*, 16 April 1831.
29.   *Norfolk Chronicle*, 2 April 1831.
30.   NRO, Keeper's Daily Journal, Norwich Castle, MF/RO 576/1.

31 *Norfolk Chronicle*, 12 July 1831.
32 *Ibid*, 3 April 1830.
33 *Ibid*, 20 March 1830.
34 *Norfolk Chronicle* and *Norwich Mercury*, 16 April 1831.
35 Chambers *Biographical Dictionary*, 2nd edn, (Chambers Harrup, Edinburgh, 1997).
36 *Bury Post*, 30 March 1831.
37 *Norfolk Chronicle* and *Norwich Mercury*, 16 April 1831.
38 Dent, H C, *The Life and Characters of Charles Dickens*, (Odhams Press, 1930).
39 *Bury Post*, 30 March 1831.
40 *Norfolk Chronicle*, 2 April 1831.
41 *Norfolk Chronicle* and *Norwich Mercury*, 16 April 1831.
42 *Bury Post*, 13 April 1831.
43 *Norwich Mercury*, 16 April 1831.
44 *Norfolk Chronicle*, 16 April 1831.
45 *Norwich Mercury*, 2 April 1831.
46 *Norfolk Chronicle* and *Norwich Mercury*, 16 April 1831.
47 Jones, D J V, 'Thomas Campbell Foster and the Rural Labourer: incendiarism in East Anglia in the 1840s', *Social History*, vol.1:1, (1976), pp. 5-43.
48 *Bury Post*, 13 April 1831.

IX. THE BRITISH CHOLERA RIOTS OF 1832

Sean Burrell and Geoff Gill

INTRODUCTION

In the early 1830s, Britain has been described as 'near to revolution'.[1] From 1830 to 1832 the Captain Swing riots erupted in response to rural unemployment. They were characterised by threats, intimidation, arson and crowd violence; though beginning in localised areas of the south of England, they spread to the Midlands and the north, and even into Scotland.[2] During the same period, a slow struggle towards electoral and Parliamentary reform was taking place. Frustration at the pace and extent of change erupted during the passage of the Reform Bill through Parliament in 1832, with major civil disturbances, particularly in Birmingham and Bristol. Troops were required to stop the riots, and there were several hundred deaths.[3] Furthermore, the issue of grave robbing and the provision of bodies for anatomical dissection led to much trouble. Whilst the Anatomy Act of 1832 (commonly known as the 'Dead Body Bill') was being debated, angry crowds rioted outside Parliament.[4]

Arguably the least-known and most poorly described of the disturbances around this time are the Cholera Riots.[5] Cholera had arrived in Britain for the first time in late 1831 and, before its disappearance about a year later, it swept the country in the most dramatic and frightening epidemic since the Great Plague. This essay will examine the chain of events that led to the Cholera Riots in Britain in 1832, and explore their relationship with the socio-political climate of the time, along with the other riots and disturbances that occurred during this turbulent period in British history.

THE 1831-32 CHOLERA EPIDEMIC

The disease that reached Britain in late 1831 was known as 'Asiatic cholera'. The term 'cholera' was already in common use throughout the country by medical practitioners, simply referring to a diarrhoeal disease of any sort.[6] Thus, diagnoses of 'summer cholera', 'autumnal cholera' and 'English cholera' were commonly made prior to 1831. The term 'cholera morbus' was used to refer to more serious diarrhoeal disease. A much more severe and acute form of the disease was known, mostly occurring in the south Asian sub-continent, and hence referred to as 'Asiatic cholera'. The cause and nature of transmission of this disease was completely unknown in 1831, though we now know it is caused by a bacteria (*Vibrio cholerae*) and transmitted faeco-orally, usually by infected water. Today, the disease is simply known as 'cholera'. Clinical manifestations of cholera are acute and profuse diarrhoea, often with abdominal cramps. Litres of watery faeces (often referred to as a 'rice-water stool') may be passed, leading to severe dehydration and collapse. Death can occur within twenty-four hours of the onset of symptoms if vigorous rehydration is not given. In the end stage of the disease, characteristic features such as sunken eyes, hollow cheeks, and cyanosis (blue tainted skin, secondary to circulatory shock and de-oxygenation) become apparent. To those witnessing this for the first time, the sight of cholera victims must have been quite shocking. Illustration IX.a illustrates a cholera victim from 1831. Though the disease was unknown in Britain prior to 1831, some doctors had experienced it during army service in India.

Illustration IX.a. The 'blue stage of cholera'. This dramatic engraving, which later became known as the 'Blue Girl', appeared in the *Lancet* in 1832.[7]

The epidemic, which reached Britain in late 1831, probably originated in Bengal in 1826. It spread (slowly initially) to mainland Europe, Russia and the Baltic.[8] Its arrival in Britain seemed inevitable; Longmate refers to the autumn of 1831 as 'waiting for cholera', and churches even prayed for deliverance from the disease.[9]

> O Almighty God, who hast visited the nations with the sudden death of thousands, spare, we beseech Thee, this Thy favoured land.[10]

The first case of Asiatic cholera was recorded in Sunderland. The patient awarded this dubious honour was William Sproat, who developed diarrhoea, stomach cramps and vomiting on Saturday 23 October 1831. He assumed that he had 'summer cholera' and did nothing, but by the next day was seriously ill. A surgeon, Mr Holmes, was called, who attended Sproat and found him desperately ill and deteriorating rapidly. Mr Kell, a second surgeon who had seen cholera during military service in India, confirmed the diagnosis of Asiatic cholera. Sproat held on agonisingly for three days before slipping into a coma and succumbing.[11] The cholera history of the British Isles had begun - the disease was to spread rapidly round the country and eventually kill over 30,000 people.[12]

Cholera spread initially through the north of England and into Scotland, and by early 1832 began a steady move south. The first case in London was announced on 14 February 1832.[13] The reasons for the rapid geographic spread of the disease were not, of course, understood. There developed two major theories: a 'contagionist' view, whose protagonists believed in spread by contact; and a 'miasmatic view', whereby the disease was believed to spread by foul vapours or 'miasma'.[14] The latter recognised an association of the disease with filth and poor sanitation. Although the aetiology of the disease was unknown, noble attempts were made to help understand its mechanism of spread. In a remarkable report on the Leeds outbreak in 1832, a surgeon named Robert Baker noted a cluster of cases 'on the uncleansed and close streets occupied by the labouring classes'.[15] Filth was certainly part of the early Victorian way of living, especially in urban environments. Cities in the 1830s harboured expanding populations, which could not be safely contained. Whole families frequently lived in damp, unlit and undrained cellars; and sewage and rubbish littered the streets (Illustration IX.b).[16]

Illustration IX.b. 'A Court for King Cholera'. This cartoon depicting the squalor of urban living appeared in *Punch* on 25 September 1852.[17]
(By permission of The British Library P.P.5270 pG 139 VOL 23)

The accompanying stench, and association of such areas with disease, gave strong support for the miasmatic theory, which became supported by most doctors. It should be mentioned that an alternative, though perhaps complementary theory existed - that the whole affair was a visitation by God on a sinful country.[18]

Concerning the response to this new and frightening epidemic, there were three important fraternities - the Government, the medical profession, and the people. The Government acted through the Privy Council (which Morris called the 'odd job man of the constitution').[19] A Cholera Bill was passed in February 1832, and a Central Board of Health established. In October 1831 the Central Board published key recommendations to combat the disease, which included the formation of local boards of health, quarantine on ships travelling from neighbouring shores, foundation of 'Cholera' hospitals, and the provision of segregated burial grounds for cholera victims (some of these were focal elements in the riots which were to follow).[20] The medical profession, via the Central Board of Health, made a valid attempt at collecting and disseminating information about the disease, publishing a regular newsletter (the *Cholera Gazette*) at one shilling a copy (with an offer of free postage!). Through this publication, reasonable attempts were made at information gathering, for example the question:

> Has the disease in your district been observed to spread from known
> points slowly, or regularly; or did it break out at many distinct points at
> the same time?

appeared in an early edition.[21] However, overall, the medical response was not impressive. As well as having no real idea of the cause or transmission of cholera, attempts at treatments were at best arbitrary, and at worst dangerous quackery. Bleeding and purgation were particularly popular and, of course, worsened the dehydration. Brandy and opium (used on William Sproat in Sunderland and many others later) may at least have made the patients feel a little better! Quack remedies abounded, and money was made out of the epidemic, especially by those with unscrupulous motives. Even locally agreed 'cholera fees' for doctors were generous - for example five shillings per case in Wallasey, Cheshire,[22] and a retainer of ten pounds per week at the height of the epidemic in York. However, even this was insufficient to retain the services of some doctors who fled in fear they should fall prey to cholera.[23] This easy money came from parishes, often ultimately from donations and even church collections.[24] In the midst of this therapeutic ineptitude, amazingly one doctor discovered a form of rehydration treatment basically the same as that used today. William Brooke O'Shaughnessy described and practised a crude form of intravenous fluid therapy:

> [...] throwing into blood vessels a quantity of water, with salt and
> albumen sufficient to supply the deficiency in the blood [...][25]

Sadly, this treatment did not achieve acceptance or widespread practice - emphasising the inherent lack of objectivity, and conservatism of the 1832 medical profession.

Public response to the epidemic has to be seen in the context of political and medical activity (or inactivity). Though the Government made attempts at containment, their actions frequently had negative effects on the population. Enforced quarantine of ships in ports, though understandable, had major financial impacts on merchants and ship-owners, particularly in London and Liverpool. In many towns and cities, the graveyards rapidly filled with the bodies of cholera victims, and local boards responded variably. Some enforced burial in remote out-of-town spots; others arranged multiple burials in pits. Precious clothes were often forcibly removed from victims and burned, and the traditional 'wakes' of the Irish were frequently curtailed and early burial enforced.[26] Above all, people felt an unprecedented fear and terror of this new disease, which was killing friends and family so rapidly and in such a horrible manner. Doctors were visibly impotent, so much so that many stories of 'medical howlers' circulated. For example, a Glasgow physician was reputed to have diagnosed cholera in a young barmaid, only to find out the next day that she had been in the early stages of labour, and had given birth to a healthy baby boy![27]

The epidemic gathered pace in the spring of 1832, and the number of cases and deaths escalated and peaked in the high summer (July-September). Nearly 9,000 died in August alone, and the overall mortality during this period approached one-third (Table IX.I).[28]

TABLE IX.I
Cholera cases and deaths in Britain, 1831-1832

Year	Month	Total cases	Deaths	Mortality (%)
1831	November	416	97	23
	December	979	282	29
1832	January	2,763	614	22
	February	3,070	708	23
	March	4,707	1,519	32
	April	4,109	1,401	35
	May	2,448	748	30
	June	4,942	1,363	28
	August	32,726	8,875	27
	September	18,095	5,479	30
	October	13,355	4,080	31
	November	2,968	802	27
	December	468	140	30
Grand Totals		**108,024**	**30,924**	**Av 28**

The warm weather may have increased infection rates, as by late autumn numbers of cases had dropped precipitously. Or, as epidemics do, perhaps it had simply run its course. Though the outbreak is generally regarded as having ended in December 1832, there were sporadic cases in early 1833, and also reports of locally occurring cases in 1834.[29] However, on Sunday 14 April 1833, the Government ordered a day of thanksgiving, and crowds packed churches giving praise to God for 'removing from us that grievous disease'.[30]

THE CHOLERA RIOTS OF 1832

It was during the most intense time of the epidemic, when numbers of cases and deaths were at their height, that a series of riots occurred throughout Britain. The first took place in February 1832 in Glasgow, the last in September 1832 in Manchester. Most however, occurred between June and August. In this essay we have discussed those that occurred in Glasgow, Edinburgh, Liverpool, Leeds, Exeter, Bristol, and Manchester. However, other riots were also reported in London, Birmingham, Sheffield, and Dumfries.[31] The disturbances were of variable magnitude and seriousness, but police involvement was frequently needed to restore peace, and on occasions troops were summoned. Riots did not occur during the later cholera epidemics of 1849, 1854 and 1866, and fear of the new and often fatal malady was thus clearly an important factor. The timing of the main riots with the peak of the epidemic would appear to support this. Disillusionment with an ineffective medical profession was undoubtedly a further precipitant, and indeed, in most of the riots, doctors and medical attendants were the object of abuse and attacks.[32] Issues over burial rights were important stimulators of riots in some towns.

A particular issue associated with the medical profession was 'Burking', the term originating from the Burke and Hare dissection murders in Edinburgh in 1828. These two notorious individuals murdered sixteen people, selling the bodies of their victims to the medical school in Edinburgh for dissection. Hare turned King's evidence to save himself, and Burke was publicly hanged on 28 January 1829, and later dissected for all to see.[33] Before the introduction of the Anatomy Act in mid-1832, it had always been difficult for the medical profession to obtain bodies for dissection. Bodies were often sold to schools of anatomy by 'body-snatchers', or 'resurrectionists' as they were known, who obtained the bodies by robbing graves of recently interred (and some not so recently interred) corpses. The practice was encouraged by the continuing demand for bodies and a 'no questions asked' attitude by the schools. After the Burke and Hare case came to light, it seems that body-snatchers were regarded as having the potential to murder, because of their motive for profit, and that the process of murder was just one step down the line from body-snatching.[34] This was proven to be true, as the dissection issue did not die with the hanging of Burke in 1829, but was re-ignited by another high-profile case in 1831, just as cholera arrived in Britain. Two individuals, Bishop and Williams, were found guilty of strangling a poor Italian boy and attempting to sell the corpse. At their trial at the Old Bailey, Bishop confessed that: 'he had been, he said, in the habit of supplying the schools of anatomy with subjects for dissection, and had, in the course of twelve years, sold from 500 to 1000 bodies, only three of these, he solemnly declared, had been murdered'.[35,36]

Bishop and Williams can perhaps be thought of as the English Burke and Hare! Their crime was certainly a high-profile one, even though they (supposedly!) murdered fewer people. In journal and newspaper articles of the time, Burke and Bishop are often written about synonymously.[37] Furthermore, it was unfortunate that the Anatomy Act of mid 1832 coincided with the height of the cholera epidemic. The Act aimed to outlaw body-snatching, allowing unclaimed bodies from work-houses and hospitals to be freely made available for anatomical dissection. Many of the cholera rioters feared that when patients were removed to cholera hospitals for 'treatment', they would be 'Burked' by doctors for the purposes of dissection.[38]

Finally, it must be emphasised that rioting in response to cholera also occurred on mainland Europe. Interestingly, the issues here were much more related to class and government, than the British issues of burial and 'burking'. The disturbances themselves, however, were often much more serious than those in Britain. They began in Russia in 1830, and spread to the rest of continental Europe the following year.[39] In Russia, several military officers were killed, and in Hungary castles were attacked and nobles massacred (the crowds believed that they had caused cholera). Serious property and fire damage occurred in Paris. Throughout Europe there was a pervading belief that the epidemic basically represented the rich poisoning the poor.[40]

Returning to the British disturbances, we will now examine the riots in selected towns in more detail. We will then draw these experiences together, and attempt to give an overview of the factors leading to the riots, particularly in relation to other contemporary violent responses - notably Reform, Anatomy and Swing.

Glasgow

According to official statistics, the first case of cholera in Glasgow occurred on 12 February, and the last on 4 November. A large number of cases (6,198) were recorded, with a death toll of 2,994 people, an extraordinary mortality rate of some 48%.[41]

The first riot, a major event in Gorbals, took place on 16 March, and was reported the next day in the *Glasgow Courier*.[42] An elderly lady developed cholera, and word spread that the surgeons would soon attend. It seems the progress of the surgeons was obstructed by a large crowd that had gathered in the street outside her house. The crowd declared she should escape the clutches of the 'medical murderers' and within thirty minutes had increased in size to an estimated 2,000 people (apparently mostly Irish labourers and, according to the newspaper, idle, 'ill-tongued women'). Upon arrival of the surgeon, a Mr Stewart, there ensued a general riot outside her house and he was 'saluted with simultaneous bursts and groans and hisses; struck on the back with pieces of mud; forcibly prevented from entering the house; and eventually compelled to take refuge in a shop'. But for the generosity of the shopkeeper, it is supposed he 'would have fallen a sacrifice to the fury of the mob'. The police were called, to stand sentry over the shop, and the surgeon was imprisoned for almost three hours. They (the police) were apparently afraid of the ringleaders of the mob, who were allowed to escape without apprehension. Upon leaving the shop, Mr Stewart was again assailed by several of the mob who had remained. Three of them were arrested for throwing stones at him, and taken into custody. It was lamented that 'a resolute rascal, who, at the commencement of the affray, was collared while about to let fly a brick-bat at the head of the doctor, was allowed to make his escape'. The woman cholera victim, having been found in the later stage of the disease, died soon after, medical assistance only being called for at the last moment (as was often the case). Although no medicines were administered to aid her, rumour soon spread that the surgeons had forced a drug down her throat, some of which fell onto a piece of cloth and dissolved it.[43]

The *Courier* made an interesting link between this riot and the reform issue. It went on to attack the irresponsible attitude of the Editor of the *Reformer's Gazette*, stating that:

> the poisonous matter [reform] that is weekly dealt forth to its silly-minded readers, by that infamous, rascally, and contemptible publication - the *Reformer's Gazette*, - the Editor of which has done all in his power to administer to the foolish prejudices, and vulgar appetites of his numerous (for we admit they are unfortunately so) reforming, but woefully ignorant, patrons. As an illustration of the fact, we may just state, that in the midst of the riot yesterday, that precious piece of balderdash - the *Gazette* - was toasted most vociferously, while 'Cholera Humbug,' ever and anon rung in the ears of the terrified surgeons.

Such were the concerns over this matter, the *Courier* suggested (as they had heard suggested by a surgeon) that 'the city authorities should step forward, and, for the safety of the medical gentlemen, as well as for the sake of the morals of the poorer classes, adopt measures to prevent the further publication of this nauseating and demoralising print'.[44] It is interesting to note the *Courier's* strong attack on the *Reformer's Gazette*, regarding the influence it apparently wielded over the rioters. The rioters may well have been influenced by this publication and held views sympathetic to it, however, the extent to which it contributed to the rioting is unclear. If the paper is to be believed, it was a major contributing factor, though it could be that the paper held an anti-reform stance.

Another point that can be extracted from the *Courier* is the extreme reluctance of people to call for assistance. It describes several cases where patients were near to death before any help was called for. Even when aid was accepted, it was done so with suspicion. For example, the mistress of a 'house of bad fame', upon reaching a state of near collapse called for a surgeon's assistance. Upon arrival, he found her in bed surrounded by 'a crowd of unfortunate females who domicile in such houses', most of whom fled upon a diagnosis of cholera being made. The mistress refused all medicines offered, except brandy, and refused even to take that unless the surgeon drank some before her.

Prejudice and mistrust abounded, illustrated by the insulting comment made by a passer-by to one the surgeons leaving the hospital, who was heard to remark:

How many have you got in the slaughter-house now?[45]

The riot in Gorbals was also reported by the *Scotsman*, and descriptions of events are elucidated further in that paper.[46] Apparently the surgeon, Mr Stewart, was unable to enter the house of the cholera victim because the crowd were:

Uttering horrid yells, vowing vengeance upon all Boards of Health, and vociferating 'Cholera Humbug', - a cry which some of the low publications of the day have wickedly taught them to repeat.

The whole of the main street became completely occupied by:

A dense mass of human beings, so much excited.

Local shops shut, and the medical gentleman was forced to take evasive action. The report goes on:

A general hunt after the medical gentlemen was speedily commenced, in which we regret to state that the female portion of the rioters took a very prominent part, throwing mud, missiles, and every impurity which they could lift from the street

as well as uttering 'oaths and imprecations' and expressing a determination to murder Mr Stewart. He narrowly escaped, but not before receiving a head injury from 'a stone or some other article thrown at him'.[47] A later report in the *Scotsman* details that Hugh Drummond, one of the mob who assaulted Mr Stewart, was tried and sentenced to sixty days imprisonment in Bridewell. To endorse the punishment, he was to be fed on alternate weeks with bread, then water.[48]

About ten days after the riot in Gorbals, a further riot took place in Paisley. This appears to have started when shovels, a rope and small iron hook were discovered at the burial ground for cholera patients. Crowds hurried to the burial-ground to ascertain if any bodies had been stolen, and it was found that out of seven coffins, all but one were empty. The crowd rapidly gathered in size, and the Sheriff, magistrates, and police officers marched to meet the crowd in an attempt to allay their feelings. Before long, things started to get out of hand, the crowd digging up another coffin and placing it on the shoulders of some porters, as well as uprooting fence posts which they 'shouldered like muskets', calling for vengeance on the doctors. Marching back into the town, two police officers bravely attempted to stop the procession but became victims themselves (of actual bodily harm) and 'were very much cut'. The window of a house, where one of the officers took refuge, was stoned and severely damaged. A stone was sent through a surgeon's window in the midst of the riot. The *Courier* described the events in detail, again relating links to the reform issue.

During the most stormy period of the tumult and while the work of devastation was proceeding with alarming energy, a dirty copy of that line on periodicals, and stain on the literature of the West of Scotland, the misnamed Loyal Reformer's Gazette, was exhibited by one of the rioters as the warrant for their lawless proceedings, while the yell of 'Cholera Humbug' was vociferated by the infatuated and demagogue-ridden miscreants, - the Editor of which print, it would appear, is the acknowledged oracle of the low, the depraved and degraded classes of the population.

The quote goes on to call, once again, for the *Reformer's Gazette* to be banned, stating 'a remedy should be applied to this moral pestilence'. It also details the industrious publication and display of 'incendiary placards' bearing the words 'Cholera Impostures', in the same region in the week prior to the riots.[49]

The day after the first riot in Paisley, a further riot took place there. This was possibly one of the most violent of the cholera riots to take place in Britain. Once more, it started following an empty coffin being found, after it had been exhumed for examination. The windows of several medical practitioners and members of the Board of Health in Paisley were smashed, with at least eleven instances recorded. This path of destruction continued to the cholera hospital, where the gates were forced and doors and windows destroyed. Having broken through the doors, the cholera hearse, or 'carrying cart', was carried off in triumph by the mob who, amongst hideous yells, carried it down to the canal to throw it in, but changed their mind and demolished it instead. One of the mob was captured while attempting to release the 'medical victims' from the hospital, prior to the mob setting fire to the 'tenement' (it is not clear whether this was the hospital, but had all the patients been 'freed' undoubtedly the hospital would have been their objective). A patient in the hospital was unfortunately struck on the head by a stone thrown through one of the windows, and 'died almost instantaneously from the effects of the blow'. The violence became so out of control that troops were called in. By 5 pm things had quietened down and the troops returned to barracks, with special constables mustered to maintain the peace. Fear of further events during the night were so great that a troop of the 4th Dragoon Guards was sent from central Glasgow to Paisley, though there was no further breach of the peace. A fifty-pound reward was offered for apprehension of the persons who had removed the body from the coffin.[50] These riots in Paisley were also reported in the *Scotsman*,[51] and had a startling effect on the local district surgeons, the Board of Health finding itself in receipt of some twenty-two resignations at a meeting held in Paisley on 27 March.[52]

Edinburgh

According to official statistics, the cholera was present in Edinburgh for almost a year, with the first case reported on 22 January, and the last case on 26 December 1832. There were a total of 1,886 cases, and 1,065 deaths. The mortality rate of 56% was even more extraordinary than that seen in the Glasgow area.[53]

Threat of the arrival of cholera excited fear and subsequent rioting. On one of the first occasions that a riot occurred, in early February, the recipients of the crowd's anger were not members of the medical profession, but three unwitting residents of Falkirk, who had taken leave to visit relations in Musselburgh (officially cholera had been present there since 18 January, slightly earlier than in Edinburgh). Upon the return of the three to Falkirk, Board of Health officers detained them at a local pub. Soon, a crowd of several hundred collected around the pub, giving vent to their indignation with loud threats, and the mob remained in the street for several hours. The surgeons attended the three, and without threat to themselves, ordered that they be fumigated and then allowed to return to their own houses upon condition that they submit to a temporary confinement there.[54]

On 22 February, the *Scotsman* reported 'considerable excitement' over a new cholera burial-ground 'in the Moss, near the Toll Bar on the Greenock Road'. A boy who had died of cholera was in the process of being transported to the burial ground by the cholera cart, there having been some delay and reluctance to agree to this by the family beforehand. On the way to the burial ground, the procession was attacked by a mob throwing stones, who turned back the cart and removed the body back to the house from which it had come. Later in the day the Sheriff and some magistrates arrived. They placed themselves at the head of the procession, which left again and this time the body was interred without further ado.[55]

By late February:

> the narrow minded and absurd prejudice against the surgeons, still prevails to a very hurtful extent among those who most require their services at the present crisis. The cry still is, that the Doctors are killing people for the sake of their bodies; and it is in consequence with the greatest difficulty that the men appointed to inter the bodies of those who die of cholera, can get their duty performed. Wherever they appear to remove the remains of any cholera patient, they are hooted and threatened, and even pelted on all sides by the ignorant rabble, and in several instances have been beat off without accomplishing their object.[56]

The *Scotsman* described another two instances of affray, one where those transporting the bodies to the burial ground were attacked and stoned, and another where the men were beaten off before even obtaining the body. In a further disturbance, the father of a child who had died of cholera, having been told that authority had been given by the Sheriff and magistrates to bury the body, laid siege with a knife, brandishing it and threatening to stab anyone who dared take away the body.[57]

In early March there had been no improvement in the situation, the *Scotsman* reporting that:

> An attempt at riot was made at the Dalmarnock Road Hospital on Saturday night, on the removal of two dead bodies for interment, which might have been attended with serious consequences, but for the vigorous interference of the Carlton Police, who kept the rabble that had collected completely in check. A few stones were thrown at the hospital, and many imprecations were heaped on the heads of the Doctors by the ignorant mob; but no other mischief was permitted by the police. The Sheriff and the Provost were, we understand, both in the neighbourhood, watching the motions of the mob.[58]

On the Sunday afternoon, 'another most disgraceful outrage was committed'. The body of a woman who had died of cholera, was being transported for burial in a 'one horse caravan' accompanied by her husband, six assistants and a fumigator. A crowd of around two hundred had assembled and:

> Immediately saluted the men with the most horrid threats, imprecations, and a volley of stones, which broke the window of the caravan, and knocked out one of the teeth of the fumigators.

The husband tried in vain to calm the 'infuriated miscreants', and the burial party were forced to abandon the task and flee for their lives. This was not the end of the fracas, as 'the poor fellows were followed by the crowd, who continued incessantly to pelt them with stones till they came to the Phoenix Foundry. Nearly all of the assistants were more or less injured, and the indentations on the body of the caravan show that the missiles were thrown with right good will.'[59]

Similar events were commonplace at around this time.

> Some disgraceful scenes took place at the Water of Leith, on the first appearance of the disease in that village. The servants of the Board were pelted, and even the medical gentlemen who had gone down to render professional assistance, were insulted and ill-treated.[60]

Another took place at the hospital in Castle Hill. While a female patient was being carried to hospital in a horse driven van, showers of stones thrown by an angry mob assailed the van and its driver. An oilcloth covering the van was completely destroyed, the driver abused and the patient considerably frightened. However, the van managed to convey the patient to hospital. Here, the crowd broke several panes of the hospital windows, and:

> Had the diabolical suggestions of a number of females been attended to, the building would now have been in a heap of ruins.

Upon returning, the driver decided to change his route to avoid the crowd, but his exertions were to no avail. He was assailed again, this time by an even bigger crowd. At this point in the proceedings:

> A ruffian fellow rushed forward, seized the reins, and by a desperate effort, stopped the horse, and brought the driver to the ground.

Having obtained possession of the van, the crowd made for the canal, where it was unceremoniously thrown into the water. Some order was restored upon the arrival of the Sheriff and Superintendent of Police with accompanying officers. It was claimed by the crowd that the woman taken to hospital had simply been drunk, and not suffering from cholera, and that:

Doctors took cholera patients under their care merely to experiment upon them!

Two of the principal rioters were apprehended.[61]

A further report of this incident stated the people's discontent was fuelled further by the setting up of a 'Quarantine Hospital' in Fountainbridge Street, and the placement of several families from the Water of Leith there. Also, some of the 'wretches' had been threatening to set fire to the hospital in Castle Street, where the riot occurred.[62]

Another separate riot occurred towards the end of March, at Greyfriars churchyard. A man who had died from cholera was conveyed there in his coffin, followed by a large crowd of people. Every effort was made to conserve the peace, but upon arrival at the churchyard the mob:

> Burst open the churchyard gates, and even threw stones and other missiles at the men who carried the coffin.

The crowd was more inflamed by the claims of:

> An old beldame who said there was no corpse in the coffin, and that she had seen stones brought to fill it. The mob were outraged, and one ruffian fellow had the temerity to break open the coffin, after it had been lowered into the grave, to satisfy himself and others.

It was reported that 'the majority who form these mobs are the veriest sweepings of Ireland'.[63]

Further events were recorded, one in particular occurring in late May. Two surgeons, with police assistance, decided to remove an old lady, suffering with cholera, from St. Mary's Wynd to the hospital. On the way to the hospital a crowd gathered, and a riot ensued. Two young men were apprehended.[64] One of them was sentenced to pay a fine of ten pounds, or suffer eighty days' confinement, the other five pounds and a caution about his future behaviour.[65]

Liverpool

The cholera riots in Liverpool have been explored in some detail and are notable for the fact that they exploded over a short period of time. There were some eight or more events that took place in a ten-day period in late May and early June.[66]

Cholera was officially declared present in the city on 17 May 1832, and prevailed until September. In that time, 4,977 cases were recorded with 1,523 deaths, a mortality rate of some 31%.[67] However, there is much controversy and speculation over a cover-up relating to the declaration of cholera in Liverpool. It seems this declaration was delayed for several weeks, almost certainly because the Board of Health in Liverpool was comprised not only of medical gentlemen, but also of several influential merchants with vested interests in the shipping trade.[68] Several pieces of evidence confirm the presence of cholera in Liverpool weeks prior to it being declared by the Board. An article in the *Liverpool Journal* entitled 'Suspected case of cholera in Liverpool' reported two cases on 5 May.[69] These were undoubtedly true Asiatic cholera, one detailing the rapid death of a young man from symptoms of the disease. Also, local doctor Thomas Weatherill reported several cases in the *Lancet,* which occurred prior to the declaration being made.[70] Further evidence is provided by another local doctor, James Collins, who states cholera was present in Liverpool in April.[71] The Board were certainly aware of these cases. Reportedly, fees paid to the Board of Health for clean bills of health, amounted to upwards of two thousand pounds per year,[72] equivalent to some one hundred and eight thousand pounds today.[73] However, even when the Board had knowledge of cholera in the city, ships were still allowed to sail with clean bills of health. For example, the *Brutus* was allowed to sail from Liverpool on 18 May with a clean bill of health, but cholera broke out on board with devastating consequences, leading to one hundred and seventeen cases and eighty-one deaths.[74] The issuing of clean bills of health at this time was irresponsible, potentially allowing cholera to be spread to other parts of the globe via the shipping routes. Although not discussed further here, the cover-up has been explored in greater detail elsewhere.[75]

Finally, the Board of Health was forced to recognise the presence of the disease, having been warned to do so by the collector of customs.[76] They put out a statement in the *Liverpool Journal*, as follows:

> The Board of Health, on Monday last, officially recognised the existence of cholera in Liverpool [...] the presence of the malady has happily created no alarm here.[77]

Unfortunately the sentiment expressed by the Board was not to hold true for long.

TABLE IX.II
Chronology and locations of the Liverpool Cholera Riots 1832[78]

In total, eight serious events were reported: -

1	Tuesday, 29 May	Perry Street and Toxteth Park
2	Friday, 1 June	Great Oxford Street North
3	Friday, 1 June	Lime Street and Islington
4	Saturday, 2 June	Addison Street (near Vauxhall Road)
5	Saturday, 2 June	Lime Street and Shaw's Brow
6	Wednesday, 6 June	Barter Street
7	Friday, 8 June	Vauxhall Road
8	Sunday, 10 June	Chisenale Street and Great Howard Street

By the end of May, cholera had really taken hold on the local population, mostly amongst the poorer classes, especially the Irish. It was at this time that a sudden series of violent clashes with the authorities occurred. The first of these took place on 29 May 1832. The *Liverpool Chronicle* reported:

> A most disgraceful instance of combined ignorance, prejudice, and folly occurred in Toxteth Park on Tuesday evening last.[79]

The report went on to describe an incident at the Toxteth Park cholera hospital, which had been set up by the local Board of Health. As a patient was being conveyed to hospital, a mob, comprised mostly of women and boys, followed his progress there, yelling abuse at members of the medical profession accompanying him. The man was admitted to the hospital, but the crowd remained outside, increasing in size until more than a thousand people were present. Suddenly, all hell broke loose and the crowd, hurling abuse, such as 'Bring out the Burkers' and 'There go the murderers', began to throw stones and brick-bats at the hospital. Windows were smashed, including those where the patient, now dying, lay resident. The attending doctor was forced to retire, and other individuals, thought to be related to the profession, were attacked and injured.[80]

Within days further disturbances took place, and each time members of the medical profession and their assistants were targeted. On Friday 1 June two more riots took place.

During the second:

> [...] a poor woman, who had been seen coming out of the Cholera-Hospital yard, in Lime Street, was attacked by the crowd, who threw mud at her, exclaiming that she was 'a Burker!' The mob followed her into Islington, where she escaped from her ignorant and brutal pursuers, by taking refuge in the yard of Mr. Whitter, the joiner, the gates of which were instantly shut.[81]

In another violent incident:

> [...] the palanquin from the hospital was brought for the patient, accompanied by a mob of persons, who on its arriving at the place, broke it into pieces, and put the attendants to flight [...] the brutal and insensitive mob displayed much violence, not only towards the persons connected with the hospitals, but against every person whom they took to be a medical man; and our informant himself experienced much difficulty in escaping from their clutches.[82]

A palanquin was a type of cart on which cholera patients were conveyed to hospital. It was often a frequent object of attack for the crowd, who saw it as a means of conveying their brethren to hospital and delivering them into the hands of the 'Burkers'. In the last reported riot:

The palanquin, on its return, was attacked in Great Howard Street, by a mob of men and boys, who would have broken it into pieces, if the constables had not come up to the assistance of the carriers.[83]

Apart from the universal fear of Burking, why the riots in Liverpool erupted with such fury over this short period of time can perhaps be explained by two significant local scandals that had occurred prior to the cholera epidemic, both of which would have been common knowledge amongst the local population. In October 1826, an event reported on the front page of the *Liverpool Mercury* caused great shock and consternation to the local populace. Under the heading 'Wholesale Resurrectionists' the *Mercury* described in detail the discovery of thirty-three dead bodies. Eleven were found in casks labelled 'Bitter Salts' on the Liverpool docks, awaiting shipment to Scotland. These were almost certainly headed for the medical school in Edinburgh for the medical students to use for the purposes of dissection.[84] Further information about this discovery details the grotesque discovery of several babies pickled in brine, a fact which proved so unpalatable for one of the jury members hearing the case of the accused, that he was taken ill and forced to retire from the court for some time afterwards.[85]

Within a year, the second scandal occurred, and the foundations of an already fragile interface with the medical profession put to the test once more. The event was reported in the *Liverpool Mercury*:

'Another discovery of this inhuman traffic, which, some months ago excited so great a sensation in this town, was made on Wednesday.'[86]

The report described a grave robbing, which occurred in the Walton area of the City, that of the recently interred daughter of a local publican. Police traced the body back to a house in Seel Street, where the publican identified it. Four bodies were found in the house, that of eminent local surgeon Mr William Gill, who was taken into custody.[87]

Gill was tried at the Liverpool quarter sessions in February 1828, and found guilty of having the body in his possession. In court he was allowed grace to read a long paper in defence of his actions. Amongst other things, he cited that the attainment of anatomical knowledge was an essential foundation for the practice of medicine and surgery, done for the greater good of the public. He was sentenced to pay a fine of thirty pounds, which he paid immediately and was discharged.[88] In the weeks and months after this event, similar cases were brought to trial in other parts of the country. In response, a committee was formed in order to help alleviate the great costs incurred to members of the profession as a consequence of legal proceedings. The committee put out a request for subscriptions in the *London Medical Gazette* in May of 1828.[89]

After 10 June 1832, the violence exhibited by the crowds receded as quickly as it had first appeared. Probably the key explanation for the decline in violence was the involvement of the Catholic Church in the situation.

> On Saturday last his worship the Mayor received an anonymous letter,
> signed 'An Irishman', full of threats, stating that himself and others had
> resolved to do several wicked things if the doctors persisted in
> removing people to the hospital. His worship very properly invited the
> attendance of the clergy at the Board of Health, and next day the
> catholic clergy addressed their congregations on the subject of the
> pestilence. With proper feeling they followed this up by an 'address'
> which will be found in another column, and the result has been most
> gratifying. The Board of Health has passed a vote of thanks to each of
> the rev. gentleman. We are permitted to copy the one sent to the Rev.
> Glover, as well as the note accompanying it.[90]

The address was quite long, and seemed to convince the locals of the errors of their
thinking. It made it clear that cholera was not merely an invention of the doctors used for the
purposes of obtaining bodies, and that the doctors were certainly not hurrying patients to
their deaths. It encouraged them to seek assistance from the doctors as soon as the symptoms
became apparent, and reassured them over their concerns about the cholera hospitals. People
were informed that relatives would be allowed to visit patients in the hospital daily, assuming
certain infection control measures were adhered to, and also to view the bodies of those
dying from cholera before their coffins were closed, as well as being allowed to then take the
coffin away for burial.[91]

The involvement of the church at this moment must surely have been a crucial event,
helping quell the feelings of discontent that had prevailed for so long. Their address was
given to Catholic congregations all over Liverpool. Many of those involved in the riots were
Irish Catholics, and almost certainly devout churchgoers. It is easy to understand why the
address had a big effect on calming their fears.

One further contribution to the decline in violence may have been made by Dr
Collins, mentioned earlier, who wrote a long letter to allay the fears of the public and explain
to them why they were misplaced. The *Liverpool Journal* of 16 June stated:

> We beg to call the attention of the public to an address from Dr. Collins
> in another page. It is a sensible and familiar appeal to the poor in their
> present trying situation, and would effect much good if circulated
> amongst those for whom it is intended.[92]

Dr Collins's letter, dated 15 June, was entitled 'A Few Words To Those Most Exposed
To Cholera'. He wrote at length on the fears expressed by the crowds, attempting to explain
why they were invalid. Speaking of these, he states:

> I do not say this by way of charge against you [...] You unconsciously
> fell into the following errors - 1. You persuaded yourself that there was
> no cholera in Liverpool. 2. You thought that the doctors wanted to kill

the sick purposely; and 3. That those who were taken to the Cholera
Hospital were 'burked'.[93]

The fact that people did not believe cholera was present in Liverpool would not have
been helped by the 'cover-up' alluded to earlier, and Collins writes:

> The disease has been weeks in Liverpool before it was declared.

Regarding the second point, doctors were accused of murdering their patients, having
'hastened them into eternity, by giving them black stuff out of a bottle'.
This association was made because the dead bodies of cholera patients turned a 'livid
blue' colour (a previously unseen phenomenon). Furthermore, 'monstrous reports' circulated
about the cholera hospital, which was rumoured to contain many trap doors behind which the
patients disappeared, never to be seen again.
He went on to try and allay these fears, pointing out that there were very few medical
students in Liverpool, hence little need for bodies, and even if there had been the bodies of
those dying from cholera would never have been used for dissection anyway.[94] His letter
certainly seems to have had some effect. On 23 June, the *Liverpool Journal* reported that:

> The address of Dr Collins, which appeared in our paper on Saturday,
> has done much good. It ought to have been printed for distribution.[95]

It is interesting to note that Dr Collins, whose letter appeared to have good effect, was
an Irishman himself.[96]
By 30 June, things were under control, the *Journal* reporting:

> We are happy to perceive that the foolish prejudice of the poor people
> has totally disappeared. They now evince no reluctance to be taken to
> the cholera hospital; and their treatment there is of a nature to inspire
> every confidence. The rev. gentlemen who have had to visit the patients
> there, speak in the highest possible terms of the cleanliness of the place,
> and the indefatigable attendance of the physicians and nurses.[97]

Leeds

The story of the epidemic in Leeds is an interesting one. The spread of the disease is
elucidated superbly in the Board of Health report of that town, written by Robert Baker,
district surgeon.[98] Published in January 1833, it gives a comprehensive overview of the
cholera in Leeds. With an expanding population of around 76,000, Leeds at this time was at
the heart of the new wave of manufacturing districts. The first case of 'pure cholera' occurred
in June in a small *cul-de-sac* of some twenty houses, named the Blue Bell Fold. This was
occupied mainly by poor families, many of whom were Irish, and it was situated in an angle
between the main river and an 'offensive beck or streamlet'.[99] This conveyed the refuse

water from numerous industries for more than a mile and a half upstream from the beck. The first victim was a poor infant, two years of age, of Irish parents. The following day, the 'play fellow' of the first child was struck down and also died. In the following days, three other cases were reported some distance from the Blue Bell Fold, but then the disease rampaged through the Fold before spreading with considerable rapidity to other parts of the town, taking a general hold by the beginning of July. It was at its height in August, and district surgeons reported cases to the Board of Health up until 12 November 1832.[100]

The Board recognised the link between poorly drained, filthy streets and those cleaner districts, some with sewers. It was noted that for a row of houses occupied by some 386 persons (including many cellar dwellers), there were 'but two small single privies'. The Board went on to comment that it was in streets such as these that there had been the highest number of cholera attacks.[101] Writing the report, Robert Baker, one of the district surgeons, noted that he:

> Never once met with a town, where in certain parts, so large a quantity
> of offensive matter was allowed to accumulate in the streets, and where
> the cholera raged so nearly in proportion to the population, as it has
> done in Leeds.

Furthermore, he noted that out of approximately 1,650 cases of cholera that occurred in Leeds, some 1,200 of these occurred in streets destitute of 'good common sewerage', drainage, and pavements where 'refuse water' from the dwelling houses lingered.[102]

The report provides a fascinating insight into the impact of cholera in Leeds. It is perhaps one of the finest pieces of epidemiology of its time, acknowledged by Edwin Chadwick in his report into the sanitary condition of the labouring population in Britain.[103] Baker's meticulous mapping of cholera cases in the city linked the disease to watercourses and areas of poor sanitation (Map IX.i) and, with amazing foresight, he even called for an Act of Parliament to address the problem.[104] This largely forgotten work predated John Snow's mapping of the Broad Street pump area in London by over twenty years.[105]

The Board of Health declared cholera to be present in the town, with a message dated 6 June 1832, published in the *Leeds Intelligencer* of 14 June, stating:

> It is our painful duty to express our decided opinion that the disease
> called spasmodic Cholera has extended to this town.[106]

The report in the *Intelligencer* goes on to describe several cases of cholera in detail, including attempts by physicians to revive patients using 'saline'. Up to fourteen pints of water were infused in some cases, along with salt and bicarbonate of soda, but unfortunately with little success.

A cholera hospital was set up in St Peters Square, to the dissatisfaction of other inhabitants and owners of property there. Several meetings were held to protest about the location of the hospital, although no action to resolve the issue was taken. On Saturday, 9 June, a 37-year-old Irishwoman developed symptoms of cholera, and was visited in the community by a surgeon. She was administered 'suitable remedies', before being conveyed to the cholera hospital at two in the afternoon. At this time she was constantly vomiting clear fluid. Accompanied by her husband, both seemed satisfied by her need for admission to the hospital. However, having left the hospital, the husband was so influenced by rumours and suspicions conveyed to him by the locals, he returned in case his wife should be murdered in the hospital. This implies he thought she was going to be killed by the doctors for dissection purposes, although the term 'burking' is not mentioned in the report. He insisted on her immediate removal but, having been reassured by the resident surgeon, he decided to leave again. However, by this time a large crowd was gathering near the hospital, perhaps seeing they could use him as a tool of protest for their own misgivings about the hospital. The man returned again, this time accompanied by the mob that had terrified him with their insinuations of murder, and had also promised him food, money, lodgings and medical attention for his wife and family. He secured the release of his wife, who had by this time been starting to recover in the hospital, but this did not stop the anger of the mob. Soon, vollies of stones began to fly and many of the hospital windows were broken. A tumultuous assembly of people remained around the hospital throughout the evening. During the night 'parties of ruffians' (operating with military precision, it seems!) raided the hospital at intervals, throwing further 'vollies of stones'. By morning, these renewed attacks had caused considerable damage. The crowds remained on the Sunday, continuing to voice their angry feelings through offensive shouts and threats.[107]

On the Monday, the Board of Health posted a note offering a reward of three guineas for information leading to the arrest and conviction of those responsible for breaking the windows. On the Wednesday, a bill-sticker, William Thomas, was apprehended by a constable while posting a placard throughout the town proclaiming that the woman had not had cholera at all, but was merely suffering the effects of drunkenness and hence had been absconded by the doctors for their own unscrupulous purposes. It claimed that her husband had been denied access to the hospital, and accused the surgeon of being anxious to retain his 'PRETENDED cholera patient'. Apparently she only escaped by running down the stairs of the hospital and leaping from a window, being unable to escape via the door, before walking to her lodgings. Bystanders were invited to attend the address to verify the story. Furthermore the placard accused the surgeons of:

> Such a display of surgical ignorance to say the least of it (for this was
> pronounced a decided case of cholera) and if not ignorance something
> so bad that the English Language cannot furnish us with words
> sufficiently strong to paint it in abominably audacious colours.

It further accused the doctors of wanting to use the cholera hospital for 'private purposes', and said the woman was grateful to those who 'had been the means of rescuing her from a premature death'.[108]

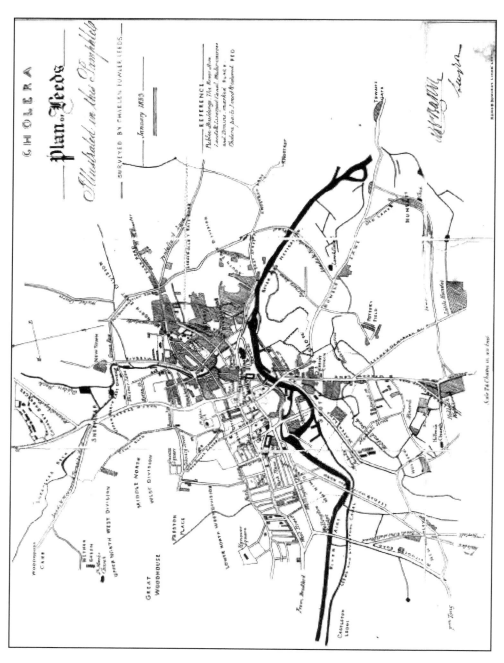

Map IX.i. Cholera map of Leeds[110]

The placard helps elucidate the story further. It may well be that the woman was misdiagnosed, and did escape by leaping through a window. These events, of course, play into the hands of those willing to promote the story further to achieve their own ends, although whether it was merely mistruth used to incense the people further, or had a degree of factual basis, is not clear. The Board of Health were quick to refute the allegations and put their side of the story in order to allay the fears of those concerned, and the bill-sticker was promptly convicted and sentenced to pay a bill of five pounds for posting bills without a printers name on them. In default of payment, it was ordered that he be committed to the house of correction at Wakefield for a period of three months.[109]

The Board of Health, in considering the concerns regarding the hospital, discussed its 'inconvenient position and imperfect nature' and decided upon new premises at a more appropriate location (with few dwellings near it), which they resolved to purchase for five hundred and fifty pounds. The mayor, vicar and other local respectable people gave guarantees and the sum of money duly required was obtained from the bank. A committee was named to oversee the preparation of the new hospital, but news of this proposed new cholera hospital soon spread, and a large crowd, composed of both sexes, assembled and conducted themselves with a tendency to much rudeness and further violence. A member of the new committee, upon leaving the new hospital, was struck violently in the face by an Irishman, receiving a severe blow to his eye. Officers who attended the scene restored order, and the Irishman responsible (coincidentally named Burke) was taken into custody. He too was fined five pounds, which he was unable to pay, and sent to the house of correction for two months.[111]

Exeter

Accounts of the cholera epidemic and its effects in Exeter are superbly illustrated in contemporary works by Shapter[112] and Brewer.[113] Shapter was a doctor in Exeter at the time of the epidemic, and his book *The Cholera In Exeter In 1832* provides a very detailed insight into what happened there.

The cholera riots in Exeter were centred mainly on problems arising from the burial of cholera victims, and the provision of burial-grounds specifically for cholera victims. There were two already crowded places of interment - Bartholomew and Southernhay burial grounds.[114] The Bartholomew burial ground was so named because it was appropriated and consecrated on Bartholomew's day, 1637, to replace the Cathedral yard (formerly the common cemetery of the city). Southernhay was consecrated in 1664.[115] The authorities in Exeter were aware of the suggestion by the Central Board of Health for provision of burial grounds exclusively for those dying of cholera, but did little about it until the epidemic arrived, when burials took place in ordinary grounds, thus exciting much commotion and alarm among local residents, so much so that the Board of Health was assailed by a barrage of complaints. By 25 July the subject had created so much alarm that a deputation began a remonstration, forwarding a memorial to the Secretary of the Board demanding that a meeting of the Board of Health be brought forward in order to discuss the matter urgently. The Board met the following day and agreed to purchase a piece of land from the

Corporation of the Poor, in the north-west corner of a place called Bury Meadow (apparently 'too publicly situated, and too near a populous neighbourhood for burial-grounds to meet this anticipated calamity'), as a holding measure until a further, more appropriate, piece of land could be found. The land was staked out in readiness, and under the impression that it had been agreed that this was to be the new cholera burial-ground, an order was given to bury the body of a cholera victim there, and the grave-digger instructed accordingly. It was on this day, 26 July, that a riot took place. Local parishioners of St David's, where the ground lay, felt aggrieved at this use of ground in their parish, and turned their attentions on the poor grave-digger. A riot ensued and 'the grave-digger's webs were cut to pieces, his tools scattered abroad, he himself assaulted, and even eventually obliged to fly; while the warden of the parish retained many persons in his own house during the night, in order to prevent any further attempt at the interment'.[116] The burial was abandoned, as it became clear this was not yet a legally constituted burial ground, and took place the following day in the Bartholomew burial ground. However, this was the scene of further violence. Those employed to assist were only able to perform their duties with great difficulty, and 'On the coffin appearing in the street supported by webs 'underhand', great indignation arose, and the procession proceeded followed by a large concourse of turbulent persons, and attended, amidst swearing, hooting, and abuse, with much confusion and excitement'.[117] Subsequently, the situation was further inflamed two days later, when a clergyman refused to bury a cholera victim in one of the 'ordinary burial grounds, or in any other place than the Bury Meadow' stating that the Board of Health had procured this for the sole purpose of burying cholera victims, and that there was an Order in Council prohibiting the interment in the normal burial grounds of those certified as having died of cholera by the medical practitioners. The Mayor intervened to try and smooth the situation by saying that perhaps the clergy should continue burials as normal until the new burial ground had been legalised and that all parties should show restraint and reflect upon their objections.[118]

At a public meeting on 10 August a Cemetery Committee was appointed to solve the problem, and they resolved that the Bury Meadow site was still the only suitable location but that it needed licensing by the bishop. Unfortunately the bishop was not in Exeter at the time, so a deputation was sent to seek his views. He agreed to the plans proposed, and sent a communication to the mayor and churchwardens informing them of his consent and stating that burials could begin there in his absence.[119] Both the bishop and the mayor came in for criticism from the local press over the delay and indecision regarding the new burial grounds.[120] There was a further minor hitch, when the legal advisor to the Corporation of the Poor, the owners of the ground, expressed doubts as to the power of the Corporation to appropriate the ground for this purpose. The Commissioners of the Corporation, however, gave their assent, and finally on 16 August it was:

> Resolved that the spot of ground in Little Bury Meadow, which is now staked out, be now appropriated for the interment of persons dying of cholera [...][121]

However, local parishioners still entertained objections, and appointed a deputation to lobby the bishop. They were overruled, but the excitement that had been raised continued, resulting in a public meeting on 23 August.[122] Concerns were raised over the depreciation in value of private property in the parish, as well as concerns over health. It was stated that:

> The removal of cholera bodies through crowded streets, from all the distant quarters of the City, for the purpose of interment at one place only, must be attended with danger to the public, is offensive and oppressive to the parishioners of St David's, and not to be justified in such a city as Exeter.[123]

Calls were made for the Board of Health to procure new burial grounds. Action was duly taken and a second cholera burial ground obtained in Pester-lane (originally 'Pester-house Lane', as in 1625 a 'pest-house' was cited there for the benefit of plague victims),[124] which was licensed by the bishop on 25 August.[125] This may have gone some way to appeasing the parishioners of St David's.

The carrying of coffins 'underhand' (referred to previously) inflamed the passions of the poor. Before the epidemic, bodies of poorer people had been carried to the grave on the shoulders of bearers, but due to opinions relating to the nature of cholera it was felt this no longer appropriate, so the first few victims were carried underhand, as mentioned. This provoked great outrage, because not only was it contrary to the normal custom, but also it was seen as a mark of humiliation and disrespect. To resolve the issue, the Corporation for the Poor decided to procure a horse-drawn hearse, devoted specifically to cholera victims, which was provided on 24 July 1832. However, at the height of the epidemic, with burials taking place during the morning, noon, and evening of each day, one hearse was found to be insufficient. The clergymen had to wait a considerable time between each funeral, so the Cemetery Committee of the Board of Health recommended provision of a second hearse, which became the topic of much discussion and several resolutions. The Corporation of the Poor would not pay for the hearse, so it was eventually procured at the expense of the Board of Health.[126]

Other unpopular practices imposed included spreading the surface mounds of recently interred cholera dead with white lime, which produced a startling effect on those passing the burial-grounds, making it obvious the numerous deaths that were occurring.[127] Also, because of the frequency of funerals during the earlier stages of the epidemic, ceremonies often had to be performed at night. It was not unusual to see the coffin being carried underhand to the grave, with the clergymen performing their last duty of religion to the victim 'at a good distance off from the grave' (presumably to reduce the risk to themselves). By night, these scenes must have looked particularly eerie, performed by the light of flickering lanterns and moonlight (Illustration IX.c).[128]

Whilst much of the violence in Exeter may be attributed to discontent over burial grounds and the carrying of coffins 'underhand', the medical profession was, as in other towns and cities, not immune from accusations. Brewer writes:

In relating the account of the awful visitation the Author cannot come to a conclusion without comment on the ILL-DESERVED abuse which the Medical Gentlemen experienced on its first appearance, the language and conduct of the lower classes of the inhabitants is the point alluded to. It was reported that the Medical Gentlemen were destroying their patients by the application of poisonous medicines for the purpose of taking the bodies for dissection; also that laudanum was administered in such quantities as caused a protracted sleep, so that many were buried alive by immediate interment, and various other expressions unfit for this print.[129]

Illustration IX.c. 16 August 1832. The last cholera corpse buried in Bartholomew yard.[130]

Shapter also highlighted the ignominy heaped upon the medical profession:

The medical attendants ministering to its (cholera's) necessities were accused of 'inducing the unknown symptoms, and even of being the murderers of the people; drunkenness prevailed; derisive, blasphemous,

and wanton songs were sung; rioting and opposition to the enactments
of the law took place [...]'[131]

A further riot on 26 July was instigated when the bodies of a man and his wife were
removed from their house to be buried, with the practice of 'carrying underhand' adopted.
This strongly aroused the indignation of the crowd, whose claims included 'They were
buried alive', 'they were murdered' and 'it was like burying a dog', etc. Upon arrival at
Southernhay burial ground, the size of the crowd had increased, much commotion was
excited, and the officers of justice who had been summoned to resolve the situation, were
themselves assaulted. Shapter himself recalls the scene:

> The burial ground was crowded with an excited, buzzing people; the
> police were protecting those engaged with the funeral; the clergyman,
> rendered conspicuous by his surplice, standing at a distance from the
> grave, proceeded with the service, his voice unheard, and the body
> lowered at the proper part of the service by a signal given. The
> ringleaders of this tumult were summoned before the magistrates, and
> cautioned against any recurrence of such acts.[132]

It seems likely it is the scene that is captured in Illustration IX.d. Who the artist was
is unclear, although Shapter's work is elucidated by several eye-catching illustrations,
perhaps his own work.

He goes on to describe another 'similar scene of tumult' on 13 August, when the body
of a man, who had fallen victim to cholera, was attempted to be removed from his house
(there was an order in place, sanctioned by an Act of Parliament, that the bodies of cholera
victims should be interred within twenty-four hours after death, in order to prevent the spread
of further infection).[134] The man's friends insisted the body was being removed too soon, and
violence ensued. The attempt to remove the body was abandoned, and could only be effected
the next day with assistance from the police. Shapter describes how these events were
connected to 'insult and abuse heaped upon the medical men, and originating in the most
extraordinary misconceptions and unnatural suspicions'. On one occasion, Shapter himself
experienced 'lowering and suspicious looks and gestures, and overheard observations
expressive of doubts of my purpose and intentions'.[135]

The local press attempted to come to the assistance of the profession. For example, a
piece in the *Exeter Gazette* stated:

> We regret to state that the most unfounded and shameful reports have
> been circulated respecting the conduct of some of the medical
> gentlemen of this City, who have attended the few cases of Cholera that
> have taken place. We can state from our own personal knowledge, that
> their anxiety and exertion to stay the progress of the disease has been
> beyond all praise.

Illustration IX.d. A cholera riot in Exeter[133]

The newspaper went on to criticise the 'mischievous individuals' who were spreading rumours, and referred to similar anti-medical outcries abroad, notably in Paris.[136]

Further petty riots and altercations were connected to the removal and destruction of clothes of those who had died of cholera, and on one particular occasion:

In the lower part of the City, much uproar and tumult arose.[137]

The bedding and clothes of victims of the disease were destroyed, by special order, and their value reimbursed to the relatives of the deceased upon application.[138] Initially, the clothes were burnt at midday, but concerns over this 'terrific and disgusting' operation (relating to fumes permeating local residences) led to strong objections.[139] Later, the process was changed, and clothes, etc., were buried in pits and covered in lime.[140]

The *Western Times* commented on the fact that a separate burial ground had not been agreed upon at an earlier stage, also relating concerns over the contagiousness of the disease: 'Even in passing a corpse to the grave, groups of people, of all ages, have been permitted to follow and congregate close around the bier. In one instance we saw upwards of two hundred infatuated persons following the mournful procession of a victim. Surely such dangerous contact as this ought to have been prevented'.[141] Regarding the discontent with the medical profession, it stated:

> There is one subject connected with this malady, that grieves us more than any other - namely, the treatment of the medical gentleman by the ignorant and besotted portion of the poorer classes of the community. In many instances they have been assailed with opprobrious epithets and even menaces - those for whose benefit they act having got hold of the notion that they wish to encompass their death. One gentleman the other night was called - one of the gang of bloody murderers who did all the mischief, and such was the diabolical feeling manifested towards him, that he was justly alarmed for his personal safety, who after this will deny that the poor want education?[142]

By mid to late August, the press were reporting a change in attitude. The *Western Times* wrote:

> Too much praise cannot be bestowed upon the medical men, who have been indefatigable in the performance of their arduous task. Their conduct seems duly appreciated by the poor, who now look upon them as their benefactors.[143]

Even after the fears of the people had calmed, incidents were still happening that must have caused them great alarm and suspicion, even if they did not show it. For example, there is the fascinating tale of the woman and her young son struck down by cholera, related in the *Western Times*. The son, after laying apparently lifeless for several hours was buried. The woman herself worsened:

> 'became insensible and motionless' so was put in a coffin to be buried. Just as the undertakers were about to screw down the lid, she 'revived and pushed off the lid, and very soon recovered'.

On enquiring about her son, and having heard he had been buried, she insisted upon his exhumation. Her wishes were obeyed, and:

> The horror of spectacles can scarcely be imagined, when on opening the coffin it was found the child had turned round, and torn its face almost to pieces with agony, having, it must of course be supposed, come to life in this dreadful situation.[144]

A strikingly similar case was reported to have occurred in Islington, when the body of another male, interred prematurely, was found upside down, the face also torn in agony. Further cases of premature interment were reported in *The Times*.[145]

In retrospect, it is easy to understand the fears of the people, especially when stories such as the above are related. By late August things were certainly much calmer, the *Western Times* reported:

> The Medical Gentlemen have set an example of attention and humanity that will never be forgotten. At the commencement of the disease, the most ignorant thought it was a humbug of the doctors, to which they were led in some measure by the thoughtlessness, to say the least of it, of many persons of a superior station in life, who affected to believe that cholera would not come to Exeter; and when they found their customers running away to the coast, they began to abuse the Doctors and the Editor of the *Exeter Gazette* (a notorious plague) of a scheme to alarm the public for the purpose of profiting by the *Doctoring and the Newsmongering*. The fatal truth forced itself upon the public, and the result has been that the Medical Gentlemen have 'won golden opinions of all men'. The poor everywhere hail them as benefactors, and no men ever had more confidence reposed in them than they now enjoy.[146]

Of course, it should be acknowledged that the press at this time were undoubtedly biased, being pro-professions and anti the poor. However, the view that now prevailed must at least have allowed the doctors to go about their daily business with a new fervour, safe in the knowledge they were now free from accusations such as:

> You kill your cholera patients first, and bury them alive afterwards![147]

Bristol

According to official statistics the first case in Bristol occurred on 16 July and the last on 23 November 1832. A total of 1,612 cases occurred, with 626 deaths.[148]

As in other cities, an unremitting fear of the disease prevailed, as well as a more deep-rooted distrust of doctors. St Peter's Hospital in Bristol was the scene of several disturbances, as reported in the *Bristol Gazette* of 9 August 1832:

Every attention has been paid to the poor sufferers, and all that medical skill could effect has been attempted to stop the pestilence; it is therefore with great pain that we are obliged to state that some of those mischievous and wickedly-disposed individuals, who never suffer an opportunity, however awful, to pass, wherein they can excite the bad passions of the uneducated part of the people, to rouse them to deeds of violence; consequently there have been numbers crowding round the hospital, and following the corpses, and opening by force the coffins of the victims; thereby exposing themselves to the chance of contagion, and thus doing everything in their power to spread the disease. If such people could be reasoned with, they would not commit such egregious folly - we therefore call upon heads of families and heads of establishments to control all within their influence from attending such scenes. The task of waiting upon the sick and burying the dead is melancholy enough, without having it embittered by execrations and threats from angry, ignorant, and bigoted idlers, who interfere on every occasion to obstruct the efforts of the benevolent and charitable.[149]

It is interesting to note that St Peter's Hospital was a place of residence for six hundred local paupers, which had been adapted to the needs of cholera victims.[150] The *Bristol Journal* stated:

With a view to giving as much information as possible to our readers, with regard to the all-engrossing topic of cholera in St. Peter's Hospital, we trust the following particulars will not be unacceptable. Perhaps we have not been sufficiently explicit in stating that the Mint or St. Peter's Hospital is at once the work or poor-house, the bedlam, and the receptacle of vagrants in this city. The number of inmates commonly consists of about six hundred, with proper accommodation for not more than half that number. From the great antiquity of the building, the wards are low, crowded together, and badly ventilated.

It was here, not surprisingly, where the greatest number of cases seems to have occurred, the *Journal* stating:

Where never poor-house ought to be allowed to remain, and where such a mass of aged and helpless humanity, whom the charities of our nature ought deeply to compassionate, should never have been located.[151]

Furthermore, this newspaper reported continuing violent events, and a belief amongst the crowds that deliberate poisoning and burying alive of victims was occurring. In consequence of this belief, several instances occurred where bodies were disinterred, and further insults and threats of violence against the medics followed. The paper also reported that the Armoury in the city, which had been purchased by the Corporation of the Poor as a work-house, was 'since the riots occupied as a barrack for troops'.[152] This certainly implies that there had been a number of riots, and that the authorities were concerned enough to bring in troops to control the situation should it get out of hand.

Attempts were certainly made in Bristol to relieve the suffering of the poor, under the auspices of the 'Anti-Cholera Association'. A house was opened where gruel and rice were provided, under a scheme whereby poor people presented a ticket sponsored by the more wealthy members of Bristol society, entitling them to receive 'a portion of this wholesome and nutritious aliment'. Further acts of benevolence occurred, for example the Bristol Society of Friends gave up their Meeting House so that it be utilised as a cholera hospital.[153]

Although officially the last case of cholera in Bristol occurred in November 1832,[154] the Governor of St Peter's Hospital stated on 20 August 1832 that:

> It is with great pleasure I inform my fellow citizens, that not a single
> case of cholera now remains in this house.[155]

Whether the hospital was really free of cholera is uncertain, and almost certainly cases were occurring in other parts of the city. The *Gazette* highlighted the overcrowding, which undoubtedly contributed to the hold which cholera took at St Peter's, stating that:

> At the time the epidemic first appeared, that there were in the girls ward
> 58 individuals sleeping in 10 beds - in one bed there were 8. At the
> same period the number in the boys' ward varied from 70 to 80, where
> there were 18 beds for their accommodation, including that of the man-
> nurse and his wife. This we conceive to be sufficient cause for the great
> mortality which has taken place amongst them.[156]

Another point of interest relating to Bristol was that St James's Fair, an annual event of much reputation locally, was cancelled. The authorities were so concerned that they resolved to send a petition to Whitehall asking for:

> An order of His Majesty's Most Honourable Privy Council to be issued,
> to prohibit the holding of Saint James's Fair, at Bristol, on 1 September.

This petition included the signatures of the Mayor and several magistrates as well as 8,500 of the 'most respectable Inhabitants of the City', its objective being to:

> Prevent the destructive effects which are universally apprehended from
> the assembling together of great numbers of persons during the present
> alarming prevalence of the Cholera Morbus.

It was endorsed by the Board of Health:

Whose opinions are entitled to every consideration from their knowledge of all the local circumstances and the acquaintance with which leads them to fear the most disastrous consequences, if the Fair takes place in the usual manner, and is of the customary duration .

Another event, 'Temple Fair', was also to be cancelled.[157]

It is interesting to note that associations of riots with fairs have been recorded, notably one particular incident in Essex in 1830, where a 'wage riot' took place four days after the local fair at Helions Bumpstead.[158] Whether or not the authorities in Bristol were aware of events such as these is another matter, although they had obviously made their own deductions that the fair was a potential meeting place for a large gathering of people, who had already shown a disposition to riotous behaviour. Their motives were most likely aimed at reducing the risk of further rioting, although cancelling the Fair may also have helped minimise the potential for further spread of disease.

Manchester

At least two cholera riots occurred in Manchester.[159] The first took place at Knott Mill in May, the second at the Swan Street cholera hospital in early September. The September riot was particularly violent, and not only was it reported in the national press, but those in Manchester remembered it for many years after. The *Manchester Chronicle* of 8 September 1832 details it as follows:

A child, an Irish boy named Brogan, was taken ill with cholera on Friday 31 August and admitted to the Swan Street Hospital. Unfortunately he died that same evening. The burial, along with several other cholera victims, was to take place on the Sunday morning, 2 September. At the graveyard, suspicions were aroused that there was no name on the little coffin, although there were names on the others. The child's grandfather became suspicious, and the coffin was forced open. To his amazement and disgust, the child's head had been severed and replaced instead with a brick. Shavings had been placed in the coffin too, in order to absorb any blood which might have haemorrhaged from the wound.[160]

In view of the grotesque findings, it was rumoured that the child had been murdered in the hospital. As the day went on, a great and frenzied crowd visited the cemetery, once more the coffin was removed from its grave, the lid torn off and the mutilated corpse of the poor boy exhibited for the gaze of the horrified onlookers. The crowd demanded retribution for the 'Burking', calling for the hospital to be burnt down. The coffin was shouldered and the crowd made for the hospital, increasing tenfold in size on the way. Upon arrival at the hospital, the gates were forced and the mob immediately set about demolishing the premises. Beds and furniture were thrown out into the street and demolished, the cholera van was dragged out into the street, bludgeoned and set on fire. The patients, some twenty-five in number, began to be conveyed out from the hospital by the crowd. It seems that had it been possible to remove all of them, the building itself would have been set on fire. The resident medical officers, including a Mr Lynch and Mr Gaskell, managed to secure a retreat, although the crowd were very vocal in calling for them, and it was reported that 'if Mr Lynch had fallen into the hands of the populace, he would certainly have been murdered'. Police at the local 'lock-up', consisting of some twenty officers, attempted to intercede, with some difficulty. Eventually, they succeeded in apprehending several of the lead rioters. However, the mob then attacked the prison itself, 'and the windows were speedily demolished'. Shortly after this the Riot Act was read by one of the magistrates. A young Irish priest, Reverend Hearne, addressed the crowd, and his efforts had much influence in calming them. Shortly after, troops of the 15th Hussars arrived and 'with great coolness proceeded to disperse the assembly'. They remained in the neighbourhood during the night, in case of further trouble.[161]

It was subsequently found out that a young man named Robert Oldham, 'the resident dispenser of medicines', had been responsible for severing the head. He fled, but the head was traced to a house of a person he had visited, and recovered. Mr Lynch, the surgeon, re-attached the head at the town hall in the presence of Reverend Hearne.[162]

The above event was of such abhorrence and magnitude that not only was it reported locally, but also nationally. *The Times* reported it in detail, also noting that nine prisoners were taken for trial to the New Bailey in connection with the riot.[163] It further reported that in fact twelve had been detained 'as the ringleaders of the riot and outrage at the Cholera Hospital in this town', most of whom were Irishmen. A warrant was also issued for the arrest of Mr Oldham, who had been responsible for severing the head.[164] The outrage even provoked letters to *The Times*, one stating 'I have never read anything which pained me more than your remarks on the Manchester riots'.[165] Further detailed reports of the Manchester riot occurred in other papers, including the *Scotsman*.[166]

This event lived on for many years in the minds of the local populace. As long afterwards as 1890 it was still recalled in vivid detail by those who had witnessed it in their youth. For example, one eyewitness recalls seeing the cholera van smashed and burnt. Another recalls someone attempting to make a journey with his mother, and coming across 'a woman being carried in a chair, followed in quick succession by several other persons of both sexes' (presumably cholera patients) as well as seeing that 'a dense crowd filled Swan-street, and that overhead smoke and flames were ascending'.[167] Another recalls that the boy whose head was severed was about four years of age, and that having first ascertained the gruesome tale was true, the crowd intended to wreak vengeance on the 'Burkers' and vowed to 'Burn the hospital'. He estimated the size of the crowd at three to four thousand, recalling them attempting to demolish the buildings and raising the cry of 'Bring out the van and let us burn it!', which was done. He recalled that the Reverend Hearne's address went some way to satisfying the crowd, who began to disperse. According to this witness, Oldham 'was not heard of again, so it is supposed he left the country'. Another lady added a detail, which may help explain the event further. Apparently one of the surgeons at Swan Street hospital had an idea that the disease (cholera) originated in the head, and that the head had been removed 'In order to ascertain the fact or fallacy'. She also recalls looking through the iron railings at the churchyard and seeing the coffins, and the Irish raising the cry that the doctors were killing the cholera patients. Her aunt ordered her to run for her father and get him to 'go for *Lavender's men*' (i.e. the police). Upon returning to the house she recalls seeing the mob from an upstairs window, recalling 'such a sight I hope few others have ever to behold. The hooting, yelling bearers of the coffin were drunk, and, jostled by a crowd in like condition, upset the poor little headless body out into the muddy roadway. It was picked up and replaced'.[168] Others recall more facts, for example that the doctors escaped by jumping over the wall at the back of the hospital. Also, the driver of the burial van was greeted with the comment from the boys grandfather of 'Give me my child's head and I'll give you the brick', before being assailed by a shower of bricks and himself having to make an escape over the back wall. Beds and bedding were set on fire too, as well as the cholera van, the damage supposed to have been about one hundred pounds. Father Hearne's address is recalled, as is the arrival of the military: 'three troops of the 15th Hussars rode up and people fled in all directions'. The subsequent showing of the corpse in the coffin to obtain money was allegedly done so on behalf of the parents, although it may be reasonable to be suspicious of this motive! Robert Oldham, the culprit, was apparently nineteen years of age and had only started at the hospital twelve days before, having been appointed 'compounder and dispenser of medicine'.[169]

Another witnessed the event as a thirteen-year-old, when working as a druggist in nearby Oldham Street, confirming the accounts of those above and also himself seeing the cholera van burn and the police apprehending some of the rioters.[170]

A later summary of events adds further detail to the story. Apparently the policemen were almost powerless to cope with the mob, so infuriated was it. Someone suggested they should 'Send for Father Hearne', who 'exercised a wonderful influence not only over his own large and ever-increasing flock of Irish immigrants, then steaming over from the sister Isle in battalions, but also over the non-Catholic portion of the community'. Father Hearne addressed the crowd from the front of the Hospital, explaining that the dreadful act had been committed by one person, a medical attendant named Oldham, for the purposes of selling the head for dissection. This had been done without knowledge of, and was contrary to the express orders of the medical board. Oldham had absconded in order to avoid the consequences of his act, but Father Hearne reassured the crowd that every effort was being made to trace him, and to return the head of the boy. The day the body was re-interred, Father Hearne acted as the officiating clergyman. There was an immense number of people at the funeral, and at the conclusion of the ceremony Father Hearne addressed the great crowd, urging them to depart in peace. They took his advice, hence closing one of the most gruesome episodes of the cholera riots of 1832.[171]

It is interesting that this event was almost certainly the last cholera riot of 1832, which, if eyewitness accounts are to be believed, involved perhaps three to four thousand people. Not only was it on a grand scale, but it was gruesome in its detail. Furthermore, it was so memorable that it provoked several responses to requests for information about it almost sixty years after the event, from those who had witnessed it as children and young adults. Perhaps then, this is why it was reported nationally in papers such as *The Times*, whereas many of the other cholera riots, such as those in Liverpool, were not. It is also interesting that, as in Liverpool too, the power of the clergy to allay the fears of the people was effective in its utmost, perhaps reflecting the large number of Irish who held strong religious beliefs.

CAUSES OF THE RIOTS

The preceding sections have included local causes for specific riots. In summary, these included issues such as burial grounds (Exeter), locally occurring scandals (Liverpool), possible incitement by Reformers (Glasgow and Edinburgh), discontent over the location of cholera hospitals (Leeds), and the gruesome discovery of the child's headless corpse in Manchester. Here, we attempt to draw these causes together, and introduce wider issues, which contributed to the disturbances. The major factors are as follows.

Class and Race

The rioters were certainly mostly poor city-dwellers, and in ports such as Liverpool, frequently Irish. Some of the popular contemporary reports, however, were probably biased. For example, a Liverpool newspaper described the mob there as 'of the lowest order', and 'low Irish'.[172] At the time, Liverpool's Irish community made up about 10% of the city's population, and many were in fact skilled workers.[173] Interestingly, a Birmingham surgeon giving evidence to a Royal Commission on the Irish Poor in 1836, described the Irish in Birmingham as the 'very pests of society'.[174] Class issues were not a direct cause of the cholera riots, but were a contributing factor. Durey suggests that the disturbances in part reflected 'a desire amongst the poor to demand social justice'.[175] Ironically, cholera did kill at least some of the upper and middle classes, who often drank equally polluted water as the poor; and in this respect the disease was not a respecter of class in the way, for example, that typhus was. Nevertheless, if only because of the overwhelming numbers of the poor, most deaths occurred in this class of society. Trapped in a cycle of destitution, frightened by the plague, and faced with helpless and ineffective medical and political leaders, the threshold to riot was low.

Burial practices

Cholera legislation in 1832, both central and local, interfered in a number of ways with the traditional ritual of death, and the practices of burial. These included removal and burning of victim's clothes, burial within twenty-four hours of death (and from July 1832 within twelve hours), the use of mass graves, and burial outside graveyards in unconsecrated grounds.[176] Such edicts were, unsurprisingly, intensely unpopular for a variety of reasons. The clothes of the dead were valuable assets to their friends and relatives. Rapid burial interfered with normal family gatherings and funeral services. The use of unconsecrated ground for burial was a particular issue for a lower class, which, at the time, was generally devoutly and traditionally religious. The rapidity of interment was especially problematic. In many parts of England, burial was delayed commonly for a week or more. Many of these factors were inflammatory to the people at the time of their great sadness of the death of loved ones, friends and colleagues, as particularly illustrated in the passage about Exeter. The Irish 'wake' was specifically interfered with, and at least one riot in Liverpool was partly related to this.[177]

Dissection and body-snatching

Medical education flourished in the early 19th century, and was heavily anatomy-based. Dissection required bodies, and these were not always easy to obtain. An illicit trade in bodies developed in the 1820s, with a number of high-profile legal cases and scandals. The best known was of course that of William Burke and William Hare, who are discussed earlier.[178] Thousands of people attended Burke's execution on 28 January 1829, and the term 'burking' entered the English language - a word frequently on the lips of cholera rioters in various cities, particularly Liverpool. The implication was that doctors were removing cholera patients to hospital to murder or 'burke' them, and then use the bodies for dissection. In fact, murder was an unusual way of procuring such bodies - mostly they were removed from graves or morgues, and sold to medical schools on a 'no-questions-asked' basis. The most famous of these 'resurrectionists' were Bishop and Williams, also convicted of murder, as discussed earlier. Interest in this case was very intense, and an estimated one hundred thousand people crowded the Old Bailey 'hastening to witness the final exit of the burkers'. The executions were described in detail in the press, it being noted that 'The moment the drop fell, the mob that had continued yelling and shouting, gave several tremendous cheers'.[179] Such was the impression created by this pair, that apart from the term 'burking', another expression, 'bishopping' was utilised. For example, a man who had not been seen in Glasgow for some time was suspected to have been 'Burked or Bishopped!'[180] The press were certainly keen to utilise terms and tales like this to increase their sales but, unfortunately, they stuck in the minds of their readers, adding to the hysteria that already existed. There followed a period of what some newspapers termed 'burkophobia'.[181] Of course, they, in part, were responsible for this. One commented that:

> Scarcely a day passes but reports are circulated of the supposed sacrifice of fresh victims to the interest of science.[182]

Fears of burking were so prevalent throughout the country, that people were sometimes moved to take drastic actions. For example, 'A mob of 20,000 persons destroyed, on Monday week, an anatomical theatre, in Aberdeen, under the impression it was a 'Burking Shop'. A surgeon and tw1o medical students narrowly escaped being murdered.'[183]

As Bishop and Williams were being hanged in London, cholera was beginning to spread throughout the north of England, and would soon reach the south. Scarcely more than six months after the execution, the Cholera riots would affect many towns and cities, and it is therefore not surprising that burking was a frequent issue. The Government's response to these events was to introduce the Anatomy Act, which eventually became law in June 1832. This Bill sought to outlaw body-snatching, by making the bodies of the poor potentially more easily available for dissection - in particular the unclaimed dead from hospitals, prisons and work-houses.[184] The legislation became commonly known as the 'Dead Body Bill' and was deeply unpopular. This act, and prevailing air of 'burkophobia', clearly had major instigating effects on the Cholera riots of mid-1832.

'On the brink of civil war'

From Table IX.III, it can be seen that the 1832 Cholera riots were at the fulcrum of a series of civil disturbances in the first half of the 19th century.[185] They were preceded by the Luddite movement (with disturbances mainly in 1812), the Swing riots (1830-1832), and the Welsh Rising in 1831. Anatomy riots and Reform Bill riots occurred in the same year as the cholera disturbances (1832), and Chartism was to erupt in 1837 and last until 1848, with the Rebecca Riots occurring between the years of 1839-1844. Luddism and Swing shared similar origins, though the former was essentially urban and the latter rural. Luddite violence was mostly machine-breaking as an act of revolt against industrial mechanisation and the general status of urban workers.[186] At the height of Luddism, in mid-1812, over 12,000 troops were stationed in the main Luddite area, between Leicester and York, in an attempt to quell violence. The 'Captain Swing' disturbances began in the south of England in early 1830, as a response initially to the introduction of threshing machines, leading to rural unemployment. A localised, but serious, rising occurred in South Wales in the summer of 1831. Centred on Merthyr Tydfil, it was a dispute between industrial workers and employers, characterised by a strike, a subsequent 'lock-out', and riots.[187]

TABLE IX.III
Civil disturbances in Britain 1812-1848

Luddism	1811-1816
'Captain Swing'	1830-1832
Welsh Rising	1831
Reform Bill riots	1831-1832
Cholera riots	1832
Anatomy riots	1832
Chartism	1837-1848
Rebecca riots	1839-1844

Note: In addition there was variable anti-Corn Law agitation between 1813 and 1846 (including, for example, a riot in London in 1815)

The Swing riots extended well into the midlands and north of England, and even into Scotland. Though mainly rural, they did affect cities occasionally, and frequently occurred in the urban hinterlands. There were overlaps between the locations where Swing and Cholera rioting occurred. For example, several Swing incidents occurred in South Lancashire and Cheshire (close to Liverpool) in 1830, and there was a Swing-related arson attack in the city itself in December 1830.188 The Swing disturbances continued in 1831, and even into 1832, well into the time of the cholera epidemic and its own riots. Factors that contributed to the Swing riots may well have been relevant also in the cholera riots. In 1833 a Royal Commission into the Poor Laws was established and in an attempt to understand factors that might have contributed to the Swing riots, they sent questionnaires to all rural parishes in England and Wales. One of the questions posed was 'To what do you attribute the cause of the recent agricultural rioting?' Interestingly, responses from parishes in Lancashire included perceived causes, such as unemployment and 'foreigners' (i.e. immigrants, particularly the Irish).189 In Liverpool, where the cholera rioting was at its most intense, the Irish were often implicated.

The Anatomy riots were relatively minor disturbances outside Parliament in the months leading up to the passing into law of the Anatomy Act (the 'Dead Body Bill') in June 1832. They are important, however, as they clearly reflected the anti-medical feeling and 'burkophobia' widespread in the country, and are likely to have contributed to the outbreak of Cholera rioting. The Reform riots were much more widespread and serious, reflecting concern and frustration over the slow progress of Parliamentary reform, as mentioned in the introduction. Links between cholera rioting and the reform issue appear stronger than those with the Swing disturbances. In Glasgow, this was particularly apparent, with calls of 'Cholera Humbug' (i.e. invention) and alleged incitement by pro-reform publications.190 When cholera first arrived in Sunderland in late 1831, it was even considered to be a ploy by the Government to divert attention away from the reform issue, and it was reported in the *Lancet* that:

> 'A great number of persons considered the 'Sunderland affair' as a 'government hoax' got up for the purpose of producing a counter-revolutionary excitement, and distracting the attention of the people away from the reform bill. It is certain that a farce of this sort was once played off with great effect during the riots in Lord G. Gordon's time, or Wilkes's, which quieted the people as effectively as the largest military force could have done'.191

The Reform Bill was finally passed in mid-1832, but had been preceded by serious rioting, notably in London and Bristol. In one riot in Bristol, four hundred citizens were killed, with four hundred thousand pounds of property damage.192 Reports of this event circulated, the *Liverpool Journal* stating:

> 'Bristol has been the scene of one of the most disgraceful and disastrous riots that the press has had to record since the destructive proceedings of Lord George Gordon, in London, in 1780. Property has been destroyed, it is stated, to the amount of £400,000; and the number

of persons killed, burnt, and buried in the ruins of falling houses,
exceeds, it is reported, (we hope inaccurately,) four hundred'.[193]

Notwithstanding the immense loss of life, in today's terms the cost of the property
damage would equate to a staggering £21.6 million.[194]

The Cholera riots of mid 1832 need to be viewed in the context of this past, present
and future violence. As Royle has observed, there was clearly a revolutionary situation in
1830-32.[195]

CONCLUSIONS

The 1832 British Cholera riots can be seen as a series of disturbances, which broke out
during a period of near-revolution, in a culture of violent rebellion. Each town affected had
particular local causes, but interference with burial rituals and the dissection issue were
frequent precipitants. Anger against doctors was common - the medical profession had
distanced themselves from their patients and the people by their insensitive handling of the
problem, and their ineffective response to the cholera epidemic. They paid for this aloofness
in the summer of 1832 by having 'stones and brickbats' hurled at them.[196] The year 1832 is
not the only time that the medical profession have experienced such anger directed at them,
especially in Liverpool. The recent scandal at Alder Hey hospital, where organs of dead
children and infants were retained without their parents' permission, provoked a similar
response of much outrage, although without the violence. There were major demonstrations
outside the hospital, a lot of adverse media coverage, and subsequent litigation against the
hospital and doctors.[197] A further scandal occurred in Bristol, where paediatric cardiac
surgeons continued to operate on babies even though their rates of mortality were
unacceptable, and they too retained organs without consent. They were only forced to
discontinue after an anaesthetist, at considerable cost to his own career, blew the whistle on
them.[198] The fact that both the Alder Hey and Bristol scandals involved children, was almost
certainly a further inflammatory factor. In the same way that issues relating to dissection and
'Burking' forced the Government in 1832 to press the Anatomy Act forward more quickly,
something positive has also come from the Alder Hey and Bristol scandals, encouraging a
new openness and better consent procedures.

It is strange that the Cholera riots have received so little attention in historical
writings. They occupy a central place in the revolutionary scenario between 1830 and 1832,
and also represent a fascinating social response to a single disease. They stimulated central
and local Government authorities to respond to the threat of cholera returning after it abated
in late 1832. In this way, cholera and the riots were integral components of the pathway that
led to public health reform, eventually bringing sewage pipes and clean water to the vast
majority of the British population by the end of the 19th century, reaping enormous benefits
for the health of the people.[199]

NOTES

1   Rudé, G, *The Crowd in History: A Study of Popular Disturbances in France and England 1730-1848*, (Serif, London 1995), p. 267; *see also* Royle, E, *Revolutionary Britannia? Reflections on the threat of revolution in Britain 1789-1848*, (Manchester University Press, Manchester, 2000).

2   Hobsbawm, E and Rudé, G, *Captain Swing*, (Phoenix Press, London 1969); *see also* Royle, E, (2000), pp. 83-88; and the 'Swing' project, www.fachrs.com.

3   Pearce, E, *Reform! The fight for the 1832 Reform Act*, (Jonathan Cape, London 2003); *see also* Royle, E, (2000), pp. 67-91; Fraser, D, The agitation for parliamentary reform., In Ward, J T, (ed.), *Popular Movements c1830-1850*, (MacMillan, London, 1970), pp. 31-53.

4   Richardson, R, *Death, Dissection and the Destitute*, (Phoenix Press, London 2001), p. 202.

5   Gill, G, Burrell, S and Brown, J, Fear and Frustration - the Liverpool Cholera Riots of 1832, *Lancet*, 2001, 358: 233-37; *see also for a more general overview of the riots*: Durey, M, *The Return of the Plague. British Society and the Cholera 1831-2*, (Gill and MacMillan Ltd, Dublin, 1979), pp. 155-84.

6   For a useful discussion on cholera terminology, *see*: Rowson, G S and Haycock, D B, Coleridge's cholera - cholera morbus. Asiatic cholera and dysentery in early nineteenth century England. *Bulletin of Historical Medicine*, 2003, 77: 298-331.

7   *Lancet*, (1832); 1: 669.

8   Morris, R J, *Cholera 1832*, (Holmes & Meier, New York, 1976), pp. 21-37.

9   Longmate, N, *King Cholera. The biography of a disease*, (Hamish Hamilton, London, 1966), pp. 11-19.

10 *Ibid*, p. 11.

11 *Ibid*, pp. 25-27.

12 Morris, R J, (1976), p. 75.

13 *The Cholera Gazette*, 14 February 1832.

14 Henriques, R Q, *Before the Welfare State - social administration in early industrial Britain.*, (Longman, London, 1979), p. 126.

15 Baker's work is quoted in Chadwick's 1842 report: Chadwick, E R, *Report on the Sanitary Conditions of the Labouring Population in Great Britain*, (London, 1842), p. 160.

16 A vivid description of the appalling living conditions in urban Britain in 1832 is James Kay's report on Manchester: Kay, J P, *The Moral and Physical Condition of the Working Classes*, (Manchester, 1832).

17 A Court For King Cholera - Cartoon by John Leech, *Punch*, 25 September 1852.

18 The 'visitation from God' theory re-emerged in ensuing cholera epidemics; *see:* Morris, R J, Religion and medicine; the cholera pamphlets of Oxford, 1832, 1848 and 1854, *Medical History*, 1975, 19: 256-70.

19 Morris, R J, (1976), p. 23.

20 *London Gazette*, 25 October 1831.

21 *Cholera Gazette* (No.2), 28 January 1832.

22 Gill, G V, *Cholera and Public Health Reform in mid-Victorian England with special reference to the Parish of Wallasey 1845-1866*, (Unpublished MA dissertation, University of Liverpool, 1999), p. 48.

23 Durey, M, The Spasmodic Cholera in York 1832. *University of York Borthwick Papers*, no 46, (1974).

24 Generosity for cholera care was often remarkable. A single church collection on 5 August 1832 in Wallasey (a poor parish in Cheshire) realised £16 7s 0d specifically for cholera: *see* Gill (1999), p. 48.

25 O'Shaughnessy, W B, Proposal of a new method of treating the blue epidemic cholera, *Lancet,* 1831-32, 1: 366-70.
26 Longmate, N, (1966), pp. 52-53 and 130-32; *see also:* Morris, R J, (1976), p. 105.
27 Wohl, A S, *Endangered Lives - Public Health in Victorian Britain,* (Harvard University Press, Cambridge, Massachussetts, 1983), p. 119.
28 Morris, R J, (1976), p. 75.
29 Shapter, T, *The Cholera In Exeter In 1832,* (John Churchill, London and Adam Holden, Exeter, 1849), Republished by S R Publishers, Wakefield and London, 1971; *see:* 'Map of Exeter in 1832 - Shewing [*sic*] the localities where the Deaths caused by Pestilential Cholera occurred in the years 1832, 1833 & 1834'. This illustrates at least twenty deaths from cholera in 1834, carefully marked to show the precise locations.
30 Longmate, N, (1966), p. 133.
31 Durey, M, (1979), pp. 158-59.
32 Gill, G, Burrell, S and Brown, J, (2001), p. 235.
33 Bold, A and Gittings, R, *The Book of Rotters,* (Mainstream Publishing,Edinburgh, 1985), pp. 176-78; *see also:* Richardson, R, (2001), pp. 131-58; for a more comprehensive and carefully researched account *see:* Bailey, B, *Burke And Hare - The Year Of The Ghouls,* (Mainstream Publishing, Edinburgh and London, 2002).
34 Richardson, R, (2001), p. 195.
35 *Liverpool Journal,* 12 November 1831.
36 *Ibid,* 10 December 1831.
37 Share Of The Council In The Late Burkings, *Lancet* 1831, 1: 565-8.
38 Gill, G, Burrell, S and Brown, J, (2001), p. 236; *see also:* Durey, M, (1979), pp. 176-78.
39 Evans, R J, Epidemics and revolutions: cholera in nineteenth century Europe, In Ranger, T, and Slack, P, (eds) *Epidemics and Ideas: essays on the historical perception of pestilence,* (Cambridge, 1992), pp. 149-73.
40 *Ibid,* pp. 163-64; Durey, M, (1979), p. 183.
41 TNA, Privy Council Papers, PC 1/108.
42 *Glasgow Courier,* 17 March 1832.
43 *Ibid.*
44 *Ibid.*
45 *Ibid.*
46 *The Scotsman,* 17 March 1832.
47 *Ibid.*
48 The *Scotsman,* 28 March 1832.
49 *Glasgow Courier,* 27 March 1832.
50 *Ibid.*
51 The *Scotsman,* 28 March 1832.
52 *Glasgow Courier,* 29 March 1832.
53 TNA, Privy Council Papers, PC 1/108.
54 *The Scotsman,* 8 February 1832.
55 *Ibid,* 22 February 1832.
56 *Ibid,* 29 February 1832.
57 *Ibid.*
58 *Ibid,* 7 March 1832.
59 *Ibid.*
60 *Ibid,* 14 March 1832.
61 *Ibid,* 17 March 1832.

62 *Edinburgh Evening Courant,* 17 March 1832.
63 The *Scotsman,* 28 March 1832.
64 *Ibid,* 30 May 1832.
65 *Ibid,* 2 June 1832.
66 Gill, G, Burrell, S and Brown, J, (2001).
67 TNA, Privy Council Papers, Ref. PC 1/108.
68 Collins, J, Notes and Observations on the loss of lives from cholera on board the ship Brutus; And on the Conduct and Constituency of the Board of Health in Liverpool, *London Medical Gazette,* 1832, 10: 412-15.
69 *Liverpool Journal,* 5 May 1832.
70 *Lancet,* 2 June 1832.
71 Collins, J, (1832), pp. 412-15.
72 *Liverpool Journal,* 28 January 1832.
73 Web site for converting UK currency dating back to A.D.1264. http://eh.net/hmit/ppower/
74 *Liverpool Journal,* 9 June 1832.
75 Burrell, S and Gill, G V, The Liverpool Cholera Epidemic of 1832 and Anatomical Dissection - Medical Mistrust and Civil Unrest, *Journal of the History of Medicine,* (Forthcoming).
76 Collins, J, (1832), pp. 412-15.
77 *Liverpool Journal,* 26 May 1832.
78 Gill, G, Burrell, S and Brown, J, (2001).
79 *Liverpool Chronicle,* 2 June 1832.
80 *Ibid.*
81 *Liverpool Courier,* 6 June 1832.
82 *Liverpool Mercury,* 8 June 1832.
83 *Liverpool Courier,* 13 June 1832.
84 *Liverpool Mercury,* 13 October 1826.
85 *Ibid,* 3 November 1826.
86 *Ibid,* 26 October 1827.
87 *Ibid.*
88 *Liverpool Chronicle,* 16 February 1828.
89 *London Medical Gazette,* 1828, 1: 744.
90 *Liverpool Journal,* 23 June 1832.
91 *Ibid.*
92 *Liverpool Journal,* 16 June 1832.
93 *Ibid.*
94 *Ibid.*
95 *Liverpool Journal,* 23 June 1832.
96 *Ibid,* 28 April 1832.
97 *Ibid,* 30 June 1832.
98 Report of the Leeds Board of Health, (1833). Printed by Hernaman and Perring, at the *Intelligencer* office, Leeds, 1833.
99 *Ibid,* p. 6.
100 *Ibid,* p.7.
101 *Ibid,* p. 10.
102 *Ibid,* p. 11.
103 Chadwick, E R, *The Sanitary Condition of the Labouring Population in Great Britain,* (London, 1842); *see also:* Hamlin, C, *Public Health and Social Justice in the Age of Chadwick,* (Cambridge University Press, Cambridge, 1998).

104 Report of the Leeds Board of Health, (1833), p. 20.

105 Brown, P E, John Snow - the autumn loiterer, *Bulletin of the History of Medicine*, vol. 35, (1961), pp. 519-28; *see also:* Brody, H, Russel, M, Vinten-Johansen, P, Paneth, N and Rachman, S, Map-making and myth-making in Broad Street: the London cholera epidemic, 1854, *Lancet,* 2000, 356: 6468.

106 *Leeds Intelligencer*, 14 June 1832.

107 *Ibid.*

108 *Ibid.*

109 *Ibid.*

110 Map supplementary to Leeds Board of Health Report, 1833. Surveyed by Charles Fowler, Leeds, January 1833. Printed by Kemp and Sowerby, Leeds. Reproduced by kind permission of Leeds Local Studies Library.

111 *Leeds Intelligencer*, 14 June 1832.

112 Shapter, T, *The Cholera In Exeter In 1832*, (John Churchill, London and Adam Holden, Exeter, 1849), republished by S R Publishers Ltd, Wakefield and London, 1971.

113 Brewer, J, *An Account of the Cholera Morbus in the City Of Exeter*, printed for the author by E Woolmer and Co. [1833].

114 Shapter, (1971), pp. 142-43.

115 *Western Times*, 11 August 1832.

116 Shapter, (1971), pp. 144-45.

117 *Ibid*, pp. 145-46.

118 *Ibid*, p. 147.

119 *Ibid*, p. 149.

120 *Western Times*, 18 August 1832.

121 Shapter, (1971), p. 154.

122 *Ibid*, p. 160.

123 *Ibid*, p. 162.

124 *Ibid*, p. 148.

125 *Ibid*, pp. 163-68.

126 *Ibid*, pp. 171-72.

127 *Ibid*, p. 173.

128 *Ibid*, pp. 173-74.

129 Brewer, (1833), pp. 20-21.

130 Shapter, (1971), p. 174.

131 *Ibid*, p. 235.

132 *Ibid*, pp. 236-37.

133 *Ibid*, p. 236.

134 Brewer, (1833), p. 18.

135 Shapter, (1971), p. 237.

136 *Exeter Gazette*, 28 July 1832.

137 Shapter, (1971), p. 237.

138 Brewer, (1833), pp. 15-16; comprehensive overview in Shapter, (1971), pp. 179-84.

139 *Western Times*, 11 August 1832.

140 Shapter, (1971), p. 180.

141 *Western Times*, 4 August 1832.

142 *Ibid.*

143 *Western Times*, 18 August 1832.

144 *Ibid*, 25 August 1832.

145 Durey, M, *The Return of the Plague,* (1979), p. 168.
146 *Ibid.*
147 *Exeter Gazette*, 4 August 1832.
148 TNA, Privy Council Papers. PC 1/108.
149 *Bristol Gazette,* 9 August 1832.
150 *Felix Farley's Bristol Journal,* 11 August 1832.
151 *Ibid.*
152 *Ibid.*
153 *Bristol Gazette,* 16 August 1832.
154 TNA, Privy Council Papers. PC 1/108.
155 *Bristol Gazette,* 23 August 1832.
156 *Ibid.*
157 *Bristol Gazette,* 30 August 1832.
158 ERO, List of Fairs and Markets D/DDu 459 and Quarter Sessions Papers Q/SBd 6/1.
159 Durey, M, (1979), p. 158.
160 *Wheelers Manchester Chronicle*, 8 September 1832.
161 *Ibid.*
162 *Ibid.*
163 *The Times*, 5 September 1832.
164 *Ibid,* 6 September 1832.
165 *Ibid,* 8 September 1832.
166 The *Scotsman,* 5 September 1832.
167 *Manchester Weekly Times,* 12 September 1890.
168 *Ibid,* 19 September 1890.
169 *Ibid,* 26 September 1890.
170 *Ibid,* 3 October 1890.
171 *Manchester City News,* 24 December 1904.
172 *Liverpool Chronicle*, 2 June 1832.
173 MacRaild, D M, *Irish Migrants in Modern Britain 1750-1922,* (New York, 1999), pp. 51-52.
174 BPP, Report of the Poor Enquiry (Ireland) Commission; Appendix G, Report on the State of the Irish Poor in Great Britain, (1836); *see also:* Scully, G, The very pests of society: the Irish and 150 years of public health in England, *Clinical Medicine,* 2004, 4: 77-81.
175 Durey, M, (1979), p. 183.
176 *Ibid*, pp. 164-66.
177 *Liverpool Courier,* 13 June 1832.
178 *See:* Bold, A and Gittings, R, *The Book of Rotters,* (Edinburgh, 1985), pp. 36-40; Richardson, R, (London, 2001), pp. 131-58; for a more comprehensive and carefully researched account *see:* Bailey, B, *Burke And Hare - The Year Of The Ghouls,* (Mainstream Publishing, Edinburgh and London, 2002).
179 *Liverpool Journal*, 10 December 1831.
180 *Glasgow Courier,* 17 March 1832.
181 Richardson, (2001), p. 197.
182 *York Chronicle,* 24 November 1831.
183 *Liverpool Journal,* 31 December 1831.
184 Durey, M, (1979), pp. 181, 212; Bynum, W F, *Science and the Practice of Medicine in the Nineteenth Century,* (Cambridge, 1994), p. 75.
185 Rudé, G, (1995), p. 79.
186 *Ibid*, pp. 70-102; *see also:* Bailey, B, *The Luddite Rebellion*, (Strand, 1998).

[187] Royle, E, (2000), pp. 79-82.

[188] Hobsbawm, E and Rudé, G, (1969), p. 351.

[189] BPP XXXIV, (1833).

[190] *Glasgow Courier,* 17 March 1832.

[191] Cholera Or No Cholera - Tricks Of Some Governments, *Lancet,* 1831, 1:377.

[192] Royle, E, (2000), pp. 68-79; Fraser, D, The Agitation for Parliamentary Reform, In Ward, J T, (ed.), *Popular Movements c 1830 - 1850,* (London, 1970), pp. 31-53.

[193] *Liverpool Journal,* 5 November 1831.

[194] Currency Conversion web site: http://eh.net/hmit/ppower/

[195] Royle, E, (2000), p. 88.

[196] Gill, G, Burrell, S and Brown, J, (2001).

[197] Redfern, M, Keeling, J W and Powell, E, *The Royal Liverpool Children's Enquiry Report,* HMSO, (2001); *see also:* Bradbury, J, Consent for requirements for necropsy may change in the UK, *Lancet,* 1999, 354: 2055; Gill, G, Burrell, S and Brown, J, (2001).

[198] *See:* Dyer, C, Doctors' Arrogance Blamed for Retention of Children's Organs, *British Medical Journal,* (2000), 320, 1359; *also:* http://www.bristol-inquiry.org.uk

[199] Gill, G, Cholera and the fight for public health reform in mid-Victorian England, *The Historian,* 2000, 66: 10-16.

X. THE REVEREND SWING!

Clive Leivers

The parson was one of the common targets for Swing protesters. Hobsbawm and Rudé identified twelve cases out of 202, where the identified victim of an arson attack was a clergyman. In the case of anonymous threatening letters, nineteen of the victims were parsons.[1] FACHRS researchers identified nearly ninety incidents where the victims were clergymen; these covered instances of the full range of Swing protest: arson attacks; threatening letters; machine-breaking; wage riots; and, particularly directed at the Anglican minister, tithe riots (Table X.I).

TABLE X.I
Offences involving clergymen[2]

Offence	No.
Attempted incendiarism	2
Incendiarism	18
Machine-breaking	6
Anon. threatening letters	11
Tithe riots	23
Assaults	4
Wage riots	8
Threats	1
Robberies	11
Miscellaneous (e.g. damage to property)	4

These incidents occurred in seventeen English counties, with the majority taking place in the areas where Swing protest was rife - from Dorset and Hampshire, through Sussex and Kent into East Anglia. Twenty-three Norfolk parsons were the targets of Swing incidents, almost 30% of the national total involving clergymen. This geographical concentration supports the statement by Hobsbawm and Rudé that 'the tithe and wage riots were centred mainly south and south-east of Norwich'.[3]

There was a growing breach between the labouring classes and the established clergy during the century preceding the Swing years. This was partly due to the identification of clergy with the local 'establishment', who were involved in action to maintain the social *status quo* - the 'squarson' figure embodying this attitude - and to the increase in the number of clergymen appointed as magistrates, so placing them in an official role of law enforcers. By 1832 twenty-two per cent of magistrates were clergymen, with even greater proportions found in Lincolnshire, Cambridgeshire and Bedfordshire.[4] It was, therefore, not surprising that the parson was identified as one of the local unpopular figures who became protest targets.

Added to this general antipathy was the specific concern over tithes; it was for the tithe-consuming clergy that the especial hatred of the rural community was reserved - the Swing rioters felt that the minister's tithe income was at the expense of farming profits and thus a factor in keeping their wages at a low level. As a result of Swing protests, tithes were reduced in several areas, often after some collaboration between farmers and their labourers.[5]

Typical of these protests was a letter sent from Bridport to the Rev. Dr Rudge, rector of Hawkchurch in Dorset, in December 1830, that read:

> 'Wrote this to you to tell you if you don't loer your tythes and all your
> prmies shall be burnt on the 20 of som month in a short time, for we
> poor dresstress solls will no suffer no longer for your passons and
> landholders, and Mr Barnes shall be destroyed likewise, from your
> friend in a short time
> Swing'[6]

At Haddiscoe in Norfolk, the Reverend Elliston ultimately agreed to reduce the tithes after being locked in a room at the Crown Inn, where he had gone to receive his tithes. The Reverend Boycott, rector of Burgh, was visited by a deputation of labourers, who asked him to reduce the tithes to enable their employers to increase wages; he was assured by the farmers that any reduction would be passed on to their work force.[7]

But the recent FACHRS research has identified one unique case, where a clergyman of the established church was not the target, but was accused as being the instigator of a Swing protest.

On 1 February 1831, John Coke, the High Sheriff of Nottinghamshire (Illustration X.a), received a threatening letter at his home in Mansfield Woodhouse. The letter dated the previous day and sent from Mansfield, read:

> 'Sir, If you do not abandon your villainous attempt upon advancing the
> price of coals here, your house and every thing belonging to you shall
> be burned to the ground.
> Yours, Swing
> No further notice to be given'

Nottinghamshire had a number of incidents during the Swing years of 1830-1832, which appeared to stem from agricultural unrest. For example, at the end of December 1830, Job Severn, a farmer at Strelley, received a letter directing him to destroy his threshing machine. In October 1831 a haystack belonging to the rector of Plumtree was set on fire.[8]

The grievance behind the letter sent to Coke was, however, obviously specific to the town of Mansfield, with the Swing signature one example of the copy-cat attachment of the appellation to any and every kind of protest during the time when the local and national press carried almost weekly reports of the machine-breaking and arson, which were attributed to Captain Swing and his followers.

The clergyman concerned was the Reverend William Bowerbank, aged about sixty, who was headmaster of the Free Grammar School in Mansfield and curate in the neighbouring parish of Pleasley, just across the Derbyshire border.

Suspicion fell on Bowerbank at an early stage for, by 11 February, he had been committed to the county gaol in Nottingham to await his trial at the forthcoming assizes, after 'a patient examination' by three local magistrates, including the Duke of Portland. Recognising his social position, he was given apartments in the house of the gaol governor, where he was attended by one of his daughters, who accompanied him to prison.[9]

Illustration X.a. John Coke, High Sheriff of Nottinghamshire

The grievance behind the threat to John Coke was a proposal by the trustees of the turnpike road, from Mansfield to Alfreton (in Derbyshire), to erect another toll bar along the route near the outskirts of Mansfield, whose inhabitants feared that this would raise the cost of coal that was carried into the town along the road. A public meeting was held in the town on 20 January 1831 to encourage opposition to the proposal, and it was agreed that a deputation from the town should attend the next trustees' meeting. Coke was one of the trustees, and his family had major interest in collieries in and around the Erewash Valley along the Nottinghamshire/Derbyshire boundary, particularly the Pinxton colliery. Coke also had a significant interest in the Mansfield and Pinxton Railway, which had opened in 1819 and which, within five years of its opening, was delivering almost 35,000 tons of coal and coke to Mansfield.[10] Coal traffic on the turnpike was likely to be much below this figure and, thus, any additional tolls would arguably have had only a marginal effect on the price of coal in the town. Perhaps Coke was singled out to receive the threat in view of his official position in the county and because his home at Debdale, a mile and a half from Mansfield, was well known to the anonymous correspondent. But the writer of the letter must surely have expected that Coke would not ignore the letter and would attempt to discover and prosecute the perpetrator.

Bowerbank was reportedly very active on the side of the opposition and he made many extremely indiscreet speeches and remarks. On the day the letter was written, he had attended the meeting at Sutton in Ashfield, presumably as a member of the Mansfield delegation, in the hope of being elected a trustee of the turnpike. But at his trial he denied having had any personal dealings with Coke at any time, nor any reason to bear malice towards him. In the event, no decisions were taken at that meeting, and a further meeting was scheduled for the end of February to discuss the proposal further.[11]

However, the two men almost certainly moved in the same social circles in the Nottinghamshire town where Bowerbank had lived for the past thirty-six years. He had been appointed as headmaster of the free grammar school, founded in the reign of Elizabeth I, in 1794, having previously conducted the Classical Department at Winthorpe Academy, near Newark on Trent. The school was open to boys from the town without charge for tuition, apart from a small entrance fee, no age requirement for admission, nor separate classes. At the time of his appointment there was only one boy in the upper school.[12]

Advertising for pupils in December that year, he assured the public that the utmost care and attention shall be exerted on behalf of the religious and moral conduct of his pupils, as well as the conduct of their education (Illustration X.b). Boarding fees, together with instruction in Latin and English were sixteen guineas per year; writing and accounts could be taught at seven shillings a quarter, for a guinea a quarter the pupils could be taught dancing. French tuition cost a little more at £1 11s 6d a quarter, and the cost of washing was £1 10s 0d a year.[13]

These terms apparently attracted an increase in the number of pupils, both boarders and day boys; at one stage there were thirty boys under the tuition of the assistant master. However, by 1818, Bowerbank seemed to have abandoned taking boarders. This was attributed to Mansfield being more a manufacturing place than it formerly was, with little demand for classical learning, which had 'a pernicious effect upon the morals and manners of the inhabitants'. Whilst both Bowerbank and his second master were stated to be of highly respectable character, neither of them were graduates. Bowerbank then had no scholars and his assistant only a few, and those primarily to receive but an English education.[14]

In 1820 the headmaster's salary was seventy pounds per year, with the usher receiving half that amount. These fixed salaries were supplemented by a share of rental income from property owned by the school trustees, with the head receiving two-thirds and the usher a third; the historian of the school has estimated that this rental income added around one hundred and fifteen pounds per annum to the headmaster's income during the final years of

Bowerbank's tenure. Further income came from fee-paying pupils, with the second master usually better placed to augment his income than was the headmaster, and this was one of the underlying causes of the frequent friction between them. This reliance on income from private pupils was said to be one of the reasons for the complaints about the poor standard of tuition by the parents of the 'free' pupils.[15]

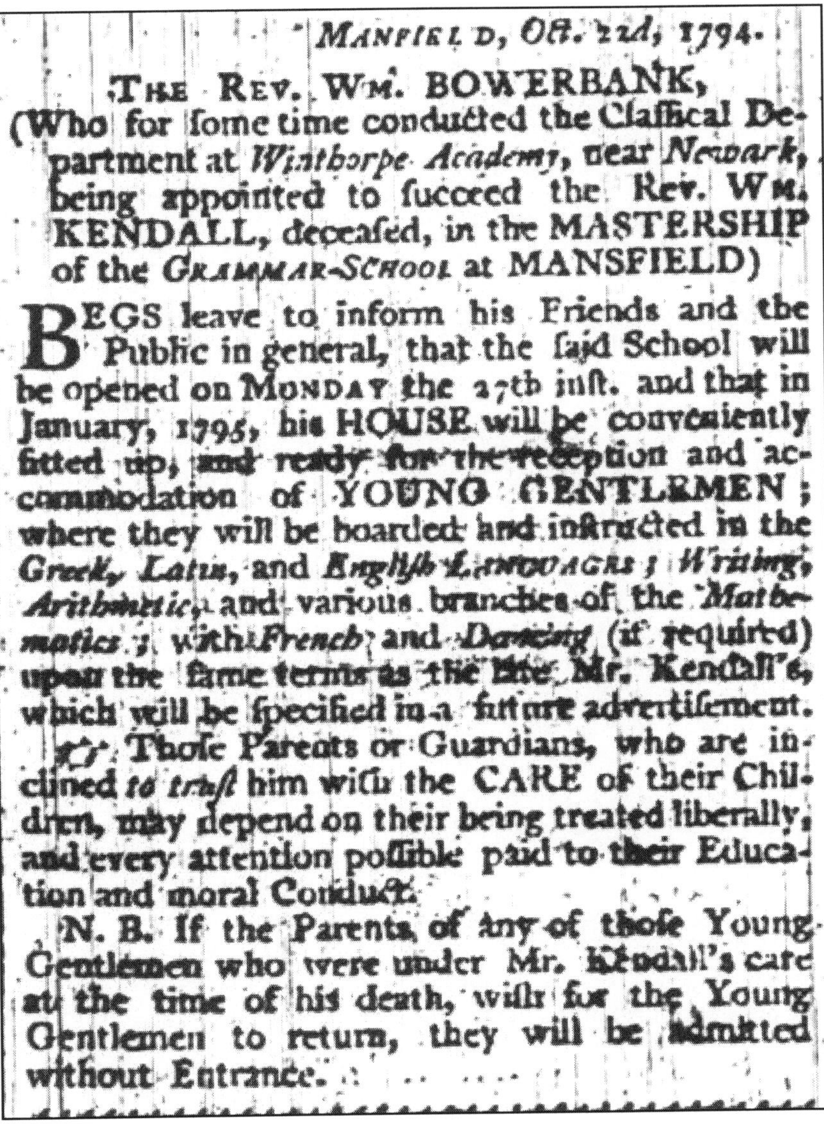

MANSFIELD, Oct. 22d, 1794.

THE REV. WM. BOWERBANK,

(Who for some time conducted the Classical Department at *Winthorpe Academy*, near *Newark*, being appointed to succeed the Rev. WM. KENDALL, deceased, in the MASTERSHIP of the *GRAMMAR-SCHOOL* at MANSFIELD)

BEGS leave to inform his Friends and the Public in general, that the said School will be opened on MONDAY the 27th inst. and that in January, 1795, his HOUSE will be conveniently fitted up, and ready for the reception and accommodation of YOUNG GENTLEMEN; where they will be boarded and instructed in the *Greek*, *Latin*, and *English* LANGUAGES; *Writing*, *Arithmetic*, and various branches of the *Mathematics*; with *French* and *Dancing* (if required) upon the same terms as the late Mr. Kendall's, which will be specified in a future advertisement.

☞ Those Parents or Guardians, who are inclined *to trust* him with the CARE of their Children, may depend on their being treated liberally, and every attention possible paid to their Education and moral Conduct.

N. B. If the Parents of any of those Young Gentlemen who were under Mr. Kendall's care at the time of his death, wish for the Young Gentlemen to return, they will be admitted without Entrance.

Illustration X.b. Reverend William Bowerbank's advertisement for Mansfield Grammar School, 1794

When the Parliamentary Commission into Charities for the Education of the Poor reported in 1834, they referred to the neglected condition of the school, which in 1821 had been the subject of complaint by the local inhabitants, with a formal reprimand given by the Governors to the under-master, the Rev. William Goodacre, appointed in 1812. The Commissioners concluded that the establishment was utterly useless to the town. In 1830 Goodacre was persuaded to resign his office by the school governors, after repeated complaints about his neglect and inattention.[16]

Goodacre himself recorded the pressures imposed by his three clerical appointments at Mansfield Woodhouse, Skegby and Sutton in Ashfield in a poem penned in 1825. After breakfasting at 8.30 he left home for Mansfield Woodhouse 'where began the labours of this toilsome day'. He inspected the Sunday Schools, preached in the church at 10.30, and after seeing four couples about their weddings and churching a woman, left for Skegby at 12.30. There he gave the Eucharist to a sick parishioner, led a service and then went on to Sutton arriving at 3 o'clock. After two baptisms, he preached at service, published seven banns and then baptised two more children. He then returned to Mansfield Woodhouse to conduct a burial, conducted evening service and performed two private baptisms. He paid a sick call, and then 'my duty done with joy I found' he was provided with a meal, which 'dinner or my supper call' by a friend. He finally returned home and, at midnight, his 'day's labours' ended, the 'past fatigue secures my rest'. This, presumably, was a typical Sunday but the responsibilities for three parishes would place considerable demands on a conscientious clergyman during the rest of the week, and one can readily see how little time Goodacre might have had to devote to his pupils at the grammar school.[17]

Goodacre was to be one of the principal prosecution witnesses at the trial of Bowerbank, and it seems clear that relationships between the two men and the reputation of the school left a great deal to be desired in the years leading up to the writing of the letter. This breakdown in the relationship between headmaster and usher was apparently no new feature at the school, with Bowerbank and Goodacre continuing the perennial struggle regarding the allocation of duties.[18]

Bowerbank's curacy at Pleasley had lasted for twenty-five years and, on the evidence of the parish registers, appeared to have ended in 1820; he also had a living in Lincolnshire. He was also a director of the local savings bank, 'in which institution he took a great interest [...] [and] was very busy with the affairs of the town'.[19]

By the time Bowerbank appeared before the assize court, the proposal for the additional tollgate had been abandoned. The turnpike trustees had faced opposition from local magnates, such as the Dukes of Devonshire and Portland, as well as the people of Mansfield, and it was probably the arguments of the landowners that had the major impact on the decision not to proceed.

The proceedings at the assizes were reported in great detail by the local press and the following account is based mainly on the reports in the *Nottingham Journal* and *Nottingham and Newark Mercury*, which appeared in the editions of 19 March 1831.

The prosecution case essentially rested on the identification of the handwriting in the letter as that of Bowerbank, although counsel for the prosecution also pointed out that the phrasing of the letter indicated that someone of no common education had written it. From the evidence given, it appeared that Coke had shown the letter on the day of receipt to William Woodcock, a Mansfield solicitor, who was also an assistant master at the grammar school. Woodcock stated that he initially recognised Bowerbank's handwriting from the address and his belief was confirmed when reading the contents. He had then shown the letter to the Reverend Goodacre, who shared his view as to the attribution of the letter to Bowerbank. Coke had also taken the letter to the postmaster at Mansfield, William Holt, who immediately judged it to be in the prisoner's hand, on the basis of Bowerbank having sent newspapers through his office to a son in Jamaica.

Other prosecution witnesses included: the national schoolmaster at Kirkby in Ashfield, who had also taught at Bowerbank's school for many years; Robert Barker, a Mansfield surgeon, who had known the defendant for seventeen or eighteen years; and a local Sunday-school teacher. All these witnesses claimed familiarity with Bowerbank's handwriting and considered the letter to be in his hand, though a little disguised.

The most revealing evidence, however, came from two clergymen - the aforesaid William Goodacre and the Reverend John Unwin, incumbent of Langar in south Nottinghamshire. Their evidence, whilst supporting the identification of the handwriting, was revealing in the airing of what seemed to be Bowerbank's disputatious and intriguing nature. This had led, certainly as far as Goodacre was concerned, to what can almost be described as a clerical and academic feud.

Unwin, now aged thirty-three, had been a pupil at the grammar school for some seven years from about the age of eighteen. He was a native of Pleasley, the village where Bowerbank was curate, and had been in very humble circumstances, employed briefly as a writer in a lawyer's office before beginning his studies at the grammar school. His tuition at the school was free and he mainly studied under Goodacre. On being ordained, he became curate to Goodacre (Illustration X.c) and was then presented to his present living at Langar by Bowerbank. From the evidence of the parish registers, this appeared to be at the beginning of 1825. Included in the terms of the presentment was an agreement that he would resign the living when Bowerbank's son came of age, for whom the next presentation had been bought. He had signed a letter of resignation, which the Archbishop of York had refused to accept. There had been a dispute with Bowerbank about dilapidations, but Unwin felt no anger against him; he had had no correspondence with the defendant for the past three years.

Bowerbank had also interfered with the distribution of a charity in the parish; he received the endowment dividends and had retained the half of the proceeds that should have been passed on to the rector (Unwin). It was only after a letter from the Commissioners that Bowerbank released the overdue monies.[20]

Unwin resigned his benefice in 1834 (he was not succeeded by Bowerbank junior!) and, after living in poverty, was found dead in the Nottingham canal three years later.[21]

Goodacre had been assistant curate at Skegby and Mansfield Woodhouse from 1812. In 1820 he had been appointed perpetual curate for the two parishes and became incumbent at Sutton in Ashfield.[22] In his evidence he stated that he had been under-master at the school for fourteen years until his resignation the previous summer, and had known Bowerbank for eighteen or nineteen years. From the time of his presentation to his incumbency Bowerbank had never spoken to him, and they had had no communication of any kind for the last three or four years. This complete failure in communication between the two chief masters over a prolonged period had clearly been a major contributory factor behind the school's lack of success.

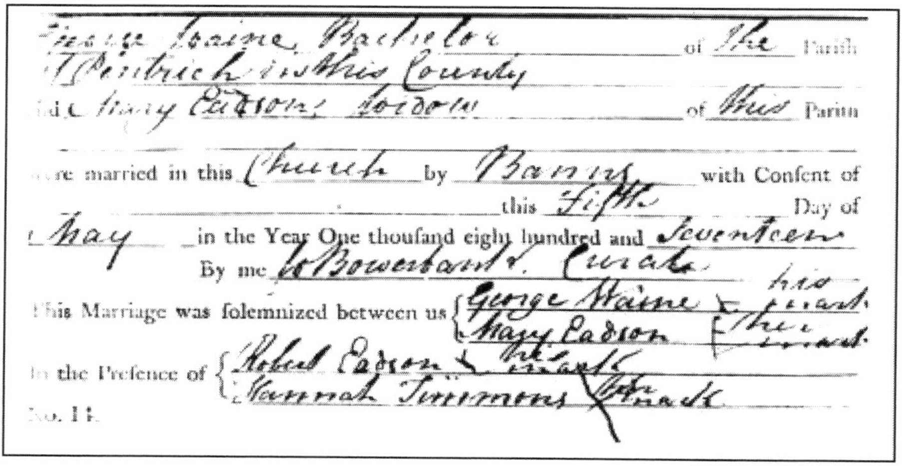
George Waine Bachelor of the Parish
of Pentrich in this County
and Mary Eadson Widow of this Parish
were married in this Church by Banns with Confent of
this Fifth Day of
May in the Year One thoufand eight hundred and Seventeen
By me J Bowerbank Curate
This Marriage was folemnized between us { George Waine his mark / Mary Eadson her mark
In the Prefence of { Robert Eadson his mark / Hannah Timmons her mark
No. 11.

Illustration X.c. Extract from Pleasley parish register 1817 showing Bowerbank as curate

Goodacre went on to say that he had received many personal offences from Bowerbank. He admitted that he might have threatened that he could have had Bowerbank removed from his Lincolnshire living. (Bowerbank had been presented as rector of Salmonby, near Horncastle in 1827.)[23]

Within the past four months he had received a letter signed Swing, which he had assumed came from Bowerbank, who was well known as an anonymous-letter writer. The subject of the letter was trifling. Another witness remarked that it advised Goodacre to be more friendly to the soap boilers and the text was given in the issue of the *Nottingham Journal*, which contained the trial report:

> Sur - I heres as ow u does not use sope wen u washes uresen. if u doant
> curage that trad u will here moar from *Swing*
> To Mr Godaker, Sutton in Hashfield, Nots

It seems quite clear that this was written as some kind of joke with its obvious misspellings and use of local dialect, and Goodacre admitted that he had since been informed that the letter had indeed been written by some pupils at the school run by Mr Cursham, the Vicar of Mansfield. At the trial one of the pupils involved gave evidence to confirm this.

All this suggests that Goodacre was acutely sensitive about the perceived insults and ill usage he had suffered at the hands of Bowerbank, almost to the point of paranoia in attributing any further slurs on his reputation to his *bête noire*. It is almost impossible to untangle the rights and wrongs of this dispute, but his parishioners in Sutton reputedly held Goodacre in high regard. A memorial tablet in the parish church pays tribute to his 'long and useful service' over thirty-nine years and a history of that town written about forty-five years after his death, in 1859, argues that he did more hard work for the parish than any other recent incumbent.[24]

Bowerbank had prepared a written statement of defence, which was read out to the court. He argued that no motive could be attributed to him that would indicate his involvement with the sending of the letter. He had not at any time had any dealings or intercourse with Coke, nor did he have the 'slightest reason to entertain any feeling of ill will towards him [...] [n]ever having at any time entertained one hostile or unchristian thought towards him'. The argument over the toll-gate was a matter of little moment to him since he was totally unconnected with all trade and manufacture, and was no more interested than any other person in the affair. His assertions on this score sit uneasily with reports that he was one of the leading opponents of the proposal and had sought to be elected as a turnpike trustee, but they apparently went unchallenged.

His personal circumstances were easy, if not affluent, and his duties at the school and as a clergyman fully occupied his time. (This despite the lack of pupils at the school!) During the evenings he retired 'to the bosom of my family, where the greater part of my leisure hours is spent and where my chief happiness this side of the grave is centred'. He pointed to his position in society as headmaster and clergyman; in the latter role, as well as his own curacy, he had officiated at more than thirty churches in Nottinghamshire and neighbouring counties, this surely suggested the good reputation in which he was held by fellow members of the cloth. He had a devoted wife and four 'dutiful and affectionate daughters, the pride of my life and the solace of my declining years'. Was it likely that he should put his character, family and personal liberty at risk through such an action?

He then turned to the evidence given by the prosecution witnesses. He pointed to the difficulty in the identification of handwriting, which was known to change over time. The value of the evidence given by Woodcock, his former attorney, must surely be doubtful; they had not been in contact for eighteen years, during which time the witness had received no letter from Bowerbank nor seen him write.

As regards the evidence given by Goodacre, he urged that it be treated with great caution coming as it did from a person who had admitted 'living on bad terms with me', a fact that was 'notorious to the whole neighbourhood'. A defence witness would assert that Goodacre had indeed threatened to interfere with Bowerbank's living in Lincolnshire and even to employ personal violence against him. Goodacre could then not be regarded as a fair and impartial witness, this was surely evident from his attributing the letter he had received to Bowerbank, and this attribution proved the inability of the witness to identify his (Bowerbank's) handwriting.

He had educated Unwin gratuitously and treated him with all kindness; he did not therefore envy his former pupil's feelings on appearing as a prosecution witness. No mention was made of the dispute between them!

He would call witnesses of unimpeachable credit and character, who knew his handwriting well, to rebut the evidence given for the prosecution; other witnesses would show that he could not have posted the letter in question. He was confident that as a result the jury would:

> procure me an honourable acquittal and restore me to the domestic comforts of my family.

The defence witnesses called to give evidence on handwriting were: John Andrews, a Mansfield draper and former scholar at the school; John Sellars, the parish clerk of Mansfield who delivered the rental income to Bowerbank and obtained signed receipts for the same; Benjamin Richards of Alfreton, an attorney; John Brown, a churchwarden at Mansfield; the Rev. John Peatfield, curate to Goodacre, who also confirmed that the prisoner and Goodacre were at variance; and Mr Flower, the defendant's present solicitor.

John Greaves, a pupil at the school run by Dr Cursham, the vicar of Mansfield, admitted that he had posted the anonymous letter to Goodacre, which had been written by a fellow pupil. He was severely reprimanded by the court for writing impertinent letters to a clergyman!

A series of witnesses then gave evidence to show that Bowerbank had been fully occupied during the time when the postmaster had stated the letter had been received at the post office (between noon and 10 pm on 31 January). His servant confirmed that Bowerbank had attended the trustees' meeting at Sutton on the day in question in the company of Mr Andrews and did not return home until 4 pm. He then remained at home in slippers and gown, and the witness locked up at 9.30. He had not seen his master leave the house after his return home. Andrews confirmed the attendance at Sutton; he had dined with Bowerbank and his family, staying with the defendant until 6 pm. A servant girl and all four of the Bowerbank daughters gave corroborative evidence that the defendant could not have been absent from the house long enough to post the letter without their knowledge.

After a trial lasting from 11 am to 7 pm, Bowerbank was found not guilty, a verdict received with general satisfaction, and which excited a burst of applause from every part of the court.

But the case continued to have repercussions. In the following August Bowerbank charged one of the prosecution witnesses, Robert Barber the Mansfield surgeon, with assault. Barber was found guilty and fined five pounds.[25]

These various proceedings clearly did little for the reputation of Bowerbank or the grammar school. In March 1832 there was only one pupil at the school, and in April of that year Bowerbank resigned his headmastership. The newspaper report stated that the resignation was at the behest of the Parliamentary Commissioners. The editor subsequently received a letter, believed to have come from Bowerbank, which denied any pressure from the Commissioners and asserted that 'an amicable remunerating agreement' had been reached with the governors. This brought a rejoinder from the author of the original report, who claimed that the Commissioners had indeed recommended Bowerbank's resignation, and had suggested proceedings to compel this step if he did not leave voluntarily. This seems to have been correct, for the Commissioners noted in their report that the resignation had obviated the need for them to make 'further observation' on the deplorable state of the school.[26]

With this account of what seems to have been a typical Bowerbank argument, the reverend gentleman leaves the Nottinghamshire scene. He appears to have retired to his Lincolnshire living with something of a golden handshake from the doubtless relieved governors of the grammar school. He was buried at Salmonby in November 1840 aged seventy. One wonders what his feelings were when he learned of the apparent suicide of his one-time protégé, Unwin; it seems unlikely that there would have been any pangs of remorse over his actions, which had caused Unwin so much trouble during his time at Langar.

This whole saga provides an insight into small town 'politics' in the early 19th century and Bowerbank's scheming as regards his colleagues at the grammar school, and his fellow clergymen are reminiscent of the worst clerical manipulations portrayed in Trollope's *Barchester Chronicles*.

It has little significance in the overview of the Swing years, being completely unrelated to the fundamental causes of that unrest. But it does perhaps indicate the influential role of the provincial press during the period in disseminating the exploits of Swing in all their various ramifications - with the result that those with any kind of grievance (and even schoolboys playing jokes) jumped on the bandwagon and used the *nom de plume* for their own ends.

NOTES

1   Hobsbawm, E J and Rudé, G, *Captain Swing*, (Lawrence & Wishart, London, 1969), p. 229.
2   FACHRS Swing Project.
3   Hobsbawm and Rudé, p. 157.
4   Evans, E J, *The Contentious Tithe: the tithe problem and English agriculture, 1750 to 1850*, (Routledge and Kegan Paul, 1976), p. 11.
5   Thompson, E P, *The Making of the English Working Class,* (Penguin, London, 1988), p. 257; Mingay, G E, *Land and Society in England 1750- 1980*, (Longman, London, 1994), p. 79; Hobsbawm and Rudé, p. 230.
6   *Derby Mercury,* 29 December 1830 (from *Dorset Chronicle*).
7   Hobsbawm and Rudé, p. 158.
8   *Nottingham and Newark Mercury,* 24 December 1830; 5 November 1831.
9   *Ibid,* 12 February 1831.
10 Vanags, J, *The Mansfield and Pinxton Railway,* (Old Mansfield Society, 2000), p. 25.
11 Buxton, A S, *Mansfield 100 Years Ago,* (Willman, Mansfield, 1932), p. 85.
12 Brettle, I, *History of Queen Elizabeth's Grammar School,* (Mansfield, 1961), p. 51; VCH - *Nottinghamshire,* Vol. ii, p. 246.
13 *Nottingham Journal,* 6 December 1794.
14 VCH, p. 248.
15 Brettle, pp. 49-51.
16 VCH, p. 248.
17 Lindley, L, *History of Sutton in Ashfield,* (Sutton, 1907), pp. 10-11.

18 Brettle, p. 49.
19 Buxton, p. 84.
20 BPP, Report of the Commissioners appointed to Inquire into Charities for the Education of the
    Poor, XXV (1834), p. 377.
21 Local Studies Library, Nottingham, Langar folder, unattributed newspaper cutting 26 March
    1949.
22 Thoroton Society Record Series XV, Clergy of Central Nottinghamshire.
23 Lincolnshire Archives, PD 183/64.
24 Lindley, pp. 9-10.
25 *Nottingham Journal*, 6 August 1831.
26 *Nottingham and Newark Mercury,* 12 May 1832; VCH, p. 248.

XI. TRANSPORTATION OF PRISONERS AND THE SETTLING OF SYDNEY COVE

Reay Ferguson

At 3 am on the morning of 13 May 1787 eleven ships sailed from Portsmouth bound for an unknown land, carrying a total of 1,398 men, women and children. Amongst those on board were 192 women prisoners, aged from thirteen to eighty-six years of age, plus twenty-seven children of women convicts and naval personnel (Table XI.I).

TABLE XI.I
Age in years of women sentenced and transported in First Fleet

Age	No. of women	Age	No. of women
13 or under	2	30	3
15	2	31	3
16	1	32	6
17	2	33	4
18	4	34	0
19	1	35	2
20	2	36	3
21	4	37	1
22	8	38	1
23	10	39	1
24	6	43	1
25	9	46	1
26	5	47	1
27	3	48	1
28	8	55	1
29	7	86	1

The crimes committed by the women prisoners ranged from theft, embezzlement, perjury, stealing livestock, highway robbery and burglary. The theft of goods up to the value of forty shillings meant being given a sentence of seven years' transportation and for goods over that value a sentence of fourteen years' transportation, or death if violence was involved. Occasionally death sentences were commuted to fourteen years' transportation, depending on the circumstances of the crime and on the whim of the Court.

Many of the women had been in prison for some time and some had given birth there. Prisoners were dependent on warders selling them food or friends providing for them. They lived in extremely unhygienic surroundings, as about half of the jails were privately owned and run for profit, therefore little expense was available for cleaning. No attempt was made to segregate men and women and so in one cell could be a mixture of murderers, thieves, rapists and debtors.

John Howard, the Quaker campaigner for prison reform, wrote a report for the Government entitled *The State of Prisons in England and Wales* hoping to effect some reform of the law and encourage the building of new jails.[1] The Government of the day, however, had other plans and the present disposition of criminals appeared to them to be the solution for overflowing cells.

Transportation was not a new idea, since it dated back to Elizabethan times when a law of 1597 'An Acte of Punishment of Rogues, Vagabonds and Sturdy Beggars' commuted death sentences to shipment for work on American plantations.[2]

The introduction of machinery on farms and in industry meant loss of work and often homes. Many were travelling about looking for employment and London was becoming very overcrowded. To add to this influx were Irish immigrants, also looking for work and who had crossed the sea to England and settled in London. Life for them was miserable, living amongst disease, crime, drunkenness and prostitution, and sporadic outbursts of violence and riots broke out, alarming citizens who urged for action to be taken to cut the numbers of criminals on the streets.

Drinking in order to forget the harshness of life, or selling sexual favours in order to eat, were not crimes in themselves but appalled the super-righteous and often duplicitous morality of the gentry, who pressed for the banishment of these street people. Transportation appeared to be the best way to rid the country of dissenters, trouble makers and vagabonds, and had provided the Government with a method of reducing the cost of maintaining jails and the old hulks of ships used as prisons.

This was the antithesis of the picture of Georgian England of the period with elegant town houses, garden squares, beautiful silver and leisurely lifestyle. The gulf between east and west was great. Whilst west London enjoyed life in pleasurable surroundings, east London had slums, sewers running into open drains and nowhere to bury the dead except in large open pits!

Punishment at the time consisted of methods other than transportation, namely whipping, branding, burning and mutilation, such as slitting nostrils or cutting off ears or a trip to the gallows. No distinction there between men and women. This was a picture of life in London when the First Fleet sailed for *Terra Australis*.

Convicts were brought to Plymouth and Portsmouth by wagon from all over the country (Table XI.II), many of them chained, and taken on board. About two months before sailing typhus broke out, but was contained, and did not spread through the fleet. Because of the bad publicity during this outbreak, the contractor appointed to victual the ships, Duncan Campbell, found he had to provide ample beef and vegetables, instead of his usual practice of skimping on food for the prisoners.

TABLE XI.II
Place of sentencing of convicts on the First Fleet

Old Bailey	106	Worcester	8	Winchester	3	New Sarum	3	Derby	2
Maidstone	2	Wigan	1	Cambridge	1	Mold	1	York	1
Lancaster	1	Surrey	2	Gloucester	3	Liverpool	1	Wells	1
Shrewsbury	4	Lincoln	4	Exeter	7	Middlesex	2		
Taunton	3	Bristol	4	Durham	1	Cheshire	1		
Manchester	5	Newcastle upon Tyne		1		St Edmonds	1		
Thetford	1	Kingston upon Thames		7		Unknown	1		

Many of the women prisoners were scantily clad, shivering from cold and rain, and some were ill from venereal disease because of their lifestyle. Two of the prostitutes were mentioned by name by the magistrate when being sentenced. Mary Allan was described as 'an unfortunate girl' and Ann Mather as 'a poor, unhappy woman of the town'. Conditions on board were extremely crowded, with four women sharing a wooden slatted shelf with two other shelves above and alongside. The women were confined below decks unless working outside on deck (Illlustration XI.a).

Illustration XI.a. Bunks holding three or four women on each platform, three storeys' high

Transportation of women has been described as 'for the comfort of the seamen' and many cohabited, either voluntarily or not, in order to escape the conditions below decks. While some of the girls had been working as prostitutes, many had been working girls or married women raising a family, who had succumbed to the temptation to steal (Table XI.III). There are names of women on the shipping lists with no history attached and one can assume that they had either been taken off the ships at the last moment because of illness or advanced pregnancy, or had died. On that first voyage twenty-three people died including two children.

The ships had to sail with the prevailing winds and at times were becalmed, but eventually anchored in Rio de Janeiro for repairs to the vessels and to take on supplies. This was a welcome break for crew and prisoners alike, giving them fresh food and some fresh air. Two seamen were put ashore in order to return to England and another seaman deserted his ship. The other stop on the voyage was in South Africa, again to do repairs and stock up not only with food but also with animals to use as the foundation stock for farms when the Fleet reached its destination. The ships were subjected to many storms on the crossing from Rio de Janeiro to Cape Town, the journey taking two months eight days, and sailing 3,300 miles. From there to Botany Bay was another 6,500 miles, which took three months seven days to complete.[3]

TABLE XI.III
Occupations of women transported in the First Fleet

Servant	61	Milliner	3
Hawker	9	No occupation	16
Dealer	3	Book stitcher	1
Lace maker	2	Mantua maker	6
Tambour maker	1	Needlewoman	7
Glove maker	1	Stay maker	1
Show binder	1	Clog maker	1
Pin header	1	Furrier	1
Watch-chain maker	1	Nurse	1
Artificial-flower maker	1		

118 women listed occupations and 73 were unknown, possibly housewives or prostitutes.

On arrival in Botany Bay, Commander Phillip discovered the scanty soil was of poor quality and unsuitable for cultivation, and also a source of drinking water was hard to find. The Aboriginal tribe in the area was decidedly unfriendly and did their best to drive out the foreigners. It was decided to explore further north, where eventually safe anchorage at Sydney Cove was found, which was large enough to take all the ships in the Fleet (Illustration XI.b).

During the first weeks in Sydney Cove the male prisoners were put to clearing undergrowth and putting up huts and tents using whatever skills they had. At the time, it was discovered that crushed shells mixed with water held the mud bricks together!

Illustration XI.b. Drawing of Sydney Cove, 1788

The women prisoners were confined to the ships until sufficient accommodation had been built or tents made ready before they were allowed to disembark. Waiting on shore were men eager to have wives or servants. The authorities were equally eager to hand the women over in order to save the expense of clothing and feeding them. If a woman agreed to live with or marry a man, then the responsibility for her upkeep and behaviour transferred to the husband from the authorities. Should she agree to being a servant, the same responsibility was given to her master, although he could return her to the Governor should she swear at him, be lazy, drunk or refuse to work, or sexually misbehave, or refuse him her bed! The woman would then be punished, probably by being jailed on a diet of bread and water. One of the first buildings to be erected was the Female Factory, where women were kept until hired out or given in marriage or brought back for punishment.

Flogging was common and punishment harsh and swift. A prisoner could be in court one day, sentenced the next and flogged or hanged the following day! Women were seldom hanged and few flogged, but they had their hair cut off as a punishment. A sentence of twenty-five lashes was common but could kill, and many sentences handed out were 200 lashes. These were administered in stages, the flogging being stopped when ordered by the doctor, and then resumed a few days later. These lashes were administered with the prisoner tied to an A-frame and continued until the requisite number of lashes had been given.

Frequently women were returned to the Female Factory because of pregnancy, often due to their master's attentions, to await the birth of the child, who was allowed to stay with the mother until weaned, and then removed and put into the Orphan School and the woman hired out again. The only way for the woman to have her children back was to marry and have a husband willing to take responsibility for the child, or to wait until her sentence was served.

Prior to embarkation women were advised to say they were single, as this gave them the opportunity to find a partner and eventually have children in their new homeland. Since common-law marriage was quite usual this did not create problems. Women who had been married in Church were advised to do likewise, although in rare instances husband and wife were both transported and occasionally able to get back together again on release.

An interesting fact is that the children born in the colony grew up to be remarkably honest and law abiding. The majority of women seemed to relish the second chance they had been given and made something of their lives after release.

On completion of sentence, both male and female prisoners were given the opportunity of applying for an acre of land and a convict to help develop it. It was possible to ask that the convict be husband or wife, and for some this was a chance to be independent, growing enough food for their own needs and having some left over to sell to the Government.

Many of the male prisoners were allocated positions of authority in the developing colony, in order to create jobs and build up the economy of the country. This, in turn, allowed boys from the orphan school to be apprenticed and learn a trade. One of the prisoners, George Howe, who had been a printer before transportation, was appointed by the Governor in 1803 to set up an old printing press in order to edit and print a newspaper, and so the *Sydney Gazette and New South Wales Advertiser* was born. Howe received no pay and was subject to censorship by the Government. The newspaper sold for six pence a copy and was produced weekly. Copies of that paper give a fascinating insight into early life in Sydney Cove.

Everyone had to adapt to life in a country where there are more insects and animals with lethal bites than anywhere in the world. Many died from wounds but also from sicknesses, such as malaria and cholera. The local Aboriginal tribe, the Carigees, fought the incomers and harassed them, but they also fell victim to diseases brought by the sailors, and within a few years their tribe had been decimated.

Starvation was the greatest peril for a time. Promised supplies failed to arrive from Britain and the poor soil made it difficult to grow enough food. A search had to be made for arable land in order to feed the colony. Governor Phillip took a search party up the peninsula to the north and discovered suitable land up the Hawkesbury River, and, by 1789, Hawkesbury farms were producing food and shipping it to Sydney Cove. In time, other industries sprang up, such as timber felling, shingle cutting, fishing and mining. However, Hawkesbury district also became the home of smugglers, illegal distillers and escapees!

West to Parramatta produced good farming land and barracks were built there, as well as large houses and estates for marine officers and Government officials. It was to be some time, however, before a way through the Great Dividing Range was found and lush farming land discovered.

A letter written home to England in 1788 describes some of the hardships. Hunger was common, as supplies often failed to materialise, and starvation was endured from 1789 until the first half of 1790. There was also a shortage of clothes, but the greatest deprivation seemed to be the lack of tea, and ground ivy leaves were used to make a brew of sorts.

Chickweed was eaten as a vegetable and kangaroo and small animals for meat, while the lack of salt and sugar made food insipid.

The first settlements fanned outwards from Sydney Cove, through Parramatta, and by 1813 had extended into the foothills of the Great Dividing Range. Later, Blaxland, Lawson and Wentworth climbed from Emu Plains, cutting a way through to the lush farmland beyond, and in time, William Cox built a road over the mountains and settlers moved inland to form large farming communities. However, this was all in the future.

To continue: it is interesting to read the Hawkesbury Pioneer Register and to follow the lives of some of the women convicts who turned their lives around to become respected citizens.

One of these women was Margaret Darnell, alias Dowling, Darnel or Darling. She was sentenced at the Old Bailey on 18 April 1787 for the theft of one dozen knives and forks from an ironmonger in Chancery Lane. The cutlery was valued at six shillings and she was given a sentence of seven years' transportation. During the voyage out she formed a liaison with Marine Charles Green and became pregnant. Her son, Charles, was born on 17 December 1788. Margaret went on to marry a seaman, Owen Cavenough, who adopted her son. In 1810 he wrote to Governor McQuarrie describing himself as a sober, industrious man wishing to settle on his own land and he was given an initial grant of one hundred acres of land in the Hawkesbury District. In 1808, according to the local newspaper, Margaret had sold land and a garden in Sydney for twenty pounds, which had probably been her first land grant. This money could have founded their new agricultural life in the Hawkesbury. They went on to have five boys and two girls, who all married in the area, the last traced to 1885. Margaret remained a respectable wife and mother until she died in 1834. This story could be replicated many times over.

Ann Huxley (née Forbes) was sentenced to death for theft in 1787. This sentence was commuted to seven years' transportation and she sailed on the ship *Prince of Wales* in the First Fleet (Appendix XI.A). Her accomplice in the theft was Lydia Munro, who also sailed on the same ship.

Ann Forbes met George Bannister, a fellow convict, and they had a daughter who was christened in Sydney on 15 November 1789. In 1792 Ann then married William Butler, a seaman, and by 1793 they had a son and a daughter. Ann then married William Dring and had another two daughters and a son, before she married Thomas Jones or Huxley. She seemed to settle down then and she went on to have five more daughters and five more sons to Thomas Huxley, the last of whom was born in 1818; ninety grandchildren and thirty-three great-grandchildren have so far been traced (Appendix XI.B).[4]

When the Second Fleet arrived in 1790 it carried free settlers, among whom was Elizabeth, the wife of Lieutenant MacArthur of the New South Wales Corps. Elizabeth was an educated woman with a small child, accompanying her husband, who was originally appointed to the post of Regimental Paymaster and later Inspector of Public Works.

The MacArthurs were given land at Rose Hill, later Parramatta, where they established Elizabeth Farm, which still stands and is now a museum. MacArthur was a fiery character and, after a duel with William Patterson, he was sent back to England in 1801 to face a court martial. He did not appear to receive any punishment and returned to Sydney

Cove. Meantime, Elizabeth had taken over the running of their farm, despite having a young family, and between them they encouraged the development of sheep farming and the wool industry. MacArthur resigned from the Army in 1805 and was granted a further 5,000 acres of land at Cow Pastures, where he bred merino sheep from imported stock. This property was named Camden Park. In 1808, at the time of the Rum Rebellion, he sailed for England once more, taking his eldest son and leaving Elizabeth to manage the farm. Due to her good management she was able to expand the wool export business and, when MacArthur returned, he also developed a wine growing and bottling business. He was created a Councillor before becoming insane in 1830. Elizabeth had nine children and was responsible for much of the progress made in the country in sheep farming and the export of wool.

The Reverend Richard Johnston, the first Chaplain to arrive in Sydney Cove, sailed out with the Second Fleet. He was horrified at the conditions on board the ships, as the contractors had over-filled the vessels with prisoners. Reverend Johnston wrote a letter to a friend describing the shocking facts he had discovered whilst going amongst the prisoners. They were without clothing and were chained. On arrival at Sydney Cove, some of the men died while being put ashore and their bodies were thrown overboard, to lie on the rocks and along the shoreline. Reverend Johnston made an official complaint about what he had seen, with the result that those who had died were given a burial on the north shore. Many of the convicts were so weak they could not walk off the ships. Some fainted on being brought up into the fresh air. Most of these prisoners had sailed on the *Neptune*.

Scant information is available about the conditions the women suffered, but eleven women died on the journey and they had been kept in irons. Governor Phillip wrote to the Secretary of State giving him the facts and informing him of the parlous condition of the convicts on arrival, blaming the contractors for over-crowding the ships and demanding more humane conditions for prisoners in the future.

The work of Elizabeth Fry changed the lives of women transported overseas. In the later Fleets, there was a matron supervisor, who was in the women's quarters on the transport ships. The women were taught to sew, and thereby had a trade of sorts on arrival.

Elizabeth Hawkins, the wife of Purser Hawkins, made that journey out. Purser Hawkins had been appointed Officer in Charge of Government Stores at Bathurst, where he was allocated a house for his family. Elizabeth's mother and her children and servants made the trip, taking with them bedding, household utensils and some agricultural implements, along with a cart and two drays, one horse-drawn and one drawn by bullocks. Elizabeth spearheaded the army of women who followed their men to establish farming inland.

Many of the women who arrived as free settlers were educated gentlewomen who had emigrated to teach, open businesses or look for husbands. Cheap passages were offered from England for those prepared to go to the new colony in order to populate it. By the 1830s, settlers were arriving frequently, due to the assisted passage scheme put in place by the British Government in order to deal with overcrowding and lack of work in that country.

While it was a hard life for these new Australians, it was a chance to make a completely new start. The strict laws put in place by the first Governors had created a fairly disciplined community, and it was only as the free settlers arrived, with the English emphasis on morality, respectability and class-consciousness, that people became ashamed of their roots.

Now the reverse is true as everyone looks for a convict ancestor!

The dichotomy between the feckless nature of the original convicts and the respectability they gained through their hard work and economic achievements is the basis of Australian society and applies equally to men and to women.

NOTES

1   Hughes, Robert, *The Fatal Shore*, (Pan Books, London), p. 40.
2   *Ibid*, p. 38.
3   *Ibid*, Map of the Route of the First Fleet to Australia, May 1787 - January 1788.
4   Family history of Ann Huxley, researched mainly from the Hawkesbury Family History Society Journal.

APPENDIX XI.A. Officers, Men and Passengers Sailing with the First Fleet (according to the Official Shipping List)

Flagship   *HMS Sirius*

1 Commander - Arthur Phillip
2 Captains - John Hunter and another
2 Masters   1 sent home from Rio de Janeiro
2 Quartermasters
1 Commissary
1 Surgeon
1 Judge Advocate
7 Marines' wives
2 Children
107 Marines and Seamen   1 died on voyage
                                          2 sent home from Rio de Janeiro

Total: 126

Naval Tender   *HMS Supply*

1 Captain
1 Master
1 Surgeon
1 Quartermaster
1 Commodore
1 Convict
21 Marines and Seamen   1 Marine Corporal died on voyage

Total 27

Convict Transport   *HMS Alexander*

1 Master
1 Assistant Surgeon
2 Ships' boys
1 Contractor's agent
21 Marines and Seamen
209 Male convicts   21 convicts died on voyage.

Total 235

Convict Transport   *HMS Scarborough*

1 Master
1 Assistant Surgeon
1 Child
3 Marines' wives   1 died on voyage
35 Marines and Seamen
208 Convicts

Total 249

Convict Transport   *HMS Prince of Wales*

1 master
1 Surveyor
1 Ship's boy
12 Marines and Seamen   1 Seaman fell overboard
3 Marines' wives
1 Marine's child
1 Male convict
50 Female convicts
2 Convicts' children

Total 72

Convict Transport   *HMS Charlotte*

1 Master
1 Surgeon General
12 Marines and Seamen   1 marine died on voyage
1 Marine's wife
19 Female convicts
1 Convict child
87 Male convicts   4 male convicts died on voyage

Total 122

Convict Transport   *HMS Friendship*

1 Master
1 Assistant Surgeon
30 Marines and Seamen   2nd Mate died on voyage
77 Male convicts   1 male convict died on voyage
20 Female convicts   1 female convict died on voyage
3 Children of convicts

Total 132

Convict Transport   *HMS Lady Penrhyn*

1 Master
4 Quartermasters
2 Ships' boys
2 Assistant Surgeons
1 Settler (first migrant named James Smith)
107 Female convicts
21 Convicts' children   1 died before Fleet sailed
28 Marines and Seamen   3rd Mate died before Fleet sailed
                                          1 Seaman deserted at Rio de Janeiro

Total 166

Store Ship   *HMS Fishburn*

1 Master
1 Seaman
1 Cook

Total 3

Store Ship   *HMS Golden Grove*

1 Master
1 Chaplain
1 Chaplain's wife
1 Clerk
1 Mate
1 Midshipman
1 Steward
1 Seaman

Total 8

Store Ship   *HMS Borrowdale*

1 Master
2 First Mates
1 Seaman

Total 4

Troop Ship   *HMS Unknown*

1 First Lieutenant
141 Marines and Seamen
21 Marines' wives
18 Marines' children
1 Female convict
1 Male convict

Total 183

Total personnel   1,327 on shipping list.

APPENDIX XI.B. Family tree of Ann Forbes or Butler or Huxley

Ann was born in 1772 and sentenced to be hanged for theft but was reprieved and sailed on the First Fleet. She and another convict had a daughter who was christened in Sydney in 1789.

In 1792 Ann ?married William Butler, a seaman, and by 1793 they had a son and daughter.

Ann (Butler) born 1792 - died 1795.
Elizabeth born 1794 - died when she fell into a fire.
Charles born 1796.

Ann then married Thomas Jones or Huxley. The children of that marriage were:

Jane born 1798 died 1833. Married Robert Jackson Arndell 1817.
Thomas born 1801 died 1859. Married Mary Evans 1822.
Charlotte born 1802 died 1885. Married:
    (1) James Neale 1819: James died 1848.
    (2) Francis da Silva.
    (3) Richard Ellem 1842 who died 1857.
Male child (unnamed) 1804 died 1806.
Ann born 1805 died 1869. Married Thomas Wall 1822.
James born 1809 died 1894. Married:
    (1) Margaret Hayman 1828. Margaret died 1847.
    (2) Ann Reason 1852. Ann died 1883.
Samuel born 1811 died 1894. Married Mary Mitchell 1834.
John Richard born 1813 died 1860. Married Susannah Martin 1841 who died 1878.
Esther born 1817 died 1884. Married James Cavenough 1831. James died 1858.
Sophia born 1818 died 1866. Married James Bligh Ridge 1835. James died 1886.

Grandchildren:

Children of Jane and Robert Arndell:
Robert born 1822.
Jane born 1823.
Thomas born 1824 died 1858. Married Harriet Butler 1850.
John born 1827 died 1905. Married:
    (1) Catherine Clines or Clynes 1851.
    (2) Amelia King 1879.
    (3) Jane Young 1898.

Children of Charlotte and James Neale:
Jane born 1829 died 1897. Married Richard Woodberry/Woodbury.

Children of Ann and Windsor Thomas Wall:
Thomas born 1823 died 1897. Married:
> (1) Ann Ridge 1850.
> (2) Martha Elizabeth Woolley 1854.

Richard born 1824 died 1881. Married Elizabeth Harriet Jones 1853 who died 1905.
John born 1826 died 1888. Married Ann Blundell 1853.
Alice born 1827 died 1902. Married John Lamb 1844 who died 1908.
George born 1829 died 1897.
Eliza born 1830.
Samuel born 1831 died 1892. Married Izetta Hayman 1856 who died 1899.
Charlotte born 1833 died 1907. Married George Hayman 1856.
William born 1837 died 1893.
Jonah born 1838 died 1907.
Sophia born 1842.
Mary Ann born 1845.
Elizabeth Ann born 1851 died 1887. Married Mountford Hector Rowley 1877.
James Charles born 1852.

Children of Thomas and Mary Wall:
Thomas born 1823 died 1898. Married Margaret Rose Robertson 1922.
Richard born 1825 died 1878. Married Ellenor Dodd who died 1877.
Mary Ann born 1827 died 1903. Married Thomas Durrington.
Sophia born 1828 died 1909. Married Peter Kemp 1846 who died 1898.
William born 1830 died 1847.
Matilda born 1832 died 1904. Married Samuel Ardnell who died 1895.
Elizabeth born 1834 died 1908. Married:
> (1) Edward Lawler.
> (2) George Houlton.

Charles born 1835 died 1903. Married Mary Lee 1920.
Louisa born 1838 died 1925. Married Edward Gosper 1854 who died 1906.
Emma Marie born 1840 died 1841.
Eliza Jane born 1842 died 1876. Married Wiliam John 1862.
John Henry (twin) born 1845 died 1858.
Esther (twin) born 1845.
Edward Prosper born 1848 died 1921. Married Amy Susannah Eather 1873 died 1943.

Children of James and Margaret Huxley:
Louisa born 1830 died 1877. Married William Tye who died 1882.
Phoebe born 1833. Married to George Austin Goodwin Brenchley 1856.
James William born 1835 died 1898. Married to Margaret Ann Stevenson 1857 who
> died 1920.

Cyrus born 1837 died 1920. Married to Mary Jane Plunkett 1857 who died 1920.
Frederick Thomas born 1840 died 1920. Married Eliza Cornwell 1862 who died 1930.

Lucinda born 1843 died 1845.
David born 1845 died 1932. Married Elizabeth Sophia Peck 1862 who died 1910.

Children of Esther and James Cavenough:
Elizabeth born 1832 died 1839.
Sophia Isabella born 1833 died 1894. Married Richard William Buttsworth 1855.
George born 1834 died 1835.
James born 1833 died 1900. Married Mary Dunstan 1858 who died 1923.
Thomas born 1837 died 1863. Married Josie Butterworth who died 1914.
Ann born 1839 died 1866.
Charles born 1840.
Samuel born 1841 died 1903. Married:
>   (1) Helen Buchanan.
>   (2) Charlotte Wright.

Richard born 1843 died 1883.
Elizabeth born 1844 died 1907. Married George Greentree.
Mary Ann born 1845 died 1902. Married John Gilbert Gillard, who died 1863.
Margaret Jane born 1848 died 1867. Married George McGinnis Colcroft died 1865.
John Henry born 1849 died 1851.
John born 1851 died 1901. Married Annie Josephine Brosnan/Bronsan 1882.
Esther Amelia born 1853 died 1869. Married Charles Halpin 1869.
William Henry born 1855. Married Ellen B Oliver 1894.
Frederick Robert born 1856 died 1931. Married Mary Ann Deighton who died 1901.

Children of Samuel and Mary Huxley:
Edwin born 1835 died 1907. Married Hannah Demaine 1859 who died 1871.
Andrew born 1836 died 1896. Married Carrie Maria Dall 1878 who died 1932.
Esther Sophia born 1839 died 1905. Married Hugh Wilson 1861 who died 1919.
Robert John born 1841 died 1899. Married Jane Masterton 1868 who died 1931.
Samuel born 1843 died 1922. Married Sarah Smallwood 1877 who died 1920.
Jane born 1846 died 1846.
William Henry born 1847. Married Mary Jane Carter 1876.
Thomas James born 1849 died 1925. Married Mary Owens.
Richard Ernest born 1854 died 1900. Married Jane Amelia Whitton 1877 died 1920.
Louanna Jane born 1856 died 1890. Married daniel Obadiah Weaver 1879 died 1927.

Children of John Richard and Susanna Huxley:
Albert born 1842 died 1938.
Eliza Ann born 1845 died 1866.
Lavinia born 1847. Married:
>   (1) Charles Glanwell Bennet 1868.
>   (2) William Rich 1875.

Emily born 1849.

William Charles born 1853 died 1920. Married Christina Myles 1879.

Children of Sophia and James Bligh Ridge:
Sophia born 1836 died 1906. Married Henry Robinson who died 1910.
Margaret Ann born 1837 died 1915. Married James Alderson 1865 who died 1900.
Isabella Jane born 1840. Married James Alexander Gough.
James Bligh born 1841 died 1913. Married Lydia Hayes 1901 who died 1942.
Richard born 1843 died 1925. Married Margaret Mckinnon 1881 who died 1942.
Martha born 1845 died 1893.
Esther Amelia born 1846 died 1884. Married Charles Henry Newman 1876.
Victoria born 1848 died 1923. Married William Edward Gilbert Flemming 1871.
William Bligh born 1852 died 1853.
Emily Adelaide born 1854 died 1883. Married Harry Parkin Thornthwaite 1881.
William Bligh born 1856 died 1905. Married Mary Therese Hennessey.
Henrietta born 1859 died 1859.

Children of Martha Ridge:
John born 1876 died 1877.
Leo born 1878 died 1951. Married Emily Elizabeth Bailey 1902.
Irwin George born 1880 died 1893.

Great-grandchildren:

Children of Margaret Ann Alderson and James Ridge:
John Bligh born 1867 died 1956. Married Laura Winifred Barlow who died 1974.
Margaret born 1865.   Married Charles Short.
Lettricia born 1868 died 1904 unmarried.
Austin born 1871 died 1872.
Pearl R born 1873. Married Alfred George Smith 1902.
James Bligh born 1875 died 1939. Married Ada Morecroft 1905 who died 1954.

Richard Ridge born 1875 died 1879.
William Tarleton born 1881 died 1948.

Children of Isabella Jane Ridge (daughter of Sarah Gough) born 1840:
Charles baptised 1864.
Victoria E baptised 1865.
Isabella Jane baptised 1866.
James Bligh baptised 1867.
Frederick Charles born 1867 died 1878.
John Richard born 1870 died 1945. Married Mary Winkle.
Charles Alexander born 1872. Married Clarine A Gough.
Emily Louise born 1875.

Amelia Ann born 1876 died 1882.
Louise born 1883.
Florence born 1885.

Great-great-grandchildren:

Children of Sophie Robinson born 1836:
Henry Bligh born1856 died 1910.
Edward James born 1857 died 1933 unmarried.
Alfred John born 1858. Married Ethel Matilda Gemmell who died 1931.
Jane Sophia born 1861 died 1894 unmarried.
Clare Martha born 1863 died 1893 unmarried.
William Richard born 1865.
Albert George born 1867 died 1928. Married Ellen Ethel Hale 1898 died 1953.
Richard Belmore born 1869. Married Marie D'Arcy.
Austin Bligh born 1871 died 1941 unmarried.
Sydney Charles born 1873 died 1953 unmarried.
Emmeline Alice born 1874 died 1950. Married Patrick D'Arcy 1897.
Jessie Amelia born 1876 died 1949 unmarried.
Florence Sophia born 1879 died 1906. Married Massey Warren who died 1929.
Evelyn Ridge born 1881 died 1955 unmarried.

BIBLIOGRAPHY

Primary Sources:
Dee Why Library, Pittwater Road, Dee Why, New South Wales 2099.
Do not have catalogue numbers, etc.

Newspapers:
Sydney Gazette and Advertiser, 1803-1804.
The Australian.
Sydney Gazette, 1995-1999.
Manly Daily, 1995-1999.

Books:
Bateson, C, *The Convict Ships 1787 - 1868,* (Glasgow, 1959).
Champion, S and G, *Manly, Warringah, Pittwater 1788 - 1858.*
Chapman, D, *1788 The People of the First Fleet,* (Sydney, 1988).
Clarke, P and Spender, D, *Life Lines,* (Allan & Unwin, 8 Napier Street, Sydney 2059, 1992).
Clarke, M, *His Natural Life,* (Penguin Books, London, 1970).
Cobley, J, *The Crimes of the First Fleet Convicts,.* (Sydney, 1970).
Chronicle of Australia, (Chronicle Australian Pty Ltd, 487 Maroondah Highway, Ringwood, Victoria 3134, 1993).
Davidson, G, Hirst, J and Macintyre, S, (eds), *The Oxford Companion to Australian History,* (Oxford University Press, Australia).
Dixson, M, *The Real Matilda: Women and Identity in Australia 1788-1975,* (Melbourne, 1976).
The Hawkesbury Pioneer Register, (Hawkesbury Pioneer Group, Windsor, New South Wales).
Hughes, R, *The Fatal Shore,* (Pan Books Ltd, London, 1986).
King, J, *Australia's First Fleet. The Voyage and Enactment of 1788/1988,* (Robertsbridge Ltd, 12 Berry Street, North Sydney 2060).
Mowle, L M, *A Genealogical History of Pioneer Families of Australia,* (Rigby, 5th edn).
McClelland, J, *McClelland's Convict/Pioneer and Immigrant Series of Australia,* (J McClelland Research, 1 Silverdale Road, Silverdale, New South Wales 2750).
Needham, A, Riddler, L, Hadley, M and Scott, P, *The Women of the 1790 Neptune,* (A Needham, PO Box 60, Dural, New South Wales 2150).
Nicholas, (ed.), *Convict Workers: Reinterpreting Australia's Past.*
Pownall, E, *Australian Pioneer Women.*
Prentis, M D, *The Scots in Australia: A Study of New South Wales, Victoria and Queensland 1788- 1900,* (Sydney, 1983).
Prentis, M D, (ed.), *Warringah History,* (Warringah Shire Council, Civic Centre, Dee Why, New South Wales 2099).
Rees, Sian, *The Floating Brothel,* (Headline Book Publishing, 2001).
Robinson, P, *The Women of Botany Bay: Reinterpretation of the Role of Women.*
Summers, A, *Damned Whores and God's Police: The Colonisation of Women in Australia,* (Penguin Books, Pelican edn, 1975).
Tardif, P, *Notorious Strumpets and Dangerous Girls,* (Collins/Angus and Robertson Publications, Australia).
Tench, W, *A Complete Account of the Settlement at Port Jackson in New South Wales,* (London, 1793).

Wollstonecroft, M, *Vindication of the Rights of Women*, (1792).

The Hatch and Brood of Time: *A Study of the First Generation of Native-born White Australians 1788 -1828* Vol. 1, (Melbourne, 1985).

The Land of Exiles: The Scots in Australia, (Her Majesty's Stationery Office, Edinburgh).

School for Seniors History Class notes, Dee Why, New South Wales.

DATE	PARISH	COUNTY	SURNAME	FORENAME
13/12/30	GREAT CLACTON	ESSEX	ABBOTT	JAMES
27/11/30	COLTON	NORFOLK	ABLE	GEORGE
13/12/30	GREAT CLACTON	ESSEX	ABLETT	SAMUEL
26/11/30	WADDESDON	BUCKS	ABRAHAM	WILLIAM
23/11/30	WICKHAM	HANTS	ABRAHAM	WILLIAM
26/11/30	UPPER WINCHENDON	BUCKS	ABRAHAM	WILLIAM
8/12/30	WALTON-LE-SOKEN	ESSEX	ACRES	WILLIAM
29/10/30	LANGLEY	KENT	ADAMS	JAMES
23/11/30	OWLESBURY	HANTS	ADAMS	RICHARD
21/11/30	LITTLETON	HANTS	ADAMS	JOHN
26/11/30	FAIRFORD	GLOUCS	ADAMS	HENRY
29/10/30	BOUGHTON	KENT	ADAMS	JOHN
27/11/30	EASTLEACH MARTIN	GLOUCS	ADAMS	THOMAS
11/11/31	EASTLEACH MARTIN	GLOUCS	ADDINGTON	WILLIAM
4/12/30	WILSHAMPSTEAD	BEDFORDSHIRE	AGGERS	JOHN
13/12/30	LINGWOOD	NORFOLK	AILETT	WILLIAM
2/31	GREAT CLACTON	ESSEX	ALDRIDGE	JOHN
23/11/30	IVER	BUCKS	ALEXANDER	JOHN
22/11/30	PUSEY	WILTSHIRE	ALLEN	JOHN
20/11/30	PENTON GRAFTON	HANTS	ALLEN	JOHN
26/11/30	WALTHAM ST LAWRENCE	BERKS	ALLEN	SOLOMON
29/11/30	WADDESDON	BUCKS	ALLEN	JAMES
3/1/31	CAWSTON	NORFOLK	ALLEN	WILLIAM
12/12/30	SOUTHROP	GLOUCS	ALLEN	JOSEPH
12/7/30	TILNEY	NORFOLK	ALLEN	ROBERT
13/12/30	DEEPING FEN	LINCS	ALLEN	CLIPSHAM
13/12/30	BECCLES	SUFFOLK	ALLINGTON	CHARLES
29/11/30	LONG MELFORD	SUFFOLK	AMBROSE	RICHARD
30/11/30	LONG MELFORD	SUFFOLK	AMBROSE	ROBERT
9/11/30	ROUGHTON	NORFOLK	AMIS	LEE
25/10/30	EAST TUDDENHAM	NORFOLK	ANDERSON	THOMAS
10/12/30	WINGHAM	KENT	ANDREWS	HENRY
19/11/30	WINGHAM	KENT	ANDREWS	HENRY
22/11/30	ARKESDEN	ESSEX	ANDREWS	WILLIAM
24/11/30	BARTON STACEY	HANTS	ANNALLS	JAMES
19/12/31	VERNHAM DEAN	HANTS	ANNETTS	JAMES
7/12/30	EAST WOODHAY	HANTS	ANNETTS	JOHN
23/11/30	SIXPENNY HANDLEY	DORSET	ANSTEY	WILLIAM
	LOUND	NOTTS	APPLEBY	GEORGE
	GREAT CLACTON	ESSEX	ARLOTT	SAMUEL
	REDENHALL	NORFOLK	ARMS	EDWARD

DATE	PARISH	COUNTY	SURNAME	FORENAME
29/5/32	WITCHINGHAM	NORFOLK	ARMS	CHRISTOPHER
1831	COLWICK	NOTTS	ARMSTRONG	JOHN
23/11/30	FORDINGBRIDGE	HANTS	ARNEY	WILLIAM
23/11/30	FORDINGBRIDGE	HANTS	ARNEY	JOSEPH
29/8/30	LYMINGE	KENT	ARNOLD	DAVID
20/9/30	BARHAM	KENT	ARNOLD	DANIEL
3/12/30	WESTON	LINCS	ASHTON	
24/11/30	REDBRIDGE	HANTS	ASTELL	THOMAS
19/11/30	BASINGSTOKE	HANTS	ASTRIDGE	WILLIAM
27/11/30	BISHOPSTONE	BUCKS	ATKINS	WILLIAM
29/11/30	MARSH GREEN	BUCKS	ATKINS	STEPHEN
25/1/31	BASILDON	ESSEX	ATKINS	GEORGE
11/2/31	WRITTLE	ESSEX	ATKINS	CHARLES
16/11/30	BENENDEN	KENT	AUSTEN	WILLIAM
8/7/32	MILDENHALL	SUFFOLK	AVES	ISAAC
7/32	MILDENHALL	SUFFOLK	AVES	ISAAC
29/11/30	STOUR PROVOST	DORSET	AYLES	GEORGE
24/11/30	WROTHAM	KENT	AYLING	JOHN
26/11/30		SOMERSET	AYRES	ISAAC
6/12/30	STEEPLE BUMPSTEAD	ESSEX	BACON	GEORGE
29/5/32	WITCHINGHAM	NORFOLK	BADCOCK	CORNELIUS
30/11/30	EAST TUDDENHAM	NORFOLK	BAGG	JOHN
10/12/30	CHEVINGTON	SUFFOLK	BAILEY	WILLIAM
10/12/30	CHEVINGTON	SUFFOLK	BAILEY	GEORGE
28/1/32	HAPPISBURGH	NORFOLK	BAILEY	JOHN
8/2/31	MONKS ELEIGH	SUFFOLK	BAKER	ROBERT
22/11/30	LECKFORD	HANTS	BAKER	JOHN
22/11/30	ROMSEY EXTRA	HANTS	BAKER	MOSES
22/11/30	WOOTON ST LAWRENCE	HANTS	BAKER	JAMES
5/12/30	GREAT HOLLAND	ESSEX	BAKER	HENRY
23/11/30	EAST WOODHAY	HANTS	BAKER	WILLIAM
24/4/32	RICKINGHALL SUPERIOR	SUFFOLK	BAKER	GEORGE
6/10/31	ST BRIAVELS	GLOUCS	BALDWYN	JAMES
26/11/30	HORSLEY	GLOUCS	BALL	ROBERT
9/11/30	HAWKHURST	KENT	BALLARD	JOHN
8/1/31	DANBURY	ESSEX	BANNISTER	FRANCIS
25/1/31	TISBURY	WILTS	BANSTONE	SAMUEL
30/11/30	KINGSUTTON	NORTHANTS	BARBER	WILLIAM
5/3/31	ROPSLEY	LINCS	BARBER	WILLIAM
8/12/30	LITTLE CLACTON	ESSEX	BAREHAM	DANIEL
13/12/30	HENHAM	ESSEX	BARKER	JAMES
29/11/30	THURGARTON	NORFOLK	BARKER	JOHN

FORENAME	SURNAME	COUNTY	PARISH	DATE
RICHARD	BELL	SUFFOLK	STOKE BY NAYLAND	25/8/30
GEORGE	BELL	NORTHANTS	WARMINGTON	26/11/30
W	BELLORN	WORCS	DEFFORD	12/30
ALFRED	BENEY	SUSSEX	BATTLE	11/30
ALFRED	BENEY	SUSSEX	NINFIELD	9/11/30
THOMAS	BENNETT	HANTS	BASINGSTOKE	22/11/30
ROBERT	BENNETT	HANTS	SELBORNE	22/11/30
RICHARD	BENWELL	GLOUCS	EASTLEACH MARTIN	27/11/30
CHARLES	BERKENS	NOTTS	COLWICK	1831
THOMAS SNR	BERRIMAN	HANTS	STRATTON	19/11/30
THOMAS	BERRIMAN	HANTS	BARTON STACEY	18/12/31
WILLIAM	BETTS	SHROPSHIRE	WHITCHURCH	12/9/31
ROBERT	BETTS	SUFFOLK	BACTON	20/11/30
WILLIAM	BICKNELL	HANTS	HEADLEY	23/11/30
WILLIAM	BIGLAND	GLOUCS	BEVERSTONE	26/11/30
ARTHUR	BINSTEAD	SUSSEX	BOSHAM	17/11/30
GEORGE	BINSTEAD	SUSSEX	BOSHAM	17/11/30
WILLIAM	BIRCH	HANTS	ANDOVER	22/11/30
GEORGE	BIRCHER	SUSSEX	KINGSTON	5/12/30
GEORGE	BIRD	ESSEX	ARKESDEN	10/12/30
THOMAS	BIRT	GLOUCS	ST BRIAVELS	6/5/31
THOMAS	BIRT	WILTS	TISBURY	25/1/30
HENRY	BISH	NOTTS	MANSFIELD	12/30
WILLIAM	BISH	NOTTS	MANSFIELD	12/30
HENRY	BISH	SUSSEX	MARESFIELD	9/11/30
WILLIAM	BISH	SUSSEX	MARESFIELD	9/11/30
GEORGE	BISHOP	KENT	BLEAN ST COSMUS	21/11/30
THOMAS	BISHOP	HANTS		26/11/30
THOMAS	BISHOP	GLOUCS	HORSLEY	1/12/30
JOHN	BISS	SOMERSET	HENSTRIDGE	26/11/30
JAMES	BLACKMAN	HANTS	ITCHEN ABBAS	1/12/30
JEREMIAH	BLAKE	NORFOLK	WRAMPLINGHAM	22/11/30
JOHN	BLAKEY	SURREY	OXTED	29/11/30
JAMES	BLANDFORD	WILTS	TISBURY	22/10/30
JOSEPH	BLANDFORD	HANTS	UPPER CLATFORD	25/11/30
RICHARD	BLATCH	DORSET	BLANDFORD	20/11/30
THOMAS	BLEATHAM	BUCKS	CHEPPING WYCOMBE	17/10/31
MARY	BLIZZARD	ESSEX	WEST BERGHOLT	29/11/30
WILLIAM	BLOOMFIELD	ESSEX	GREAT CLACTON	18/7/31
SAMUEL	BLOOMFIELD	NORTHANTS		7/12/30
JOHN	BLOWS	CAMBS	SHINGAY	12/31
SAMUEL	BLUNDELL	NORTHANTS	FINENDON	30/11/30
ISABELLA	BLUNT	CAMBS	MARCH	25/12/30

DATE	PARISH	COUNTY	SURNAME	FORENAME
29/11/30	SPARHAM	NORFOLK	BARLEY	BENJAMIN
8/9/31	SEVENOAKS	KENT	BARNARD	JOHN
23/11/30	OWLESBURY	HANTS	BARNES	WILLIAM
12/30	EASTERGATE	SUSSEX	BARNES	JOHN
24/11/30	FOULSHAM	NORFOLK	BARNES	FRANCIS
24/11/30	FOULSHAM	NORFOLK	BARNES	WILLIAM
18/12/30	NORTH WALSHAM	NORFOLK	BARNET	JAMES
29/11/30	CHEPPING WYCOMBE	BUCKS	BARRETT	CHARLES
25/11/30	TISBURY	WILTS	BARRETT	SAMUEL
25/11/30	TISBURY	WILTS	BARRETT	JOHN
9/11/30	HAWKHURST	KENT	BARROW	GEORGE
9-11/12/30	SWIMBRIDGE	DEVON	BARROW	RICHARD
22/11/30	ROMSEY EXTRA	HANTS	BARTHOLEMEW	BENJAMIN
3/8/32	CROYDON	CAMBS	BARTLE	SAMUEL
29/11/30	CHEPPING WYCOMBE	BUCKS	BARTON	EDMUND
29/11/30	CHEPPING WYCOMBE	BUCKS	BARTON	JAMES
29/11/30	LOUDWATER	BUCKS	BARTON	DAVID
22/11/30	HINDOLVESTON	NORFOLK	BARTRAM	SAMUEL
25/11/30		NORFOLK	BASNER	FRANCIS
24/11/30	FIELD DALING	NORFOLK	BASTERD	JOHN
23/11/30	OWLESBURY	HANTS	BATCHELOR	BENJAMIN
27/11/30	BISHOPSTONE	BUCKS	BATES	E
27/11/30	BISHOPSTONE	BUCKS	BATES	FRANCIS
27/11/30	BISHOPSTONE	BUCKS	BATES	WILLIAM
27/11/30	BISHOPSTONE	BUCKS	BATES	THOMAS
20/11/30	BARTON STACEY	HANTS	BATT	GEORGE
19/11/30	MICHELDEVER	HANTS	BATT	THOMAS JNR
20/11/30	BARTON STACEY	HANTS	BATTEN	CHARLES
22/11/30	WOOTON ST LAWRENCE	HANTS	BATTEN	JOHN
19/11/30	STRATTON	HANTS	BAVERSTOCK	THOMAS
12/7/30	BECCLES	SUFFOLK	BAXTER	JOHN
4/12/30	ATTLEBOROUGH	NORFOLK	BAXTER	JAMES
7/12/30	GREAT CLACTON	ESSEX	BAXTER	ROBERT
29/11/30	SOUTHROP	GLOUCS	BAYLISS	BENJAMIN
29/11/30	SOUTHROP	GLOUCS	BAYLISS	ROBERT
6/8/31	ST BRIAVELS	GLOUCS	BEACH	JOHN
9/11/30	HAWKHURST	KENT	BEALE	JOHN
13/12/30	LONG MELFORD	SUFFOLK	BEALES	JAMES
19/12/32	BEESTON	NOTTS	BECK	GEORGE
23/11/30	QUARLEY	HANTS	BECKINGHAM	RICHARD
20/11/30	UPPER CLATFORD	HANTS	BECKINGHAM	THOMAS
3/12/30	HENSTRIDGE	SOMERSET	BELBIN	CHARLES

DATE	PARISH	COUNTY	SURNAME	FORENAME
1/12/30	DRAYCOTT	SOMERSET	BOARD	FREDERICK
20/11/30	MARTYR WORTHY	HANTS	BOLTER	WILLIAM SNR
22/11/30	SELBORNE	HANTS	BONE	HENRY
6/31	DAGENHAM	ESSEX	BONHAM	DAVID
3/12/30	WORTHING	SUSSEX	BONIFACE	JAMES
8/3/32	BECCLES FEN	SUFFOLK	BORRETT	CHARLES
12/9/31	WHITCHURCH	SHROPSHIRE	BOTTS	WILLIAM
24/3/32	BENTLEY	YORK (WR)	BOULTON	THOMAS
26/11/30	FAIRFORD	GLOUCS	BOULTON	ISAAC
19/11/30		HANTS	BOUND	BENJAMIN
5/2/31	MANSFIELD	NOTTS	BOWERBANK	WILLIAM
29/11/30	CHEPPING WYCOMBE	BUCKS	BOWLES	THOMAS
30/11/30	EAST TUDDENHAM	NORFOLK	BOWLES	GEORGE
6/10/31	DILHAM	NORFOLK	BOWMAN	JONATHON
17/11/30	BOSHAM	SUSSEX	BOXALL	THOMAS
13/12/30	HOXNE	SUFFOLK	BOYCE	JONATHON
23/11/30	OWLESBURY	HANTS	BOYES	WILLIAM
23/11/30	EAST WOODHAY	HANTS	BRACKSTONE	WILLIAM
22/11/30	THRUXTON	HANTS	BRACKSTONE	WILLIAM
22/11/30	PENTON GRAFTON	HANTS	BRAILSFORD	JOHN
18/1/31	SHEFFIELD	YORKS (WR)	BRATCHER	CHARLES
25/11/30	FAWLEY	HANTS	BRAZIER	SAMUEL
8/3/31	WRITTLE	ESSEX	BRIGHT	BENJAMIN
20/12/30	FOULMIRE	CAMBS	BRIGHT	WILLIAM
24/11/30	HAEDLEY	HANTS	BRIGHT	JAMES
23/10/30	BEAKESBOURNE	KENT	BRISTOW	JOHN
6/31	HALSTED	KENT	BROADHURST	WILLIAM
23/11/30	EAST WOODHAY	HANTS	BROOKS	WILLIAM
4/12/30	LINGWOOD	NORFOLK	BROOKS	MARTIN
4/12/30	LINGWOOD	NORFOLK	BROWN	WILLIAM
20/11/30	MARGATE	KENT	BROWN	JOHN
21/11/30	HOUGHTON	HANTS	BROWN	J
8/11/30	HOOE	SUSSEX	BROWN	DANIEL
6/12/30	COLCHESTER	ESSEX	BROWN	BENJAMIN
22/11/30	NEW ALRESFORD	HANTS	BROWN	OLIVER
19/7/30	PRIEST HUTTON	LANCS	BROWN	THOMAS
2/31	MAIDFORD	NORTHANTS	BROWN	THOMAS
11/30	FLETCHING	SUSSEX	BROWN	THOMAS
23/11/30	REDENHALL	NORFOLK	BROWN	HENRY
23/11/30	SIDMONTON	HANTS	BROWN	JOHN
25/11/31	BESTHORPE	NORFOLK	BROWN	JOHN
26/11/30	LITTLE WALSINGHAM	NORFOLK	BROWNE	CHARLOTTE
26/11/30	LITTLE WALSINGHAM	NORFOLK	BROWNE	THOMAS
29/5/32	WITCHINGHAM	NORFOLK	BROWNE	THOMAS
29/5/32	WITCHINGHAM	NORFOLK	BROWNE	JOHN
22/11/30	GREAT COGGESHALL	ESSEX	BROWNING	JOHN
22/11/30	UPHAM	HANTS	BRUMMELL	CHARLES
28/11/30	OUNDLE	NORTHANTS	BRUNSWICK	ROBERT
29/11/30	CHEPPING WYCOMBE	BUCKS	BRYANT	JOSEPH
23/11/30	DROXFORD	HANTS	BRYANT	CHARLES
29/11/30	CHEPPING WYCOMBE	BUCKS	BRYANT	WILLIAM
17/10/30	HARTFIELD	SUSSEX	BUCKWELL	GEORGE
17/11/30	BOSHAM	SUSSEX	BUDDEN	GEORGE
1/12/30	STALBRIDGE	DORSET	BUGBY	GEORGE
6/12/30	COLCHESTER	ESSEX	BUGGS	WILLIAM
2/7/32	STODY	NORFOLK	BULLOCK	J
22/11/30	WOOTON ST LAWRENCE	HANTS	BULPITT	JOHN
26/11/30	FAWLEY	HANTS	BUNDY	HENRY
25/11/30	FAWLEY	HANTS	BUNDY	SAMUEL
25/10/30	FLETCHING	SUSSEX	BUNN	THOMAS
22/11/30	MOTTISFONT	HANTS	BURBAGE	WILLIAM
23/8/31	GUESTLING	SUSSEX	BURFORD	THOMAS
17/11/30	BOSHAM	SUSSEX	BURGE	CHARLES
27/11/30	BISHOPSTONE	BUCKS	BURGESS	WILLIAM
23/11/30	MONK SHERBORNE	HANTS	BURGESS	WILLIAM
23/11/30	DROXFORD	HANTS	BURGESS	JESSE
5/1/32	NEWBURGH	YORK (NR)	BURNETT	FRANCIS
2/12/30	WAVENDON	BUCKS	BURROWS	THOMAS
13/12/30	HOXNE	SUFFOLK	BURROWS	JAMES
24/3/32	BENTLEY	YORK (WR)	BURTON	WILLIAM
12/31	SHINGAY	CAMBS	BURTON	JOSEPH
29/8/31	OAKINGTON	CAMBS	BURTON	WILLIAM
1830	NEW FISHBOURN	SUSSEX	BUSBY	WILLIAM
28/11/30	EAST PRESTON	SUSSEX	BUSHBY	JOHN
3/11/30	BATTLE	SUSSEX	BUSHBY	EDMUND
20/11/30	MARGATE	KENT	BUSHELL	EDMUND
20/11/30	MARGATE	KENT	BUSHELL	STEPHEN
24/11/30	WROTHAM	KENT	BUSS	WILLIAM
26/11/30	EXBURY & LEAPE	HANTS	BUTCHER	JAMES
22/11/30	BIGHTON	HANTS	BUTCHER	JOHN
16/11/30	BENENDEN	KENT	BUTLER	ISAAC
29/11/30	MARSH GREEN	BUCKS	BUTLER	JAMES
29/11/30	MARSH GREEN	BUCKS	BUTLER	WILLIAM
7/12/30	WENDEN LOFTS	ESSEX	BUTTON	STEPHEN

FORENAME	SURNAME	COUNTY	PARISH	DATE
GEORGE	CHOLOCOMBE	HANTS	ROMSEY EXTRA	22/11/30
WILLIAM	CHRISFORD	KENT	HAWKHURST	9/11/30
J	CHURCH	SUFFOLK	HOXNE	13/12/30
CHARLES JNR	CHURCHER	HANTS	OWLESBURY	23/11/30
JOHN	CHURCHER	NOTTS	CARBURTON	15/12/30
WILLIAM	CHURCHILL	DEVON	SIDMOUTH	1/1/31
GEORGE	CHURCHILL	DEVON	SIDMOUTH	1/1/31
JOB	CLAPHAM	NORTHANTS	FINENDON	30/11/30
JAMES	CLAPPEN	GLOUCS	FAIRFORD	26/11/30
ABRAHAM	CLARINGBOLD	KENT	WINGHAM	9/11/30
JOSEPH	CLARK	BUCKS	BISHOPSTONE	27/11/30
RICHARD	CLARK	SOMERSET	KENN	8/30
GEORGE	CLARK	HANTS	WOOTON ST LAWRENCE	22/11/30
ROBERT	CLARK	DORSET	PRESTON	29/11/30
GEORGE	CLARK	HANTS	FORDINGBRIDGE	23/11/30
ELIJAH	CLARK	ESSEX	GREAT COOGESHALL	22/11/30
JOHN	CLARKE	BUCKS	LITTLE BRICKHILL	1/12/30
JOHN YOUNGER	CLARKE	BUCKS	LITTLE BRICKHILL	1/12/30
GEORGE	CLARKE	HANTS	FORDINGBRIDGE	23/11/30
JAMES	CLARKE	NORFOLK	DOCKING	29/11/30
CHARLES	CLEMENT	BUCKS	IVER	1/12/30
THOMAS JNR	CLIFTON	CAMBS	COVENEY	17/11/31
ALLEN	CLIPSHAM	LINCS	DEEPING FEN	10/12/30
THOMAS	COBB	KENT	RUCKINGE	16/11/30
JOHN	COBB	HANTS	SELBOURNE	22/11/30
THOMAS	COBB	KENT	WINGHAM	9/11/30
WILLIAM	COBB	NORFOLK	ROUGHAM	22/11/30
ROBERT	COCKERILL	NORFOLK	LINGWOOD	4/12/30
JOSEPH	COCKLIN	ESSEX	WEST HAM	11/32
WILLIAM	COKER	BUCKS	BISHOPSTONE	27/11/30
WILLIAM	COLE	ESSEX	LITTLE CLACTON	8/12/30
SAMUEL	COLE	NORTHANTS	HARDINGTON	1831
ROBERT	COLE	NORFOLK		24/11/30
RICHARD	COLE	GLOUCS	COLN ROGERS	29/11/30
RICHARD	COLEBROOK	KENT	BENENDEN	16/11/30
GEORGE	COLEBROOK	KENT	BENENDEN	16/11/30
GEORGE	COLEMAN	HANTS	MARTYR WORTHY	22/11/30
THOMAS	COLES	BUCKS	WADDESDON	26/11/30
WILLIAM	COLES	SOMERSET		6/31
JOHN	COLESHILL	BUCKS	IVER	1/12/30
THOMAS	COLINS	BUCKS	WAVENDON	2/12/30
SAMUEL	COLLINS	KENT	SEVENOAKS	8/9/31

DATE	FORENAME	SURNAME	COUNTY	PARISH
27/11/30	ROBERT	BYE	NORFOLK	FOXLEY
21/11/30	JOHN	CAIN	HANTS	HOUGHTON
5/12/30	ROBERT	CALLENDAR	ESSEX	RAMSEY
22/11/30	JAMES	CAMIS	HANTS	NEW ALRESFORD
22/11/30	JOHN	CANNINGS	HANTS	ITCHEN ABBAS
5/8/31	JOHN	CANNON	KENT	RIPPLE
29/11/30	ROBERT	CAREY	BUCKS	MARSH GREEN
12/30	RICHARD	CARLILE	LONDON	LONDON
29/11/30	JOHN	CARMAN	NORFOLK	WHINBURGH
28/8/30	CHARLE	CARSWELL	KENT	LOWERHARDRES
20/9/30	CHARLES	CARSWELL	KENT	BARHAM
19/11/32		CARTER	BERKS	LAMBOURNE
27/11/30	JOSEPH	CARTER	BUCKS	BISHOPSTONE
19/11/30	JOSEPH	CARTER	HANTS	EAST STRATTON
21/11/30	GEORGE	CARTER	HANTS	VERNHAM DEAN
22/11/30	GEORGE	CARTER	HANTS	ITCHEN ABBAS
27/11/30	GEORGE	CARTER	BUCKS	BISHOPSTONE
26/1/31	JAMES	CARVER	GLOUCS	FAIRFORD
26/1/31	THOMAS	CASS	ESSEX	GREAT HALLINGBURY
7/12/30	JAMES	CASS	ESSEX	GREAT CLACTON
27/11/30	RICHARD	CASTLE	BUCKS	STONE
29/11/30	WILLIAM	CATCHPOLE	NORFOLK	WHINBURGH
13/12/30	JOHN	CAUSTON	ESSEX	GREAT CLACTON
25/11/30	HENRY	CAVELL	HANTS	FAWLEY
20/10/32	WW	CAWSON	KENT	RAINHAM
20/10/32	J	CAWSON	KENT	RAINHAM
22/11/30	JOHN	CHALK	HANTS	DURLEY
7/12/30	JOB	CHALLIS	ESSEX	ELMDON
7/12/30	THOMAS	CHALLIS	ESSEX	ELMDON
29/5/32	JOHN	CHAPLIN	NORFOLK	WITCHINGHAM
1/12/30	JAMES	CHAPMAN	BUCKS	IVER
12/30	JOHN	CHAPMAN	NOTTS	NORTON
28/10/30	EDWARD	CHAPMAN	KENT	HOLLINGBOURNE
24/11/30	JAMES	CHAPMAN	NORFOLK	FOULSHAM
26/11/30	JOSEPH	CHAPMAN	NORTHANTS	WARMINGTON
12/30	W	CHECKETTS	WORCS	DEFFORD
17/10/31	JOHN	CHERETT	DORSET	BLANDFORD
23/10/30	ABRAHAM	CHERRYBOLD	KENT	BEAKESBOURNE
5/8/31	WILLIAM	CHIDDICK	KENT	RIPPLE
22/11/30	ABRAHAM	CHILDS	HANTS	CORHAMPTON
10/31	JOHN	CHIPMAN	WARWICKSHIRE	RUGBY
19/11/32		CHIVERS	BERKS	LAMBOURNE

DATE	PARISH	COUNTY	SURNAME	FORENAME
22/11/30	MICHELMERSH	HANTS	COLLINS	GEORGE
22/11/30	MICHELMERSH	HANTS	COLLINS	JOHN
19/11/30	MICHELDEVER	HANTS	COLLIS	DAVID
26/11/30	HORSLEY	GLOUCS	COMPTON	GEORGE
26/11/30	BEVERSTONE	GLOUCS	COMPTON	HENRY
1/12/30	HENSTRIDGE	SOMERSET	CONDON	WILLIAM
21/11/30	KIMPTON	HANTS	CONDUIT	WILLIAM
4/2/31	WHITCHURCH	SHROPSHIRE	COOK	THOMAS
1/31	MAIDSTONE	KENT	COOK	
22/11/30	ITCHEN ABBAS	HANTS	COOK	THOMAS
22/11/30	WOOTON ST LAWRENCE	HANTS	COOK	JAMES
22/11/30	ROMSEY EXTRA	HANTS	COOKE	HENRY
21/11/30	MICHELDEVER	HANTS	COOKE	ROBERT
21/11/30	VERNHAM DEAN	HANTS	COOKE	HENRY
1830			COOLING	RICHARD
1/31	LUSBY	LINCS	COOMBS	CHARLES
27/11/30	BUCKLAND NEWTON	DORSET	COOPER	
17/12/30	SELBOURN	HANTS	COOPER	JOHN
22/11/30	ITCHEN ABBAS	HANTS	COOPER	THOMAS
10/5/30	CHIPPING CAMDEN	GLOUCS	COOPER	JAMES THOMAS
7/12/30	FORDINGBRIDGE	HANTS	COOPER	CHARLES
8/30	BURY ST EDMUNDS	SUFFOLK	COOPER	JAMES
23/11/30	EAST WOODHAY	HANTS	COOPER	RICHARD
20/12/30	MORETON IN THE MARSH	GLOUCS	COPCUTT	JOHN
26/11/30	WADDESDON	BUCKS	COPELAND	JOHN
23/11/30	NORTH WALSHAM	NORFOLK	COPHAM	JAMES
3/12/30		NORFOLK	COSTELLO	DANIEL
27/11/30	STONE	BUCKS	COWELL	ELIJAH
26/11/30	WADDESDON	BUCKS	COWELL	JOHN
7/12/30	WENDEN LOFTS	ESSEX	COWLEY	ROBERT
26/11/30	FAIRFORD	GLOUCS	COWLEY	JOHN
24/11/30		NORFOLK	COX	JOHN
12/31	ASTON CLINTON	BUCKS	COX	WILLIAM
26/11/30	HORSLEY	GLOUCS	COX	WILLIAM
20/12/31	BARSTON	WARWICKSHIRE	COX	DAVID
27/11/30	EASTLEACH TURVILLE	GLOUCS	COXON	THOMAS
24/11/30	RODSLEY	DERBY	CRAYTHORN	HENRY
26/11/30	WARMINGTON	NORTHANTS	CRAYTHORN	JOHN
19/11/30	WESTBOURNE	SUSSEX	CROCKFORD	HURLOCK
29/11/30	LONG CRENDON	BUCKS	CROOK	JOHN
29/11/30	SOUTHROP	GLOUCS	CROOK	ROBERT
22/11/30	UPHAM	HANTS	CROPP	JAMES

DATE	PARISH	COUNTY	SURNAME	FORENAME
5/31	LENTON	NOTTS	CROSS	WILLIAM
7/12/30	GREAT CLACTON	ESSEX	CROSS	JAMES
29/11/30	CHEPPING WYCOMBE	BUCKS	CRUTCH	JOHN
19/12/31	BASSINGBOURN	CAMBS	CUBISS	MARTHA
19/12/31	BASSINGBOURN	CAMBS	CUBISS	GEORGE
26/11/30	FAWLEY	HANTS	CULL	ROBERT
25/10/30	WINGHAM	KENT	CULL	JOSEPH
25/11/30	FAWLEY	HANTS	CULL	ROBERT
7/12/30	GREAT CLACTON	ESSEX	CULLENDER	JAMES
24/10/31	SIDDINGTON	CHESHIRE	CUMBERLIDGE	WILLIAM
8/12/30	LITTLE CLACTON	ESSEX	CURTIS	WILLIAM
10/31		YORK (ER)	CURTIS	RICHARD
15/11/30	GOUDHURST	KENT	CUTBUSH	JOHN
26/11/30	BEVERSTONE	GLOUCS	CYPHER	JOHN
29/11/30	MARSH GREEN	BUCKS	DAFTER	JOHN
29/11/30	CHEPPING WYCOMBE	BUCKS	DANDRIDGE	JOHN
27/11/30	BISHOPSTONE	BUCKS	DANIELS	WILLIAM
27/11/30	BISHOPSTONE	BUCKS	DANIELS	JOHN
27/11/30	BISHOPSTONE	BUCKS	DANIELS	WILLIAM (YOUNGER)
3/8/32	CROYDON	CAMBS	DARNEL	SAMUEL
4/12/30	YARDLEY	HERTS	DARTON	JASPER
4/12/30	YARDLEY	HERTS	DARTON	JASPER ELDER
4/12/30	YARDLEY	HERTS	DARTON	JOHN
8/12/30	KIRBY-LE-SOKEN	ESSEX	DAVEY	GEORGE
8/12/30	KIRBY-LE-SOKEN	ESSEX	DAVEY	ROBERT
8/12/30	WALTON-LE-SOKEN	ESSEX	DAVEY	ROBERT
29/11/30	EAST STOWER	DORSET	DAVIDGE	JAMES
9/11/30	WINGHAM	KENT	DAVIDSON	A
9/1/31	SWANTON MORLEY	NORFOLK	DAVIDSON	JOSIAH
9/1/31	SWANTON MORLEY	NORFOLK	DAVIDSON	DAVID
12/30	ALTON BARNES	WILTS	DAVIS	
26/11/30	WADDESDON	BUCKS	DAVIS	ISAAC
21/11/30	CANTERBURY	KENT	DAVY	GEORGE
8/12/30	WALTON-LE-SOKEN	ESSEX	DAVY	GEORGE
11/30	RANSKILL	NOTTS	DAWSON	
14/12/30	FINCHINGFIELD	ESSEX	DAWSON	WILLIAM
27/11/30	TAVERHAM	NORFOLK	DAWSON	HENRY
22/11/30	ROMSEY EXTRA	HANTS	DAY	WILLIAM
22/11/30	WOOTON ST LAWRENCE	HANTS	DAY	HENRY
23/11/30	FORDINGBRIDGE	HANTS	DEADMAN	AARON
27/11/30	COLN ST ALDWYN	GLOUCS	DEBANK	WILLIAM

DATE	PARISH	COUNTY	SURNAME	FORENAME
26/11/30	WADDESDON	BUCKS	DEELEY	JOHN
29/11/30	CHEPPING WYCOMBE	BUCKS	DELL	JOHN
23/11/30	SHERFIELD	HANTS	DENNETT	JOSEPH
22/11/30	FOXLEY	NORFOLK	DENNEY	JAMES
26/4/31	TRUNCH	NORFOLK	DERSING	JAMES
30/11/30	FINENDON	NORTHANTS	DESBOROUGH	JOHN
27/11/30	BISHOPSTONE	BUCKS	DEWBERRY	JOSEPH
27/11/30	STONE	BUCKS	DEWBERRY	WILLIAM
28/11/30	BOUGHTON	NORFOLK	DEWING	J
23/11/30	PAMBER	HANTS	DIBLEY	JAMES
26/11/30	EXBURY & LEAPE	HANTS	DICKSON	JAMES
29/5/32	WITCHINGHAM	NORFOLK	DIGBY	CHARLES
6/12/30	GREAT THURLOW	SUFFOLK	DISS	WILLIAM
29/11/30	THURGARTON	NORFOLK	DIX	ROBERT
5/8/31	RIPPLE	KENT	DIXON	MARK
11/31	EASTRY	KENT	DIXON	RICHARD
12/31	EASTRY	KENT	DIXON	ROBERT
6/8/31	ST BRIAVELS	GLOUCS	DOBBS	THOMAS
19/12/31	BASSINGBOURNE	CAMBS	DOCWRA	WILLIAM
16/11/30	BENENDEN	KENT	DODGE	JOHN
18/12/30	NORTH WALSHAM	NORFOLK	DOE	WILLIAM
30/1/30	BILLINGHAY	LINCS	DONNELLY	JAMES
29/11/30	STOUR PROVOST	DORSET	DORE	JOHN
1830	FUNTINTON	SUSSEX	DOREY	JOHN
24/11/30	CAWSTON	NORFOLK	DOVE	WILLIAM
7/12/30	GREAT CLACTON	ESSEX	DOVERCOURT	WILLIAM
29/3/32	STAPLEFORD TAWNEY	ESSEX	DOW	JOSEPH
19/3/31	DENBY	YORKS (WR)	DOWNING	WILLIAM
22/12/30	CHARTERIS	CAMBS	DRAKE	JOHN
4/12/30	YARDLEY	HERTS	DRAPER	JOSEPH
26/11/30	FARFORD	GLOUCS	DRAPER	JOHN
8/12/30	WALTON-LE-SOKEN	ESSEX	DRAPER	SAMUEL
18/11/30	HAVANT	HANTS	DUKE	JOHN
15/12/30	WHITCHURCH	SHROPSHIRE	DUMOIR	JOHN
24/11/30	THANET	KENT	DUNK	JAMES
8/9/31	SEVENOAKS	KENT	DUNKS	WILLIAM
6/12/30	GREAT HOLLAND	ESSEX	DUNNETT	CHARLES
27/11/30	BUCKLAND NEWTON	DORSET	DURRANT	WILLIAM
11/12/30	SHUTLANGER	NORTHANTS	DURRANT	EDWARD
7/12/30	TENDRING	ESSEX	DURRANT	WILLIAM
13/12/30	LONG MELFORD	SUFFOLK	DURRENT	ALEXANDER
3/31	POLSTEAD	SUFFOLK	DYER	WILLIAM

FORENAME	SURNAME	COUNTY	PARISH	DATE
JOHN	DYKE (@ FIELD)	KENT	BEARSTED	10/11/30
STEPHEN	EADE	ESSEX	GREAT CLACTON	7/12/30
JAMES	EARLE	NORFOLK	HICKLING	25/11/30
	EASON	KENT	THROWLEY	31/10/31
JOHN	EAST	BUCKS	CHEPPING WYCOMBE	29/11/30
DAVID	EASTLAND	SUSSEX	BATTLE	11/30
DAVID	EASTLAND	SUSSEX	NINFIELD	9/11/30
STEPHEN	EAVES	KENT	GOUDHURST	9/11/30
GEORGE	EAVIS	SOMERSET	HENSTRIDGE	1/12/30
WILLIAM	EBBEN	NORFOLK	WINFARTHING	23/11/30
ROBERT	EBSWORTH	GLOUCS	EASTLEACH MARTIN	27/11/30
JOHN	EDGEWORTH	GLOUCS	BILBURY	29/11/30
THOMAS	EDGEWORTH	GLOUCS	BIBURY	29/11/30
JAMES	EDGEWORTH	GLOUCS	BIBURY	29/11/30
JOSEPH	EDGINGTON	GLOUCS	COLN ST ALDWYN	27/11/30
WILLIAM	EDWARDS	BUCKS	LONG CREDON	29/11/30
BENJAMIN	EDWARDS	SUFFOLK	WESTLETON	30/4/31
	EDWINSTOW	NOTTS	OLLERTON	23/8/31
WILLIAM	ELDRIDGE	KENT	ORPINGTON	10/4/30
HENRY	ELDRIDGE	HANTS	FORDINGBRIDGE	23/11/30
HENRY	ELDRIDGE	GLOUCS	EASTLEACH MARTIN	27/11/30
JOHN	ELDRIDGE	GLOUCS	SOUTHROP	29/11/30
	ELEPHANT	SUFFOLK	POLSTEAD	12/11/30
WILLIAM	ELKINS	HANTS	FORDINGBRIDGE	23/11/30
HARRY	ELKINS	DORSET	CANN	30/11/30
GEORGE	ELKINS	DORSET	CANN	30/11/30
GEORGE JUN	ELKINS	DORSET	CANN	30/11/30
JOSEPH	ELLERM	CAMBS	GREAT SHELFORD	15/12/31
JOHN	ELLIOTTS	GLOUCS	BEVERSTONE	26/11/30
JOSEPH	ELLIS	HANTS	UPPER CLATFORD	20/11/30
JOHN	ELLISON	WILTSHIRE	SWINDON	5/11/31
EDWARD	ELSMORE	GLOUCS	ST BRIAVELS	6/8/31
WILLIAM	ENDALL	NOTHANTS	UPPER BEDINGTON	3/12/30
WILLIAM	ENDELL	NORTHANTS	UPPER BEDDINGTON	3/12/30
ERNEST	ERBST	SUSSEX	BATTLE	11/30
GEORGE	ESAM	NOTTS	BULWELL	6/31
WILLIAM	ESAM	NOTTS	BULWELL	6/31
RICHARD	ETHERINGTON	HANTS	DURLEY	22/11/30
JOHN	EVANS	SHROPSHIRE	RABINS WOOD	7/2/31
	EVANS	KENT/SUSSEX		1830
WILLIAM	EVANS	BUCKS	IVER	1/12/30
JOHN	EVANS	BUCKS	WADDESDON	26/11/30

DATE	PARISH	COUNTY	SURNAME	FORENAME
1830	FRAMFIELD	SUSSEX	EVANS	BENJAMIN
10/12/30	CHEVINGTON	SUFFOLK	EVERED	JOHN
6/12/30	WITHERSFIELD	SUFFOLK	EVERITT	THOMAS
6/12/30	WITHERSFIELD	SUFFOLK	EVERITT	JAMES
5/11/30	RAYLEIGH	ESSEX	EWEN	JAMES
19/12/31	LOUND	NOTTS	EXBY	WILLIAM
22/11/30	PENTON GRAFTON	HANTS	EYLES	ISAAC
25/11/30	TISBURY	WILTS	EYRES	SAMUEL
16/11/30	ASHLEY	KENT	FAGG	MICHAEL
29/1/31	RUCKINGE	KENT	FAGG	WILLIAM
8/9/30	WESTERHAM	KENT	FAIRBURN	GEORGE
22/11/30	WOOTON ST LAWRENCE	HANTS	FARMER	WILLIAM
22/11/30	VERNHAM DEAN	HANTS	FARMER	JEREMIAH
6/12/30	COLCHESTER	ESSEX	FARROW	THOMAS
20/11/30	UPPER CLATFORD	HANTS	FAY	CHARLES
12/30	LUTTON	LINCS	FENDLEBOW	
26/11/30	BEVERSTONE	GLOUCS	FERRABEE	RICHARD
26/11/30	FAIRFORD	GLOUCS	FERRIS	CHARLES
10/11/30	THURNHAM	KENT	FIELD	JOHN
22/11/30	MICHELMERSH	HANTS	FIELDER	ARTHUR
28/8/30	LOWER HARDRES	KENT	FILE	STEPHEN
9/2/30	BURSTALL	SUFFOLK	FINCH	EDWARD
				BOLTON
4/12/30	MARSH GREEN	NORFOLK	FISH	THOMAS
29/11/30	HONING	BUCKS	FISHER	THOMAS
25/11/30	WHITWELL	NORFOLK	FISHER	JOHN
25/11/30	BRESSINGHAM	NORFOLK	FISHER	EDWARD
4/12/30	RIPPLE	KENT	FISKE	THOMAS
5/8/31	CHEVINGTON	SUFFOLK	FITTAL	GEORGE
10/12/30	ROYDON	NORFOLK	FLACK	ROBERT
1831	ORSETT	ESSEX	FLATMAN	EDWARD
3/12/30	BATTLE	SUSSEX	FLETCHER	MEYRICH
11/30	BATTLE	SUSSEX	FOORD	STEPHEN
9/11/30	NINFIELD	SUSSEX	FOORD	LEVI
9/11/30	NINFIELD	SUSSEX	FOORD	STEPHEN
30/11/30	SHAFTESBURY	DORSET	FOOTE	LEVI
21/11/30	CRAWLEY	HANTS	FORD	CHARLES
9/11/30	WINGHAM	KENT	FORD	JAMES
26/11/30	BEVERSTONE	GLOUCS	FORD	GEORGE
1/1/32	ALPHINGTON	DEVON	FORD	JOHN
20/11/30	BACTON	SUFFOLK	FORD	WILLIAM
				ROBERT

FORENAME	SURNAME	COUNTY	PARISH	DATE
CHARLES	FORDER	HANTS	BROUGHTON	22/11/30
JOHN	FOSTER	KENT	THANET	24/11/30
JOSEPH	FOWLER	BUCKS	WADDESDON	26/11/30
JAMES	FOX	GLOUCS	BIBURY	29/11/30
EDWARD	FOX	NORFOLK	WRAMPINGTON	29/11/30
SUSAN	FRAMPTON	DORSET	SYDLING ST NICHOLAS	30/5/30
BEN	FRANCIS	BUCKS	MARSH GREEN	29/11/30
JOHN	FREELAND	SUSSEX	WESTBOURNE	19/11/30
AMBROSE	FREEMAN	NORTHANTS	FINENDON	30/11/30
NICHOLAS	FREEMANTLE	HANTS	CORHAMPTON	22/11/30
JOHN	FROST	ESSEX	HENHAM	13/12/30
JEREMIAH	FRY	GLOUCS	BEVERSTONE	26/11/30
JAMES	FRYER	HANTS	FORDINGBRIDGE	23/11/30
JOHN	FULFORD	HANTS	FORDINGBRIDGE	23/11/30
JOHN	FULFORD	HANTS	FORDINGBRIDGE	23/11/30
WILLIAM	FULLER	ESSEX	GREAT DUNMOW	10/12/30
JOHN	FULLER	ESSEX	HENHAM	13/12/30
WILLIAM	FULLER	NORFOLK	NORTH WALSHAM	18/12/30
THOMAS	FULLER	NORFOLK	NORTH WALSHAM	5/32
CHARLES	FULLER	NORFOLK	WITCHINGHAM	29/5/32
JAMES	FUSSELL	ESSEX	OWLESBURY	23/11/30
WILLIAM	GAGE	ESSEX	GREAT COGGESHALL	22/11/30
HENRY	GALE	HANTS	BROUGHTON	22/11/30
THOMAS	GAMBILL	KENT	WINGHAM	9/11/30
THOMAS	GAMBRILL	KENT	BEAKESBOURNE	23/10/30
JAMES	GAPES	ESSEX	ARKESDEN	10/12/30
WILLIAM	GARDENER	KENT		1830
RICHARD	GATHERCOTE	NORFOLK	MATTISHALL	29/11/30
GEORGE	GEOFFREY	ESSEX	ELMDON	7/12/30
GEORGE	GERRARD	WILTS	FONTHILL BISHOP	25/11/30
JOHN	GIBBS	BUCKS	LONG CREDON	29/11/30
JOHN	GIBBS	WILTS	STEEPLE ASHTON	1831
THOMAS	GIBBS	HANTS	FARRINGDON	22/11/30
THOMAS	GIBBS	NORFOLK	HICKLING	25/11/30
JOHN	GIBSON	BUCKS	MARSH GREEN	29/11/30
DAVID	GILBERT	HANTS	FORDINGBRIDGE	23/11/30
AMOS	GILBERT	LINCS	LEAKE	15/12/31
JOHN	GILBERT	NORFOLK	EAST TUDDENHAM	30/11/30
JAMES	GILES	HANTS	CRAWLEY	21/11/30
CHARLES	GILLETT	GLOUCS	FAIRFORD	26/11/30
JOHN	GILMORE	HANTS	UPPER CLATFORD	20/11/30
DANIEL	GLADDING	SUFFOLK	BURSTALL	9/2/30

DATE	PARISH	COUNTY	SURNAME	FORENAME
13/12/30	GREAT CLACTON	ESSEX	GLADWELL	JOSEPH
7/12/30	GREAT CLACTON	ESSEX	GLADWIN	JOSHUA
22/11/30	CORHAMPTON	HANTS	GLASSPOLE	JAMES
17/11/30	BOSHAM	SUSSEX	GOBLE	EDWARD
11/1/31	STANDON	HERTS	GODDARD	JAMES
12/30	ALDBOURNE	WILTS	GODDARD	THOMAS
2/12/31	RUGELEY	STAFFS	GODWIN	SAMUEL
9-11/12/30	SWIMBRIDGE	DEVON	GOFF	GEORGE
2/32	BRETTINGHAM	SUFFOLK	GOFF	BENJAMIN
29/11/30	DOCKING	NORFOLK	GOLASON	JAMES
29/11/30	DOCKING	NORFOLK	GOLASON	EDWARD
29/11/30	DOCKING	NORFOLK	GOLASON	CHARLES
19/11/30	BASINGSTOKE	HANTS	GOLD	JOHN
15/11/30	ISLE OF THANNET	KENT	GOLDER	THOMAS
20/11/30	MARGATE	KENT	GOLDER	WILLIAM
5/8/31	RIPPLE	KENT	GOLDER	THOMAS
5/8/31	RIPPLE	KENT	GOLDER	RICHARD
26/11/30	BEVERSTONE	GLOUCS	GOLDING	WILLIAM
20/11/30	UPPER CLATFORD	HANTS	GOODALL	JOHN
20/11/30	UPPER CLATFORD	HANTS	GOODALL	THOMAS
2/12/30	WAVENDON	BUCKS	GOODHALL	WILLIAM
1/1/31	SIDMOUTH	DEVON	GOODING	THOMAS
1830	BATHLEY	NOTTS	GOODMAN	THOMAS
11/1830	BATTLE	SUSSEX	GOODMAN	THOMAS
1/12/30	LITTLE BRICKHILL	BUCKS	GOODSON	JAMES
22/11/30	GREAT COGGESHALL	ESSEX	GOODSON	THOMAS
29/3/31	DONYATT	SOMERSET	GOSLING	SAMUEL
26/11/30	WARMINGTON	NORTHANTS	GOSS	WILLIAM
22/11/30	GREAT COGGESHALL	ESSEX	GOULD	ISAAC
4/3/31	BUXTON	NORFOLK	GOULD	JOHN
23/11/30	FORDINGBRIDGE	HANTS	GOULDING	JOSEPH
15/3/32	FORDWICH	KENT	GRANT	HEZEKIAH
29/11/30	WINFRITH	DORSET	GRANT	WILLIAM
12/2/31	ARNE	DORSET	GRANT	JAMES
8/12/30	WALTON-LE-SOKEN	ESSEX	GRANT	THOMAS
8/12/30	WALTON-LE-SOKEN	ESSEX	GRANT	JOHN
8/12/30	WALTON-LE-SOKEN	ESSEX	GRANT	JAMES
22/11/30	BROUGHTON	HANTS	GRANT	WILLIAM
20/11/30	MARTYR WORTHY	HANTS	GRANTHAM	J
2/7/32	STODY	NORFOLK	GRAVELAND	JOHN
31/7/31	BARHAM	KENT	GRAVES	
18/1/30	DEIGHTON	YORK (ER)	GRAY	WILLIAM

DATE	PARISH	COUNTY	SURNAME	FORENAME
3/8/32	CROYDON	CAMBS	GREAVES	WILLIAM
23/8/31	OLLERTON	NOTTS	GREAVES	JOHN
3/8/32	CROYDON	CAMBS	GREEN	JOHN
20/11/30	UPPER CLATFORD	HANTS	GREEN	THOMAS
8/12/30	STOKE BY CLARE	SUFFOLK	GREEN	RICHARD
15/5/32	WINFARTHING	NORFOLK	GREEN	CHRISTOPHER
22/11/30	QUARLEY	HANTS	GREGORY	THOMAS
13/10/30	STANSTED MOUNTFITCHET	ESSEX	GRIGGS	JOSHUA
12/9/31	WHITCHURCH	SHROPSHIRE	GRINDLEY	JOSEPH
12/9/31	WHITCHURCH	SHROPSHIRE	GRINDLEY	S
5/1/31	LITTLEDEAN	GLOUCS	GRINDOLL	SAMUEL
6/8/31	ST BRIAVELS	GLOUCS	GRINDOLL	GEORGE
27/4/31	KNAPTON	NORFOLK	GRIX	SARAH
12/30	DEFFORD	WORCS	GROVE	T
29/11/30	DOCKING	NORFOLK	GROVES	JOSEPH
24/11/30	DOCKING	NORFOLK	GUILDING	RICHARD
1/12/30	STALBRIDGE	DORSET	GULLIVER	GEORGE
3/32	BARNWELL	CAMBS	GUNN	JAMES
30/11/30	EAST TUDDENHAM	NORFOLK	GUNTON	JAMES
30/11/30	EAST TUDDENHAM	NORFOLK	GUNTON	SAMUEL
4/32	WITCHINGHAM	NORFOLK	GUYMER	ROBERT
24/12/30	STRUMPSHAW	NORFOLK	GYMER	THOMAS
8/12/30	LITTLE CLACTON	ESSEX	HACKSHELL	BENJAMIN
11/31	BRIGSTOCK	NORTHANTS	HADLAND	JOSEPH
29/5/32	WITCHINGHAM	NORFOLK	HAINSWORTH	CHRISTOPHER
29/11/30	MARSH GREEN	BUCKS	HALL	MOSES
27/7/32	BLACKER	YORK (WR)	HALL	JOSEPH
22/11/30	CHEPPING WYCOMBE	BUCKS	HALL	JAMES
22/11/30	HURSTBOURNE TARRANT	HANTS	HALL	JOSEPH
29/11/30	SOUTHROP	GLOUCS	HALLAM	JAMES
2/32	BRADMORE	NOTTS	HALLAM	WILLIAM
29/10/30	BOUGHTON	KENT	HALLIWELL	
10/12/30	CHEVINGTON	SUFFOLK	HAMMOND	ABRAHAM
22/11/30	ARKESDEN	ESSEX	HAMMOND	WILLIAM
29/11/30	ITCHEN ABBAS	HANTS	HAMPTON	GEORGE
6/10/31	MARSH GREEN	BUCKS	HANCOCK	WILLIAM
24/11/30	DILHAM	NORFOLK	HANNANT	D
23/11/30	WROTHAM	KENT	HARDING	THOMAS
22/11/30	HEADLEY	HANTS	HARDING	AARON
22/11/30	SELBOURNE	HANTS	HARDING	BENJAMIN
9/11/30	UPHAM	HANTS	HARDING	FAULKNER
	WINGHAM	KENT	HARDING	

DATE	PARISH	COUNTY	SURNAME	FORENAME
25/11/30	FONTHILL BISHOP	WILTS	HARDING	WILLIAM
6/12/30	COLCHESTER	ESSEX	HARDWICK	ISAAC
6/12/30	GREAT THURLOW	SUFFOLK	HARGRAVE	FREDERICK
6/12/30	WHEPSTEAD	SUFFOLK	HARIS	JOHN
27/11/30	GREAT THURLOW	SUFFOLK	HARLOCK	ISAAC
29/11/30		NORFOLK	HARNELL	WILLIAM
19/12/31	LONG CRENDON	BUCKS	HARPER	JAMES
30/7/32	BASSINGBOURNE	CAMBS	HARRADENE	WILLIAM
1/12/30		CAMBS	HARRADINE	JOHN
23/11/30	STALBRIDGE	DORSET	HARRIS	JOHN
16/6/31	EAST WOODHAY	HANTS	HARRIS	JOHN
10/12/30	ST BRIAVELS	GLOUCS	HARRIS	WILLIAM
8/12/30	ARKESDEN	ESSEX	HARRIS	WILLIAM
3/1830	LITTLE CLACTON	ESSEX	HARRISON	THOMAS
23/11/30	RAUNDS	NORTHANTS	HARRISON	JOHN
5/12/30	BREAMORE	HANTS	HART	JOHN
9/31	RAMSEY	ESSEX	HART	HENRY
9/31	WRITTLE	ESSEX	HART	SAMUEL
26/11/30	WRITTLE	GLOUCS	HARVEY	CHARLES
24/11/30	FAIRFORD	NORFOLK	HARVEY	JAMES
11/32	CAWSTON	ESSEX	HARWOOD	JOSEPH
29/11/30	WEST HAM	DORSET	HATCHER	DAVID
29/11/30	STOUR PROVOST	DORSET	HATCHER	STEPHEN
22/11/30	EAST STOWER	KENT	HAWKER	
10/12/30	WOODNESBOROUGH	ESSEX	HAYDEN	JAMES
10/12/30	ARKESDEN	ESSEX	HAYDEN	CHARLES
22/11/30	ARKESDEN	HANTS	HAYES	JOHN
7/12/30	WENDEN LOFTS	ESSEX	HAYES	JOSIAH
8/12/30	KIRBY-LE-SOKEN	ESSEX	HAYHOE	SAMUEL
23/11/30	FORDINGBRIDGE	HANTS	HAYTER	CHARLES
4/12/30	YARDLEY	HERTS	HEAD	WILLIAM
1830	BREDE	SUSSEX	HEALEY	THOMAS
19/12/32	BEESTON	NOTTS	HEARSON	GEORGE
23/11/30	HEADLEY	HANTS	HEATH	JOHN
24/11/30	WROTHAM	KENT	HEAVER	G
27/11/30	BISHOPSTONE	BUCKS	HEDGES	GEORGE
24/11/30	BINSTED	HANTS	HEIGHES	WILLIAM
24/11/30	BINSTED	HANTS	HEIGHES	THOMAS
9/11/30	WINGHAM	KENT	HEIGHT	THOMAS
3/12/30	HENSTRIDGE	SOMERSET	HELIER	JAMES
8/3/32	BECCLES FEN	SUFFOLK	HELLEN	HENRY

FORENAME	SURNAME	COUNTY	PARISH	DATE
THOMAS	HEPBURN	KENT	MARGATE	20/11/30
ERNEST	HERLEST	SUSSEX	NINFIELD	9/11/30
WILLIAM	HIBBERD	HANTS	BIGHTON	22/11/30
DANIEL	HIBDEN	SUFFOLK	BECCLES FEN	8/3/32
JAMES	HICKS	SUSSEX	BREDE	1830
HENRY	HICKS	GLOUCS	SOUTHROP	29/11/30
WILLIAM	HIGH	NORFOLK	TILNEY	3/1/31
RICHARD	HIGHAM	NORFOLK	DOCKING	29/11/30
GEORGE	HIGNELL	GLOUCS	FAIRFORD	26/11/30
ISAAC	HILL	HANTS	MICHELDEVER	19/11/30
ISAAC SNR	HILL	HANTS	MICHELDEVER	19/11/30
WILLIAM	HILL	HANTS	BURGHCLERE	23/11/30
GEORGE	HILLESDON	BUCKS	WADDESDON	26/11/30
JAMES	HILLESDON	BUCKS	WADDESDON	26/11/30
JOHN	HILTON	YORK (WR)	BLACKER	27/7/32
ROBERT	HILTON	NORFOLK	WHINBURGH	29/11/30
RICHARD	HINDES	SUFFOLK	BECCLES FEN	8/3/32
HENRY	HIPKIN	NORFOLK	DOCKING	29/11/30
JOHN	HITCHCOCK	HANTS	ITCHEN ABBAS	22/11/30
RICHARD	HOAR	HANTS	OWLESBURY	23/11/30
WILLIAM	HOARE	HANTS	BURITON	22/11/30
THOMAS	HOARE	HANTS	SELBORNE	22/11/30
JAMES	HOBBS	DORSET	STALBRIDGE	1/12/30
RICHARD	HODD	SUSSEX	WITHYAM	1830
THOMAS	HODSON	HANTS		19/11/30
ROBERT	HOLDAWAY	HANTS	HEADLEY	23/11/30
ROBERT	HOLDAWAY	HANTS	HEADLEY	23/11/30
EDWARD	HOLLAND	ESSEX	COLCHESTER	6/12/30
THOMAS	HOLLAND			
JOSEPH	HOLLAND	BUCKS	WADDESDON	26/11/30
GEORGE	HOLLANDS	KENT	THANET	24/11/30
JOHN	HOLLANDS	KENT	THANET	24/11/30
RICHARD	HOLLOWAY	HANTS	CRAWLEY	21/11/30
DAVID	HOLMES	NORFOLK	LINGWOOD	4/12/30
GEORGE	HOLT	HANTS	MARTYR WORTHY	20/11/30
JOHN	HOOK	NORFOLK	REDENHALL	23/11/30
ISAAC	HOOKER	WILTS		12/30
THOMAS	HOOPER	HANTS	SOUTH STONEHAM	23/11/30
HENRY	HOPCRAFT	BUCKS	LONG CRENDON	29/11/30
ROBERT	HOPCROFT	BUCKS	WADDESDON	26/11/30
THOMAS	HOPES	CAMBS	BASSINGBOURNE	19/12/31

DATE	PARISH	SURNAME	FORENAME	COUNTY
20/12/30	FOULMIRE	HOPGOOD	BENJAMIN	CAMBS
19/11/30	ANDOVER	HOPGOOD	JOHN	HANTS
21/11/30	VERNHAM DEAN	HOPGOOD	GEORGE	HANTS
22/11/30	ITCHEN ABBAS	HOPKINS	CHRISTOPHER	HANTS
3/8/32	CROYDON	HOPKINS	JOHN	CAMBS
20/12/30	FOULMIRE	HOPWOOD	B	CAMBS
17/10/31	BLANDFORD	HORLOCK	JOHN	DORSET
22/11/30	ITCHEN ABBAS	HORN	JAMES	HANTS
20/11/30	WALTHAM ST LAWRENCE	HORTON		BERKS
25/10/30	WINGHAM	HORTON		KENT
22/11/30	DURLEY	HOUGHTON	PETER	HANTS
22/11/30	DURLEY	HOUGHTON	JAMES	HANTS
26/11/30	WADDESDON	HOUNSLOW	JOHN	BUCKS
24/11/30	BUCKLAND NEWTON	HOUSE	ABRAHAM	DORSET
24/11/30	BUCKLAND NEWTON	HOUSE	JAMES	DORSET
17/11/30	SOUTHOVER	HOWARD		SUSSEX
17/11/30	SOUTHOVER	HOWARD		SUSSEX
28/11/30	BISHOPS WALTHAM	HOWE	HENRY	HANTS
24/11/30	CAWSTON	HOWES	GEORGE	NORFOLK
25/11/30	KERDISTON	HOWES	EDWARD	NORFOLK
25/11/30	HICKLING	HOWES	GEORGE	NORFOLK
27/11/30	BISHOPSTONE	HOWLETT	ROBERT	BUCKS
29/11/30	BURNHAM THORPE	HUBBARD	WILLIAM	NORFOLK
15/5/32	WINFARTHING	HUBBARD	ROBERT	NORFOLK
18/11/30	WARBLINGTON	HUDSON	JOHN	HANTS
20/11/30	MARGATE	HUGHES	WILLIAM	KENT
27/11/30	BISHOPSTONE	HUGHES	THOMAS	BUCKS
20/12/30	BARSTON	HUGHES	JOHN	WARWICKSHIRE
20/12/30	BARSTON	HUGHES	JOSEPH	WARWICKSHIRE
23/10/30	BEAKESBOURNE	HULKES	HENRY	KENT
26/11/30	WARMINGTON	HUMBERSTONE	WILLIAM	NORTHANTS
20/11/30	BARTON STACEY	HUNT	HENRY	HANTS
10/12/31	BARTON STACEY	HUNT	HENRY	HANTS
9/1/31	SWANTON MORLEY	HUNT	ROBERT	NORFOLK
27/11/30	EASTLEACH TURVILLE	HUNT	JOHN	GLOUCS
29/11/30	SOUTHROP	HUNT	BENJAMIN	GLOUCS
8/12/30	LITTLE CLACTON	HURRELL	BENJAMIN	ESSEX
28/12/30	BARFORD	HURRELL	ISAAC	NORFOLK
10/12/30	ARKESDEN	HURRELL	ALAN	ESSEX
8/12/30	LITTLE CLACTON	HURRELL	THOMAS	ESSEX
9/3/31	BRIDPORT	HUSSEY	S	DORSET
11/12/30	HANLEY WILLIAM	HYDE	JOHN	WORCS

FORENAME	SURNAME	COUNTY	PARISH	DATE
RICHARD	HYDON	SOMERSET	CHARD	4/31
BAKER	IGGULDEN	KENT	SHOREHAM	12/1/232
STEPHEN	ILLSLEY	HANTS	ITCHEN ABBAS	22/11/30
DAVID	ILOTT	CAMBS	CROYDON	3/8/32
WILLIAM	INGRAM	ESSEX	WALTON-LE-SOKEN	8/12/30
JOHN	INSKIPP	SUSSEX	BATTLE	22/11/30
CHARLES	ISLES	HANTS	KIMPTON	21/11/30
ISAAC	ISTED	SUSSEX	WARBLETON	1830
WILLIAM	IVESON	YORK (ER)	BEVERELY	1/12/30
FRANK	JACKSON	DORSET	BUCKLAND NEWTON	27/11/30
GEORGE	JACKSON	SHROPSHIRE	WHITCHURCH	9/31
JAMES GREEN	JACKSON	DORSET	BLANDFORD	17/10/31
THOMAS	JACOBS	SUFFOLK	HOXNE	13/12/30
JOHN	JAMES	HANTS	HEADLEY	23/11/30
HENRY	JAMES	GLOUCS	ST BRIAVELS	6/8/31
WARREN	JAMES	ESSEX	WALTON-LE-SOKEN	8/12/30
ABRAHAM	JARVIS	BUCKS	WADDESDON	26/11/30
STACEY	JARVIS	BUCKS	UPPER WINCHENDON	26/11/30
JOSEPH	JARVIS	BUCKS	WADDESDON	29/11/30
EDMUND	JEFFERIES	GLOUCS	BILBURY	10/12/30
WILLIAM	JEFFERY	ESSEX	ARKESDEN	10/12/30
GEORGE	JEFFERY	ESSEX	ARKESDEN	11/12/30
JOSEPH	JEFFERY	ESSEX	CLAVERING	11/12/30
THOMAS	JEFFERY	ESSEX	CLAVERING	8/12/30
JOSHUA	JEFFERY	ESSEX	WALTON-LE-SOKEN	13/12/30
JOB	JEFFRIES	SUFFOLK	HOXNE	18/11/30
WILLIAM	JEFFRIES	HANTS	HAVANT	18/11/30
WILLIAM	JENMAN	HANTS	WARBLINGTON	17/11/30
GEORGE	JENMAN	SUSSEX	BOSHAM	24/3/31
WILLIAM	JENNER	ESSEX	WRITTLE	23/3/20
WILLIAM	JENNINGS	SUFFOLK	BRANDON	25/11/30
JACOB	JEPHTA	WILTS	TISBURY	8/2/31
CHARLES	JERRARD	SUFFOLK	MONKS ELEIGH	29/11/30
ISAAC	JOHNSON	BUCKS	LONG CREDON	29/11/30
EDWARD	JOHNSON	NORTHANTS	KINGSUTTON	30/11/30
RICHARD	JOHNSON	NORFOLK	REDENHALL	23/11/30
JOHN	JOHNSON	NOTTS	SNEITON	3/31
WILLIAM	JOLLEY	BUCKS	LITTLE BRICKHILL	1/12/30
WILLIAM	JOLLY	SUFFOLK	EYE	19/4/30
SAMUEL	JOLLY	SUFFOLK	GREAT THURLOW	6/12/30

DATE	PARISH	SURNAME	COUNTY	FORENAME
12/30	WINFARTHING	JOLLY	NORFOLK	SUSANAH
9/11/30	WINGHAM	JONES	KENT	SAMUEL
26/11/30	FAIRFORD	JONES	GLOUCS	WILLIAM
5/1/31	LITTLEDEAN	JONES	GLOUCS	THOMAS
29/11/30	THURGARTON	JORDAN	NORFOLK	SIMON
11/12/30	CLAVERING	JOSLIN	ESSEX	JAMES
29/11/30	WHINBURGH	JUDE	NORFOLK	GEORGE
29/11/30	WHINBURGH	JUDE	NORFOLK	JAMES
17/12/30	OSPRINGE	JUDGE	KENT	JAMES
19/4/30	EYE	JUFF	SUFFOLK	JOHN
7/11/30	NORTHFLEET	JULL	KENT	SAMUEL
22/11/30	GREAT COGGESHALL	JUNIPER	ESSEX	JAMES
19/11/30	WALTON-LE-SOKEN	KAMIS	HANTS	ROBERT
8/12/30	FORDWICH	KEEBLE	ESSEX	JOHN
15/3/32	WOOTON ST LAWRENCE	KEEN	KENT	RICHARD
22/11/30	MONK SHERBOURNE	KEENS	HANTS	WILLIAM
23/11/30	BROUGHTON	KEENS	HANTS	JOHN
22/11/30	CLAVERING	KELSEY	ESSEX	GEORGE
11/12/30	LITTLE BOWDEN	KEMP	NORTHANTS	JOHN
2/1830	COLN ST ALDWYN	KENDALL	GLOUCS	WILLIAM
27/11/30	BLANDFORD	KENT	DORSET	CHARLES
17/10/31	CRAWLEY	KENT	HANTS	JOHN
21/11/30	MICHELDEVER	KERBY	HANTS	ELIAS
19/11/30	SIXPENNY HANDLEY	KERR	DORSET	EDWARD
24/11/30	FAIRFORD	KETTLE	GLOUCS	JOHN
26/11/30	WADDESDON	KEYLOCK	BUCKS	WILLIAM
26/11/30	ATTLEBOROUGH	KEYS	NORFOLK	JOHN
4/12/30	CROYDON	KIDDLE	CAMBS	JOHN
23/11/30	FORDINGBRIDGE	KIDMAN	HANTS	ROBERT
6/12/30	WITHERSFIELD	KIMBER	SUFFOLK	WILLIAM
6/12/30	WITHERSFIELD	KIMMENCE	SUFFOLK	WILLIAM
23/11/30	SOUTH STONEHAM	KIMMENCE	HANTS	JAMES
1/12/30	LITTLE BRICKHILL	KINCHIN	BUCKS	WILLIAM
12/31	SHINGAY	KING	CAMBS	HENRY
26/11/30	BEVERSTONE	KING	GLOUCS	WILLIAM
1830	CROWHURST	KING	SUSSEX	JAMES
1830	CROWHURST	KING	SUSSEX	WILLIAM
25/11/30	WHITWELL	KING	NORFOLK	JOHN
23/11/30	GREATHAM	KINGSHOTT	HANTS	JOHN
27/11/30	BISHOPSTONE	KIRBY	BUCKS	ROBERT
27/11/30	BISHOPSTONE	KIRBY	BUCKS	WILLIAM

DATE	PARISH	SURNAME	COUNTY	FORENAME
27/11/30	BISHOPSTONE	KIRBY	BUCKS	JAMES
27/11/30	BISHOPSTONE	KIRBY	BUCKS	GEORGE
22/11/30	ITCHEN ABBAS	KIRCHER	HANTS	RICHARD
19/11/30		KITCHEN	HANTS	WILLIAM
29/11/30	CHEPPING WYCOMBE	KNIBBS	BUCKS	WILLIAM
1832	SHEPSHED	KNIGHT	LEICS	JOHN
22/11/30	ROMSEY EXTRA	KNIGHT	HANTS	GEORGE
23/11/30	GREATHAM	KNIGHT	HANTS	JOHN
7/30	AYTHORPE RODING	KNIGHT	ESSEX	CHARLES
12/32	GULDEN MORDEN	KNIGHTS	CAMBS	RICHARD
7/30	WROTHAM	LAING	KENT	ROGER
29/5/32	WITCHINGHAM	LAKEY	NORFOLK	THOMAS
22/11/30	NEWTON TONEY	LAMB	WILTS	MARY
11/12/30	BARROW	LAMBERT	WORCS	JAMES
1831	WINGFIELD	LANCASTER	BEDFORDSHIRE	JAMES
25/11/30	FAWLEY	LANE	HANTS	RICHARD
25/11/30	FAWLEY	LANE	HANTS	WILLIAM
12/30	NEWARK	LANE	NORTHANTS	JOHN
19/11/32	BAYDON	LANGFORD	WILTS	STEPHEN
10/12/30	WEST MERSEA	LAPPAGE	ESSEX	WILLIAM
29/11/30	CHEPPING WYCOMBE	LARNEY	BUCKS	JOHN
29/11/30	WRAMPINGTON	LASKY	NORFOLK	HENRY
22/11/30	ITCHEN ABBAS	LAWRENCE	HANTS	GEORGE
6/12/30	BALSHAM	LAWRENCE	CAMBS	WILLIAM
21/11/30	HOUGHTON	LAWRENCE	HANTS	JOSEPH
9/31	WHITCHURCH	LEA	SHROPSHIRE	JAMES
22/11/30	VERNHAM DEAN	LEADER	HANTS	JAMES
12/9/31	WHITCHURCH	LEAR	SHROPSHIRE	JAMES
29/11/30	BURNHAM THORPE	LEATHERSTICK	NORFOLK	JOHN
26/11/30	LITTLE WALSINGHAM	LEEDER	NORFOLK	CHARLES
27/11/30	BUCKLAND NEWTON	LEGG	DORSET	JOHN
27/11/30	BUCKLAND NEWTON	LEGG	DORSET	GEORGE
21/11/30	CANTERBURY	LEMAR	KENT	WILLIAM
24/11/30	CAWSTON	LEMMON	NORFOLK	BENJAMIN
4/12/30	YARDLEY	LEVENS	HERTS	JOHN
1830		LEVINGTON	CORNWALL	
6/12/30	STEEPLE BUMPSTEAD	LEVITT	ESSEX	SAMUEL
6/12/30	STEEPLE BUMPSTEAD	LEVITT	ESSEX	STEPHEN
26/11/30	FAIRFORD	LEWIS	GLOUCS	JOHN
24/11/30	THANET	LILLEY	KENT	WILLIAM
6/12/30	COLCHESTER	LILLY	ESSEX	SAMUEL
9/2/30	BURSTALL	LILLY	SUFFOLK	ROBERT

FORENAME	SURNAME	COUNTY	PARISH	DATE
THOMAS	MATTHEWS	BUCKS	BISHOPSTONE	27/11/30
GEORGE	MATTHEWS	ESSEX	CLAVERING	11/12/30
WILLIAM	MAY	GLOUCS	FAIRFORD	26/11/30
HENRY	MAYER	NORFOLK	DOCKING	29/11/30
	MAYES	NORFOLK	DOCKING	29/11/30
GEORGE	MEAD	ESSEX	HENHAM	13/12/30
	MENDHAM	CORNWALL		1830
JAMES	MERRETT	GLOUCS	BILBURY	29/11/30
WILLIAM	MILES	BUCKS	BISHOPSTONE	27/11/30
JOHN	MILES	BUCKS	BISHOPSTONE	27/11/30
GEORGE	MILES	BUCKS	BISHOPSTONE	27/11/30
JAMES	MILES	BUCKS	CHEPPING WYCOMBE	29/11/30
ROBERT	MILES	GLOUCS	EASTLEACH MARTIN	27/11/30
JAMES	MILLER	BUCKS	BISHOPSTONE	27/11/30
SAMUEL	MILLER	SUSSEX	ALFRISTON	12/31
JOHN	MILLER	BUCKS	STONE	27/11/30
WILLIAM	MILLS	ESSEX	RAMSEY	5/12/30
JOHN	MILLS	ESSEX	GREAT CLACTON	7/12/30
ANDREW	MINTRAM	HANTS	FAWLEY	25/11/30
SILAS	MITCHELL	DORSET	BUCKLAND NEWTON	27/11/30
JOHN	MITCHELL	DORSET	BUCKLAND NEWTON	27/11/30
JACOB	MITCHELL	DORSET	BUCKLAND NEWTON	26/11/30
JOHN	MITCHELL	GLOUCS	FAIRFORD	26/11/30
THOMAS	MITCHELL	GLOUCS	FAIRFORD	27/11/30
WILLIAM	MITCHELL	GLOUCS	EASTLEACH TURVILLE	27/11/30
JOHN	MONK	BUCKS	STONE	27/11/30
JOHN	MOODY	BUCKS	MARSH GREEN	29/11/30
JOHN	MOODY	BUCKS	CHEPPING WYCOMBE	29/11/30
JAMES	MOODY	BUCKS	EAST DELLOW	24/11/30
GEORGE	MOODY	HANTS	FORDINGBRIDGE	23/11/30
THOMAS	MOODY	HANTS	CRAWLEY	21/11/30
WILLIAM	MOODY	BUCKS	MARSH GREEN	29/11/30
JOHN	MOODY	HANTS	MOTTISFONT	22/11/30
GEORGE	MOORE	KENT	THANET	24/11/30
WILLIAM	MOORE	DORSET	CANN	30/1/30
ELIZABETH	MOORE	NOTTS	SNEITON	28/3/32
GILES	MOORE	SUFFOLK	WITHERSFIELD	6/12/30
DAVID	MOORE	SUFFOLK	WITHERSFIELD	6/12/30
JOHN	MOORES	BUCKS	BISHOPSTONE	27/11/30
SAMUEL	MORLEY	HANTS		19/11/30
	MORRIS	LINCS	LUTTON	12/30
WILLIAM	MORTIMER	NORFOLK	COLTON	27/11/30

DATE	PARISH	COUNTY	SURNAME	FORENAME
7/12/30	GREAT CLACTON	ESSEX	LILLY	JOHN
29/11/30	SPARHAM	NORFOLK	LINCOLN	ROBERT
7/32	INGATESTONE	ESSEX	LINDSELL	HENRY
8/3/31	WRITTLE	ESSEX	LINES	GEORGE
8/3/31	WRITTLE	ESSEX	LINES	SAMUEL
11/12/30	SHUTLANGER	NORTHANTS	LINNELL	JAMES
8/12/30	LITTLE CLACTON	ESSEX	LINNETT	THOMAS
21/1/31	SWINDON	STAFFS	LLOYD	THOMAS
17/10/31	BLANDFORD	DORSET	LONG	GEORGE
7/31	CROYDON	CAMBS	LONGHURST	JOHN
17/10/31	CANFORD MAGNA	DORSET	LONNEN	CHARLES
21/11/30	SALISBURY	WILTS	LOOKER	WILLIAM
29/11/30	BIBURY	GLOUCS	LOOKER	HARMAN
29/11/30	BIBURY	GLOUCS	LOOKER	HENRY
1830	NEW FISHBOURN	SUSSEX	LOUR	GEORGE
22/11/30	GREAT COGGESHALL	ESSEX	LOVE	WILLIAM
7/12/30	WENDEN LOFTS	ESSEX	LOVEDAY	JOHN
7/12/30	WENDEN LOFTS	ESSEX	LOVEDAY	JAMES
27/11/30		NORFOLK	LOVELL	WILLIAM
12/31	ALFRISTON	SUSSEX	LOWE	SAMUEL
13/12/30	GREAT CLACTON	ESSEX	LUNNETT	THOMAS
29/11/30	CHEPPING WYCOMBE	BUCKS	LUNNON	DAVID
22/11/30	BROUGHTON	HANTS	LUSH	JOHN
22/11/30	ROMSEY EXTRA	HANTS	MABEY	JOSEPH
12/30	LUTTON	LINCS	MACEY	CHRISTOPHER
23/11/30	MONK SHERBOURNE	HANTS	MAILE	CHARLES
26/11/30	BEVERSTONE	GLOUCS	MANN	WORTHY
20/11/30	UPPER CLATFORD	HANTS	MANNS	ISAAC
20/11/30	UPPER CLATFORD	HANTS	MANNS	JAMES
17/11/30	FRANT	SUSSEX	MANTELLOW	THOMAS
26/11/30	WARMINGTON	NORTHANTS	MARRIOTT	THOMAS
25/10/30	WINGHAM	KENT	MARSH	JOHN
23/11/30	HEADLEY	HANTS	MARSHALL	THOMAS
22/11/30	ITCHEN ABBAS	HANTS	MARSHEM	GEORGE
22/11/30	NEWTON TONEY	WILTS	MARTIN	MARY
17/11/31	COVENEY	CAMBS	MARTIN	JOHN JNR
23/11/30	BURGHCLERE	HANTS	MARTIN	JAMES
14/12/30	FINCHINGFIELD	ESSEX	MARTIN	WILLIAM
19/11/30	EAST STRATTON	HANTS	MASON	JOSEPH
19/11/30	EAST STRATTON	HANTS	MASON	ROBERT
22/11/30	WEYHILL	HANTS	MASTERS	HENRY
25/11/30		NORFOLK	MATTHEW	WILLIAM

DATE	PARISH	COUNTY	SURNAME	FORENAME
23/11/30	FORDINGBRIDGE	HANTS	MORTON	JAMES
7/12/30	GREAT CLACTON	ESSEX	MOSS	JOHN
1/31	LUSBY	LINCS	MOTLEY	THOMAS
27/11/30	STONE	BUCKS	MOTT	RICHARD
30/11/30	FINENDON	NORTHANTS	MOULD	JOHN
25/11/30	TISBURY	WILTS	MOULD	JAMES
25/11/30	TISBURY	WILTS	MOULD	JAMES
25/11/30	TISBURY	WILTS	MOXAM	ANDREW
8/9/31	SEVENOAKS	KENT	MUGGERIDGE	ROBERT
22/11/30	ITCHEN ABBAS	HANTS	MULLENS	HENRY
30/11/30	FINENDON	NORTHANTS	MUNNS	JOSEPH
30/11/30	FINENDON	NORTHANTS	MUNNS	MICHAEL
30/11/30	FINENDON	NORTHANTS	MUNNS	ROBERT
29/11/30	BILBURY	GLOUCS	MUSTO	EDWARD
9/11/30	WINGHAM,	KENT	MUTER	EDWARD
9/11/30	WINGHAM	KENT	MUTTER	EDWARD
23/10/30	BEAKESBOURNE	KENT	MUTTON	JAMES
9/11/30	WINGHAM	KENT	MUTTON	EDWARD
12/8/31	HULL	YORK (ER)	MYERS	HARRIETT
20/11/30	UPPER CLATFORD	HANTS	MYLAND	GEORGE
3/8/32	CROYDON	CAMBS	NASH	JOHN
23/11/30	BURGHCLERE	HANTS	NASH	JOHN
5/12/30	RAMSEY	ESSEX	NEAL	ABRAHAM
2/7/32	STODY	NORFOLK	NEAL	W
2/7/32	STODY	NORFOLK	NEAL	J
2/7/32	STODY	NORFOLK	NEAL	T
29/3/31	DONYATT	SOMERSET	NEALD	JOHN
21/11/30	VERNHAM DEAN	HANTS	NEALE	THOMAS
26/4/31	TRUNCH	NORFOLK	NEALE	JAMES
26/4/31	TRUNCH	NORFOLK	NEALE	ROBERT
29/12/30	COXWOLD	YORK (NR)	NEEDHAM	W
6/12/30	COLCHESTER	ESSEX	NEVARD	SAMUEL
5/12/30	RAMSEY	ESSEX	NEVARD	JOHN
27/11/30	BUCKLAND NEWTON	DORSET	NEW	JAMES
27/11/30	BUCKLAND NEWTON	DORSET	NEW	JASPER
11/30	WESTBOURNE	SUSSEX	NEWLAND	JAMES
24/11/30	SELBORNE	HANTS	NEWLAND	JOHN
11/12/30	CLAVERING	ESSEX	NEWLAND	ROBERT
12/31	SHINGAY	CAMBS	NEWMAN	WILLIAM
3/8/32	CROYDON	CAMBS	NEWMAN	RICHARD
23/11/30	ROCKBOURNE	HANTS	NEWMAN	JOHN
23/11/30	FORDINGBRIDGE	HANTS	NEWMAN	WILLIAM

DATE	PARISH	COUNTY	SURNAME	FORENAME
14/12/30	FINCHINGFIELD	ESSEX	NEWMAN	JAMES
7/12/30	GREAT CLACTON	ESSEX	NEWMAN	THOMAS
7/12/30	GREAT CLACTON	ESSEX	NEWMAN	ABRAHAM
23/11/30	FORDINGBRIDGE	HANTS	NEWTON	WILLIAM
8/3/32	BECCLES FEN	SUFFOLK	NICHOLLS	WILLIAM
		CORNWALL	NIGHTINGALE	
1830	BREDE	SUSSEX	NOAKES	THOMAS
1830	BREDE	SUSSEX	NOAKES	DAVID
24/11/30	CAWSTON	NORFOLK	NOBES	MATTHEW
22/11/30	BROUGHTON	HANTS	NOBLE	WILLIAM JNR
12/30	BRESSINGHAM	NORFOLK	NOBLE	JOSEPH
9/1/31	SWANTON MORLEY	NORFOLK	NOCKOLDS	RICHARD
13/8/32	WHISTON	YORK (WR)	NORBURN	SAMUEL
23/11/30	MONK SHERBOURNE	HANTS	NORMAN	PETER
26/11/30	WADDESDON	BUCKS	NORMAN	JOHN
1830	ERISWELL	SUFFOLK	NORMAN	WILLIAM
27/11/30	COLTON	NORFOLK	NORMAN	WILLIAM
1831	UPWELL	CAMBS	NORTH	MICHAEL
22/11/30	ROMSEY EXTRA	HANTS	NOTLEY	CHARLES
10/12/30	CHEVINGTON	SUFFOLK	NUNN	THOMAS
23/11/30	FORDINGBRIDGE	HANTS	NUTBEAN	EDWARD
22/11/30	BROUGHTON	HANTS	OFFER	CHARLES
20/11/30	MARGATE	KENT	OLIPHANT	ISAAC
22/11/30	ITCHEN ABBAS	HANTS	OLIVER	RICHARD
22/11/30	BURITON	HANTS	OLIVER	BEN
28/7/32	CHIVERELL	WILTS	ORCHARD	BARNARD
20/11/30	BACTON	SUFFOLK	OSBORNE	ROBERT
20/11/30	MARTYR WORTHY	HANTS	OVER	GEORGE
20/11/30	MARGATE	KENT	OVERY	THOMAS
30/1/30	BILLINGHAY	LINCS	OWEN	JOHN
1/10/30	SURFLEET	LINCS	OXMAN	JOHN
19/11/30		HANTS	PACE	GEORGE
21/11/30	BLEAN ST COSMUS	KENT	PACKMAN	WILLIAM
21/11/30	BLEAN ST COSMUS	KENT	PACKMAN	HENRY
19/11/30	CUCKFIELD	SUSSEX	PAGDEN	JOHN
24/11/30	DOCKENFIELD	HANTS	PAGE	THOMAS
23/11/30	SOUTH STONEHAM	HANTS	PAGE	RICHARD
17/11/30	FRANT	SUSSEX	PAIGE	THOMAS
22/11/30	WOOTON ST LAWRENCE	HANTS	PAIN	CHARLES
3/8/32	CROYDON	CAMBS	PAIN	THOMAS
23/11/30	HEADLEY	HANTS	PAINTER	JAMES

DATE	PARISH	COUNTY	SURNAME	FORENAME
24/11/30		HANTS	PAINTER	JOHN
20/10/32	RAINHAM	KENT	PALMER	THOMAS
20/10/32	RAINHAM	KENT	PALMER	J
22/11/30	MICHELMERSH	HANTS	PALMER	GEORGE
13/12/30	HENHAM	ESSEX	PALMER	ISAAC
29/11/30	SOUTHROP	GLOUCS	PALMER	EDWARD
27/11/30	FOXLEY	NORFOLK	PALMER	JOHN
30/11/30	BURNHAM OVERY	NORFOLK	PALMER	GEORGE
22/11/30	NEWTON TONEY	WILTS	PARKER	MARY
24/11/30	WROTHAM	KENT	PARKER	THOMAS
27/11/30	BISHOPSTONE	BUCKS	PARKER	WILLIAM
26/11/30	BEVERSTONE	GLOUCS	PARKER	ELIZABETH
27/11/30	EASTLEACH MARTIN	GLOUCS	PARKER	ROBERT
8/12/30	WALTON-LE-SOKEN	ESSEX	PARKER	CHARLES
24/11/30	FIELD DALING	NORFOLK	PARNELL	HENRY (JUN)
24/11/30	FIELD DALING	NORFOLK	PARNELL	HENRY (SNR)
10/12/30	ARKESDEN	ESSEX	PARRISH	JOSEPH
2/31	MAIDFORD	NORTHANTS	PARSONS	THOMAS
11/30	WESTBOURNE	SUSSEX	PATCHENS	WILLIAM
28/8/30	LYMINGE	KENT	PATERSON	JOHN
29/8/30	LYMINGE	KENT	PATTERSON	JOHN
27/11/30	FOXLEY	NORFOLK	PATTERSON	JOHN
29/10/30	BOUGHTON	KENT	PATTMAN	
23/11/30	HIGHCLERE	HANTS	PAYNE	DANIEL
23/11/30	EAST WOODHAY	HANTS	PAYNE	JOHN
10/12/30	GREAT DUNMOW	ESSEX	PAYNE	CHARLES
8/1/31	DANBURY	ESSEX	PAYNE	THOMAS
6/12/30	COLCHESTER	ESSEX	PEACHALL	EDWARD
27/11/30	BISHOPSTONE	BUCKS	PEACOCK	JAMES
27/11/30	BISHOPSTONE	BUCKS	PEACOCK	JOHN
19/11/30	EAST STRATTON	HANTS	PEARCE	JAMES
1830	FUNTINTON	SUSSEX	PEARCE	JOHN
7/1830	LITTLE BOWDEN	NORTHANTS	PEBODY	JOHN
12/30	WORCESTER	WORCS	PEE	WILLIAM
30/11/30	BODIAM	SUSSEX	PENNELLS	RICHARD
20/12/30	FOULMIRE	CAMBS	PERKISS	JOSEPH
20/12/30	FOULMIRE	CAMBS	PERKISS	WILLIAM
10/12/31	BARTON STACY	HANTS	PERRIMAN	THOMAS
19/11/32	LAMBOURNE	BERKS	PERRY	WILLIAM
19/11/32	BAYDON	WILTS	PERRY	H
	HOXNE	SUFFOLK	PERRY	
3/8/32	CROYDON	CAMBS	PETERS	JAMES

DATE	PARISH	COUNTY	SURNAME	FORENAME
28/1/31	KIRTLING	CAMBS	PETTET	JOHN
4/12/30	YARDLEY	HERTS	PHILIPS	WILLIAM
8/12/30	WALTON-LE-SOKEN	ESSEX	PHILLIPS	JOHN
23/11/30	FORDINGBRIDGE	HANTS	PHILPOTT	JOHN
23/11/30	FORDINGBRIDGE	HANTS	PHILPOTT	GEORGE
11/12/31	BEDMOND	HERTS	PHILPOTT	DORCAS
8/12/30	WALTON-LE-SOKEN	ESSEX	PHIPPS	JOHN
26/11/30	LEEK	STAFFS	PICKFORD	ANDREW
1/12/30	LITTLE BRICKHILL	BUCKS	PIGGOTT	JOHN
22/11/30	ITCHEN ABBAS	HANTS	PIKE	GEORGE
29/11/30	STOWER PROVOST	DORSET	PIKE	ROBERT
25/10/30	STOURMOUTH	KENT	PILCHER	STEPHEN
11/30	WESTBOURNE	SUSSEX	PILES	GEORGE
23/11/30	HIGHCLERE	HANTS	PIPER	JOHN
9/11/30	WINGHAM	KENT	PITCHER	STEPHEN
25/11/30	TISBURY	WILTS	PITMAN	R
5/2/31	HICKLING	NORFOLK	PLATTEN	JOHN
28/11/30	HICKLING	NORFOLK	POLL	HENRY
25/11/30	HICKLING	NORFOLK	POLLARD	JAMES
21/11/30	ALVERSTOKE	HANTS	POLLEXSIN	HENRY
26/11/30	FAIRFORD	GLOUCS	PONTING	CHRISTOPHER
26/11/30	HORSLEY	GLOUCS	POOLE	JOHN
24/11/30	SIXPENNY HANDLEY	DORSET	POPE	JOSEPH
5/12/30	RAMSEY	ESSEX	PORTER	GEORGE
1/6/30	ORPINGTON	KENT	PORTER	PHILIP
10/12/30	GREAT DUNMOW	ESSEX	PORTER	JOHN
6/12/30	WITHERSFIELD	SUFFOLK	POTTER	CROMWELL
17/11/30	FRANT	SUSSEX	POULTER	
22/11/30	THANET	HANTS	POYNDER	JOHN
24/11/30	EAST WELLOW	KENT	POYNTER	JAMES
24/11/30	BROMSBERROW	HANTS	PRAGNELL	ALEXANDER
1/11/31	CROYDON	GLOUCS	PREDDY	JOHN
3/8/32	GOUDHURST	CAMBS	PRESSLIN	JOHN
9/11/30	ASH	KENT	PRICE	ROBERT
25/10/30	STOCKBURY	KENT	PRICE	STEPHEN
27/10/30	EAST MALLING	KENT	PRICE	ROBERT
3/11/30	CHEPPING WYCOMBE	BUCKS	PRICE	ROBERT
29/11/30	UPHAM	HANTS	PRIEST	JOSEPH
22/11/30	MICHELDEVER	HANTS	PRIMER	WILLIAM
19/11/30	MICHELDEVER	HANTS	PRIOR	GEORGE SNR
19/11/30	HANLEY WILLIAM	HANTS	PRIOR	THOMAS JNR
11/12/30		WORCS	PRITCHARD	MARK

DATE	PARISH	SURNAME	COUNTY	FORENAME
18/11/30	MICHELDEVER	PUMPHREY	HANTS	JAMES
25/11/30	SOUTHREPPS	PYE	NORFOLK	DAVID
8/3/31	WRITTLE	QUINN	ESSEX	WILLIAM
23/11/30	FORDINGBRIDGE	QUINTON	HANTS	SAMUEL
19/11/30	FORDINGBRIDGE	RACE	HANTS	GEORGE
27/11/30	COLTON	RADFORD	NOTTS	SAMUEL
26/11/30	BEVERSTONE	RADFORD	GLOUCS	JOHN
13/12/30	LONG MELFORD	RAISIN	SUFFOLK	WILLIAM
10/12/30	GREAT DUNMOW	RALPHE	ESSEX	DANIEL
8/31	SHIMPLING	RAMPLING	SUFFOLK	HENRY
22/11/30	WOOTON ST LAWRENCE	RAMPTON	HANTS	RICHARD
6/12/30	STEEPLE BUMPSTEAD	RANDALL	ESSEX	WILLIAM
3/12/30		RANSOME	NORFOLK	GEORGE
9-11/12/30	SWIMBRIDGE	RAWCLIFF	DEVON	THOMAS
6/12/30	GREAT THURLOW	RAWLINSON	SUFFOLK	JOSEPH
24/11/30	SIXPENNY HANDLEY	RAYMOND	DORSET	JAMES
23/11/32	HAREWOOD	RAYNER	YORK (WR)	THOMAS
2/7/32	STODY	RAYNER	NORFOLK	A
2/7/32	STODY	RAYNER	NORFOLK	W
20/11/30	MARGATE	READ	KENT	WILLIAM
23/11/30	CRANBOURNE	READ	DORSET	JOHN
23/11/30	FORDINGBRIDGE	READ	HANTS	CHARLES
19/11/30	WESTBOURNE	READ	SUSSEX	THOMAS
9/11/30	WINGHAM	READ	KENT	THOMAS
28/8/30	LOWER HARDRES	READ	KENT	HENRY
28/8/30	LOWER HARDRES	READ	KENT	EDWARD
25/10/30	WINGHAM	READ	KENT	THOMAS
12/31	CHIPPENHAM	READS	LINCS	WILLIAM
31/3/30	ALFRISTON	REDHEAD	SUSSEX	JOHN
12/31	BISHOPSTONE	REEVES	BUCKS	DAVID
27/11/30	SOUTH STONEHAM	REEVES	HANTS	JOHN
23/11/30	TWINEHAM	REEVES	SUSSEX	RICHARD
23/11/30	CHEPPING WYCOMBE	REYNOLDS	BUCKS	JOHN
29/11/30	ELSENHAM	REYNOLDS	ESSEX	THOMAS
19/2/32	ELSENHAM	REYNOLDS	ESSEX	EDWARD
4/2/31	WHITCHURCH	RICHARDSON	SHROPSHIRE	THOMAS
24/11/30	WROTHAM	RICHARDSON	KENT	SIMEON
24/11/30	WROTHAM	RICHARDSON	KENT	ISAAC
22/11/30	VERNHAM DEAN	RICHARDSON	HANTS	THOMAS
5/11/30	RAYLEIGH	RICHARDSON	ESSEX	JONATHON
29/11/30	WRAMPINGTON	RICHARDSON	NORFOLK	JAMES
10/3/32	SNETTISHAM	RICHARDSON	NORFOLK	LEEDS

FORENAME	SURNAME	COUNTY	PARISH	DATE
JOSEPH	RICKLEWOOD	ESSEX	GREAT CLACTON	7/12/30
JOSEPH	RIDGEWAY	BUCKS	WADDESDON	26/11/30
JAMES	RITCHIE	SURREY	CHEAM	12/12/30
HENRY	RIX	NORFOLK	WITCHINGHAM	29/5/32
THOMAS	RIXEN	WILTS	TISBURY	25/11/30
THOMAS	ROBINSON	HANTS	HEADLEY	23/11/30
WILLIAM	ROBINSON	KENT	HOLLINGBOURNE	28/10/30
JOHN	RODWELL	SUFFOLK	HOXNE	13/12/30
NICHOLAS	ROE	LINCS	SURFLEET	1/10/30
WILLIAM	ROGERS	HANTS	ROMSEY EXTRA	22/11/30
HENRY	ROGERS	HANTS	MICHELMERSH	22/11/30
ROGER	ROLFE	NORTHANTS	SILVERSTONE	1/32
JOHN	ROLFE	BUCKS	STONE	27/11/30
WILLIAM	ROSE	HANTS	ROMSEY EXTRA	22/11/30
JAMES	ROSE	WARWICKSHIRE	PRIORS SALFORD	1/2/32
J	ROSE	SUFFOLK	HOXNE	13/12/30
RICHARD	ROULFE	KENT	BEAKESBOURNE	23/10/30
JOHN	ROWLAND	ESSEX	RAMSEY	5/12/30
GEORGE	ROWLEY	SOMERSET	KENN	8/30
J	RULE	ESSEX	WENDEN LOFTS	7/12/30
JOHN	RUMP	NORFOLK	DILHAM	6/10/31
WILLIAM	RUSSELL	KENT	YALDING	11/11/30
THOMAS	RUSSELL	BUCKS	MARSH GREEN	29/11/30
THOMAS	RUSSELL	GLOUCS	BROMSBERROW	1/11/31
LUKE	RYE	NORFOLK	ROUGHAM	22/11/30
WILLIAM	SADLER	YORKS (WR)	SHEFFIELD	18/1/31
ARTHUR	SAGE	KENT	HOLLINGBOURNE	31/10/30
JAMES	SALMON	ESSEX	FINCHINGFIELD	14/12/30
WILLIAM	SALTER	BUCKS	MARSH GREEN	29/11/30
JAMES	SAMSON	SOMERSET	HENSTRIDGE	1/12/30
WILLIAM	SAMUELS	NORFOLK	LITTLE WALSINGHAM	26/11/30
THOMAS	SAMWAYS	DORSET	BUCKLAND NEWTON	27/11/30
SAMUEL	SANDERS	ISLE OF WIGHT	FAWLEY	23/11/30
JOHN	SANSOM	HANTS	HOUND	9/12/30
GEORGE	SANSOME	DORSET	BUCKLAND NEWTON	27/11/30
JOHN	SANSOMS	DORSET	STALBRIDGE	1/12/30
JOHN	SARNEY	BUCKS	CHEPPING WYCOMBE	29/11/30
JAMES	SAUNDERS	BUCKS	LONG CRENDON	29/11/30
JOHN	SAUNDERS	ESSEX	ARKESDEN	10/12/30
JOHN	SAVAGE	LINCS	SURFLEET	1/10/30
JAMES	SAVAGE	HERTS	YARDLEY	4/12/30
GEORGE	SAVAGE	HERTS	YARDLEY	4/12/30

DATE	PARISH	COUNTY	SURNAME	FORENAME
13/11/30	BLUNTISHAM	HUNTS	SAVILLE	JOSEPH
29/11/30	LONG CRENDON	BUCKS	SAWYER	EDWARD
22/11/30	EAST WELLOW	HANTS	SCAMMELL	THOMAS
9/11/30	WINGHAM	KENT	SCATH	HENRY
23/11/30	SHERFIELD	HANTS	SCOATES	THOMAS
23/11/30	SOUTH STONEHAM	HANTS	SCOREY	WILLIAM
27/11/30	BISHOPSTONE	BUCKS	SCOTCHINS	RICHARD
27/11/30	BISHOPSTONE	BUCKS	SCOTCHINS	JOHN
27/11/30	STONE	BUCKS	SCOTCHINS	ROBERT
27/11/30	STONE	BUCKS	SCOTCHINS	WILLIAM
27/11/30	EASTLEACH MARTIN	GLOUCS	SCOTFORD	EDWARD
26/11/30	WADDESDON	BUCKS	SCOTT	THOMAS
26/11/30	WADDESDON	BUCKS	SCOTT	JAMES
26/11/30	HORSLEY	GLOUCS	SEAL	SAMUEL
1/12/30	IVER	BUCKS	SEALS	WILLIAM
7/10/30	OTFORD	KENT	SEAMAN	JOHN
7/12/30	ELMDON	ESSEX	SEAMAN	JONATHON
27/11/30	BISHOPSTONE	BUCKS	SEARCH	GEORGE
23/10/30	BEAKESBOURNE	KENT	SEATH	HENRY
1830	BREDE	SUSSEX	SELMES	SPENCER
5/12/30	RAMSEY	ESSEX	SEXTON	SAMUEL
1/12/30	HENSTRIDGE	SOMERSET	SEYMOUR	JOSEPH
9-11/12/30	SWIMBRIDGE	DEVON	SHADDICK	PHILIP
8/3/32	BECCLES FEN	SUFFOLK	SHARMAN	JOSEPH
14/12/30	FINCHINGFIELD	ESSEX	SHEAD	SAMUEL
14/12/30	FINCHINGFIELD	ESSEX	SHEAD	JAMES
14/12/30	FINCHINGFIELD	ESSEX	SHELFORD	WILLIAM
1831	COLWICK	NOTTS	SHELTON	THOMAS
10/12/30	HAWKWELL	ESSEX	SHEPHERD	JOHN
22/11/30	ANDOVER	HANTS	SHEPHERD	WILLIAM
23/11/30	FORDINGBRIDGE	HANTS	SHEPHERD	CHARLES
27/11/30	BUCKLAND NEWTON	DORSET	SHEPPARD	JOSEPH
5/12/30	RAMSEY	ESSEX	SHIP	THOMAS
7/12/30		SUFFOLK	SHIP	STEPHEN
27/11/30	STONE	BUCKS	SHOWLER	GEORGE
29/11/30	LONG CREDON	BUCKS	SHRIMPTON	EMANUEL
29/11/30	CHEPPING WYCOMBE	BUCKS	SHRIMPTON	WILLIAM
9/11/30	WINGHAM	KENT	SIDDERS	WILLIAM
25/10/30	ASH	KENT	SIDDONS	WILLIAM
19/11/30	NORTHINGTON	HANTS	SILCOCK	JOHN
27/11/30	COLN ST ALDWYN	GLOUCS	SILK	JAMES
19/11/30		HANTS	SIMMS	J

FORENAME	SURNAME	COUNTY	PARISH	DATE
W	SIMMS	HANTS		19/11/30
D	SIMMS	HANTS		19/11/30
HANNAH	SIMONS	SHROPSHIRE	WHITCHURCH	2/12/31
WILLIAM	SKELTON	HANTS	ROMSEY EXTRA	22/11/31
BENJAMIN	SKINNER	KENT	SHOREHAM	11/32
WILLIAM	SLADDEN	KENT	WINGHAM	9/11/30
JOHN	SLADE	HANTS	ROCKBOURNE	23/11/30
THOMAS	SLAUGHTER	WORCS	ELMLEY LOVETT	12/30
THOMAS	SMALL	BUCKS	BISHOPSTONE	27/11/30
JOHN	SMART	DORSET	BUCKLAND NEWTON	24/11/30
THOMAS	SMITH	WARWICKSHIRE	RUGBY	10/31
J	SMITH	BUCKS	MARSH GREEN	29/11/30
THOMAS	SMITH	BUCKS	CHEPPING WYCOMBE	29/11/30
JOHN	SMITH	HANTS	WICKHAM	23/11/30
THOMAS	SMITH	HANTS	SOUTH STONEHAM	23/11/30
JOHN	SMITH	CAMBS	LITTLEPORT	28/11/30
BENJAMIN	SMITH	HANTS	SELBORNE	22/11/30
WILLIAM	SMITH	HANTS	BARTON STACEY	19/11/30
JAMES	SMITH	SUSSEX	BOSHAM	17/11/30
STEPHEN	SMITH	SUSSEX	FUNTINTON	1830
JASPER	SMITH	HERTS	YARDLEY	4/12/30
JOHN	SMITH	KENT	BEAKESBOURNE	23/10/30
ALLEN	SMITH	SUFFOLK	BURSTALL	9/2/30
JOHN	SMITH	KENT	RAINHAM	20/10/32
WILLIAM	SMITH	YORK (ER)	BOSTON	31/12/30
GEORGE	SMITH	BUCKS	CHEPPING WYCOMBE	29/11/30
THOMAS	SMITH	NORFOLK	EASTLEACH MARTIN	24/11/30
JOHN	SMITH	GLOUCS	GREAT DUNMOW	10/12/30
WILLIAM	SMITH	ESSEX	WEST MERSEA	10/12/30
WILLIAM	SMITH	ESSEX	BILSTON	1831
JOHN	SMITH	STAFFS	COCKFIELD	12/30
SAMUEL	SMITH	SUFFOLK	COCKFIELD	12/30
JAMES	SMITH	SUFFOLK	BURNHAM OVERY	30/11/30
SAMUEL	SMITH	NORFOLK	LINGWOOD	4/12/30
SAMUEL	SMITH	NORFOLK	LINGWOOD	4/12/30
ROBERT	SMITH	NORFOLK	ATTLEBOROUGH	4/12/30
ROBERT	SMITH	ESSEX	CLAVERING	11/12/30
EDMUND	SMITHHEN	NORFOLK	WRAMPINGTON	29/11/30
JAMES	SMITHSON	NORFOLK	CAWSTON	24/11/30
WILLIAM	SNOOK	WILTS	TISBURY	25/11/30
WILLIAM	SNOW	SUSSEX	BOSHAM	17/11/30

DATE	PARISH	COUNTY	SURNAME	FORENAME
3/12/30	HADDISCOE	NORFOLK	SOAM	JOHN
20/11/30	WALTHAM ST LAWRENCE	BERKS	SOLOMON	WILLIAM
29/11/30	WINFRITH	DORSET	SOMERS	WILLIAM
19/11/30		HANTS	SOMERSLEY	JAMES
24/11/30	CAWSTON	NORFOLK	SOUTHGATE	BARNARD
29/11/30	DOCKING	NORFOLK	SOUTHLAND	BENJAMIN
29/11/30	DOCKING	NORFOLK	SOUTHLAND	JANE
26/11/30	FAIRFORD	GLOUCS	SPARROW	WILLIAM
3/31	BESTWOOD	NOTTS	SPENCER	RICHARD
26/11/30	WADDESDON	BUCKS	SPENCER	RICHARD
29/11/30	BIBURY	GLOUCS	SPENCER	WILLIAM
27/11/30	PULHAM	DORSET	SPICER	HENRY
29/8/30	LYMINGE	KENT	SPICER	WILLIAM
11/12/30	HANLEY WILLIAM	WORCS	SPILSBURY	WILLIAM
30/11/30	EAST TUDDENHAM	NORFOLK	SPRAGGS	FRANCIS
12/30	DEFFORD	WORCS	SPRUCE	A
18/11/30	BOXGROVE	SUSSEX	SQUIRES	WILLIAM
29/11/30	STOUR PROVOST	DORSET	STACEY	JAMES
21/11/30	HOUGHTON	HANTS	STACEY	THOMAS
4/12/30	ATTLEBOROUGH	NORFOLK	STACEY	JAMES
29/11/30	WRAMPLINGHAM	NORFOLK	STAFF	HENRY
29/11/30	WRAMPLINGHAM	NORFOLK	STAFF	WILLIAM
24/11/30	DROXFORD	HANTS	STAGG	THOMAS
26/11/30	BEVERSTONE	GLOUCS	STANCOMBE	JOHN
9/11/30	GOUDHURST	KENT	STANDEN	WILLIAM
10/11/30	HORSMONDEN	KENT	STANDEN	WILLIAM
27/11/30	BISHOPSTONE	BUCKS	STANLEY	JAMES
5/11/30	SWINDON	WILTSHIRE	STANLEY	THOMAS
27/11/30	STONE	BUCKS	STANLEY	JOHN
20/11/30	UPPER CLATFORD	HANTS	STANMORE	WILLIAM
25/10/30	WINGHAM	KENT	STANNARD	JOHN
25/10/30	ASH	KENT	STANNARD	JOHN
1830	HELLESLEY	SUFFOLK	STANNARD	JOHN
15/3/32	FORDWICH	KENT	STANNER	
1/12/30	IVER	BUCKS	STAPPS	JAMES
30/7/32		CAMBS	STEARS	JAMES
23/11/30	SIDMONTON	HANTS	STEEL	ISAAC
1/12/30	FORDINGBRIDGE	HANTS	STEELE	GEORGE
23/11/30	COLN ROGERS	GLOUCS	STEPHENS	JOSHUA
29/11/30	COLN ROGERS	GLOUCS	STEPHENS	ROBERT
1/11/31	BROMSBERROW	GLOUCS	STEPHENS	GEORGE
1/12/30	LITTLE BRICKHILL	BUCKS	STEVENS	SAMUEL

DATE	PARISH	COUNTY	SURNAME	FORENAME
9/11/30	WINGHAM	KENT	STICKELLS	RICHARD
20/10/32	GREAT SWAFFHAM	NORFOLK	STICKWOOD	WILLIAM
24/11/30	SIXPENNY HANDLEY	DORSET	STOKES	WILLIAM
29/11/30	CHEPPING WYCOMBE	BUCKS	STONE	JAMES
25/10/30	ASH	KENT	STONE	WILLIAM
25/10/30	STOURMOUTH	KENT	STONE	WILLIAM
9/11/30	WINGHAM	KENT	STONE	THOMAS
22/11/30	DURLEY	HANTS	STONEAGE	JOHN
3/8/32	CROYDON	CAMBS	STOREY	ANDERSON
9/11/30	WINGHAM	KENT	STOWE	THOMAS
29/11/30	MARSH GREEN	BUCKS	STRATFORD	HENRY
29/11/30	CHEPPING WYCOMBE	BUCKS	STRETTON	JAMES
9/11/30	WINGHAM	KENT	STROAD	THOMAS
25/10/30	WINGHAM	KENT	STROOD	THOMAS
25/10/30	WINGHAM	KENT	STROUD	THOMAS
23/11/30	BURGHCLERE	HANTS	STROUD	WILLIAM
30/4/31	WESTLETON	SUFFOLK	STROWGER	JAMES
11/30	BIRCHINGTON	KENT	STUDHAM	ELIZABETH
21/11/30	LITTLETON	HANTS	STURGESS	GEORGE
7/12/30		SUFFOLK	SUBTLE	JOHN
25/1/31	BASILDON	ESSEX	SUCH	JOSEPH
22/11/30	LECKFORD	HANTS	SUMMERBEE	WILLIAM
29/11/30	CHEPPING WYCOMBE	BUCKS	SUMMERFIELD	SAMUEL
23/11/30	FORDINGBRIDGE	HANTS	SUTTON	WILLIAM
18/9/30	UPPER HARDRES	KENT	SWAINE	INGRAM
20/10/32	RAINHAM	KENT	SWAN	SAMUEL
21/1/31	SWINDON	STAFFS	SWATKINS	JOHN
18/11/30	WARBLINGTON	HANTS	SYDENHAM	EDWARD
27/11/30	BUCKLAND NEWTON	DORSET	SYMES	CHARLES
27/11/30	BUCKLAND NEWTON	DORSET	SYMONDS	JOHN
20/11/30	BACTON	SUFFOLK	SYRETT	THOMAS
26/11/30	WADDESDON	BUCKS	TACK	GEORGE
26/11/30	WADDESDON	BUCKS	TACK	FRANCIS
18/11/30	WARBLINGTON	HANTS	TADD	GEORGE
25/11/30	TISBURY	WILTS	TARGETT	JOHN
19/11/30	MICHELDEVER	HANTS	TARRANT	EDWARD
1/10/30	SURFLEET	LINCS	TAYLOR	EDWARD
9/11/30	WINGHAM	HANTS	TAYLOR	DANIEL
23/10/30	BEAKESBOURNE	KENT	TAYLOR	DANIEL
12/30	PRESTEIGNE	RADNORSHIRE	TAYLOR	JAMES
10/12/30	ARKESDEN	ESSEX	TAYLOR	THOMAS
10/12/30	ARKESDEN	ESSEX	TAYLOR	WILLIAM

FORENAME	SURNAME	COUNTY	PARISH	DATE
JOHN	TRIM	SUSSEX	NEW FISHBOURN	1830
JOHN	TRIMMING	HANTS	SELBORNE	22/11/30
THOMAS	TRINDER	GLOUCS	BIBURY	29/11/30
JEMMY	TRUMPS	KENT	DOVER	14/1/31
JOHN	TUBB	HANTS	HOUGHTON	21/11/30
JOHN	TUBBY	NORFOLK	CAWSTON	24/11/30
	TUCKER	WILTS	BAYDON	19/11/32
JOHN	TUNLERS	NORFOLK	COLTON	27/11/30
JACOB	TURNER	HANTS	BARTON STACEY	19/11/30
WILLIAM	TURNER	LINCS	CHIPPENHAM	31/3/30
THOMAS	TURNER	NORTHANTS	MAIDFORD	2/31
WILLIAM	TURNER	NORTHANTS	MAIDFORD	2/31
PURCELL C	TURNER	BUCKS	WADDESDON	26/11/30
MOSES	TURNER	BUCKS	BISHOPSTONE	27/11/30
WILLIAM	TURNER	NORFOLK	HICKLING	25/11/30
EDWARD	TURNER	SOMERSET	HENSTRIDGE	3/12/30
JOHN	TURNER	SUFFOLK	LONG MELFORD	13/12/30
GEORGE	TURNER	ESSEX	HENHAM	13/12/30
THOMAS	TURNER	GLOUCS	BIBURY	29/11/30
CHARLES	TURNER	NORFOLK	TOFT	3/12/30
JOHN	TURNER	NORFOLK	WELLINGHAM	18/12/30
GEORGE	TURRELL	SUFFOLK	BECCLES FEN	8/3/32
JOHN	TURTON	HANTS	CRAWLEY	21/11/30
	TURTON	NOTTS	RANSKILL	11/30
T	TURVEY	WORCS	DEFFORD	12/30
	TUSSEL	HANTS	EAST WOODHAY	23/11/30
THOMAS	TYERS	NOTTS	PLUMTREE	12/10/31
NATHANIEL	UNWIN	ESSEX	ARKESDEN	10/12/30
J	VALE	WORCS	DEFFORD	12/30
WILLIAM	VARNDELL	HANTS	WICKHAM	23/11/30
JAMES	VARNELL	HANTS	SOUTH STONEHAM	23/11/30
JAMES	VENEMORE	BUCKS	WADDESDON	26/11/30
THOMAS	VENEMORE	BUCKS	UPPER WINCHENDON	6/31
JAMES	VENTING	SOMERSET		1832
JOHN	VICKERSTAFF	NOTTS	BASFORD	5/11/31
PETER	VINES	WILTSHIRE	SWINDON	25/11/30
THOMAS	VINING	WILTS	TISBURY	25/11/30
THOMAS	VOWELLS	DORSET	EAST STOWER	29/11/30
ROBERT BATES	WADE	SUFFOLK	MILDENHALL	12/30
JOHN	WAINER	KENT	MEOPHAM	29/11/30
JOHN	WALDUCK	BUCKS	CHEPPING WYCOMBE	29/11/30
ELIZABETH	WALES	KENT	UPPER HARDRES	4/30

DATE	PARISH	COUNTY	SURNAME	FORENAME
30/11/30	EAST TUDDENHAM	NORFOLK	TAYLOR	JAMES
3/12/30		NORFOLK	TAYLOR	JANE
24/11/30	SIXPENNY HANDLEY	DORSET	TELLWOOD	SAMUEL
24/11/30	SIXPENNY HANDLEY	DORSET	TELLWOOD	ROBERT
3/12/30		NORFOLK	TEMPLE	MATTHEW
9/11/30	WINGHAM	KENT	TERRY	CHARLES
25/10/30	ASH	KENT	TERRY	CHARLES
25/11/30	HICKLING	NORFOLK	THAIN	WILLIAM
25/11/30	HICKLING	NORFOLK	THAIN	JAMES
1830	GREAT WALDINGFIELD	SUFFOLK	THEOBALD	JAMES
24/11/30	SIXPENNY HANDLEY	DORSET	THICK	JAMES
30/11/30	BURNHAM OVERY	NORFOLK	THOMAS	JOSHUA
3/8/32	CROYDON	CAMBS	THOMPSON	ISAAC
13/12/30	HENHAM	ESSEX	THOMPSON	THOMAS
9-11/12/30	SWIMBRIDGE	DEVON	THORN	JAMES
12/31	ARLINGTON	SUSSEX	THORNCROFT	S
24/11/30	BUCKLAND NEWTON	DORSET	THORNE	JAMES
24/11/30	BUCKLAND NEWTON	DORSET	THORNE	ADAM
12/31	ALFRISTON	SUSSEX	THORNECROFT	SAMUEL
22/11/30	ITCHEN ABBAS	HANTS	THORP	HENRY
1830		CORNWALL	THURSBY	
31/12/30	BOSTON	YORK (ER)	THURWELL	GEORGE
31/12/30	BOSTON	YORK (ER)	THURWELL	STEPHEN
29/11/30	WHINBURGH	NORFOLK	TICE	ROBERT
9/11/30	HAWKHURST	KENT	TICKNER	JOHN
7/12/30	GREAT CLACTON	ESSEX	TILLETT	JOHN
27/11/30	COLTON	NORFOLK	TIMBO	JOHN
27/11/30	EASTLEACH MARTIN	GLOUCS	TIMBRILL	BENJAMIN
21/1/31	SWINDON	STAFFS	TIMMINS	THOMAS
3/32	OUNDLE	NORTHANTS	TIMSON	WILLIAM
3/8/32	CROYDON	CAMBS	TITMARSH	SIMON
19/11/30		HANTS	TODD	GEORGE
12/30	LUTTON	LINCS	TOMLINSON	
29/11/30	WINFRITH	DORSET	TOMS	JOHN
19/11/30		HANTS	TONGS	JOHN
25/11/30	TISBURY	WILTS	TOPP	THOMAS
1832	BASFORD	NOTTS	TORR	J
17/11/30	BOSHAM	SUSSEX	TOWNSHEND	GEORGE
4/12/30	LINGWOOD	NORFOLK	TRETT	JOHN
19/11/30		HANTS	TREW	SAMUEL
23/11/30	HEADLEY	HANTS	TRIGGS	MATTHEW
17/11/30	BOSHAM	SUSSEX	TRIGGS	JOHN

DATE	PARISH	COUNTY	SURNAME	FORENAME
27/11/30	BISHOPSTONE	BUCKS	WALES	JOHN
29/11/30	CHEPPING WYCOMBE	BUCKS	WALKER	WILLIAM
29/11/30	CHEPPING WYCOMBE	BUCKS	WALKER	JOHN
29/11/30	CHEPPING WYCOMBE	BUCKS	WALKER	HENRY
12/1830	KNOTTINGLY	YOK (WR)	WALKER	SAMUEL
8/30	KENN	SOMERSET	WALL	WILLIAM
6/12/30	WHEPSTEAD	SUFFOLK	WALLIS	ROBERT
28/10/30	HOLLINGBOURNE	KENT	WALTER	MATTHEW
26/11/30	WADDESDON	BUCKS	WALTON	GEORGE
29/5/32	WITCHINGHAM	NORFOLK	WANT	JAMES
23/11/30	EAST WOODHAY	HANTS	WARD	JAMES
23/11/30	EAST WOODHAY	HANTS	WARD	WILLIAM
23/1/31	QUENBOROUGH	LEICS	WARD	JAMES
11/30	SHEPSHED	LEICS	WARD	JOHN
22/11/30	WOOTON ST LAWRENCE	HANTS	WAREHAM	WILLIAM
11/30	ALBURY	SURREY	WARNER	JAMES
10/12/30	WEST MERSEA	ESSEX	WARNER	WILLIAM
30/11/30	FINEDON	NORTHANTS	WARREN	JOHN
23/11/30	MONK SHERBOURNE	HANTS	WARWICK	THOMAS
7/1/32	CALTWAITE	CUMBERLAND	WARWICK	SARAH
13/10/30	STANSTED MOUNTFITCHET	ESSEX	WARWICK	CHARLES
1/12/30	IVER	BUCKS	WATERFIELD	RICHARD
1/12/30	IVER	BUCKS	WATERFIELD	RICHARD
20/12/30	MORETON IN THE MARSH	GLOUCS	WATERS	JOSEPH
7/12/30	GREAT CLACTON	ESSEX	WATLING	GEORGE
26/11/30	WADDESDON	BUCKS	WATSON	JONAS
26/11/30	UPPER WINCHENDON	BUCKS	WATSON	JONAS
13/12/30	HOXNE	SUFFOLK	WATTING	R
29/11/30	LOUDWATER	BUCKS	WATTS	JOHN
23/11/30	BURGHCLERE	HANTS	WATTS	WILLIAM
27/11/30	COLN ST ALDWYN	GLOUCS	WEAVING	THOMAS
29/11/30	LONG CRENDON	BUCKS	WEBB	ROBERT
22/11/30	ROMSEY EXTRA	HANTS	WEBB	RICHARD
8/11/30	HOOE	SUSSEX	WEBB	T
26/11/30	FAWLEY	HANTS	WEBB	JOHN
20/11/30	BARTON STACEY	HANTS	WEBB	THOMAS
5/12/30	GREAT HOLLAND	ESSEX	WEBB	JOHN
11/1/31	STANDON	HERTS	WEBB	WILLIAM
29/11/30	MARSH GREEN	BUCKS	WEBB	JAMES
23/11/30	ROCKBOURNE	HANTS	WEBB	GEORGE
23/11/30	FORDINGBRIDGE	HANTS	WEBB	WILLIAM
20/12/30	MORETON IN THE MARSH	GLOUCS	WEBB	ROBERT

DATE	PARISH	COUNTY	SURNAME	FORENAME
10/12/30	ARKESDEN	ESSEX	WEDLOCK	JAMES
29/11/30	CHEPPING WYCOMBE	BUCKS	WEEDON	RICHARD
23/11/30	ROCKBOURNE	HANTS	WEEKS	JOHN
9/31	BILLINGBOROUGH	LINCS	WELLDEN	JOHN
23/8/31	OLLERTON	NOTTS	WELLOW	
22/11/30	BURITON	HANTS	WELLS	HENRY
23/11/30	MONK SHERBOURNE	HANTS	WELLS	HENRY
27/11/30	EASTLEACH TURVILLE	GLOUCS	WELLS	THOMAS
11/30	WESTBOURNE	SUSSEX	WELSH	GEORGE
23/11/30	FORDINGBRIDGE	HANTS	WEST	JOSEPH
21/11/30	HOUGHTON	HANTS	WEST	HENRY
9/11/30	MAYFIELD	SUSSEX	WESTON	WILLIAM
11/12/30	CLAVERING	ESSEX	WESTWOOD	JAMES
1/12/30	IVER	BUCKS	WETHERELL	HENRY
20/11/30	WALTHAM ST LAWRENCE	BERKS	WHEELER	ROBERT
29/11/30	EAST STOWER	DORSET	WHELLER	THOMAS
27/11/30	BISHOPSTONE	BUCKS	WHIGGS	HENRY
23/11/30	REDENHALL	NORFOLK	WHISKIN	THOMAS
10/12/31	BARTON STACY	HANTS	WHITAKER	WILLIAM
29/3/30	CHILDERDITCH	ESSEX	WHITBY	WILLIAM
23/11/30	SOUTH STONEHAM	HANTS	WHITCHER	GEORGE
12/2/31	ARNE	DORSET	WHITE	JAMES
12/30	WORCESTER	WORCS	WHITE	JOPSEPH
26/11/30	BEVERSTONE	GLOUCS	WHITE	JAMES
26/11/30	BEVERSTONE	GLOUCS	WHITE	JOHN
26/11/30	UPPER CLATFORD	HANTS	WHITE	JOHN
7/11/30	NORTHFLEET	KENT	WHITE	WILLIAM
22/11/30	EAST WELLOW	HANTS	WHITE	JAMES
25/11/30	TISBURY	WILTS	WHITE	EDMUND
27/11/30	COLN ST ALDWYN	GLOUCS	WHITEHEAD	EDWARD
10/12/30	DYKE	LINCS	WHITEHEAD	JOHN
1831	WHITCHURCH	SHROPSHIRE	WHITFIELD	RICHARD
13/12/30	GREAT CLACTON	ESSEX	WHITING	GEORGE
20/11/30	BARTON STACEY	HANTS	WHITTACKER	THOMAS
25/11/30	HICKLING	NORFOLK	WHITTAKER	FAREWELL
25/11/30	HICKLING	NORFOLK	WHITTAKER	CHRISTMAS
21/11/30	CANTERBURY	KENT	WICKENDEN	BENJAMIN
1830	BUXTED	SUSSEX	WICKENS	JOHN
17/11/30	FRANT	SUSSEX	WICKS	THOMAS
23/11/30	MONK SHERBOURNE	HANTS	WIGGENS	MARK
1831	ROYDON	NORFOLK	WILBY	PHILIP

DATE	PARISH	COUNTY	SURNAME	FORENAME
6/12/30	COLCHESTER	ESSEX	WRIGHT	J
11/12/30	CLAVERING	ESSEX	WRIGHT	JAMES
24/11/30	FIELD DALING	NORFOLK	WRIGHT	STEPHEN
29/3/30	CHILDERDITCH	ESSEX	WRIGHT	ELIAS
29/3/30	CHILDERDITCH	ESSEX	WRIGHT	JAMES
29/3/30	CHILDERDITCH	ESSEX	WRIGHT	SAMUEL
29/12/30	BACTON	SUFFOLK	WRIGHT	WILLIAM
30/11/30	KINGSUTTON	NORTHANTS	WYATT	JOSEPH
5/8/31	RIPPLE	KENT	WYBURN	WILLIAM
18/1/31	SHEFFIELD	YORK (WR)	YEARDLEY	ROBERT
20/9/30	BARHAM	KENT	YONENS	GEORGE
22/11/30	ROUGHAM	NORFOLK	YOUNGS	JOHN
24/11/30	SIXPENNY HANDLEY	DORSET	ZILLWOOD	ROBERT
24/11/30	SIXPENNY HANDLEY	DORSER	ZILLWOOD	SAMUEL

DATE	PARISH	COUNTY	SURNAME	FORENAME
23/11/30	CRANBOURNE	DORSET	WILKINS	JAMES
18/11/30	LUDGERSHALL	WILTS	WILKINS	HENRY
16/11/30	STONE	HEREFORDSHIRE	WILLIAMS	HENRY
1/4/32	COLEFORD	GLOUCS	WILLIAMS	CHARLES
26/11/30	BEVERSTONE	GLOUCS	WILLIAMS	JOHN
27/11/30	STONE	BUCKS	WILLIAMS	DANIEL
6/12/30	WITHERSFIELD	SUFFOLK	WILLIAMS	WILLIAM
1/4/32	COLEFORD	GLOUCS	WILLIAMS	CHARLES
23/11/30	REDENHALL	NORFOLK	WILLIAMSON	ROBERT
26/11/30	WARMINGTON	NORTHANTS	WILLIAMSON	RICHARD
30/10/30	CANFORD MAGNA	DORSET	WILLIS	HENRY
6/32	MILTON	NORTHANTS	WILLIS	THOMAS
9/3/30	MANSTON	DORSET	WILMOT	EBENEZER
9/3/30	MANSTON	DORSET	WILMOT	JOEL
14/4/30	HADDENHAM	BUCKS	WILSON	JOSEPH
7/12/30		SOMERSET	WILTON	WILLIAM
11/1831	ALTON	HANTS	WILTSHIRE	JACOB
20/12/30	FOULMIRE	CAMBS	WILTSHIRE	E
21/11/30	VERNHAM DEAN	HANTS	WILTSHIRE	JACOB
29/11/30	CHEPPING WYCOMBE	BUCKS	WINGROVE	EDMUND
19/11/32	LAMBOURNE	BERKS	WINKWORTH	
19/11/30	MICHELDEVER	HANTS	WINKWORTH	WILLIAM
11/1/31	READING	BERKS	WINTERBOURNE	
24/11/30		NORFOLK	WISEMAN	WILLIAM
30/7/32		CAMBS	WISNEL	THOMAS
23/8/31	OLLERTON	NOTTS	WOMBWELL	GEORGE
23/8/31	OLLERTON	NOTTS	WOMBWELL	THOMAS
29/11/30	MEOPHAM	KENT	WOOD	HENRY
26/11/30	BEVERSTONE	GLOUCS	WOOD	GEORGE
27/11/30	BISHOPSTONE	BUCKS	WOODFORD	THOMAS
1831	HACONBY	LINCS	WOODFORD	PRISCILLA
26/11/30	BEVERSTONE	GLOUCS	WOODMAN	JOHN
11/30	WESTBOURNE	SUSSEX	WOODS	WILLIAM
10/3/32	SNETTISHAM	NORFOLK	WOODS	GEORGE
1/12/30	LITTLE BRICKHILL	BUCKS	WOODWARD	WILLIAM
12/31	NORMANTON	DERBYSHIRE	WOODWARD	SAMUEL
12/10/31	NORMANTON	DERBYSHIRE	WOODWARD	JOSEPH
6/8/31	ST BRIAVELS	GLOUCS	WOORE	JAMES
8/11/32	UCKFIELD	SUSSEX	WREN	GEORGE
29/11/30	CHEPPING WYCOMBE	BUCKS	WRIGHT	ARTHUR
20/12/30	FOULMIRE	CAMBS	WRIGHT	B
13/8/32	WHISTON	YORK (WR)	WRIGHT	EBENEZER

APPENDIX II: LIST OF VICTIMS OF SWING PROTEST

PARISH	COUNTY	VICTIM
AYLESFORD	KENT	ABBOTT
BARTON TURF	NORFOLK	ABBOTT
WRITTLE	ESSEX	ABBOTT
BREDE	SUSSEX	ABELL THOMAS
TUNBRIDGE WELLS	KENT	ABERGAVENNY
THURNHAM	KENT	ACKHURST
EDINGTHORPE	NORFOLK	ADAMS RICHARD
WRITTLE	ESSEX	ADDY
ARLINGTON	SUSSEX	ADE C
ALFRISTON	SUSSEX	ADE CHARLES
STOURMOUTH	KENT	ADLEY
CHINNOR	OXON	AILNUTT WILLIAM
COTON	CAMBS	AINGER
COTON	CAMBS	AINGER RICHARD
BEARSTED	KENT	AKEHURST
MESSING	ESSEX	ALBON ROBERT
HASTINGS	SUSSEX	ALDERTON H
BATTLE	SUSSEX	ALDERTON HENRY
COLNEY	NORFOLK	ALDRED & BELOE
SHIPBOURNE	KENT	ALDRIDGE
VERNHAM DEAN	HANTS	ALEXANDER MARY
COSHAM	HANTS	ALEXANDER RH
CLIFF	KENT	ALLEN
ERPINGHAM	NORFOLK	ALLEN
YALDING	KENT	ALLEN
MORETON IN THE MARSH	GLOUCS	ALLEN WILLIAM
NARBOROUGH	NORFOLK	ALLEN WILLIAM
SUTTON	NORFOLK	ALLENBY
LONG SUTTON	LINCS	ALLENBY REDMORE
LUTTON	LINCS	ALLENBY REDMORE
HENTON	OXON	ALLMOTT WILLIAM
HIGH WYCOMBE	BUCKS	ALLNUT
CHINNOR	OXON	ALLNUTT WILLIAM
ST IVES	HUNTS	ALLPRESS
MARSH GREEN	BUCKS	ALNUTT ZACHARY
CROYDON	CAMBS	ALPIN
PITMINSTER	SOMERSET	ALWAYS JAMES
AUST	GLOUCS	ALWAYS WIDOW
SILVERSTONE	NORTHANTS	AMOS EDWARD
CALDEWGATE	CUMBERLAND	ANDREW

PARISH	COUNTY	VICTIM
CARLISLE	CUMBERLAND	ANDREWS
FAWLEY	HANTS	ANDREWS JOHN
GLOUCESTER	GLOUCS	ANDREWS JOSEPH
HULL	YORK (ER)	ANDSELL FRANCES
SEIGHFORD	STAFFS	ANSELL THOMAS
DROXFORD	HANTS	APPLEBY JOHN
BURGHCLERE	HANTS	ARBUTHNOT EDWARD
FINDON	SUSSEX	ARKELL
MAIDSTONE	KENT	ARNOLD SAMUEL
ORSETT	ESSEX	ASHFORD
IVER	BUCKS	ASHLEY WILLIAM
EAST WOODHAY	HANTS	ASHWORTH JOHN H
SIDMONTON	HANTS	ASPREY JANE
REEPHAM	NORFOLK	ASTLEY JACOB
HINDOLVESTON	NORFOLK	ASTLEY JACOB SIR (BT)
ST BRIAVELS	GLOUCS	ASTON JOHN
ENGLEFIELD GREEN	SURREY	ATKINS
SHOREHAM	KENT	ATKINS JOHN
MARLOW	BUCKS	ATKINSON
ULCEBY	LINCS	ATKINSON JAMES
COLTON	NORFOLK	ATTERTON JAMES
RUCKINGE	KENT	AUSTEN ROBERT
DYKE	LINCS	AUSTIN
KENNARDINGTON	KENT	AUSTIN
WHITFIELD	KENT	AVERY
MILDENHALL	SUFFOLK	AVES ADAM
SHIPDHAM	NORFOLK	AYLMER BOB
CHIDDINGLY	SUSSEX	AYLMER JAMES
BINSTED	HANTS	BAIGENT EDWARD
NANTYGLO	MONMOUTH	BAILEY
WITCHINGHAM	NORFOLK	BAILEY
MOTTISFONT	HANTS	BAILEY SARAH
NEWTON ST LOE	SOMERSET	BAINE THOMAS
KIRBY-LE-SOKEN	ESSEX	BAKER
SHERE	SURREY	BAKER
SOUTHAMPTON	HANTS	BAKER CHARLES
SOUTHAMPTON	HANTS	BAKER CHARLES
BLEAN	KENT	BAKER GEORGE
KNOWLE	WARWICKSHIRE	BAKER PETER
KNAPTON	NORFOLK	BAKER SAMUEL
BURGHCLERE	HANTS	BAKER WILLIAM
BARSTON	WARWICKSHIRE	BAKER, PETER

PARISH	COUNTY	VICTIM
NEWTON	CHESHIRE	BALDWIN
TIBENHAM	NORFOLK	BALE EDMUND
WINFARTHING	NORFOLK	BALE EDMUND
SWANTON ABBOTT	NORFOLK	BALKE WILLIAM
WADDESDON	BUCKS	BALLARD RICHARD
MILTON ERNEST	BEDFORDSHIRE	BALLS
FALKINGHAM	LINCS	BALLY
GREAT WITCHINGHAM	NORFOLK	BALY GEORGE
DANBURY	ESSEX	BANNISTER
WINDSOR	BERKS	BANNISTER
NORTHAMPTON	NORTHANTS	BARBER J (JUN)
WARBLETON	SUSSEX	BARDEN WILLIAM
LONGPARISH	HANTS	BARING A
NORTHINGTON	HANTS	BARING BINGHAM
BACTON	SUFFOLK	BARKER
CLAVERING	ESSEX	BARKER
WEST TARRING	SUSSEX	BARKER
KNODISHALL	SUFFOLK	BARKER THOMAS
KNODISHALL	SUFFOLK	BARLOW
STONE	STAFFS	BARLOW EDWARD
HOLLINGBOURNE	KENT	BARNARD
STEEPLE BARTON	OXON	BARNARD
GREAT ELLINGHAM	NORFOLK	BARNARD JOHN
TIRLEY	GLOUCS	BARNES EDWARD
KIMPTON	HANTS	BARNES JOHN
BEESTON	NORFOLK	BARNES THOMAS
BILLERICAY	ESSEX	BARRELL JOHN
KEGWORTH	LEICS	BARROW SAMUEL
BANWELL	SOMERSET	BARROW JOHN
DOVER	KENT	BARTER
HOUGHAM	KENT	BARTER of EWELL
HADLOW	KENT	BARTON
LEVERTON	LINCS	BARTON
NORTH FRITH	KENT	BARTON
EASTLEACH MARTIN	GLOUCS	BARTON J
CORSHAM	WILTS	BARTON MRS
STAGSDEN	BEDFORDSHIRE	BASS
HEMEL HEMPSTEAD	HERTS	BATCHELOR
METHWOLD	NORFOLK	BATELEY

PARISH	COUNTY	VICTIM
THORPE	NORFOLK	BATELEY
HINDOLVESTON	NORFOLK	BATELEY W LIONEL
HADDENHAM	BUCKS	BATES
HADDENHAM	BUCKS	BATES
CARLTON	YORK (WR)	BAYLDON TS
CLIFF PYPARD	WILTS	BEAKE
SHEERING	ESSEX	BEALE
BLACKER RICHARD	YORK (WR)	BEARDCHILL
HUCKNALL TORKARD	NOTTS	BEASTALL JOHN
HICKLING	NORFOLK	BEAUMONT ABRAHAM
ASH	KENT	BECKER MICHAEL
ASH	KENT	BECKER MICHAEL
ROYSTON	HERTS	BEDAM
SPELDHURST	KENT	BEECHING THOMAS
BARRINGTON	CAMBS	BELDAM
BASSINGBOURNE	CAMBS	BELDHAM
CANTERBURY	KENT	BELL JOHN
BOREHAM	ESSEX	BELLINGHAM
BRIGHTON	SUSSEX	BELLINGHAM
SINGLEDGE	KENT	BELSEY
KEGWORTH	LEICS	BELSHAW
MOULTON	LINCS	BENNER WILLIAM
WESTON	LINCS	BENNER WILLIAM
SALISBURY	WILTS	BENNET J
SALISBURY	WILTS	BENNET JOHN MP
FONTHILL BISHOP	WILTS	BENNETT
HADLOW	KENT	BENNETT
BOSHAM	SUSSEX	BENNETT EDWARD
TISBURY	WILTS	BENNETT JOHN
ANDOVER	HANTS	BENSLEY THOMAS
WOOTON PILLINGE	BEDFORDSHIRE	BENSON
OSPRINGE	KENT	BENSTEAD
KIMPTON	HERTS	BERRETT CHARLES
BOUGHTON HILL	KENT	BERRY
CUCKFIELD	SUSSEX	BEST
AMPNEY CRUCIS	GLOUCS	BETTERTON
HORSINGTON	SOMERSET	BEWSEY LAZARUS
PLUMTREE	NOTTS	BEXON THOMAS
HIGH WYCOMBE	BUCKS	BIDDLE JOSEPH

PARISH	COUNTY	VICTIM
WOOTON ST LAWRENCE	HANTS	BIGG WITHER HARRIS
BROMSGROVE	WORCS	BIGGS
WHITWELL	NORFOLK	BILLAM JOHN
BURGESS HILL	SUSSEX	BILNEY
DRIFFIELD	YORK (ER)	BILTON
WALTON CARRS	YORK (ER)	BILTON
HORNDON-ON-THE-HILL	ESSEX	BIRD
SHOULDHAM	NORFOLK	BIRD
STEVENTON	BERKS	BITTERIDGE
ASHBY FOLVILLE	LEICS	BLACK
BOWERS GIFFORD	ESSEX	BLACK
SWANTON MORLEY	NORFOLK	BLAKE WILLIAM
ESCRICK	YORK (ER)	BLAND JOHN
NUTLEY	HANTS	BLATCH
WEASENHAM	NORFOLK	BLYTH
BRAMFORD	SUFFOLK	BLYTHE M
LONG MELFORD	SUFFOLK	BODY JOSEPH
WESTLEY	SUFFOLK	BOLDERO
CAWSTON	NORFOLK	BOND JOHN
EASTERGATE	SUSSEX	BONIFACE
TWEMLOES	CHESHIRE	BOOTH
WHITCHURCH	SHROPSHIRE	BOOTH
WEST DARLINGTON	SHROPSHIRE	BOOTH T
PREES HEATH	SHROPSHIRE	BOOTH THOMAS
LINGWOOD	NORFOLK	BOROUGHS JEREMIAH
CUERDLY	LANC'S	BOSCOE WILLIAM
WOOTON	SURREY	BOSCOWEN
GREAT HALLINGBURY	ESSEX	BOURCHIER Rev
WESTBURY	WILTS	BOURNE JAMES
WESTBURY	WILTS	BOURNE JAMES
WESTBURY	WILTS	BOURNE IAS
BUCKWORTH	HUNTS	BOWKER
WITCHINGHAM	NORFOLK	BOWLES
LOUTH	LINCS	BOWLING
VIRGINIA WATER	SURREY	BOWYER
BROUGHTON	HANTS	BOX JOHN
ATTLEBOROUGH	NORFOLK	BOYCATT WILLIAM
BURGH	NORFOLK	BOYCATT WILLIAM

PARISH	COUNTY	VICTIM
WHITCHURCH	SHROPSHIRE	BRADBURY
SWINDON	WILTS	BRADFORD
STROUD	GLOUCS	BRADFORD J
BENNINGTON	NOTTS	BRADFORD MICHAEL
MARCH	CAMBS	BRADFORD SAMUEL
SWINDON ELIZABETH	STAFFS	BRADFORD,
CARLTON	NOTTS	BRADSHAW
DUDDINGTON	NORTHANTS	BRADSHAW
SNEINTON	NOTTS	BRADSHAW
SOUTHWELL	NOTTS	BRADSHAW
SWINDON ELIZABETH	WILTS	BRAILSFORD
REDMARLEY	GLOUCS	BRAY
OVERSTONE	NORTHANTS	BRAY JOHN
SPRATTON	NORTHANTS	BRAY JOHN
GUESTLING	SUSSEX	BREEDS, T
TAPLOW	BUCKS	BREGENSHAW JOHN
BURNHAM OVERY	NORFOLK	BRETT WILLIAM
CRANBOURNE	DORSET	BREWER J
LOUGHBOROUGH	LEICS	BREWIN A
SYDLING ST NICHOLAS	DORSET	BRIDLE WILLIAM
DERBY	DERBYSHIRE	BRIERLEY
HECKINGTON	LINCS	BRIGGS
WADDESDON	BUCKS	BRIGGS JAMES
TEMPLE COMBE	SOMERSET	BRINE
HAWKWELL	ESSEX	BROCKIES
EYE	SUFFOLK	BROOM THOMAS
RUGBY	WARWICKSHIRE	BROOMWICH
BENTLEY	YORK (WR)	BROUGHTON
BENTLEY	YORK (WR)	BROUGHTON THOMAS
SIXPENNY HANDLEY	DORSET	BROUNCKER RICHARD
BUTTERWICK	LINCS	BROWN
STRADISHALL	SUFFOLK	BROWN
BESTWOOD	NOTTS	BROWN GEORGE
WARMINGTON	NORTHANTS	BROWN SAMUEL
BLANDFORD	DORSET	BRYANT WILLIAM
EDGEFIELD	NORFOLK	BSISHOP
RUDHAM	NORFOLK	BUCK JAMES
TUNBRIDGE WELLS	KENT	BUCKING THOMAS

PARISH	COUNTY	VICTIM
HOUND	ISLE OF WIGHT	BUCKLAND JOHN
COXWOLD	YORK (NR)	BUCKLE JOHN
COXWOLD	YORK (NR)	BUCKLE JOHN
HONING	NORFOLK	BUFFIN
VERNHAM DEAN	HANTS	BULL DARIUS
HARWICH	ESSEX	BULL REV SN
PULHAM	DORSET	BULLEN
BUCKLAND		BULLER ROBERT
NEWTON	DORSET	BULWER
AYLSHAM	NORFOLK	BULWER Dr
HEYDON	NORFOLK	BUNNING
EMPINGHAM	RUTLAND	BUNNY RICHARD
HURSTBORNE		EARLE
TARRANT	HANTS	BURGESS
SPALDING	LINCS	BURNSIDE, JOHN
PLUMTREE	NOTTS	BURROWS
WISBECH St MARY	CAMBS	BURTON
EGHAM	SURREY	BURITT JOSEPH
FULBECK	LINCS	BUSSEY
POCKTHORPE	NORFOLK	BUTCHER
ROPSLEY	LINCS	BUTCHER ANN
CHIVERELL	WILTS	BUTLER
EMSWORTH	HANTS	BUTLER
HAVANT	HANTS	BUTLER
RATCLIFF ON SOAR	NOTTS	BUTLER
RATCLIFF ON THE WREAK	LEICS	BUTLER RICHARD
GUILDEN MORDEN	CAMBS	BUTTERFIELD JAMES
LITTLE WIGBOROUGH	ESSEX	BYFORD
BARNET	HERTS	BYNG G
GUILDFORD	SURREY	BYNG G
St ALBANS	HERTS	BYNG G
GOUDHURST	KENT	CALDER E
EAST STRATTON	HANTS	CALENDAR FRANCIS
ANDOVER	HANTS	CALLAWAY JAMES
NEW CATTON	NORFOLK	CALVER
BUXTON	NORFOLK	CAMBRIDGE
RAMSEY	ESSEX	CAMPION
WRAMPLINGHAM	NORFOLK	CANN JS
EAST WOODHAY	HANTS	CANNING BENJAMIN
OGBOURNE ST ANDREWS	WILTS	CANNING ROBERT
HORNCASTLE	LINCS	CAPARN
MATLOCK	DERBYSHIRE	CARLISLE
HIGHCLERE	HANTS	CARNARVON
WEST PECKHAM	KENT	CARNELL
FIELD DALING	NORFOLK	CARR
THURGATON	NORFOLK	CARR EPHRAIM
MAYFIELD	SUSSEX	CARRINGTON
PETERSFIELD	HANTS	CARTER JB
NORTHALLERTON	YORK (NR)	CARTER JOHN
WEREHAM	NORFOLK	CARTER THOMAS
SANDWICH	KENT	CASTLE ROBERT
WIMBORNE	DORSET	CASTLEMAN
CHARTHAM	KENT	CATT
WALTON-LE-SOKEN	ESSEX	CAULSON
GREAT CLACTON	ESSEX	CAUVILL
LITTLE CLACTON	ESSEX	CAUVILL
FAWLEY	HANTS	CAVELL HENRY
THURSFORD	NORFOLK	CHAD CHARLES
MAIDSTONE	KENT	CHAMBERLAIN
COVENEY	CAMBS	CHAMBERS Bydall
PEWSEY	WILTS	CHANDLE Mrs
MONK SHERBOURNE	HANTS	CHANDLER THOMAS
RUDHAM	NORFOLK	CHAPMAN
LENHAM	KENT	CHAPMAN WILLIAM
CHEDZOY	SOMERSET	CHARNEY
DILHAM	NORFOLK	CHENERY B
HAGNABY LOCK	LINCS	CHERRY
LUSBY	LINCS	CHERRY, JOHN
STICKFORD	LINCS	CHERRY, JOHN
GEDLING	NOTTS	CHESTERFIELD
HELLINGLY	SUSSEX	CHICHESTER
LAUGHTON	SUSSEX	CHICHESTER
NEW ALRESFORD	HANTS	CHIDDELL JOHN
EAST WOODHAY	HANTS	CHILD THOMAS
VERNHAM DEAN	HANTS	CHILDS WILLIAM
COPAL	BEDFORDSHIRE	CHIPPERFIELD
YALDING	KENT	CHUMLEY CHARLES
ALDBOURNE	WILTS	CHURCH
NEWPORT	MONMOUTH	CHURCH JOHN
WADDESDON	BUCKS	CHURCHILL
WHITCHURCH	SHROPSHIRE	CHURTEN WILLIAM
CADMORE	BUCKS	CLANFIELD Jos
HELLINGLY	SUSSEX	CLAPSON
DENHAM	SUFFOLK	CLARGE DOUGHTY GEO
DENHAM	SUFFOLK	CLARGE DOUGHTY
CROWLAND	LINCS	CLARK
ANLABY	YORK (ER)	CLARK J
DEEPING FEN	LINCS	CLARK JAMES
DOVER	KENT	CLARKE
HARDINGHAM	NORFOLK	CLARKE
MARKET DEEPING	LINCS	CLARKE
STOWGATE	LINCS	CLARKE
SUTTON IN ASHFIELD	NOTTS	CLARKE
MICHELDEVER	HANTS	CLARKE THOMAS
HENHAM	ESSEX	CLAYDEN
BOUGHTON ALUPH	KENT	CLEMENTS MH
LENHAM	KENT	CLIFFORD CEFUS
RUGBY	WARWICKSHIRE	CLIFTON & JONES
HEMSBY	NORFOLK	CLOWES
FORDINGBRIDGE	HANTS	COATES
NETTLESTEAD	KENT	COBB
THROWLEY	KENT	COBB
SELBORNE	HANTS	COBBOLD WILLIAM R
HIGHWEEK	DEVON	COCHRAN GEORGE
FORTHAMPTON	GLOUCS	COCKS PHILIP
FORTHAMPTON	GLOUCS	COCKS PHILIP
WHAPLODE	LINCS	CODLING
ATTLEBOROUGH	NORFOLK	COE
MANSFIELD	NOTTS	COKE, JOHN
GUYHIRN	CAMBS	COLBY
HAPPISBURGH	NORFOLK	COLE
NORMANTON	DERBYSHIRE	COLE RICHARD
PLUMTREE	NOTTS	COLE RICHARD
BENENDEN	KENT	COLEBROOK
GREAT ELLINGHAM	NORFOLK	COLEBY
DONYATT	SOMERSET	COLEMAN
EWELL	KENT	COLEMAN
TRULL	SOMERSET	COLEMAN

PARISH	COUNTY	VICTIM
DOVER	KENT	COLEMAN JOHN
EWELL	SURREY	COLEMAN JOHN
LANGLEY	WILTS	COLEMAN W
RIDDINGHAM	NORFOLK	COLK ROBERT
EDDINGTON	KENT	COLLARD
MONKTON	KENT	COLLARD
MONKTON	KENT	COLLEY
FARNINGHAM	KENT	COLLIER CHARLES
CAMBRIDGE	CAMBS	COLLINS
HENSTRIDGE	SOMERSET	COMBES WILLIAM
BEAMINSTER	DORSET	CONWAY G
CHILDERDITCH	ESSEX	COOPER ROBERT
ROCKBOURNE	HANTS	COOTE EYRE
WHITGREAVE	STAFFS	CORDWELL
ULCOMBE	KENT	CORK WILLIAM
EASTERGATE	SUSSEX	CORNEY CHARLES
BARTON STACEY	HANTS	COTTON MARY
OTFORD	KENT	COUCHMAN GEORGE
THATCHAM	BERKS	COULTHORPE
BARTON STACEY	HANTS	COURTNEY WILLIAM
BLACKBURN	LANCS	COUSELL
BRIMPTON	BERKS	COVE
LEYSDOWN	KENT	COVENEY M JUN
BUCKLAND	DORSET	COWARD WILLIAM
NEWTON	BERKS	COWDERY JAMES
ABINGDON	BERKS	COX
LITCHFIELD	HANTS	COX RICHARD BETHEL
QUARLEY	HANTS	COYNEY WALTER HILL
CAVERSWALL	STAFFS	CRASKE
CAWSTON	NORFOLK	CRAWFORD R
EAST GRINSTEAD	SUSSEX	
BISHOPS STORTFORD	HERTS	
CRAWLEY		
CROWBOROUGH	SUSSEX	CRAWLEY
STANDON	HERTS	CRAWLEY, JOSEPH
DEWSBURY	YORK (WR)	CRAWSHAW P
BILLINGHAY	LINCS	CREASEY JOHN
SHERSTON	WILTS	CRESWELL GEORGE
BIBURY	GLOUCS	CRESWELL SACKVILLE
MILVERTON	SOMERSET	CROCHER
RANSKILL	NOTTS	CROFTS
EARLHAM	NORFOLK	CROSS
WHITFIELD	KENT	CROSS
KIRTLING	CAMBS	CROSS PHILIP
SIDLEY GREEN	SUSSEX	CROWHURST
DEERHURST	GLOUCS	CRUMP
HONING	NORFOLK	CUBITT T
BRANDISTONE	NORFOLK	CULLY HENRY
STOURMOUTH	KENT	CULMER
WISBEACH ST MARY	LINCS	CULY ABRAHAM
WOOTON ST LAWRENCE	HANTS	CURTIS JOSEPH
RUGELEY	STAFFS	CURZON, R
COXWOLD	YORK (NR)	CUSSONS GEORGE
NEWBURGH	YORK (NR)	CUSSONS GEORGE
COLSTON	SOMERSET	CUTLER H
RAWLEIGH	HANTS	DAGWELL, JOHN
MARTYR WORTHY	SHROPSHIRE	DALBY
LUDLOW	NORFOLK	DANIELS
STOKESBY	ESSEX	DANIELS R
WEST BERGHOLT	HUNTS	DANNS
ALCONBURY	SHROPSHIRE	DARLINGTON
PREES HEATH	CHESHIRE	DARLINGTON
TWEMLOES	SHROPSHIRE	DARLINGTON
WHITCHURCH		WILLIAM
COBHAM	KENT	DARNLEY
WOLDINGHAM	SURREY	DARTNELL
LEYTONSTONE	ESSEX	DAUBRIZ JT
SIDDINGTON	CHESHIRE	DAVENPORT DAVID
BRESSINGHAM	NORFOLK	DAVEY
FRAMLINGHAM	SUFFOLK	DAVEY
DOCKING	NORFOLK	DAVEY JOHN
KENCHESTER	HEREFORDSHIRE	DAVIES
YENSTON	SOMERSET	DAVIES
MILDENHALL	SUFFOLK	DAVIES JOHN
CHEPPING WYCOMBE	BUCKS	DAVIS
HENSTRIDGE	SOMERSET	DAVIS ROBERT
STALLBRIDGE	DORSET	DAWN
SANDFORD ORCAS	SOMERSET	DAWS
EWHURST	SUSSEX	DAWS
HATTON	LINCS	
STOCKBURY	KENT	DAWSON
STOCKBURY	KENT	DAWSON
OAKINGTON	CAMBS	DAY
WRITTLE	ESSEX	DAY
NORWICH	NORFOLK	DE CAUX
FRESHWATER	HANTS	DEAN
HENLEY-ON-THAMES	OXON	DEANE
HIGHAM FERRERS	NORTHANTS	DEARLOVE
ELSENHAM	ESSEX	DEATH WILLIAM
HILBOROUGH	NORFOLK	DEBENHAM JOHN
RUCKINGE	KENT	DEEDES CHARLES
EWELL	KENT	DELL GEORGE
NEWARK	NOTTS	DENNISON
OSSINGTON	NOTTS	DENNISON, J
FINEDON	NORTHANTS	DESBOROUGH PHILIP
TOTTINGFORD	NORFOLK	DESFORGES
CHATSWORTH	DERBYSHIRE	DEVONSHIRE
MAIDSTONE	KENT	DEVY
PRIEST HUTTON	LANCS	DICKERSON FRANCIS
WILSHAMSTEAD	BEDFORDSHIRE	DINES THOMAS
HIGH WYCOMBE	BUCKS	DIVINE REV
BLACKHEATH	KENT	DIXON
DRIFFIELD	YORK (ER)	DIXON
PRESTON	YORK (ER)	DIXON
SLAYSDALE	YORK (ER)	DIXON
SIXPENNY HANDLEY	DORSET	DIXON JAMES
NEWTON	NOTTS	DIXON W
UPPER HARDRES	KENT	DODD
UPPER HARDRES	KENT	DODD WILLIAM
FAWLEY	HANTS	DODDS LUKE
LONG CRENDON	BUCKS	DODWELL
WINFARTHING	NORFOLK	DOGGATT DANIEL
WESTLETON	SUFFOLK	DOGGETT D
YAXLEY	SUFFOLK	DOGGETT DANIEL
WESTMINSTER	MIDDLESEX	DONOLAN
STEVINGTON	BEDFORDSHIRE	DOOLEY
STOURMOUTH	KENT	DOUCE JAMES
OSMINGTON	DORSET	DOUGHTY EDWARD
WISBECH	CAMBS	DOW W
NORTHINGTON	HANTS	DOWDEN THOMAS

PARISH	COUNTY	VICTIM
THRANDESTON	SUFFOLK	DRANE
BREWHAM	SOMERSET	DREW MARTIN
YAXLEY	SUFFOLK	DROME
SWANTON MORLEY	NORFOLK	DUCKER
SWANTON ABBOTT	NORFOLK	DUCKER RICHARD
FUNTINTON	SUSSEX	DUKE CHARLES
WESTMINSTER	MIDDLESEX	DUNLOP
CHATTERIS	CAMBS	DUNN
BLACKHEATH	KENT	DUNN DIXON
SYDERSTRAND	NORFOLK	DURRELL
MORBORNE	HUNTS	EARL
STONE	BUCKS	EAST
EASTON	LINCS	EASTCROFT
CANFORD MAGNA	DORSET	EASTON
CAWSTON	NORFOLK	EASTON JAMES
EAST WELLOW	HANTS	EASTED JOHN
ELLESMERE	SHROPSHIRE	EDGE
MANCHESTER	LANCS	EDGE & PARTINGTON
WEST WALTON	NORFOLK	EDGOOSE R
GOUDHURST	KENT	EDGWORTH CHARLES
ABBEY SALFORD	WARWICKSHIRE	EDWARDS
PRIORS SALFORD	WARWICKSHIRE	EDWARDS
QUARLEY	HANTS	EDWARDS WILLIAM
KERDISTON	NORFOLK	EGLINGTON JOHN
RAUNDS	NORTHANTS	EKINS RICHARD
ELDON	DURHAM	ELDON
ISLE OF THANET	KENT	ELGAR
BROCKHURST	HANTS	ELKINS
ABBOT'S KERSWELL	DEVON	ELLIOTT
HADISCOE	NORFOLK	ELLISON THOMAS
TOFT	NORFOLK	ELLISON THOMAS
RINGSFIELD	SUFFOLK	ELLISTON E
WROTHAM	KENT	EMEADES ANN
BATTLE	SUSSEX	EMERY CHARLES
WEST STAFFORD	DORSET	ENGLAND
SOUTH WEALD	ESSEX	ESTAUGH
COLNBROOK	BUCKS	EVANS
BURGHCLERE	HANTS	EVANS THOMAS
BROTHERTOFT	LINCS	EVERARD SAMUEL
HUBBERT'S BRIDGE	LINCS	EVERARD SAMUEL
WICKHAMBROOK	SUFFOLK	EVERETT GEORGE

PARISH	COUNTY	VICTIM
MOULTON MARSH	LINCS	EVERETT, ROBERT
SINGLEDGE	KENT	EVERY JOHN
RUFFORD	OXON	EYRE
BURSTALL	SUFFOLK	FAIERS GEORGE
LEIGH	ESSEX	FAIRCHILD
CROYDON	CAMBS	FAIRCLOTH THOMAS
FULBECK	LINCS	FANE ANN HON
ICKLESHAM	SUSSEX	FARMCOMB
BISHOPSTONE	BUCKS	FARNBOROUGH J
BOSHAM	SUSSEX	FARNDELL WILLIAM
NORTH COVE	SUFFOLK	FARR JOHN LEE
BASFORD	NOTTS	FARRANDS GEORGE
STOKE BY CLARE	SUFFOLK	FARRANTS GEORGE AND MARY
MUNDHAM	NORFOLK	FARROW
CUCKFIELD	SUSSEX	FAULKNER
ODDINGLEY	WORCS	FEATHERSTONE J
GREAT HOLLAND	ESSEX	FEEDHAM
GREAT HOLLAND	ESSEX	FEEDHAM ROBERT
BURGHCLERE	HANTS	FELLOWS JAMES
BECCLES	SUFFOLK	FENN GEORGE
VERNHAM DEAN	HANTS	FERMOR HENRY
MEADS STREET	SUSSEX	FIELDER MOSS
ROCKLAND	NORFOLK	FIELDING
EASTBOURNE	SUSSEX	FILDER JOSEPH
EASTBOURNE	SUSSEX	FILDER MOSES
ARNE	DORSET	FILLITER G
BACTON	SUFFOLK	FINBOW WILLIAM
CAMBRIDGE	CAMBS	FINCH
CHARTHAM	KENT	FINCH
TILNEY ALL SAINTS	NORFOLK	FISHER
WAVENDON	BUCKS	FISHER
LYNN	NORFOLK	FISHER F
SHIMPLING	SUFFOLK	FISKE THOMAS
HIGHAM	SUFFOLK	FISON
STEEPLE BUMPSTEAD	ESSEX	FITCH FREDERICK
BARNSLEY	YORK (WR)	FITZWILLIAM
BOSTON SPA	YORK (WR)	FOBLE GEORGE
PAMBER	HANTS	FOLLETT JOHN
STALLBRIDGE	DORSET	FOOKES ROBERT

PARISH	COUNTY	VICTIM
BLANDFORD	DORSET	FORD
COLLINGBOURNE	WILTS	FORD
OXTED	SURREY	FORD
RUSHTON	DORSET	FORD
COLCHESTER	ESSEX	FORD THOMAS
WHITCHURCH	SHROPSHIRE	FORGHAM JOHN
FOWLMIRE	CAMBS	FORTUNE JAMES
BURGHCLERE	HANTS	FOSBURY JOHN
EAST WOODHAY	HANTS	FOSBURY JOHN
HIGHCLERE	HANTS	FOSBURY JOHN
TOTTENHOE	BEDFORDSHIRE	FOSSEY
HAPPISBURGH	NORFOLK	FOULK
FLITCHAM	NORFOLK	FOULKS WILLIAM SIR
OARE	WILTS	FOWLER
STOURMOUTH	KENT	FOX
BADDELY HULSE	CHESHIRE	FOXLEY SAMUEL
RENDHAM	SUFFOLK	FRANCIS MARTIN
RENDHAM	SUFFOLK	FRANCIS MARTIN
ATTLEBOROUGH	NORFOLK	FRANKLIN F
GUILDFORD	SURREY	FRANKS
ALBURY	SURREY	FRANKS JAMES
HICKLING	NORFOLK	FREEMAN JOHN
SHEPSHED	LEICS	FREEMAN WILLIAM
WINDSOR	BERKS	FREEMANTLE WH
BEAKESBOURNE	KENT	FRIDAY JOHN
NEWINGTON	KENT	FRIEND
ARNOLD	NOTTS	FRIGNALL
LONG CRENDON	BUCKS	FRYER JAMES
HOUGHTON	SUSSEX	FULLER
UCKFIELD	SUSSEX	FULLER ELEANOUR
NANTWICH	CHESHIRE	FURNIVAL
MICHELMERSH	HANTS	FUTCHER JAMES
FIRLE	SUSSEX	GAGE
RINGMER	SUSSEX	GAGE
YAXHAM	NORFOLK	GALL
LANGLEY	KENT	GAMBIER JE
CHURTON	CHESHIRE	GAMMAN THOMAS
BEAKESBOURNE	KENT	GARDNER AUSTEN
STRATFORD UPON AVON	WARWICKSHIRE	GARDNER ISAAC
MAIDFORD	NORTHANTS	GARDNER WILLIAM
ST LAWRENCE	KENT	GARRETT THOMAS

PARISH	COUNTY	VICTIM
ROTHWELL	NORTHANTS	HAFFORD WILLIAM
TEMPLE GATE	SOMERSET	HAIR & CO
HUNGERFORD	BERKS	HALCOMBE WILLIAM
HICKLING	NORFOLK	HALL
HUCKNALL TORKARD	NOTTS	HALL
SOMERTON	SOMERSET	HALL GEORGE WEBB
DRAYCOTT	SOMERSET	HALL JOHN
EATON SOCON	BEDFORDSHIRE	HALL MARTIN
LYMINGE	KENT	HAMBROOK JOHN
ASHFIELD	SUFFOLK	HAMMOND
MARGATE	KENT	HAMMOND
BOUGHTON	KENT	HAMMOND
BURWELL	CAMBS	HAND
TRENT HAY	STAFFS	HAND, THOMAS
EASTWOOD	NOTTS	HANFORD
BANWELL	SOMERSET	HANFORD WILLIAM H
BASINGSTOKE	HANTS	HANKEY CASSANDRA
HUCKNALL TORKARD	NOTTS	HANKIN ELIZABETH
MINSTER	KENT	HANNAM GEORGE
BRANDON	WARWICKSHIRE	HANSON
STINSFORD	DORSET	HARDING
FROME	SOMERSET	HARDING B
TONBRIDGE	KENT	HARDINGE C
DYKE	LINCS	HARDWICK
BOURNE	LINCS	HARDWICKE W
TENDRING	ESSEX	HARDY
BATTLE	SUSSEX	HARE
STONEHOUSE	DEVON	HARE
WHITCHURCH	SHROPSHIRE	HARPER ROBERT
BREASTON	DERBYSHIRE	HARRIMAN
BIBURY	GLOUCS	HARRIS J
LOUGHBOROUGH	LEICS	HARRIS JAMES
DERBY	DERBYSHIRE	HARRISON
HERNE	KENT	HARRISON
SANDON	STAFFS	HARROWBY
GREAT MELTON	NORFOLK	HART
HOE	NORFOLK	HART
WINFARTHING	NORFOLK	HART
HORSLEY	GLOUCS	HART HENRY
CANFORD MAGNA	DORSET	HART JOHN FILL

PARISH	COUNTY	VICTIM
RUNCTON	NORFOLK	GOODALE
RAMSEY	CAMBS	GOODBURN S
KEDDINGTON	SUFFOLK	GOODCHILD WILLIAM
TERRINGTON	NORFOLK	GOODE
GREATHAM	HANTS	GOODEVE WILLIAM
NEWARK	NORTHANTS	GOODMAN
CLATFORD	WILTS	GOODMAN I
WHITSTABLE	KENT	GOODWIN
PAINSWICK	GLOUCS	GORDAN
HENSTRIDGE	SOMERSET	GOREY
EASTBOURNE	SUSSEX	GORRINGE BROS
DUNSTABLE	BEDFORDSHIRE	GOSELOUR
SOUTH STONEHAM	HANTS	GOSLING WILLIAM
CATERHAM	SURREY	GOWER
CALVERTON	BUCKS	GRACE
DEIGHTON	YORK (ER)	GRAVES ROBERT
BUCKWORTH	HUNTS	GRAY
STALLBRIDGE	DORSET	GRAY B
BIRCHINGTON	KENT	GREAVES
HEVINGHAM	NORFOLK	GREEN
OTHAM	KENT	GREEN
TIBBERTON	SHROPSHIRE	GREEN
WHITCHURCH	SHROPSHIRE	GREEN
HEAGE	DERBYSHIRE	GREENSMITH
AYLSHAM	NORFOLK	GREGORY
CASNEWYDD-AR-WYSG	MONMOUTH	GREGORY T
CHICKSANDS	BEDFORDSHIRE	GRESHAM
MALVERN	WORCS	GRESWOLD
BIRMINGHAM	WARWICKSHIRE	GRESWOLDE
DUFFRYN	GLAMORGAN	GREY
ST LYTHANS	GLAMORGAN	GREY WB
KENCHESTER	HEREFORDSHIRE	GRIFFITHS J
BOUGHTON	KENT	GRIPPS G
SOUTH STONEHAM	HANTS	GUBBINS JOSEPH
BISHOPS WALTHAM	HANTS	GUNNER WILLIAM
HAVERHILL	SUFFOLK	GURTEEN D
DUNSTABLE	BEDFORDSHIRE	GUTTERIDGE
LOUGHBOROUGH	LEICS	GUTTERIDGE
ROPSLEY	LINCS	GUYLEE WILLIAM
TINTWISTLE	CHESHIRE	HADFIELD AND WILKINSON

PARISH	COUNTY	VICTIM
BUCKHORN WESTON	DORSET	GATEHOUSE, JOHN
SOUTH STONEHAM	HANTS	GATER WILLIAM HENRY
PENTON GRAFTON	HANTS	GAWLER HENRY
WEST PECKHAM	KENT	GEARY LADY
RIMPTON	SOMERSET	GEORGE
LITTLEDEAN	GLOUCS	GETHIN THOMAS
GREAT SWAFFHAM	NORFOLK	GIBLIN CHARLES
WALDINGFIELD	SUFFOLK	GIBLIN D
RADWINTER	ESSEX	GIBLIN ROBERT
OVER	CAMBS	GIFFORD NATHANIEL
BARSBY	LEICS	GILBERT
FREETHORPE	NORFOLK	GILBERT
POSTWICK	NORFOLK	GILBERT
BEVERLEY	YORK (ER)	GILBY WR
CANFIELD	DORSET	GILLINGHAM DAVID
MONKTON	KENT	GILLOW
BUCKLAND NEWTON	DORSET	GILPIN MATTHEW
NEWARK	NOTTS	GILSTRAP
OLD HEATH	SHROPSHIRE	GILTINS
BROUGHTON	HANTS	GIPPS GEORGE
ATTLEBOROUGH	NORFOLK	GIRLING
TENDRING	ESSEX	GIRLING
GREAT CLACTON	ESSEX	GIRLING JOHN
PASTON	NORFOLK	GIRLING JOHN
WICKHAM SKEITH	SUFFOLK	GISSING
SHREWSBURY	SHROPSHIRE	GITTINS
BERRICK	OXON	GLENDENNING
SOUTHREPPS	NORFOLK	GLOVER
BECCLES	SUFFOLK	GOAT
BARROW	WORCS	GOATMAN
SUTTON IN ASHFIELD	NOTTS	GODAKER T
CHILTON FOLIAT	WILTS	GODDARD MRS
SWINDON	WILTS	GODDARD, AMBROSE
IVER	BUCKS	GODLIMAN JOHN
MARCH	CAMBS	GOLDEN T
HARPLEY	NORFOLK	GOLDERSTONE
GOOSE GREEN	KENT	GOLDING
HUTTON	SOMERSET	GOOD JAMES

PARISH	COUNTY	VICTIM
WESTBOURNE	SUSSEX	HARTFIELD MARY
ASHBOURNE	DERBYSHIRE	HARTSHORN THOMAS
BRISTON	NORFOLK	HARVEY
COWDEN	KENT	HARVEY
DOVER	KENT	HARVEY
BARHAM	KENT	HARVEY JOHN
PATRIXBOURNE	KENT	HARVEY JOHN
FRESHWATER	HANTS	HARVEY RICHARD
SNARLTON	WILTS	HARVEY W
EASTRY	KENT	HATFIELD &
SINGLETON		
WOODFORD		
BRIDGE	ESSEX	HATTON
BULWELL	NOTTS	HAUGHTON LUKE
HOLT	NORFOLK	HAWES
LONGPARISH	HANTS	HAWKER
MARCH	CAMBS	HAWKES
DROXFORD	HANTS	HAWKINS MRS
PEEBLES	PEEBLESHIRE	HAY JOHN
HIGH WYCOMBE	BUCKS	HAYES
MARDEN	KENT	HAYES
UPHAM	HANTS	HAYGARTH JOHN
HANNINGTON	WILTS	HAYWARD B
WHITSTABLE	KENT	HAYWARD GEORGE
BEVERSTONE	GLOUCS	HAYWARD JACOB
LAVINGTON	WILTS	HAYWOOD B
CORPUSTY	NORFOLK	HAZE THOMAS
GREAT SHELFORD	CAMBS	HEADLEY HENRY
SURFLEET	LINCS	HEARDSON JAMES
BURGHFIELD	BERKS	HEARNE CHARLES
WHITCHURCH	SHROPSHIRE	HEATH
BARNSTAPLE	DEVON	HEATHCOTT
WOBURN	BEDFORDSHIRE	HEIGHINGTON
FOULSHAM	NORFOLK	HENDRY JAMES
IRBY	LINCS	HENDSLEY JOHN
TAMWORTH	STAFFS	HEWITT, ROBERT
NEWARK	NOTTS	HEWS
CAWSTON	NORFOLK	HICKLING SAMUEL
COLN ST ALDWYN	GLOUCS	HICKS BEACH MRS
SIXPENNY		
HANDLEY	DORSET	HICKS BENJAMIN
WATERSFIELD	SUSSEX	HIDE

PARISH	COUNTY	VICTIM
DEEPING FEN	LINCS	HIELY
WHITECROSS	HEREFORDSHIRE	HIGGINSON
HARROW	MIDDLESEX	HIGGS
HOUNSLOW	MIDDLESEX	HIGGS
ROBERTSBRIDGE	SUSSEX	HILDER
ALFORD	LINCS	HILL
BRISTON	NORFOLK	HILL
WOBURN	BEDFORDSHIRE	HILL ROWLAND
WHITCHURCH	SHROPSHIRE	HILLS WILLIAM
CHATHAM	KENT	HILTON
DANBURY	ESSEX	HINCHCLIFF JOHN
HOLMFIRTH	YORK (WR)	HIND
WALMER	KENT	HIRONS RICHARD
WADDESDON	BUCKS	HITCHCOCK H
ALTON	HANTS	HITCHCOCK HENRY
MANNINGFORD	WILTS	HITCHINSON WIDOW
ASGARBY	LINCS	HIX ELIZABETH
CHARD	SOMERSET	HOARE HENRY
WAVENDON	BUCKS	HODGMAN GEORGE
DUMPTON	KENT	HODGSON
NEWCASTLE	N'HUMBERLAND	HOLDEN
MANSFIELD	NOTTS	HOLDSTOCK
STODMARSH	KENT	
CARLTON ON		
TRENT	NOTTS	HOLE & TAYLOR
BREDE	SUSSEX	HOLE DR
CARRINGTON	LINCS	HOLLAND
SNETTISHAM	NORFOLK	HOLLAND ROBERT
WARBLINGTON	HANTS	HOLLOWAY G
HAVANT	HANTS	HOLLOWAY SARAH
MONKS ELEIGH	SUFFOLK	HOLMAN
WISBECH	CAMBS	HOLMES
CAWSTON	NORFOLK	HOLMES SAMUEL
EMSWORTH	HANTS	HOLLOWAY GAVAN
CARLTON ON		
TRENT	NOTTS	HOLT SAMUEL
LOWER HARDRES	KENT	HOLTUNS
TREDEGAR	MONMOUTH	HOMFRAY
MONK		
SHERBOURNE	HANTS	HOOPER WILLIAM
WOOTON ST		
LAWRENCE	HANTS	HOOPER WILLIAM

PARISH	COUNTY	VICTIM
LONG EATON	DERBYSHIRE	HOPKINS JOHN
CHAMBERLAIN		
DYMOCK	GLOUCS	HOPKINS WILLIAM
PAPPLEWICK	NOTTS	HOPPER
CANFORD MAGNA	DORSET	HORE JOHN
CHIPPING		
CAMPDEN	GLOUCS	HORN JOHN
SHUTLANGER	NORTHANTS	HORN THOMAS
HOLLINGBOURNE	KENT	HORTON
FUNTINTON	SUSSEX	HOUNSON HJ
EAST DEREHAM	NORFOLK	HOWARD WILLIAM
MIDDLETON	NORFOLK	HOWE
BRININGHAM	NORFOLK	HOWES
BESTHORPE	NORFOLK	HOWES ABRAHAM
COLN ROGERS	GLOUCS	HOWES HERMAN
HAPPISBURGH	NORFOLK	HOWES WILLIAM
LINBY	NOTTS	HOWETT WILLIAM
CROWBOROUGH	SUSSEX	HOWIS
BURCHAM	NORFOLK	HOWLETT WARNER
BANSTEAD	SURREY	HOWORTH, HUMPHREY
IDE HILL	KENT	HUBBLE
WILLINGHAM	CAMBS	HUCKLE
HADLEIGH	SUFFOLK	HUDSON JOHN
ASTON	CHESHIRE	HUGHES
ANSFORD	SOMERSET	HUMPHREYS
WINFARTHING	NORFOLK	HUMPHRIES
EAST STOWER	DORSET	HUNT MATTHEW
STOUR PROVOST	DORSET	HUNT WILLIAM
WALPOLE	SUFFOLK	HUNTINGFORD LORD
DEDHAM	ESSEX	HURLOCK WILLIAM
MILTON		
TILSTOCK	SHROPSHIRE	HUXLEY
WHITCHURCH	SHROPSHIRE	HUXLEY
WHEPSTEAD	SUFFOLK	IMAGE T
STANNINGFIELD	SUFFOLK	IMAGE THOMAS
LOWER HARDRES	KENT	INGE
BEVERLEY	YORK (ER)	INGLE JAMES
HEYDON	NORFOLK	IRELAND
THORNTON LE FEN	LINCS	IRELAND
LANGLEY	BUCKS	IVES
WOOD DALLING	NORFOLK	IVES ROBERT
FORNCETT	NORFOLK	JACK

PARISH	COUNTY	VICTIM
BARTON	CHESHIRE	JACKSON
STAMFORD	LINCS	JACKSON
STOKE BY NAYLAND	SUFFOLK	JACKSON ISAAC
OSPRINGE	KENT	JACOB
BRADMORE	NOTTS	JACQUES SAMUEL
CODDINGTON	NOTTS	JALLAND JOHN
PRESTEIGNE	RADNORSHIRE	JAMES E
MONKS ELEIGH	SUFFOLK	JAMES NATHANIEL
BACTON	NORFOLK	JARVIS
CARROW	NORFOLK	JARVIS
BUXTON	NORFOLK	JARVIS GEORGE
WICKHAMPTON	NORFOLK	JARY WILLIAM THOMAS
WILBY	SUFFOLK	JEFFERIES
FAIRFORD	GLOUCS	JENKINS JOSEPH
BURGESS HILL	SUSSEX	JENNER
WESTWELL	KENT	JENNINGS
PIDDLETOWN	DORSET	JESTY GEORGE
SPALDING	LINCS	JOHNSON
YAXHAM	NORFOLK	JOHNSON
CORPUSTY	NORFOLK	JOHNSON HENRY
CHARING	KENT	JOHNSON RICHARD
SHIFNAL	STAFFS	JONES
WINGFIELD	BEDFORDSHIRE	JONES
LLANWIT MAJOR	GLAMORGAN	JONES DANIEL
ROMSEY	HANTS	JONES, EDWARD
EATON FORD	HUNTS	JORDAN
EATON SOCON	BEDFORDSHIRE	JORDAN
OTFORD	KENT	JORDAN ISAAC
LITTLE CORNARD	SUFFOLK	JOSLIN
TAVERHAM	NORFOLK	JUBY
LINGWOOD	NORFOLK	JURY WILLIAM
CAMPDEN	GLOUCS	KEAN JOHN
WESTINGTON	GLOUCS	KEAN JOHN
SELLING	KENT	KEEN
LOWER HARDRES	KENT	KELCEY
SEVENOAKS	KENT	KELSO GEORGE
LONDON	LONDON	KEMBLE C
SWABY	LINCS	KEMP
SWAFIELD	NORFOLK	KEMP THOMAS
SHERNBOURNE	NORFOLK	KENDAL R
WITCHINGHAM	NORFOLK	KENDALL WILLIAM

PARISH	COUNTY	VICTIM
BARNSLEY	YORK (WR)	KENDRAY
HARTFIELD	SUSSEX	KENNARD W
BURGHCLERE	HANTS	KENT STEPHEN
UCKFIELD	SUSSEX	KENNARD W
BREAMORE	HANTS	KERNOTT JOHN
WROTHAM	KENT	KERR
LINCOLN	LINCS	KETTON
TONBRIDGE	KENT	KIBBLES
CHERRINGTON	GLOUCS	KILMINSTER R
HEADLEY	HANTS	KING
TADLOW	CAMBS	KING
WESTBOURNE	SUSSEX	KING JOHN
GOUDHURST	KENT	KING JW
GREATHAM	HANTS	KING MARY
PAMPISFORD	CAMBS	KING T
STONE	BUCKS	KINGHAM
BRETTINGHAM	SUFFOLK	KINGSBURY MATTHEW
BUNGAY	SUFFOLK	KINGSBURY MB
BEDALE	YORK (NR)	KIRBY W
GREAT COGGESHALL	ESSEX	KIRKHAM WILLIAM
MILDENHALL	SUFFOLK	KITCHENER THOMAS
BURNHAM THORPE	NORFOLK	KITTON GEORGE
SWANSEA	GLAMORGAN	KNEATH
BOBBING	KENT	KNIGHT
NEWTON VALENCE	HANTS	KNIGHT
SITTINGBOURNE	KENT	KNIGHT
OWLESBURY	HANTS	KNIGHT JAMES
BORDEN	KENT	KNIGHT THOMAS
WROTHAM	KENT	LABS-BAKER
NORTH WALSHAM	NORFOLK	LACEY
PINCHBECK	LINCS	LACY TIMOTHY
BOUGHTON HILL	KENT	LADD
BOUGHTON	KENT	LADD W
STODY	NORFOLK	LADELL WILLIAM
GREAT CLACTON	ESSEX	LAKE
IVER	BUCKS	LAKE
NORTH COVE	SUFFOLK	LAMMING
NORTH COVE	SUFFOLK	LAMMING JAMES
LANGTOFT	YORK (ER)	LAMPLOUGH THOMAS
HIGH WYCOMBE	BUCKS	LANE

PARISH	COUNTY	VICTIM
CHEPPING WYCOMBE	BUCKS	LANE JOHN & JOSEPH
QUARELY	HANTS	LANE JOSEPH
BEVERELY	YORK (ER)	LANGDALE
LECKONFIELD	YORK (ER)	LANGDALE JOHN
KINGSTON	SURREY	LANGLEY
CHEPPING WYCOMBE	BUCKS	LANSDALE
HIGH WYCOMBE	BUCKS	LANSDALE
GREAT CRESSINGHAM	NORFOLK	LARKMAN
CANTERBURY	KENT	LASLETT
BARROW UPON SOARE	LEICS	LATHBURY
CHICHESTER	SUSSEX	LAVIN Z
WITHERSFIELD	SUFFOLK	LAWRENCE EDWARD
MARCH	CAMBS	LAXTON WILLIAM
PEASENHALL	SUFFOLK	LAY JOHN
GOUDHURST	KENT	LE GEYT PHILIP
SIDDINGTON	CHESHIRE	LEA JOSEPH
STONHAM ASPALL	SUFFOLK	LEATHER E
ABBOT'S KERSWELL	DEVON	LEE
BARKSTONE	LINCS	LEE THOMAS
FOXLEY	NORFOLK	LEEDS THOMAS
BILSTON	STAFFS	LEIGH, WILLIAM
POTTERNE	WILTS	LENNARD
RINGSTEAD	NORFOLK	L'ESTRANGE
REDBRIDGE	HANTS	LETHBRIDGE LADY
ABINGDON	BERKS	LEYCOTT
ROMSEY EXTRA	HANTS	LINTORT WH
RODSLEY	DERBYSHIRE	LITCHFIELD JAMES
WORTHING	SUSSEX	LLOYD
THORNBURY	GLOUCS	LLOYD EDMUND
SOUTHAMPTON	HANTS	LLOYD HERBERT
OVERTON	HANTS	LONGMAN
LECKFORD	HANTS	LONGMAN-HUTTON
PENRITH	CUMBERLAND	LONSDALE
ALPHINGTON	DEVON	LORAN R
STONE	STAFFS	LOVATT GEORGE
SHOREHAM	KENT	LOVE
MARLOW	BUCKS	LOVEGROVE
BURGHCLERE	HANTS	LOVELOCK THOMAS

PARISH	COUNTY	VICTIM
CHADDERTON	LANCS	LOWE
BENENDEN	KENT	LUCK
YALDING	KENT	LUCK JOHN
BRISTON	NORFOLK	LUNNIS
CALDECOT	CAMBS	MACE
MODDERHALL	STAFFS	MALKIN ADAM
STONE	STAFFS	MALKIN, ADAM
SWINTON	YORK (NR)	MALLINSON GEORGE
BURY ST EDMUNDS	SUFFOLK	MALLOW
ELSTOW	BEDFORDSHIRE	MANNING
STUDDAL	KENT	MANSER
ASHLEY	KENT	MANSER STEPHEN
SWINESHEAD	LINCS	MANTON
SNEINTON	NOTTS	MANVERS
GUNTHORPE	NORFOLK	MARGESON
GUNTHORPE	NORFOLK	MARGESTON WILLIAM
WESTWICK	NORFOLK	MARIS
EATON	NOTTS	MARRIOTT
HARDINGTON	NORTHANTS	MARRIOTT JOHN
EAST WOODHAY	HANTS	MARSH JAMES
RIPPLE	KENT	MARSH RICHARD
HASTINGLEIGH	KENT	MARSHALL JOHN
SPILSBY	LINCS	MARSHALL THOMAS
COTESSEY	NORFOLK	MARTIN
WIGGENHALL	NORFOLK	MARTIN EDWARD
EAST PECKHAM	KENT	MARTIN THOMAS
DOWNHAM	CAMBS	MARTIN WILLIAM
RANSKILL	NOTTS	MARTIN, WILLIAM
NORBURY	DERBYSHIRE	MASKERY
BRIGHTLINGSEA	ESSEX	MASON
SHERNBOURNE	NORFOLK	MASTERS
SUNDRIDGE	KENT	MASTERS HM
ORPINGTON	KENT	MASTERS
WINGHAM	KENT	MATSON
WINGHAM	KENT	MATSON SARAH
STAINDROP	DURHAM	MAUDE JACOB
MOULTON	LINCS	MAUGHAM
ELY	CAMBS	MAWER
SOUTH RESTON	LINCS	MAWSER GEORGE
THORPE	NORFOLK	MAXWELL JAMES
HADLOW	KENT	MAY
STOKE ON TRENT	STAFFS	MAYER THOMAS

PARISH	COUNTY	VICTIM
BECCLES	SUFFOLK	MAYHEW
CALDEWGATE	CUMBERLAND	McCUTCHEON
CHIPPING NORTON	OXON	MEALINGS
CHIPPING NORTON	OXON	MEALINGS
BARROW	LEICS	MEASURES
TOFT	SUFFOLK	MEDLAR
STALLBRIDGE	DORSET	MEDLEYCOTT W
MELBOURNE	DERBYSHIRE	MELBOURNE
ARNOLD	NOTTS	MEW
TAVERHAM	NORFOLK	MICKELTHWAITE N
SPARHAM	NORFOLK	MIDDLETON
SPARHAM	NORFOLK	MIDDLETON JOHN
GOUDHURST	KENT	MILLER GILES
BEDMOND	HERTS	MILLS
STANTON ST BERNARD	WILTS	MILLS HENRY
BRASTED	KENT	MINET
KITHURST	SUSSEX	MITCHELL
PENISTONE	YORK (WR)	MITCHELL THOMAS
HACEBY	LINCS	MITCHINSON
ASEBY	LINCS	MITCHISON Mrs
HOOE	SUSSEX	MITTENS J
BANWELL	SOMERSET	MONCREIFF D
FORD	BUCKS	MONGER
HARTWELL	BUCKS	MONK
STONE	BUCKS	MONK
STONE	HEREFORDSHIRE	MONKHOUSE
GRANTHAM	LINCS	MONKS
STONE JOHN	BUCKS	MONKS CHARLES AND
ASHTON UPON TRENT	DERBYSHIRE	MOODY GEORGE
RUDSTON	YORK (ER)	MOODY W
CHORLEY	CHESHIRE	MOORCROFT
WROTHAM	KENT	MOORE G
SYSTON	LEICS	MOORE M
ANGMERING	SUSSEX	MOORE TA
BUCKLAND NEWTON	DORSET	MOREY CHRISTOPHER
GOSPORT	HANTS	MORGAN
ASHTON UPON TRENT	DERBYSHIRE	MORLEY GEORGE

PARISH	COUNTY	VICTIM
SEVENOAKS	KENT	MORPHEW
BETTESHANGER	KENT	MORRICE
SOUTHOVER	SUSSEX	MORRIS
WALSINGHAM (OLD)	NORFOLK	MORRISON
WHITCHURCH	SHROPSHIRE	MOSS
GREAT CLACTON	ESSEX	MOSS GEORGE
WHITCHURCH	CHESHIRE	MOSSES
WOOLHAMPTON	BERKS	MOUNT WILLIAM
ORPINGTON	KENT	MOYER THOMAS
CRANBOURNE	DORSET	MOYLE HENRY
HELLINGLY	SUSSEX	MUGGERIDGE
SWAFFHAM FEN	CAMBS	MUSSELL
BELPER	DERBYSHIRE	MUSSON JOHN
COLWICK	NOTTS	MUSTERS
DEPTFORD	LONDON	MYATT
BISHOPS STORTFORD	HERTS	NASH
BATLEY	YORK (WR)	NASSEY
HAYNFORD	NORFOLK	NEAL
REIGATE	SURREY	NEAL
MONCKTON	KENT	NEALE GEORGE
SELLING	KENT	NEAME JOHN
FAVERSHAM	KENT	NEANE J
MONKTON	WILTS	NEATE GEORGE
TILNEY ALL SAINTS	NORFOLK	NEEPE FRANCIS
ORDSALL	NOTTS	NELSON THOMAS
PENDOVER	SOMERSET	NEPEAN MOLINEAUX H
SANDWICH	KENT	NETHERSOLE
HORSMONDEN	KENT	NEWINGTON JOSEPH
KEMPSTON	BEDFORDSHIRE	NEWLAND ROBERT
ROMSEY	HANTS	NEWMAN
BROMSBERROW	GLOUCS	NEWMAN SAMUEL
WISBECH	CAMBS	NEWSHAM L
BENSON	OXON	NEWTON
ELMINGTON	NORTHANTS	NEWTON
SOWERBY	YORK (NR)	NICHOLLS
EDGEHILL KINETON	WARWICKSHIRE	NICHOLLS Mrs
HESLINGTON	YORK (ER)	NICHOLSON JOHN
OXENDEN	KENT	NINCH JAMES
DUMBLETON	GLOUCS	NIND
SOMERSHAM	HUNTS	NIX WILLIAM

PARISH	COUNTY	VICTIM
DURLEY	HANTS	PINK THOMAS
NORTON	SUFFOLK	PIZZY M
LOUDWATER	BUCKS	PLAISTOW RICHARD
FARNHAM	SUFFOLK	PLANT ROBERT
BRIDSTOW	HEREFORDSHIRE	PLATT
TOTTERIDGE	HERTS	POINTER
CHARLTON	WILTS	POLHILL
NORTHOWTRAM	YORK (WR)	POLLARD BENJAMIN
THRUXTON	HANTS	POLLEN JW
DREWSTEIGNTON	DEVON	PONSFORD G
KENN	SOMERSET	POOLE
COVE	DEVON	PORTER
COVENEY	CAMBS	PORTER
COLNEY	NORFOLK	POSTLE J
CRANBORNE	DORSET	POTHECARY
DUNTON	BEDFORDSHIRE	POTTON
EAST WOODHAY	HANTS	POVEY ANNA
SIDMOUTH	DEVON	POWELL
HAWKHURST	KENT	POWELL JOHN
ASHBY DE LA ZOUCH	LEICS	PRATT
EASTCHURCH	KENT	PRATT J
LOUGHBOROUGH	LEICS	PRATT WILLIAM
EASTLEACH		
MARTIN	GLOUCS	PREATER JAMES
WINFARTHING	NORFOLK	PRETTY
TINHEAD	WILTS	PRICE
LYMINGE	KENT	PRICE RALPH
QUENNINGTON	GLOUCS	PRICE ROBERT
TINHEAD	WILTS	PRICE W
IRMINGLAND	NORFOLK	PRIEST
TRUNCH	NORFOLK	PRIMROSE
CRETINGHAM	SUFFOLK	PULHAM
COLNBROOK	BUCKS	PULLEN
WOULDHAM	KENT	PYE
COLLINGBOURNE	WILTS	PYKE MRS
BATTLE	SUSSEX	QUAIFE
FALKINGHAM	LINCS	QUARNBOROUGH
ASH	KENT	QUESTED GEORGE
SHAFTESBURY	DORSET	RABBETS
MANSFIELD	NOTTS	RADFORD

PARISH	COUNTY	VICTIM
NORTH HYDE	MIDDLESEX	PARSHAM
DOWNTON	WILTS	PARSONS
KERSEY	SUFFOLK	PARTRIDGE MRS
SHEERING	ESSEX	PARVITT
BUXTON	NORFOLK	PASSON
UPPER BEDDINGTON	NORTHANTS	PAYNE, WILLIAM
BATTLE	SUSSEX	PEACOCK
NEEDHAM	SUFFOLK	PEACOCK JOHN
OXFORD	OXON	PEAKE
SCALBY	YORK (NR)	PEARSON
SELINGE LEES	KENT	PEARSON
LAYER-DE-LA-HAYE	ESSEX	PEARSON J
MANSFIELD	NOTTS	PEATFIELD JOHN
COLEFORD	GLOUCS	PEEL WILLIAM HENRY
BLEAN	KENT	PELLETT
TRUMPINGTON	CAMBS	PEMBERTON
ROMSEY	HANTS	PENLEAZE
HALSTED	KENT	PENNEL PETER
FARRINGDON	HANTS	PENTON WILLIAM
DOVER	KENT	PEPPER
HOUGHAM	KENT	PEPPER
WEYHILL	HANTS	PERRETT BRIDGET
SWINDON	STAFFS	PERRY JAMES
ALVERSTOKE	HANTS	PERVIS JOHN B
ASH	KENT	PETLEY WILLIAM
HESTON	MIDDLESEX	PETO
MOUNTNESSING	ESSEX	PETRE
MONKTON	KENT	PETT
POLSTEAD	SUFFOLK	PEYTON HENRY
EARL STONHAM	SUFFOLK	PHEAR
HIGH WYCOMBE	BUCKS	PHELPS JAMES
WESTHAY	SOMERSET	PHIPEN ROBERT
HARBORNE	WARWICKSHIRE	PHIPSON JW ESQ
BRIDLINGTON	YORK (ER)	PIERCY G
LITTLINGTON	CAMBS	PIGGETT
GALMINGTON	SOMERSET	PIGOT JOHN HUGH
SMYTH		
EASTRY	KENT	PILKINGTON HENRY
ALTON BARNES	WILTS	PILL
BARROWBY	LINCS	PINDER THOMAS

PARISH	COUNTY	VICTIM
BROADHOLME	NOTTS	NIXON JOHN
MEOPHAM	KENT	NORRIDGE
EMSWORTH	HANTS	NORRIS
HAVANT	HANTS	NORRIS
WRITTLE	ESSEX	NORRIS
LOUGHBOROUGH	LEICS	NORTH
SWIMBRIDGE	DEVON	NOTT
ARKESDEN	ESSEX	NOTTAGE
SEVENOAKS	KENT	NOUVALLE
COLCHESTER	ESSEX	NUNN
WHITCHURCH	SHROPSHIRE	NUNNERELY JOHN
CAMBRIDGE	CAMBS	NUTTER
COOLING	KENT	OAKLEY
KINGSTON	SUSSEX	OLIVER
EAST PRESTON	SUSSEX	OLIVER GEORGE
HOLLINGBOURNE	KENT	OLIVER JOSEPH
HADDON	HUNTS	OLIVER ROBERT
PEPPERSTOCK	HERTS	ORCHARD
NORTON WOODSEATS	DERBYSHIRE	OSBORNE
HURST	BERKS	OWEN
ASTON CLINTON	BUCKS	OWEN E
BROOME	KENT	OXENDEN HENRY
WHISTON	YORK (WR)	OXLEY JOHN
WINCHCOMBE	GLOUCS	PACEY (WIDOW)
PRESTWOLD	LEICS	PACKE CW
LITTLE BRICKHILL	BUCKS	PAGE ABRAHAM
FINEDON	NORTHANTS	PAGE WILLIAM
MICHELDEVER	HANTS	PAIN WILLIAM
BANBURY	OXON	PAINE
RAMSEY	ESSEX	PALMER O
OLNEY	BUCKS	PALMER WILLIAM F
HISTON	CAMBS	PAPWORTH P
MONKTON	KENT	PARAMOUR
HEADLEY	HANTS	PARKER ANN
COMBE HAY	SOMERSET	PARKHOUSE
SAWLEY	DERBYSHIRE	PARKINSON W
RUDDINGTON	NOTTS	PARKYN LADY
AYLSHAM	NORFOLK	PARMENTER R
BOSTON	LINCS	PARNHAM, JOHN
CROPWELL BUTLER	NOTTS	PARR GEORGE
TILSTOCK	SHROPSHIRE	PARRY

PARISH	COUNTY	VICTIM
QUENNINGTON	GLOUCS	RADWAY JOSHUA
CASBY	NORTHANTS	RAGSDELL RICHARD
ORPINGTON	KENT	RANFORD JAMES
LEE	KENT	RAVEN
NIDD	YORK (NR)	RAWSON B
UPPER LOVELL	WILTS	RAXWORTHY JOHN
STRADISHALL	SUFFOLK	RAY
HORTON KIRBY	KENT	RAY P
BASILDON	ESSEX	RAYNHAM JAMES
FRETTENHAM	NORFOLK	READ
LINGWOOD	NORFOLK	READ
HOUGHTON	HANTS	READ BENJAMIN
STURRY	KENT	READER
DRIFFIELD	YORK (ER)	REASTON JOHN
EAST WOODHAY	HANTS	REBBECK BENJAMIN
ARNOLD	NOTTS	REDGATE THOMAS
LOWER KINNERTON	FLINTSHIRE	REECE JOHN
REDENHALL	NORFOLK	REED ROBERT
BOUGHTON	KENT	RELF BROOKER V
WALPOLE	SUFFOLK	RENCE COL
DRIFFIELD	YORK (ER)	REYNARD H
WALPOLE ST PETER	NORFOLK	RHEYMES BARTLE
ARNOLD	NOTTS	RHODES, THOMAS
DINAS POWIS	GLAMORGAN	RICHARDS W
KINNERTON	CHESHIRE	RICHARDS WILLIAM
CATTON	NORFOLK	RICHES
BLACKGROVE	BUCKS	RICKFORD W
WADDESDON	BUCKS	RICKFORD WILLIAM
ADLINGTON	CHESHIRE	RIDGEWAY
COLATON RALEIGH	DEVON	RIDLER J
HERNE HILL	KENT	RIGDEN J
HERNE HILL	KENT	RIGDEN J
DUNNINGTON	YORK (ER)	RISDALE BENJAMIN
MARTHAM	NORFOLK	RISING BENJAMIN
CHARD	SOMERSET	RIST JOHN
GREENWICH	KENT	RITCHIE
MARTYR WORTHY	HANTS	RIVERS HENRY SIR
TITTLESHALL	NORFOLK	RIX THOMAS
BEVERSTONE	GLOUCS	ROBBINS WILLIAM
ABBEY CWM HIR	POWYS	ROBERTS

PARISH	COUNTY	VICTIM
BENNINGHOLME	YORK (ER)	ROBINSON
KELBY	LINCS	ROBINSON
SWINE	YORK (ER)	ROBINSON BENJAMIN
AYLESFORD	KENT	ROBSON
ROYDON	NORFOLK	RODWELL EDWARD
CHALLOCK	KENT	ROGERS W
BICTON	DEVON	ROLLE
EYETHORNE	KENT	ROMNEY
FRESHWATER	HANTS	ROOKLEY
MINSTER	KENT	ROOTHAM
HOLLINGBOURNE	KENT	ROPER
SHENFIELD	ESSEX	ROPER
EAST GRINSTEAD	SUSSEX	ROSE
WINGHAM	KENT	ROSE
NORTH BARSHAM	NORFOLK	ROSE JOHN
FAIRFORD	GLOUCS	ROSE RICHARD
STANSTED MOUNTFITCHET	ESSEX	ROSE THOMAS
BUCKLAND NEWTON	DORSET	ROUNT JOHN
SNELSTON	DERBYSHIRE	ROWE ANN
MARGATE	KENT	ROWE MILES
CHERHILL	WILTS	ROWLAND JOHN
HEXHAM	NOTHUMBERLAND	RUDDOCK J
HAWKCHURCH	DEVON	RUDGE
BROAD CHALK	WILTS	RUMBOLD JESSE
WHITCHURCH	SHROPSHIRE	RUSCOE JOHN
WOOD DALLING	NORFOLK	RUSH
HOUGHTON	HANTS	RUTT HENRY
RAYLEIGH	ESSEX	SACH JOHN
EAST FEN	CAMBS	SALISBURY
CALTHWAITE	CUMBERLAND	SALKELD JOHN
HOLLINGBOURNE	KENT	SALMON
MATTISHALL	NORFOLK	SALTERS WP
CALLINGTON	CORNWALL	SAMBOLLS JOHN
AYLESFORD	KENT	SAMUEL ARNOLD
HOLLINGBOURNE	KENT	SAMUEL THOMAS
HORNINGSEA	CAMBS	SAMWAY THOMAS
DEEPING FEN	LINCS	SANDERS W
ETTON	NORTHANTS	SANDERSON
BARHAM	KENT	SANDERSON P
BENENDEN	KENT	SANKEY
		SANTER

PARISH	COUNTY	VICTIM
GREENWICH	KENT	SAVILLE
FAIRFORD	GLOUCS	SAVORY JOHN
SYDERSTONE	NORFOLK	SAVORY JOHN
ALFRISTON	SUSSEX	SAXBY SCRASE
BECKHAM	NORFOLK	SAYERS SAMUEL
WOOTON ST LAWRENCE	HANTS	SCLATER WILLIAM L
GREAT HOLLAND	ESSEX	SCOTT
KNAPTON	NORFOLK	SCOTT
ROUGHAM	NORFOLK	SCOTT
WISBECH	CAMBS	SCRIMSHAW EDWARD
SEWELL	BEDFORDSHIRE	SCROGGS
MILDENHALL FEN	SUFFOLK	SEAHER
HAPPISBURGH	NORFOLK	SEILLY ANDREW
AMESBURY	WILTS	SELF
ATTLEBOROUGH	NORFOLK	SELLER THOMAS
MANSTON	DORSET	SENIOR WILLIAM
EAST DEAN	SUSSEX	SERACE R
VERNHAM DEAN	HANTS	SERGEANT MARY
STRELLEY	NOTTS	SEVERN
BASSINGHAM	LINCS	SEWARDS
EYE	SUFFOLK	SEWELL
TWINEHAM	SUSSEX	SHARP
NORTH WALSHAM	NORFOLK	SHARPE JOHN
SANDON	STAFFS	SHAW
RUDDINGTON	NOTTS	SHAW RICHARD
FLETCHING	SUSSEX	SHEFFIELD
STOCKTON	HANTS	SHEPARD
DILHAM	NORFOLK	SHEPEARD TAYLOR
HAPPISBURGH	NORFOLK	SHEPHERD
CROSTWICK	NORFOLK	SHEPHERD MARTIN
FORDINGBRIDGE	HANTS	SHEPHERD WILLIAM
BEDFONT	MIDDLESEX	SHERBOURNE
OXTON	NOTTS	SHERBROOKE WC
BEDFONT	MIDDLESEX	SHERWIN
YOXALL	STAFFS	SHIPTON THOMAS
WARSOP	NOTTS	SHORT SAMUEL
BOURNE FEN	LINCS	SHOTHOLT
BINSTED	HANTS	SHOTTER ROBERT
EWELME	OXON	SHRUBB
WALCOT	NORFOLK	SIELEY
BARROWBY	LINCS	SILLS WILLIAM

PARISH	COUNTY	VICTIM
STANTON ST BERNARD	WILTS	SIMKINS
GREENWICH	KENT	SIMPSON
CATERHAM	SURREY	SIMPSON PINDER
YIELDERSLEY	DERBYSHIRE	SINGLETON WILLIAM
GREAT HOLLAND	ESSEX	SKEEL
ASHINGTON	SUSSEX	SKINNER JOSEPH
PETWORTH	SUSSEX	SKINNER JOSEPH
NINFIELD	SUSSEX	SKINNER SAMUEL
ACLE	NORFOLK	SKOYLES SAMUEL
WISBECH ST MARY	CAMBS	SKRIMSHIRE EDWARD
PETWORTH	SUSSEX	SLATER
WESTON-UPON-TRENT	DERBYSHIRE	SLATER R
BUSHTON	WILTS	SMART JOHN
BARTON STACEY	HANTS	SMITH
BODIAM	SUSSEX	SMITH
BROOKWEIR	MONMOUTH	SMITH
ELLASTON	STAFFS	SMITH
GREAT CLACTON	ESSEX	SMITH
LOUGHBOROUGH	LEICS	SMITH
LYNN	NORFOLK	SMITH
MONKTON	KENT	SMITH
NOTTINGHAM	NOTTS	SMITH
SNEINTON	NOTTS	SMITH
WEST LYNN	NORFOLK	SMITH
NORTON	NOTTS	SMITH
POLSTEAD	SUFFOLK	SMITH BEN
DOCKENFIELD	HANTS	SMITH BENJAMIN
MEOPHAM	KENT	SMITH EDWARD
HAWKHURST	KENT	SMITH GEORGE
RICKENHALL	NORFOLK	SMITH JAMES
WINFARTHING	SUFFOLK	SMITH JAMES
EPPERSTONE	NOTTS	SMITH JAMES
NASH	BUCKS	SMITH JOSEPH
WRAMPLINGHAM	NORFOLK	SMITH LORRAME
OVER	CAMBS	SMITH MARY MRS
COLN ST ALDWYN	GLOUCS	SMITH NATHANIEL
BROCKWEIR	GLOUCS	SMITH PERCY
DENVER	NORFOLK	SMITH RICHARD
ASH	KENT	SMITH SC
POLSTEAD	SUFFOLK	SMITHER
		SMYTH
TORRINGTON ST JOHN	NORFOLK	SNITTERBY
WINFRITH	DORSET	SNOOK WILLIAM
GREAT WALTHAM	ESSEX	SNOW
GREAT WALTHAM	ESSEX	SNOW PETER
RUCKINGHALL SUPERIOR	SUFFOLK	SNOW PETER
MARR	YORK (WR)	SNOWDEN
WEST MERSEA	ESSEX	SOUTH DANIEL
ASH	KENT	SOUTHEE RICHARD
SANDWICH	KENT	SPAIN
NORTH WALSHAM	NORFOLK	SPEARING
EXBURY	HANTS	SPEDDING JOHN
LAMBOURNE	BERKS	SPICER
LYDD	KENT	SPRINGETT
BRADWELL-JUXTA-MARE	ESSEX	SPURGEON
BARNINGHAM	NORFOLK	SPURRELL
COLTISHALL	NORFOLK	ST JOHN
MOTTISFONT	HANTS	ST JOHN D
KIRKBY OVERBLOW	YORK (WR)	STABLES
STOCKBURY	KENT	STACEY COURTNEY
COSTESSEY	NORFOLK	STAFFORD
ROTHWELL	NORTHANTS	STAFFORD
HENHAM	ESSEX	STALLIBRASS
WESTLETON	SUFFOLK	STAMFORD ADOLPHUS
OWLESBURY	HANTS	STANBROOK MOSES
WESTLETON	SUFFOLK	STANFORD ADOLPHUS
BEIGHTON	DERBYSHIRE	STANIFORTH
BEIGHTON	YORK (WR)	STANIFORTH
YALDING	KENT	STARNS
HOLCOMBE	SOMERSET	STEEL JAS
OXBOROUGH	NORFOLK	STEPHENS
WHITE LACKINGTON	SOMERSET	STEPHENS
WHITE LACKINGTON	SOMERSET	STEPHENS T & W
CHIPPING CAMPDEN	GLOUCS	STEPHENS WILLIAM
BAUMBER	LINCS	STEPHENSON JOSEPH
EMSWORTH	HANTS	STEVENS
HAVANT	HANTS	STEVENS
LITTLEPORT	CAMBS	STEVENS HENRY
EAST WOODHAY	HANTS	STEVENS WILLIAM
BOUGHTON	NORFOLK	STEWARD WILLIAM
BIRCHANGER	ESSEX	STOKES JCH
BEARSTED	KENT	STOKES MICHAEL
YALDING	KENT	STONE
HENLEY-ON-THAMES	OXON	STONOR
WESTON-UPON-TRENT	DERBYSHIRE	STORER RICHARD
LIMPSFIELD	SURREY	STORR BENJAMIN
BASSINGHAM	LINCS	STORR EDWARD
BASFORD	NOTTS	STOVER THOMAS
BUDBROOK	WARWICKSHIRE	STOWE
SWINDON	WILTS	STRANGE
FORDINGBRIDGE	HANTS	STREET MICHAEL L
CHATHAM	KENT	STRONG
PAINSWICK	GLOUCS	STRONG R
HAREWOOD	YORK (WR)	STURDY
ALCONBURY	HUNTS	STURTON
GUNTON	NORFOLK	SUFFIELD LORD
RAINHAM	KENT	SUGDEN THOMAS
WICKHAMBROOK	SUFFOLK	SUTTLE
ROUGHTON	NORFOLK	SUTTON STEPHEN
	YORK (ER)	SWADILL
SPOFFORTH	YORK (WR)	SWALES
WINGHAM	KENT	SWEETLOVE JOHN
WINFARTHING	NORFOLK	SYMONDS JOHN
BURTON	STAFFS	TABBERERS
AYTHORPE RODING	ESSEX	TABRUM ROBERT
HOTHFIELD	KENT	TAPPENDEN
UPPER CLATFORD	HANTS	TASKER R & W
EAST MALLING	KENT	TASSALL ROBERT
EAST MALLING	KENT	TASSELL ROBERT
CHEAM	SURREY	TAUNTON WILLIAM
PYLE		TAYLOR
HAMPTON	MIDDLESEX	TAYLOR
RUSHTON	NORTHANTS	TAYLOR
BULKINGTON	WARWICKSHIRE	TAYLOR JONATHON
BISHOPS STORTFORD	HERTS	TAYLOR JOSEPH

PARISH	COUNTY	VICTIM
LITTLE BOWDEN	NORTHANTS	TAYLOR SAMUEL
LITTLE BOWDEN	NORTHANTS	TAYLOR SAMUEL ELD
RAINHAM	KENT	TAYLOR THOMAS
RAINHAM	KENT	TAYLOR WILLIAM
CARLETON	NOTTS	TAYLOR WILLIAM
SHEFFIELD	YORK (WR)	TAYLOR WILLIAM
HACONBY	LINCS	TEESDALE ISSAC
WEST HADDON	NORTHANTS	TERRY
HOLBEACH MARSH	LINCS	THIMBLEBY, P
LOUTH	LINCS	THISTLEWOOD
		THOMAS
WYHAM	LINCS	THISTLEWOOD
		THOMAS
HOLLINGBOURNE	KENT	THOMAS
ST LYTHANS	GLAMORGAN	THOMAS
STANNINGFIELD GREEN	SUFFOLK	THOMAS
HOLLINGBOURNE	KENT	THOMAS RICHARD
FORDINGBRIDGE	HANTS	THOMPSON
OXTED	SURREY	THOMPSON
SEVENOAKS	KENT	THOMPSON
SUNDRIDGE	KENT	THOMPSON
WESTERHAM	KENT	THOMPSON SAMUEL
FORDINGBRIDGE	HANTS	THOMPSON SAMUEL
STICKFORD	LINCS	THOMPSON W JNR
RAWDEN	YORK (WR)	THORNTON &
GLOSSOP	DERBYSHIRE	
RIDGEWAY		
GLENTHAM	LINCS	THORPE WILLIAM
GLENTHAM	LINCS	THORPE WILLIAM
GLENTHAM	LINCS	THORPE WILLIAM
KNOWSTONE	DEVON	THROGMORTON C
BURWELL	NORFOLK	THURSTON
BEANDON PARVA	NORFOLK	TICE THOMAS
ACTON	SUFFOLK	TIFFIN
HARMONDSWORTH	MIDDLESEX	TILLER
BRILL	BUCKS	TIMS
LITTLE ELLINGHAM	NORFOLK	TINGAY
LITTLE ELLINGHAM	NORFOLK	TINGAY
OULTON	SUFFOLK	TIPPLE
OULTON	NORFOLK	TIPPLE JAMES
KINGSTON	SURREY	TIRRY

PARISH	COUNTY	VICTIM
HARTWELL	BUCKS	TODD BENJAMIN
STOUR PROVOST	DORSET	TOMKINS JOHN
BRIGSTOCK	NORTHANTS	TOMLIN JOHN
HILDERSTONE	STAFFS	TOMLINSON, JOSEPH
ELMLEY LOVETT	WORCS	TOMLINSON, MRS
UXBRIDGE	MIDDLESEX	TOMPSON
SEVENOAKS	KENT	TONG
WROTHAM	KENT	TORRINGTON
AWBRIDGE	HANTS	TRAGETT TH
CHESTERTON	HUNTS	TRAYLIN
WROXHAM	NORFOLK	TREADWAY
DREWSTEIGNTON	DEVON	TREVERTON
DREWSTEIGNTON	DEVON	TREVERTON
WORTHING	SUSSEX	TRIBE WILLIAM
HESTON	MIDDLESEX	TRIMMER H
DAGENHAM	ESSEX	TUCK
FRESHWATER	HANTS	TUCKER
KEYNSHAM	SOMERSET	TUCKER
LOWER HARDRES	KENT	TUCKER HENRY
EASTLEACH		
TURVILLE	GLOUCS	TUCKWELL JOHN
APPLEBY MAGNA	LEICS	TUNADINE T
MILTON	NORTHANTS	TURLAND WILLIAM
BANSTEAD	SURREY	TURNER
WEST DEREHAM	NORFOLK	TURNER E
COLCHESTER	ESSEX	TURNER JOHN
WILTON	NORFOLK	TURNER JOSEPH
DISS	NORFOLK	TURNER ROBERT
WOODBRIDGE	SUFFOLK	TURNER ROBERT
HOUGHTON REGIS	BEDFORDSHIRE	TWEEN
WARE	HERTS	TWEEN CHARLES
EDGE	CHESHIRE	TWEMLOE
ITCHEN ABBAS	HANTS	TWITCHIN ANDREW
MICHELDEVER	HANTS	TWITCHIN RICHARD
YALDING	KENT	TWYSDEN LADY
STEVENTON	BERKS	TYRELL & STEVENS
BASSINGBOURN	CAMBS	UNITT JAMES
RAITHBY	LINCS	UPTON
STANNINGHALL	NORFOLK	UTTING THOMAS
BUCKLAND		
NEWTON	DORSET	VENABLES J
THWING	YORK (ER)	VICKERMAN

PARISH	COUNTY	VICTIM
HAPPISBURGH	NORFOLK	VINCE
BRADLE	DORSET	VOSS W
ORPINGTON	KENT	VOULES JAMES
ROUGHAM	NORFOLK	WAITE
TONBRIDGE	KENT	WAITE, JOHN
HANLEY WILLIAM BEAUCHAMP	WORCS	WAKEFIELD
ROOTHING	ESSEX	WALDEN
UPPER LAMBOURNE	BERKS	WALDRON
LONG STRATTON	NORFOLK	WALFORD
OCKBROOK	DERBYSHIRE	WALKER
SALINGHAM	NORFOLK	WALKER
BEESTON	NOTTS	WALKER Jos
BRADMORE	NOTTS	WALKER RICHARD
SAXLINGHAM	NORFOLK	WALKER W
BROUGHTON	HANTS	WALL CHARLES BARING
CHILTERN	WILTS	WALLIS
PRESTON	DORSET	WALLIS
EASTBOURNE	SUSSEX	WALTERS
SHINGAY	CAMBS	WALTERS JOHN
DOVER	KENT	WALTERS THOMAS
GREAT DUNMOW	ESSEX	WARD JOHN
WESTERHAM	KENT	WARD JOHN
YALDING	KENT	WARD JOHN
PENRITH	CUMBERLAND	WARD MICHAEL
BRANSFORD	WORCS	WARNER
OXLEY	STAFFS	WARNER
AYLSHAM	NORFOLK	WARNES JOHN JNR
LEIGH UPON MENDIP	SOMERSET	WARR GEORGE
CAISTER	NORFOLK	WARREN
KIRKBY		
UNDERWOOD	LINCS	WARREN
ATTLEBOROUGH	NORFOLK	WARRENS
ELMDON	ESSEX	WATERS
NEWPORT	MONMOUTH	WATERS THOMAS
RIPPINGALE	LINCS	WATERS W
DUFFRYN	GLAMORGAN	WATKINS MRS
WELLINGHAM	NORFOLK	WATSON GEORGE
NOTTINGHAM	NOTTS	WATTON WILLIAM
ICKLESHAM	SUSSEX	WATTS
SNEINTON	NOTTS	WATTS

PARISH	COUNTY	VICTIM
CORHAMPTON	HANTS	WATT'S JOHN
BATTLE	SUSSEX	WATT'S ROBERT
SLOUGH	BUCKS	WAY
MARLOW BOTTOM	BUCKS	WEBB RICHARD
BRAMPTON	DERBYSHIRE	WEBSTER
POLEBROOK	LINCS	WEBSTER GEORGE
FINCHINGFIELD	ESSEX	WEDD
HIGHCLERE	HANTS	WEDGE WILLIAM
GREAT CLACTON	ESSEX	WELHAM JOHN
STRATHFIELDSAYE	HANTS	WELLINGTON
WARBLINGTON	HANTS	WELLS DANIEL
TREDLINGTON	WARWICKSHIRE	WELLS EDWARD
SIXPENNY		
HANDLEY	DORSET	WELSH STEPHEN
NEWTON	HANTS	WENTMORE J
FOXLEY	NORFOLK	WEST THOMAS
SEMPRINGHAM	LINCS	WESTMORELAND
BARTON UPON		
HUMBER	LINCS	WESTOBY
BRIXWORTH	NORTHANTS	WESTON JOSEPH
EAST HARLING	NORFOLK	WESTON ROBERT
GREAT MORDEN	SURREY	WESTROPE JOSEPH
GOSPORT	HANTS	WESTWOOD
MARLOW	BUCKS	WETHERED
SWAYFIELD	LINCS	WHATTOFF MATTHEW
GREENWICH	KENT	WHEATELY
CHARD	SOMERSET	WHEATLEY JOSEPH
FROME	SOMERSET	WHEELER
OWERMOIGNE	DORSET	WHETHAM
HOUGHTON	SUSSEX	WHICHER
HUDDERSFIELD	YORK (WR)	WHITACRE &
		WOODHOUSE
ALBURY	SURREY	WHITBURN
KNOOK	WILTS	WHITE
WOODNESBOROUGH	KENT	WHITE JAMES
NEWENT	GLOUCS	WHITE WILLIAM
LANGHALL	SUFFOLK	WHITEBRED
LOUND	NOTTS	WHITEHEAD
NORTHFLEET	KENT	WHITEHEAD
WHITCHURCH	SHROPSHIRE	WHITFIELD GEORGE
WHITCHURCH	CHESHIRE	WHITFIELD GEORGE
NOTTINGHAM	NOTTS	WHITTLE JOSEPH

PARISH	COUNTY	VICTIM
EAST WINCH	NORFOLK	WICKE
NORWICH	NORFOLK	WICKES
PELDON	ESSEX	WIFFEN
EAST MALLING	KENT	WIGEN JA
MOULTON	NORFOLK	WIGGETT
MOULTON	LINCS	WIGGETT
UPPER		
WINCHENDEN	BUCKS	WIGGINS WILLIAM
GOUDHURST	KENT	WIGHT
UPWELL	CAMBS	WILES THOMAS
MILTON ABBAS	DORSET	WILKINS
REDGRAVE	SUFFOLK	WILKINSON
NORWICH	NORFOLK	WILLETT
BAYDON	WILTS	WILLIAMS
BLANDFORD	DORSET	WILLIAMS
CRESSAGE	SHROPSHIRE	WILLIAMS ELIZABETH
HARLESTON	SUFFOLK	WILLIAMS MRS
LLYNGWR	MONMOUTH	WILLIAMS REES
TREDYNOG	MONMOUTH	WILLIAMS W
ARNOLD	NOTTS	WILLIAMSON
BRISTON	NORFOLK	WILLIAMSON
LEICESTER	LEICS	WILLIAMSON
QUENBOROUGH	LEICS	WILLIAMSON
QUENBOROUGH	LEICS	WILLIAMSON
SUTTON IN		
ASHFIELD	NOTTS	WILLIAMSON JAMES
CHEAM	SURREY	WILLIS
SHOREHAM	KENT	WILLIS JAMES
FINCHINGFIELD	ESSEX	WILLOWS
SWANTON MORLEY	NORFOLK	WILSON
BARTON STACEY	HANTS	WILSON HENRY
WRIGHT		
STICKFORD	LINCS	WILSON JOHN
RADFORD	NOTTS	WILSON WILLIAM
MICHELDEVER	HANTS	WINCHCOMBE SARAH
LENHAM	KENT	WINCHELSEA EARL
OF		
WHEPSTEAD	SUFFOLK	WINFIELD
STEEPLE ASHTON	WILTS	WING WILLIAM
HOLYPORT	BERKS	WINKWORTH
FOSTON	LINCS	WINTER WILLIAM
MAIDENHEAD	BERKS	WINWORTH

PARISH	COUNTY	VICTIM
LUXBOROUGH	HANTS	WITHERS
OLLERTON	NOTTS	WOMBWELL, JOHN
ASHBOURNE	DERBYSHIRE	WOOD
NORTH COVE	SUFFOLK	WOOD
SPROUGHTON	SUFFOLK	WOODARD
MITCHELMERSH	HANTS	WOODCOCK
EASTON	WILTS	WOODCROFT
GAYTON THORPE	NORFOLK	WOODS
MIDDLETON	NORFOLK	WOODS
WINFARTHING	NORFOLK	WOODS
MARESFIELD	SUSSEX	WOODWARD GEORGE
LISS	HANTS	WOOGER
FORDWICH	KENT	WOOTON
STAPLEFORD		
TAWNEY	ESSEX	WORTERS
INGHAM	SUFFOLK	WORTLEDGE
LEAKE	LINCS	WOULD SAMUEL
BLEAN	KENT	WRAIGHT WILLIAM
HAINFORD	NORFOLK	WRIGHT
MARLOW	BUCKS	WRIGHT
RINGSTEAD	NORFOLK	WRIGHT
WINDSOR	BERKS	WRIGHT
RINGSTEAD	NORFOLK	WRIGHT BENJAMIN
BARNINGHAM	NORFOLK	WRIGHT DAVID
EAST TUDDENHAM	NORFOLK	WRIGHT THOMAS
FREISTON	LINCS	WRIGHT-COUPLAND
ALCONBURY	HUNTS	WRIGHTS
WORSTEAD	NORFOLK	WURR
COLCHESTER	ESSEX	WYNEALL WILLIAM
CARROW	NORFOLK	YARDLEY
POTTON	BEDFORDSHIRE	YARRELL
COLTON	STAFFS	YATES
CHIDDINGSTONE	KENT	YOUNG
ROMSEY	HANTS	YOUNG JAMES
PULHAM	DORSET	YOUNG JOHN
LEEK	STAFFS	YOUNG SAMUEL
HONING	NORFOLK	YOUNGMAN

CONSOLIDATED BIBLIOGRAPHY

Armstrong, A. *Farmworkers in England and Wales: A Social and Economic History, 1770 to 1980*. Batsford, London 1988.

Ashford, L.J. *History of High Wycombe from its Origins to 1880*. Routledge & Kegan Paul, London 1960.

Bailey, B. *The Luddite Rebellion*. Strand, London 1998.

Bailey, B. *Burke and Hare: the year of the ghouls*. Mainstream Publishing, Edinburgh 2002.

Barringer, C. (ed.) *Norwich in the Nineteenth Century*. Norwich 1984.

Bate, J. *John Clare*. Picador, London 2003.

Bateson, C. *The Convict Ships, 1787 to 1868*. Glasgow 1959.

Baugh, G.C. (ed.) *Victoria County History of Shropshire*. VCH, London.

Beattie, J.M. *Crime and the Courts in England, 1660 to 1800*. OUP, Oxford 1986.

Bold, A. & Gittings, R. *The Book of Rotters*. Mainstream Publishing, Edinburgh 1985.

Boyer, G.R. *An Economic History of the English Poor Law, 1750 to 1850*. CUP, Cambridge 1990.

Brayley, E.W. *A History of Surrey*. Robert Best Ede, 1844.

Brettie, I. *History of Queen Elizabeth's Grammar School*. Mansfield, 1961.

Brewer, J. *An Account of the Cholera Morbus in the City of Exeter*. E Woolmer & Co., Exeter 1833.

Briggs, A. *England in the Age of Improvement 1783-1867*. Folio Society, 1997.

Bright, J.S. *A History of Dorking*. R J Clark, 1884.

Brown, C.L. *Wellington*. SPCK, 1889.

Brundage, A. *The Making of the New Poor Law, 1832 to 1839*. Hutchinson, London 1978.

Burchardt, J. *The Allotment Movement in England, 1793 to 1873*. Royal Historical Society, Woodbridge 2002.

Buxton, A.S. *Mansfield 100 Years Ago*. Willman, Mansfield 1932.

Bynum, W.F. *Science and Practice of Medicine in the nineteenth century*. CUP, Cambridge 1994.

Chadwick, E.R. *Report on the Sanitary Conditions of the Labouring Population in Great Britain*. London 1842.

Chambers, J. *Berkshire Machine Breakers*. Jill Chambers, Herts.

Chambers, J. *Buckinghamshire Machine Breakers: The Story of the 1830 Riots*. Jill Chambers, Herts 1991.

Chambers, J. *Gloucestershire Machine Breakers*. Jill Chambers, Herts.

Chambers, J. *Wiltshire Machine Breakers Vol I The Riots and Trials, Vol II The Rioters*. Jill Chambers, Herts.

Chambers, J.D. & Mingay, G.E. *The Agricultural Revolution, 1750 to 1850*. Batsford, London 1966.

Charlesworth, A. *Social Protest in a Rural Society: the spatial diffusion of the Captain Swing disturbances, 1830 to 1831*. Liverpool University Press, Liverpool 1979.

Charlesworth, A. (ed.) *An Atlas of Rural Protest in Britain, 1548-1900*. Croom Helm, London 1983

Checkland, S.G. & E. *The Poor Law Report 1834*. Penguin, London 1974.

Clabburn, P. *Shawls*. Shire Publications, 1981.

Clarke, M. *His Natural Life*. Penguin, London 1970.

Cooper, J. *The Well-ordered Town: A Story of Saffron Walden, Essex*. Cooper Publications, Saffron Walden 2000.

Davidson, G., Hirst, J. & McIntyre, S. (eds) *The Oxford Companion to Australian History*. OUP, Melbourne 1998.

Dent, H.C. *The Life and Characters of Charles Dickens*. Odhams, London 1930.

Dixson, M. *The Real Matilda: women and identity in Australia 1788 to 1975*. University of New South Wales, Melbourne 1976.

Dunbabin, J.P.D. (ed.) *Rural Discontent in Nineteenth Century Britain*. Holmes & Meier, New York 1974.

Dunkley, P. *The Crisis of the Old Poor Law in England 1795 to 1834*. Garland, New York 1982.

Durey, M. *The Return of the Plague: British society and the cholera 1831-2*. Gill & MacMillan, Dublin 1979.

Dyck, I. *William Cobbett and Rural Popular Culture*. CUP, Cambridge 1992.

Eastwood, D. *Governing Rural England*. Clarendon, Oxford 1994.

Edwards, W.M.A. *Notes on British History 1783-1901*. Rivingtons, London 1948.

Eliot, G. *Silas Marner*. London 1861.

Emsley, C. & Walvin, J. (eds.) *Artisans, Peasants and Proletarians, 1760 to 1860*. Croom Helm, London 1985.

Ernle, Lord. *English Farming Past and Present*. Heineman, London 1961.

Evans, E.J. *The Forging of the Modern State in Early Industrial Britain*. Longman, London 1983.

Evans, E. *The Contentious Tithe: the tithe problem and English agriculture, 1750 to 1850*. Routledge & Kegan Paul, London 1976.

Evans, Rev. J. *Narrative of the Fires in Whitchurch in 1830 and 1831*. Newling, 1832.

Farey, J. *General View of the Agriculture of Derbyshire Vol 3*. London 1817.

Fraser, D. *The Evolution of the British Welfare State*. Macmillan, London 1974.

Fussell, G.E. *The Farmer's Tools: British farm implements, tools and machinery, AD 1500 to 1900*. Bloomsbury, London 1952.

Gatrell, V.A.C. *The Hanging Tree: execution and the English people, 1770 to 1868*. OUP, Oxford 1994.

Görlach, M. *English in Nineteenth Century England*. CUP, Cambridge 1999.

Green, D. *Great Cobbett: the noblest agitator*. Hodder & Stoughton, London 1983.

Gyford, J. *Men of Bad Character; the Witham fires of the 1820s*. Essex CC, Chelmsford 1991.

Hamlin, C. *Public Health and Social Justice in the Age of Chadwick*. CUP, Cambridge 1998.

Hammond, J.L. & B. *The Village Labourer, 1760 to 1832: a study of the government of England before the Reform Bill*. Longman, London 1920.

Henriques, R.Q. *Before the Welfare State: social administration in early industrial Britain*. Longman, London 1979.

Hobsbawm, E.J. & Rudé, G. *Captain Swing*. Lawrence & Wishart, London 1969.

Holderness, B.A. & Turner, M. (eds) *Land, Labour, and Agriculture, 1700 to 1920: essays for Gordon Mingay*. Hambledon, London 1991.

Holland, M. & Cooper, J. (eds) *Essex Harvest: a collection of essays in memory of Arthur Brown*. Essex CC, Chelmsford 2003.

Horn, P. *The Rural World 1780 to 1850*. Hutchinson, London 1980.

Hughes, R. *The Fatal Shore*. Pan, London 1986.

Johnson, A.H. *The Disappearance of the Small Landowner [1909]*. Merlin Press, London 1963.

Jones, E.L. *Seasons and Prices: the role of weather in English agriculture*. Allen & Unwin, London 1964.

Jones, D.J.V. *Crime, Protest, Community, and Police in Nineteenth Century Britain*. Routledge & Kegan Paul, London 1982.

Kay, J.P. *The Moral and Physical Condition of the Working Classes*. Manchester 1832.

King, P. *Crime, Justice and Discretion in England 1740 to 1820*. OUP, Oxford 2003.

Langbein, J.H. *The Origins of Adversary Criminal Trial*. OUP, Oxford 2003.

Lees, L.H. *The Solidarities of Strangers: the English poor laws and the people, 1700 to 1848*. CUP, Cambridge 1998.

Lindley, L. *History of Sutton in Ashfield*. Sutton 1907.

Longmate, N. *King Cholera: the biography of a disease*. Hamish Hamilton, London 1966.

Mackley, A. *The Poaching Priors of Blytheburgh*. Blytheburgh Society, 2002.

MacRaild, D.M. *Irish Migrants in Modern Britain 1750-1922*. Palgrave Macmillan, New York 1999.

Malcolm, W.J. & J.A. *A General View of the Agriculture of Surrey*. London 1794.

Malden, H.E. (ed.) *A History of the County of Surrey Vol 1*. Dawson, 1967.

Mingay, G. *Land and Society in England 1750-1980*. Longman, 1994.

Mingay, G.E. *The Agrarian History of England and Wales, Volume VI, 1750 to 1850*. CUP, Cambridge 1989.

Mingay, G.E. *The Unquiet Countryside*. Routledge, London 1989.

Moran, M. & Barton, J. *Dearnford Hall*. Logaston Press, 2003.

Morris, R.J. *Cholera 1832*. Holmes & Meier, New York 1976.

Moule, *English Counties in the 19c*. London 1836.

Mowat, R.B. *England in the Eighteenth Century*. Harrap, 1932.

Nicholls, G. *A History of the English Poor Law, vol 1 [1854]*. Augustus Kelley, New York 1967.

Partridge, E. *The Penguin Dictionary of Historical Slang*. Penguin, London 1982.

Peacock, A.J. *Bread or Blood: A study of the agrarian riots in East Anglia, 1816*. Gollancz, London 1965.

Pearce, E. *Reform! The fight for the 1832 Reform Act*. Jonathan Cape, London 2003.

Powell, S. *Rural Crime Dictionary*.

Prentis, M.D. *The Scots in Australia: a study of New South Wales, Victoria, and Queensland*. Sydney 1983.

Priestley, U. *The Fabric of Stuffs*. University of East Anglia, Norwich 1990.

Ranger, T. & Slack, P. (eds) E*pidemics and Ideas: essays on the historical perception of pestilence*. CUP, Cambridge 1992.

Rattue, J. *High Wycombe Past*. Phillimore, 2002.

Reay, B. *The Last Rising of the Agricultural Labourers: Rural Life and Protest in Nineteenth Century England*. OUP, Oxford 1990.

Rees, S. *The Floating Brothel*. Thorndyke Press, London 2001.

Richardson, J. *The Local Historian's Encylopedia*. History Publications, New Barnet 1985.

Richardson, R. *Death, Dissection, and the Destitute*. Phoenix Press, London 2001.

Royle, E. *Revolutionary Britannia? Reflections on the threat of revolution in Britain 1789 to 1848*. Manchester UP, Manchester 2000.

Rudé, G. *The Crowd in History: a study of popular disturbances in France and England, 1730 to 1848*. Serif, London 1995.

Saville, J. *1848: the British state and the Chartist Movement*. CUP, Cambridge 1990.

Schweizer, K.W. & Osborne, J.W. *Cobbett in his Times*. St Martins, Leicester 1990.

Shapter, T. *The Cholera in Exeter in 1832*. S R Publishers, 1971.

Smart, W. *Economic Annals of the Nineteenth Century, 1821 to 1830, vol II [1910]*. Augustus Kelley, New York 1964.

Smith, A.D. *The Derbyshire Economy in 1851*. Derbyshire CC, Matlock 1997.

Stevenson, W.W. *A General View of the Agriculture of Surrey*. York 1813.

Summers, A. *Damned Whores and God's Police: the colonisation of women in Australia*. Penguin, London 1975.

Sylvester, D. *The Rural Landscape of the the Welsh Borderland*. Macmillan, London 1969.

Theobald, W. *A Practical Treatise on the Poor Laws as altered by the Poor Law Amendment Act and other recent statutes*. London 1836.

Thompson, E.P. *Customs in Common*. Penguin, London 1993.

Thompson, E.P. *The Making of the English Working Class*. Penguin, London 1988.

Trinder, B. *The Industrial Revolution in Shropshire*. Philimore, Chichester 1973.

Turner, M. *English Parliamentary Enclosure: its historical geography and economic history*. Dawson, Folkestone 1980.

Vanags, J. *The Mansfield and Pinxton Railway*. Old Mansfield Society, 2000.

Vincent, V.H. *The Police Code and General Manual of Criminal Law*. Francis Edwards, London 1901.

Vincent, D. *Literacy and Popular Culture: England 1750 to 1914*. CUP, Cambridge 1993.

Ward, J.T. (ed.) *Popular Movements c. 1830 to 1850*. Macmillan, London 1970.

Watts, W.W. *Shropshire: the geography of the county*. Shrewsbury 1939.

Wells, R.A.E. *Insurrection: the British experience, 1795 to 1803*. Alan Sutton, Gloucester 1983.

Wells, R.A.E. *Wretched Faces: famine in wartime England, 1763 to 1803*. Alan Sutton, Gloucester 1988.

Wiener, J.H. *Great Britain, the Lion at Home: a documentary history of domestic policy, vol 1*. Chelsea House, New York 1983.

Wohl, A.S. *Endangered Lives- Public Health in Victorian Britain*. Harvard UP, Harvard 1983.

Woodward, I. *The History of Wem and its Neighbourhood*. Shrewsbury 1952.

Ziegler, P. *Melbourne: a biography of William Lamb, second Viscount Melbourne*. Collins, London 1987.

Theses

Gill, G.V. *Cholera and Public Health Reform in mid-Victorian England with special reference to the Parish of Wallasey*. Unpublished MA Dissertation, University of Liverpool 1999.

Surname Index

The index is alphabetised in word-by-word order, e.g. *Bray, William* is filed before *Braybrook.*
Page numbers are given in full form, e.g. 124-125.
Page numbers shown as 132...139 indicate sporadic, often unrelated, references throughout the range.
References to illustrations, maps and figures are given in *italics*, those for tables are given in **bold**.
Page numbers followed by bib refer to bibliographical references, either in essay *Notes* or the *Consolidated Bibliography*.

Adams (butcher), 157
Adams, G, 49
Allan, Mary, 243
Allnutt, Zachary, 131,138,139,147
Andrews, John, 238
Arbuthnot, Mr, 53
Archer (clerk to the Justices), 110
Arden, Lord, Lord Lieutenant of Surrey, 29,50,51,55
Ashby, Robert, 101
Ashford, Thomas, 11,**98**,99
Atkins, Charles, 103; Stephen, 142,**144**

Baker, Henry, **95**; Robert, 186,201-202,*204*; Samuel, **95**,96
Balls, William, 72,73
Bannister (mayor), 157; Francis, **98**,101; George, 247
Barker, George, 92; Robert, 235,238
Barlett, W, 49
Barrington, Justice J, 108,109
Barton, David, **144**; Edmund, **144**; James, 142,**144**
Beale (victim), **95**
Beamer, Samuel, 104
Bemrose, William, 123
Bennet (farmer), 163
Benyon, Samuel, 70
Bernays, Maurice, 46
Berwick, Lord, 74
Bignold, Sheriff, 178
Bird, John, 48; Sarah, 48
Bishop and Williams, 189,219
Blizzard, Mary, 146; Thomas, 135,137,139,140,142, **144**,146
Bloomfield, William, **95**,97

Blunt, Thomas, 73
Bodkin (lawyer), 137,138
Booth (owner of Twelmow's Farm), 71,84
Boscawen, Reverend J E, 48
Bothwell, Samuel, 49
Botts, William, 74,85-86
Bourchier, Rev., **98**
Bowerbank, Rev. William, 231...239
Bowles, Thomas, 137,**144**
Boycott, Rev., 230
Bradbury (stack owner), 69,75,84
Brasher, John, 127
Bray, William, 28,39
Braybrooke, Lord Lieutenant, 109
Brewitt (churchwarden), 106
Briant, Joseph, **144**; William, **144**
Bridgwater, Lady, 72,84
Broadwood, James Shudi, 50,52
Brockies, Daniel, 11,**98**,100
Brogan (cholera victim), 215
Brown, John, 238
Bryant, William, 131,137
Buckingham, Duke, 138,142
Buckland, William, 49
Burke, William and Hare, William, 189,210,219
Burrows, John, 176
Butler, John, **144**; William, **144**,247

Campbell, Duncan, 243
Camphill (farmer), 45
Campion (victim), **95**
Carey, Robert, 142,**144**
Carlile, Richard, 177

Carrington, Lord, 130
Cartwright (ironmonger), 68
Cass, Thomas, **98**,101
Cauvill (victim), **95**
Cavenough, Owen, 247
Chadwick, Edwin, 202
Chandos, Marquis, Lord Lieutenant Bucks, 128,131
Charsley (coroner), 137
Churton, William, 70
Clementin, Rev. J, 30
Clements (intelligence officer), 69
Clive, Lord, 73
Coe, John, 101
Coke, John, 230...237,*231*
Collins, C, 30
Collins, Edmund, 142; James, 197,200-201
Comber (prisoner), 45
Combes, William, 49
Compton, William, 14
Cook, Thomas, 70
Cooke, Aaron, 178
Cooper, William, 53
Cove, Rev. C, 153
Cox, William, 247
Coxon, Henry, 120,122
Crawford, William, 49,50,53
Cross (protester), **95**
Croucher, Samuel, 49
Crutch, John, **144**
Cursham, Rev., 236,238

Dafter, John, **144**
Dale, Joshua T, 86
Dandridge, John, **144**
Darling (rioter), 159
Darlington (owner of Twemlow's Hall), 71,84,86
Darnell, Margaret, alias Dowling, Darnel or Darling, 247
Davidson, Josiah, 172,178,180; Robert, 178,179,180
Davis, W R, 133,138,140
Devonshire, Duke, Lord Lieutenant, 121
Dewdney, George, 49
Drewitt, Thomas, 39,41
Dring, William, 247
Drummond, Henry, 28,30,39,43,45,48,51; Hugh, 192
Duffield, John, 173
Dumoir, John, 65
Dundas, Charles, MP, 159-160
Dunnett, Charles, **95**
Durrell (protester), **95**

Eade, Stephen, **95**
Earnshaw, Mr, 55
East, John, **144**
Edward, T, 52

Ellenborough, Lord, 154
Elliston, Rev., 230
Evans, Thomas, 161
Ewen, James, 104-105,107,110,113,114

Fairchild, Samuel, 107
Feedham, Robert, 89,**95**
Fisher, Thomas, **144**; William, 49
Fletcher, Meyrich, **98**,99,100
Flower (solicitor), 238
Forbes, Ann, *see: Huxley*
Forgham, John, 72
Fosbury, John, 160
Fowle, Rev. Fulwar Craven, 159-160
Francis, Benjamin, **144**
Franks, James, 42-43
Fry, Elizabeth, 248

Garner (victim), 123
Gaskell, Dr, 216
Gasson (labourer), 44
Gibbons, Richard, 127
Gibson, John, **144**
Gill, William, 199
Gittins, Cyrus, 68
Goodacre, Rev. William, 234...239
Goodman, Thomas, 21
Greaves, John, 238
Green, Charlie, 177,180; Marine Charles, 247
Grey, Lord, 44,51,53
Griffiths, H R, 86
Griggs, Joshua, 90
Grindley, Joseph, 71,72,73,74,75,85-86; Martha, 73;
    Samuel, 72,73,74,85-86; Sarah, 73
Gurney (banker), 176,181; (lawyer), 137,138

Hailey, Richard, 135
Hall, James, **144**
Hancock, William, 142,**144**
Hardwick (rioter), **93**
Harper, George, 72
Harriman (farmer), 121
Harris, Rev., 101
Hartshorn, Thomas, 123
Harvey, Col, 176,178,181
Hawkins, Elizabeth, 248
Hay, John, 131,132,139,140
Hearne, Rev., 215...217
Heath, William, 64,65,67,84
Higginson, Samuel, 73
Hill, Robert Chambre, 74; Sir Rowland, 70,72,73,74
Hilton (victim), **98**
Hockley, James, 96
Holland, John Staples, 108
Holmes (surgeon), 186

Holt, Moses, **144**; William, 235
Hopkins, John, 121; Rev. James, 92
Hotham, Sir Henry, 53
Howard, John, *The State of Prisons in England and Wales*, 242
Howe, George, 246
Hunt, Henry, 142; Richard, 180
Hurlock, Rev., 12,**98**,101
Huxley (tenant farmer), 68,70,84; Ann (née Forbes), 247; Ann (née Forbes), family tree, 254-258; Thomas (or Jones), 247

Jennings, William, 104
Johnston, Rev. Richard, 248
Jolly, Susannah, 14
Jones, Thomas, *see: Huxley;* William, 67
Joslin, James, 92
Justice, Rev. J, 72

Keate, Dr, 158
Kell (surgeon), 186
Kennerley (protester), 69,74,84-85
Kesterman, Col. Jeremiah, 100
Kilmorney, Earl, 72
Kirkham (overseer), 91
Knight, Charles, 90
Knox (barrister), 101

Lake (victim), **95**
Lamb, George, 122
Lane, John, 131,137,147; Joseph, 131,137,147
Langley, Mr, 67; Mrs, 48
Lansdale, Richard, 132,137,140
Lappage, William, 94
Layzell, Mary, 99
Lea, James (suspect), 69,72,73,74,75,85-86
Lee, J, 72
Leigh, Mr, 56
Lines, George, 104; Samuel, 104
Littledale, Mr Justice, 73
Lodwick, Justice J, 100,108
Lovett, Rev. Robert, 48
Lunnon, David, 137,**144**
Lynch, Dr, 216

MacArthur, Elizabeth, 247
Malmsbury, Lord, 154
Mann, Worthy, 14
Manvers, Earl, 120
Mason, Joseph, 161-162; Robert, 161; William, 122
Mather, Ann, 243
Matthews, George, 92
Maule, George, 138,*139*
McQuarrie, Governor of New South Wales, 247

Melbourne, Viscount, 28,30,41,43,45,46,48,50,53,55, 108,109,120,122,139,140,143
Middleton, Lord, 120
Miles, James, **144**
Moody, John, **144**; William, **145**
Moore, Elizabeth, 14
Moss (stackyard owner), 67,84; George, 95
Munday, Francis, 123
Munro, Lydia, 247
Murray, Colonel, 41
Mytton, Squire 'Jack', 74

Nevile, Rev. E, 72
Newland, Robert, 92
Nibbs, William, **145**
Nockolds, Richard, 170-183; William, 174
Norris (rioter), 159
Nunn, Thomas, 111
Nunnerley (farmer), 65,71,73,84,85-86

O'Shaughnessy, William Brooke, 187
Oakley (rioter), 159
Oldham, Robert, 216-217
Osborne, Mr, 123

Paine, Thomas, 174,177
Palmer, O, **95**
Park, Sir James Allen, 135,138-140
Parker, Elizabeth, 13
Patterson (overseer), 91; William, 247
Payne, Charles, **95**,96
Pearson (farmer), 89
Peatfield, Rev. John, 238
Peel, Sir Robert, 30,44,51
Penfold, James, 49
Philips, John, **95**,96
Phillip, Arthur, Commander of First Fleet, 244; Governor of Sydney Cove, 246,248
Phillips, J M, 138
Phipps (protester), **95**
Plaistowe, Richard, 127,132,139,140,147
Porter, John, 96
Portland, Duke, 231
Preater, J, 163
Priest, Joseph, **145**

Quinn, William, 104

Raynham (farmer), 105
Reid, M, 53
Reynolds, John, **145**
Richards, Benjamin, 238
Richardson (protester), 108; Thomas Salusbury, 70
Rose, Thomas, 90
Rudge, Rev. Dr, 230

Russell, William, **145**
Ruthorn, G, 46

Sach, John, 90,104
Salter, Arthur, **145**
Sarney, John, 137,139,140,142,**145**,146
Saville, Joseph, 14
Scobell, Rev. George, 130,131
Scott (victim), **95**
Scrope, Poulett, 30
Sellars, John, 238
Senior, Nassau, 30,31
Severn, Job, 231
Shepherd, Hardy, 175,177,180; John, 175-176,177,180
Sheppard, John, **98**,100
Shrimpton, Willliam, 137,**145**
Simmons, Hannah, 14,72-73
Simpson, Pinder, 46
Skeel (victim), **95**
Smallpiece, George, 41,43
Smith (victim), **95**; alias Captain Winterbourne (rioter), 156,159; John, **145**; William, 94,137
Smyth, Sir George, 93
Snow, John, 202
Somers Smith, H R, 111
South (farmer), 7,45,94
Sparkes, Timothy, 178
Springhall, William, 174,180
Sproat, William, 185-186
Spurgeon, William, 2-3,3,89,114
Stanhope, Earl, 120
Staniforth (farmer), 123
Steele, Mr, 53
Stewart (surgeon), 190-192
Stingemore, John, 162-163
Stingimore, Thomas, 163
Stone, James, **145**
Stratford, Henry, **145**
Stretton, James, **145**
Such, Joseph, 105
Summerfield, Samuel, **145**
Symonds, John, 14

Tabrum, Robert, 90
Taunton, Mr Justice, 93
Taylor, Jane, 13
Thomas, William, 203
Thompson (farmer), 32
Tidy, Richard, 43
Tillett, John, **95**
Timbrell, Benjamin, 163; Sylvia, 163
Tirry, Mr, 48

Unwin, Rev. John, 235...239

Vaughan, Baron, 161-162
Vincent, Rev., 132
Vyse, Col., High Sheriff of Buckinghamshire, 132

Walden (farmer), 89
Walduck, John, 137,**145**
Walker, Henry, **145**; John, **145**; William, **145**
Ward, John, **95**,96
Warner, James, 39,42-43,45,50,56; William, 94
Watts, John, **145**; William, 160-162
Wayne, Justice G, 108
Weatherill, Thomas, 197
Webb, James, **145**; John, **95**
Wedd (protester), **95**
Weedon, Richard, 137,142,**145**
Welham, John, **95**
Wellington, Duke, 31,44,51,120,142,154,165
Westwood, James, 92
Wheeler, Robert, 138
Whitbread, Samuel, 94
White, William, 48
Whitfield, George T, 68,72,73,74,75,85-86; John, 85-86; Richard, 72,73,84,85-86
Whitter (joiner), 198
Wiffen, Charles, 94
Wilkins, William, 49
Willett (victim), 176
Williams, Henry, 14; John, 72
Wilmot, H S, 123
Wilson, Samuel, **95**,96
Wingrove, Edmund, **145**
Winkworth (farmer), 157
Woodcock, William, 235,237
Wright (assistant overseer), 157; (victim), 176,180; Arthur, 137,**145**; James, 92,93

Young (nurserymen), 48; Arthur, 2

Subject Index

The index is alphabetised in word-by-word order, e.g. *Long Wittenham* is filed before *Longmynds*
Page numbers are given in full form, e.g. 124-125
Page numbers shown as 132...139 indicate sporadic, often unrelated, references throughout the range
References to illustrations, maps and figures are given in *italics*, those for tables are given in **bold**
Page numbers followed by *bib* refer to bibliographical references, either in essay *Notes* or the *Consolidated Bibliography*.
References to specific newspapers indicate a quote from that publication on that page.

Abingdon (Berks), 152,155,156
Abinger (Surrey), 34,42,45
Abinger Hall (Surey), 45
Aboriginal tribes, 244
Acts of Parliament, 51,53
    Allotments Act 1832, 167-168*bib*
    Anatomy Act 1832, 184
    Beerhouse Act 1830, 19,108
    Black Act 1715, 116*bib*
    Factory Act 1833, 147
    Municipal Corporation Act 1835, 63,66
    Navy Mutiny Act 1797, 166
    Parliamentary Reform Act 1884, 107*bib*
    Peel Metropolitan Police Act 1829, 63
    Poor Law Amendment Act 1834, 147,166,
      297*bib*
    Reform Act 1832, 63,147,297*bib*
    Riot Act 1715, 151,152,153
    Select Vestries Act 1819, 158
    Settlement Laws 1662, 166*bib*
    Tithe Commutation Act 1838, 166
    Transportation Act 1597, 242
    see also: relevant Act
agricultural, depression, in Surrey, 27-29
    distress, 31
    labourer, 28
    land usage, in Surrey, 39,41
    riot, 1,3
Albury (Surrey), 28,34,37,39,42,43,45,51
Albury Park (Surrey), 28,51
Alexander (ship), 250
Alfreton (Derbys), 231
Allotments Act 1832, 167-168*bib*

Althorne (Essex), 104
Anatomy Act 1832, 184,219
    riots, 220,220,221
animal maiming, 5,90
anonymous threatening letters, 5,6,11,32,48,70,92,**98**,
    120,121,123,127,157-158,178,230,231
    examples, 11-12,*12*
    geographical spread, *13*
    recipients of, **11**
Anti-Cholera Association, in Bristol, 214
Appletree Hundred (Derbys), 118
Arithmeticke Project, 23, *see also:* www.fachrs.com
Arkesden (Essex), **93**
arson, 7,32,41,45,46,48,180,231
    in Liverpool, 220
    see also: fires and *incendiarism*
Asbourne (Derbys), 118,124
Ascot (Berks), 163
Ash Hall (Shropshire), 70
assaults, on poor law officials, 5
assizes, 56,73,234
associations, funds, 51
    in Surrey, 51
Aston Green (Shropshire), 71
Aston Upon Trent (Derbys), 122,123
attacks, 176,190,194,195,197,198,199
Attingham Park (Shropshire), 74
Australia, 242
Aylesbury (Bucks), 133
Aythorpe Roding (Essex), 90

Bagshot (Surrey), 34,37,43,51
Baker, Robert, 186,201-202,*204*

Banstead (Surrey), 36,43
Barchester Chronicles, 239
Barking (Essex), **98**,99
Barrack Street, Norwich, cottages, *175*
barracks, 193,213,246
Basildon (Essex), **102**,103,105
Battle (Sussex), 21,157
Beaconsfield (Berks), 133,156,158
Beare Green (Surrey), 53
Beauchamp Roding (Essex), 89
Beauchamp Roothing (Essex), **102**
Beerhouse Act 1830, 20,108
beershop, 8
Beighton (Derbys), 123
Belgium, 22,51,52
Belper (Derbys), 122
Bengal (India), 185
Benson (Berks), 155
Berkshire Chronicle, 152
Beverstone (Glos.), 13
Bicester (Oxon), 127
bill of health, 197
Billericay (Essex), **102**
Birchanger (Essex), **102**
Birdbrook (Essex), 92, **93**
Birmingham (Warks), 189
Bishop and Williams, 189,219
    hanging, 219
bishopping, 219
Black Act 1715, 116*bib*
Blackheath (Surrey), 32,39
Bletchingley (Surrey), 31
blood riots, 87
Blue Bell Fold (Leeds), 201
Blythburgh (Suffolk), 171
Board of Health, 187,193,196,197,198,199-
    200,202,203, 205,206,207,214
bodies, elicit trade, 218-219
body-snatching, 189,190,199,218-219
    see also: grave robbing
Boreham (Essex), **102**
Borrowdale (ship), 253
Botany Bay (Australia), 244
Bowerbank, Rev. William, 231...239
    advertisement for Mansfield Grammar school,
    233
    trial, 234-238
Bowers Gifford (Essex), **102**
Bradfield (Berks), 168
Bradwell-juxta-Mare (Essex), 2,**102**
Braintree (Essex), 112
Brampton (Derbys), 123
Bray (Berks), 168
Braybrooke, Lord Lieutenant, 109
bread riots, 87

Brede (Sussex), 18
Brightlingsea (Essex), 91,**102**
Brighton Gazette, **35**
Bristol (Somerset), 189,212-215,
Bristol Gazette, 158,212,214
Bristol Journal, 213
Brockies, Daniel, 11,**98**,100
Broxted (Essex), 89, **102**
Brutus (ship), 197
Buckingham, Duke, 138,142
Bucks and Windsor Herald, 152
Bucks Gazette, 127...146
Bucks Yeomanry, 129,131
Burgh (Norfolk), 230
Burghfield (Berks), 168
burglary, 5,94,104,174 *see also: theft* and *robbery*
burials, 215,218
    alive, 211 *see also: disinterment* and *exhumation*
    rituals *see: death rituals*
Burke, William, and Hare, William, 189,210
    execution, 219
burker, 197,198
burking, 189,190,202,215,219
Burnham (Berks), 156
Burnt Stub Mansion, Chessington (Surrey), 48
Bury Post, 177,178,179
Byfleet (Surrey), 33,42

Calendar of Prisoners, *see: prisoners, Calendar of*
Camden Park, 248
Cape Town (South Africa), 244
Capel (Surrey), 34,42,53
Captain Swing, 5,220,231
Carigees (Aboriginal tribe), 246
Carlile, Richard, 177
Carlisle (Cumbria), 150
Carrington, Lord, 130
Carshalton (Surrey), 52
Caterham (Surrey), 33,41,42,46
Caterham Lodge Farm (Surrey), 46
Catholic church, 199-200
Chandos, Marquis, Lord Lieutenant Bucks, 128,131
Charles X, King of France, 155
Charlotte (ship), 251
Charsley (coroner), 137
chartism, 220,**220**
Chatsworth House (Derbys), 121
Cheam (Surrey), 36,37,43
Chelmsford (Essex), 100,109,112
Chepping Wycombe *see: High Wycombe*
Chertsey (Surrey), 27,51,156
Chessington (Surrey), 36
Chesterfield (Derbys), 122
Chiddingfold (Surrey), 35,48
Childerditch (Essex), 88

Chobham (Surrey), 38,43,45,51
cholera, 246
    Asiatic, 184-185,196-197
    autumnal, 184
    blue stage, 185,*185*,201
    burial grounds, 205,*208*
    burials, 188,189,192,193,194,196,207
        carrying underhand, 206,207,209
        live, 207,208
        use of white lime, 207
    cases and deaths 1831-32, 188,190,193,196,212
        mapping of, 202,*204 see also: Snow, John* and
        Baker, Robert
    Catholic church intervention, 199-200
    causes, 186-187,202
    cover-up, 196-197
    death rate, 186
    English, 184
    epidemics, 189
    fees, 187
    Punch cartoon, *186*
    reluctance to accept help, 191
    remedies, 187,202
    summer, 184
    symptoms, 185
Cholera Bill, 187
Cholera Gazette, 187
cholera humbug, 191,192,221
cholera morbus, 185,214
cholera riots, 7,184-228,**220**
    causes, 218-221
        burial practices, 218
        civil disturbances, 219-221
        class and race, 218
        dissection and body-snatching, 219-220
    in Europe, 190
    in Exeter, *209*
    in Liverpool, dates and locations, **198**
civil disturbances, in Britain 1812-1848, **220**
Clandon (Surrey), 42
Clare, John, *The Hue and Cry: A Tale of the Times*, 47
Clavering (Essex), 93, **93**
Clee (Shropshire), 67
Clee Hills (Shropshire), 63
clergymen, as instigators of protest, 230
    as magistrates, 230
    as Swing protester targets, 229-240
    offences, **229**
        geographic spread, 229-230
Clive, Lord, 73
cloth, 171
    bombazine, 171,173
    silk, 171
    worsted damask, 171
coal, cost as cause of protest, 232

Cobbett, William, 21,26,29,30,41,43,47,56,177,296*bib*
    The Noblest Agitator, 21
    Two-penny Trash, 21
    writings, 29-30
Cobham (Surrey), 27,33,42,43
Coke, John, 230...237,231
Colchester (Essex), 92,**93**
    Mile End, 92
    St Michael's, 92-93
Coleshill (Berks), 168
Colnbrook (Surrey), 27
Colthorp (Berks), 143
Cookham (Berks), 168
Coombe (Surrey), 33
County Chronicle, 27,29,43,45,51,52
Cow Pastures (Australia), 248
Cranleigh (*formerly* Cranley, Surrey),51
Cressage (Shropshire), 67
crimes, women prisoners, 242 *see also: prisoners,*
    women
Crowhurst (Surrey), 37,43

Dale Abbey (Derbys), 120
damage, 193,195,197,198,203,205,215,216,219,221
    costs, 55
    wilful, 5,155
Danbury (Essex), **98**
Dearnford Hall (Shropshire), 68,70,*80*
death rituals, 218,222
death sentence, 72,73,79,91,138,139,140,142,161,164,
    177,180,242 *see also: hanging* and *execution*
    criterion, 105
    petition for stay of, 141
Debdale (Notts), 232
Dedham (Essex), 12,**98**,101
Delacroix, Eugene, *Liberty Leading the People*, 22
Derby (Derbys), 124
Derby and Chesterfield Reporter, 121
Derby Mercury, 120,121,122,123,124
Derbyshire Courier, 122,123,124
Devonshire, Duke, Lord Lieutenant, 121
Dickens, Charles *see: Sparkes, Timothy*
disinterment, 214,215
dissection, 189,218-129
Ditton (Surrey), 33
Dorking (Surrey), 31-32,35,48-49,50,51,53
Drayton (Berks), 168
Dumfries (Scotland), 189
Dundas, Charles, MP, 159-160

East Hendred (Berks), 168
Eastbury (Berks), 156
Easterham (Surrey), 33
Eckington (Derbys), 124
Eddowes Salopian Journal, 64...86

Edinburgh (Scotland), 189,193-196
education, costs, 232
Egham (Surrey), **34,35,38**,43,46,55,156
Eliza (transportation ship), 160
Elizabeth Farm, Rose Hill (Australia), 247
Ellaston (Staffs), 120
Ellenborough, Lord, 154
Elmdon (Essex), **93**
Elsenham (Essex), **102**
Ely (Cambs), 150
Emu Plains (New South Wales), 247
enclosure, 1,5
Englefield Green (Surrey), **33**,42
Epping (Essex), 112
Epsom (Surrey), 29,**34**,36,42,43,48
Essex, description, 87
    location, *88*
Essex Economic Fire Association, 89
Eton (Berks), 156,158
Eton School, 13
Europe, influences, 22
execution, 56,73,104,105,146,160,179,219 *see also:*
    death sentence and *hanging*
Exeter (Devon), 189,205-212
Exeter Gazette, 209,212
exhumation, 211,213
extortion, 5

Factory Act 1833, 147
Falkirk (Scotland), 193
Farmers' Journal, 128
Farnham (Surrey), 37,43
female factory, Sydney Cove, 245
Finchingfield (Essex), **93**,112
fire engines, use of, 42,65,69,70,71,104,157
fire-fighting, methods, 41,
fires, in Derbyshire, 121,122
    in Manchester, 215
    in Shropshire, 62-86,78-79,
    in Surrey, 39-43,46-47
    methods for starting, 103,178
    produce burnt, 41-43,45,65,67,68,70,71,73,89,
        124,157,231
    see also: arson and *incendiarism*
First Fleet, details, 250-253
Fishburn (ship), 252
Flackwell Heath (Bucks), 131
food, price of, 1
food riot, 5,*10*
Fordingbridge (Hants), 127,143
France, 22,46,50,52,63,143,154
Friendship (ship), 252
Frimley (Surrey), 39
frotie, 101,116*bib*
Froxfield (Wilts), 7

Fuel Allotment Law 1832, 166

general unrest, 7
gentlemen, 146,154,155
    on horseback, 45,154,162,164
Gestingthorpe (Essex), 112
Glasgow (Scotland), 189,190-193
Glasgow Courier, 190,192
gleaning riot, 5
Glossop (Derbys), 122,124
Godalming (Surrey), 27
Godstone (Surrey), 42,43
Golden Grove (ship), 253
Goodacre, Rev. William, 234...239
    daily routine, 234
    under-master Mansfield Grammar, 234-239
Gordon Riots 1780, 151
Gosport (Hants), 150
graffiti, Norwich Castle, 181,*181*
grave robbing, 199 *see also: body-snatching*
Great Chesterford (Essex), **102**
Great Clacton (Essex), **93,95**,97
Great Coggeshall (Essex), 91,112
Great Dividing Range (New South Wales), 246,247
Great Dunmow (Essex), 95,**95**,96
Great Farringdon (Berks), 168
Great Hallingbury (Essex), **98**,101
Great Henny (Essex), 112
Great Holland (Essex), 89,**95,102**
Great Stanmore, 48
Great Waltham (Essex), **102**
Grey, Lord, 44,51,53
Guildford (Surrey), 27,28,35,37,43,49-50
guns, carrying, 178
    use of, 39,43,123,124,131,133,137,163,174,
        176,180

Haddiscoe (Norfolk), 230
handbills, 52-56,*55*,174 *see also: posters*
hanging, 42-43,151,171,189 *see also: death sentence*
    and *execution*
Hanging Bridge (Derbys), 123
Hardy (prison hulk), 142
Hare, William *see: Burke*
Harlow (Essex), 112
Harwich (Essex), **102**
Hawkchurch (Dorset), 230
Hawkesbury, 246
    pioneer register, 247
    river, 246
Hawkstone Park (Shropshire), 74
Hawkwell (Essex), **98**,100
Hayfield (Derbys), 122
headmaster, income, 232-233
    salary, 232-233

Health of Towns Commission 1844, 175
Helions Bumpstead (Essex), **93**,215
Helston (Cornwall), 10
Henham (Essex), **93**
Henley (Berks), 155
High Wycombe (Bucks), *126*,126,129
highway robbery, 5,6-7
Hill, Sir Rowland, 70,72,73,74
Hobsbawm & Rudé, 5,32,**35-36**,46,47,55,56,62,87,90,
   103,114,127,143,146,147,150,159,161,164,229,230
Holland (country), 22
Holyport (Berks), 157
Hook (Surrey), 36
Horley (Surrey), 56
Horndon-on-the-Hill (Essex), **102**,105
Horsham (Sussex), 45,50,53
hospital, Bristol, 212-213
Howard, John, *The State of Prisons in England and
   Wales*, 242
Hungary, 190
Hungerford (Berks), 7,127,155
Hurley (Berks), 168

illiteracy, 99
immigrants, Irish, 221
imprisonment, 4,13,14,16,17,49,56,70,71,89,90,92,93,
   94,97,101,**144-145**,146,156,164,176,177,190,192
   see also: sentences
incendiaries, professionals, 41
incendiarism, 5,6,47,48,87,89,92,99,102-107,**102-103**,
   see also: fires and *arson*
      attempted, 5,**102-103**
      non-agricultural premises, 7
      of hayricks, methods employed, 41,
      principal crime, 6
      produce burnt, 41-43,45,65,67,68,70,71,73,89
incitement, 5, *see also: inflammatory writers*
industries, in New South Wales, 246
inflammatory writers, 177 *see also: Carlile, Cobbett,
   Paine*
      writings, 177
Ingatestone (Essex), 112
injuries, 132,133,163,176,180,192,193,197,206,221
instigators, foreigners, 44-52,220
      French, 44-52
      of protests, 44-52,230
      strangers, 44-52,109
insurance, 55-56,68,89
      valuation, 84
interment, 218
Irish, 188,197,199,200,201,202,205,215,217,218,221
   labourers, 7,123
Ironbridge (Shropshire), 64

Kent and Essex Mercury, 152

Kidderminster (Worcs), 171
Kilmorney, Earl, 72
Kingston (Surrey), 36,42,45,48
Kintbury (Berks), 159,168
Kintbury Family History, 160,165
Kirby-le-Soken (Essex), **95**,96
Kirkby in Ashfield (Notts), 235
Knott Mill (Manchester), 215

labourers, 1,
   Irish, 7,42,
Ladt Penrhyn (ship), 252
Lambourne (Berks), 155,156,168
Lancet, 185,197,221
Langar (Notts), 235
Last Labourers' Revolt, 1,142,147
Lawford (Essex), 107,112
Layer-de-la-Haye (Essex), 89, **102**
Leeds (Yorks), 189,201-205
Leeds Intelligencer, 202
Leigh (Essex), **102**,107
Leigh (Surrey), 35,56
Leith (Scotland), 195,196
Letcombe Regis (Berks), 168
Leytonstone (Essex), **102**,105
lime (white), use on cholera burial mounds, 207
      use on cholera victim linens, 210
Limpsfield (Surrey), 35,36,39,43,50
Little Clacton (Essex), **95**,97
Little Marlow (Bucks), 135
Little Waltham (Essex), 112
Little Wigborough (Essex), 8,**93**
Liverpool (Lancs), 73,188,189,196-201
Liverpool Chronicle, 198
Liverpool Journal, 196-197,200,201,221
Liverpool Mercury, 199
living conditions, 175-176,
London, 188,189
London Medical Gazette, 199
Long Eaton (Derbys), 121
Long Wittenham (Berks), 169
Longmynds (Shropshire), 63
looms, 170...183
      draw-loom, 171,*173*
      hand-loom, 170-171
Loudwater (Bucks), 132
Loudwater Mill (Wycombe, Bucks), 127
Lower Hardres (Kent), 155
Luddism, 220,**220**
Lyng (Norfolk), 143

machine-breaking, in Essex, 95
      non-agricultural, 7,*130*,131-132,133,143,220
         geographical spread, *8*,
      other agricultural, 5,6,92,96,231
      threshing, 5,6,32,96,132,155,161, 163

Maidenhead (Berks), 156
Maidstone Journal, **33**
malaria, 246
malicious killing of livestock, 5
Malmsbury, Lord, 154
Manchester (Lancs), 73,189,215-217
Manchester Chronicle, 215
Manningtree (Essex), 111
Mansfield (Notts), 230
Mansfield and Pinxton railway, 232
Mansfield Grammar school, advertisement, *233*
    condition, 234
Mansfield Woodhouse (Notts), 230,236
Manvers, Earl, 120
Market Drayton (Shropshire), 68,69
Marlow (Bucks), 129
Marsh Green (Bucks), 131
Mason, Joseph, life of a transportee, 162
Matlock (Derbys), 123
Maule, George, letter to Home Office, *139*
McQuarrie, Governor of New South Wales, 247
meeting, in beershop, 8
    notice, *129*
    notice of resolutions, *128*,134,
    seditious, 7
Melbourne, Viscount, 28,30,41,43,45,46,48,50,53,55,
    108,109,120,122,139,140,143
Merthyr Tydfil (Wales), 220
Merton (Surrey), 34,42
Mickleover (Derbys), 121
Middleton, Lord, 120
military, 51
    use of, 49,50,64,91,131,153,163,176,184,193,
    215-216,217,220
militia, 49,50,64
mills, paper, 126-149
    powered, 172
    steam-driven, spinning, 172
        weaving, 172
Milton (Berks), 169
Molesey (Surrey), 34
Morden (Surrey), 36
Morning Herald, 140
Mounted Constabulary Association, 134
Mountnessing (Essex), **102**
Municipal Corporation Act 1835, 63,66
murder(ers), 5,7,43,70,72,189,190,197,200,202,203,
    208,211,215,219,242
Musselburgh (Scotland), 193
mutilation, 215-216,217

Napoleonic wars, *iii*,1,3,26,63,151,174
    effects on agriculture, *iii*,26
*Narrative of the Fires which occurred in the Parish of
    Whitchurch in the Years 1830-31*, 69,71

Nash (Bucks), 127
Navy Mutiny Act 1797, 166
Neptune (ship), 248
Nettlebed (Berks), 155
Newark on Trent (Notts), 232
Newbury (Berks), 152,155
Newdigate (Surrey), 49
Newlands Corner (Surrey), 43
Newport Pagnell (Bucks), 131
newspaper research, 152-158
Nockolds, Richard, 170-183
Norbury (Derbys), 123
Norfolk Chronicle, 174...181
North Walsham (Norfolk), 178
Norton Woodseats (Derbys), 123
Norwich (Norfolk), 170-183
Norwich Mercury, 179
Norwich Weavers Society, 173
Norwood (Surrey), 35
Nottingham and Newark Mercury, 123,234,239-240bib
Nottingham Journal, 234,236,239-240bib
Nottingham Review, 121

Oak Gang, 42
Ockbrook (Derbys), 122
Ockley (Surrey), 34,43,48,53
Old Bailey (London), 189,219,**243**,247
Old Heath (Shropshire), 68
Ongar (Essex), 109
Orphan School, Sydney Cove, 245,246
Orpington (Kent), 127
Orsett (Essex), 11,**98**,99
Osmaston (Derbys), 120
Otmoor (Oxon), 127
overseers, assistant, role of, 32
    victims, **17**,18
Oxshott (Surrey), 36
Oxted (Surrey), 32-33,42-45,50

Paine, Thomas, 174,177
paper-mill riots, in Berks, 143
    in Bucks, 126-149
    in Norfolk, 143
Paris (France), 190,210
parish, loan document, *4*
Parliamentary Commission into Charities for the
    Education of the Poor Report 1834, 234
Parliamentary Commissioners, 238
Parliamentary Reform Act 1884, 107bib
Parramatta (New South Wales), 246
pauper hospital, 212-213
Peasemarsh (Surrey), 39
Peel Metropolitan Police Act 1829, 63
Peel, Sir Robert, 30,44,51
Peldon (Essex), 8,93,**93**,94

petition(s), 21,27,29,118,119,120,138,140,*141*,142,160, 165,174,214
Phillip, Arthur, Commander of First Fleet, 244
    Governor of Sydney Cove, 246,248
Pinxton colliery (Derbys), 231
planaquin, 198
Pleasley (Derbys), 231,235
Pleasley parish register extract, *235*
Plymouth, 243
Pockthorpe (Norfolk), 175
police intervention, 190,192,194,195,196,205,210,215
political riot, 7
Political Register, **34**,43
poor law riot, 5,91
poor rate, in Surrey, 31
poor relief, 4,27-29,31,32,135,146,157,165,174
Poor Law, 3-4,18,142,146,166
Poor Law Amendment Act 1834, 147,166,297*bib*
Portland, Duke, 231
Portley Farm, Caterham (Surrey), 39,41-42
Portsmouth (Hants), 241,243
posters, 53,*54*,193,203 *see also: handbills*
Prees Hall (Shropshire), 74
Prees Heath (Shropshire), 65,70,71,72,73,75
Prince of Wales (ship), 247,251
prison chaplain, 176,179
    reform, 242
    sentence, *see: sentences*
    ships, 142,**144-145**
        records, 143
prison(s), 56,98,100,215,219,231
prisoner(s), 45,50,73,133,135,137,138,139,142,146, 156,161,162,215,234,238,241...260
    children, 241
    conditions, 242,248
    women, 241
        ages, **241**
        at Sydney Cove, 245
        crimes, 242
        occupations, 244,**244**
Prisoners, Calendar of, 72,135,*136*,143
Prittlewell (Essex), 112
propaganda, in Surrey, 52-56
protest, 1,
    causes, 112
    incidents, in Bucks, 131-135
    incidents, in Surrey, 1830-1832, **33-38**
    responses, 108-112,
protesters, age range, male, *16*
    capital sentencing patterns, 13-17,*16*,
    in Essex, 107
    occupations, **15**
    patterns, 13-17
    sentencing patterns, 13-17,*16*
Proteus (transportation ship), 142

Punch, 186
punishment, at Sydney Cove, 245
    methods other than transportation, 242
Pyrford (Surrey), 37,43

racial riot, 5
    Lincolnshire,7
    Northamptonshire, 7
Ramsey (Essex), **95,102**
Rayleigh (Essex), 87,90,**102**,103,112
Reading (Berks), 7,152
Reading Mercury, 152,157
Rebecca riots, 220,**220**
Reform Act 1832, 63,147,221,297*bib*
Reform Bill riots, 220,**220**,221
Reformer's Gazette, 191,192
Reigate (Surrey), 35,37,43,44,46,48
rent riot, 5
Repton and Gresley Hundred (Derbys), 118
rescue, of protesters from custody, 5
resurrectionists, 219 *see also: body-snatchers* and *body-snatching*
reward, 3,43,53,*54*,64,89,123,154
Ridgewell (Essex), 92,**93**
Rio de Janeiro (Brazil), 244
riot, legal definition, 91
Riot Act 1715, 151,152,153
Riot Act, reading of, 49,91,110,124,131,132,153, 176,215
riots, 221 *see also: blood, bread, cholera, food, gleaning, paper-mill, political, poor law, rent, subsistence, Swing, tithe, wage*
    in Surrey, 48-50
robbery, 5,6,67,177 *see also: burglary* and *theft*
Robson's *Directory*, 147
Rochester Gazette, **33**
Rochford (Essex), 110,112
Rodsley (Derbys), 120
Rose Hill (Australia), 247
roundsman system, **21**,22,88 *see also: Speenhamland System*
Royal Commission on Poor Law, 1833, (*Rural Queries*), 221
Royal Commission on the Irish Poor, 1836, 218
Royle, Professor Edward, 222,223-228*bib*
Rum Rebellion of 1808, 248
Rural Queries, 9,18-22,146,150,165,220
    Berks, 168-169
    Bucks, 146
    Essex, 112-113
    geographical responses, 19
    perceptions of causes, **21**,21-22
    principal causes, *20*
Russia, 190
Rye (Bucks), 130

Saffron Walden (Essex), **93**, 109,147
salaries, 52
    headmaster, 232-233
    usher, 232-233
Salisbury (Wilts), 163
Salmonby (Lincs), 236,239
Salop Directory, 73
Salt Hill (Bucks), 127,156,158
Sawley (Derbys), 122
scandal, medical, 222
Scarborough (ship), 251
Scarsdale Hundred (Derbys), 118
Scotsman, 191,193,194,216
Scottow (Norfolk), 178
Second Fleet, 247
Select Vestries Act 1819, 3-4,158
sentences, 65,90,98,122,142,156,170,196,199,203,242
   see also: death sentences, execution, hanging,
   imprisonment, prison, transportation
    completed in Sydney Cove, 245
sentencing places, of First Fleet convicts, **243**
Settlement Laws 1662, 166*bib*
Settlement Laws Amendment 1834, 166
Shapter, T, *The Cholera In Exeter in 1832*, 205,207-
   210
sheep farming, in Surrey, 41
Sheering (Essex), **95**
Sheffield (Yorks), 189
Sheffield Iris, 123
Shenfield (Essex), **102**
Shepperton (Surrey), 38,43
Sheppey (Isle of, Kent), 150
Shere (Surrey), 28,37,38,39,42,43
Shifnal (Shropshire), 68
ships, 241
    repairs, 244
Shottesbrook (Berks), 169
Shrewsbury (Shropshire), 63,68
Shrewsbury Chronicle, 63...86
Shrivenham (Berks), 169
Shropshire, description, 62-64
Shropshire Yeomanry, 64
Sible Heddingham (Essex), 112
Silas Marner, 172
Sirius (ship), 250
Skeel (victim), **95**
Skegby (Notts), 234,236
smock frock, 50,154,*155*,167*bib*
Snakely Mill (Loudwater, Bucks), 132,*132*
Sneinton (Notts), 14
Snow, John, 202
Société Propagande, 44
Society of Friends, Bristol, 214
South Weald (Essex), **102**,107
Southampton (Hants), 127

Southend (Essex), 87
Sparkes, Timothy, 178
special constables, 29,49,51-52,64,65,68,91,92,109,
   110,111,112,122,128,*128*, 131,133,137,153,156,193
Special Commission, 135,138,146,161
Speen (Berks), 169
Speenhamland (Berks), 160
Speenhamland System, 22,151,160,164
    variation, **21**,22,88
Spondon (Derbys), 121
St Alkmund's Church (Whitchurch, Shropshire), *81*
St James's Fair, Bristol, 214
St Mary's (Reading, Berks), 169
St Peter's Hospital Bristol, 212-213,214
stacks, looker, 7
Staines (Mddx), 45,156
Stambourne (Essex), 92,**93**
Standsted Mountfitchet (Essex), 112
Stanhope, Earl, 120
Stanmore (Mddx), 45
Stanton by Dale (Derbys), 120
Stapleford Tawney (Essex), 94, **102**
Steeple Bumpstead (Essex), **93**
Stondon Massey (Essex), 89,**102**,112
Stone (Herts), 14
strangers, 44-52,146
Strelley (Notts), 231
strike, 7
Strumpshaw (Norfolk), 7
subsistence riots, 87
Sun Assurance, 68
Sun Fire Insurance Company, 55
Sunderland, 185
Supply (ship), 250
Surrey Militia, 50
Sutton in Ashfield (Notts), 232,234,236
Sutton Wick (Berks), 169
Swan Street Hospital, Manchester, 215
Swanton Abbott (Norfolk), 172,178
Swindon (Shropshire), 68
Swing, 220,**220**
    against clergy, 9,14,18,229-240
    against women, 18
    and transportation, 241-260
    background, 1-5
    causes *see: Rural Queries*
    geographical spread, *6*
    in Berkshire, 150-169
    in Derbyshire, 118-125,*119*
    in Essex, 87-117,*90*,*106*
    in Norfolk, 170-183
    in Shropshire, 62-86,*77*
    in Surrey, 26-61
       geographical spread, *40*
    influences on, 151

Swing, non-agricultural incidents, 7
    offences, 5,
    origin of name, 5
    protests, instigators of, 44-52,146
    rioters' sentencing, 146,164
    victims, 17-18
        occupations, 17
swingel, 2,5
Sydney (NSW, Australia), 162
Sydney Cove (Australia), 241...260
Sydney Gazette and New South Wales Advertiser, 246

Tasmania (Australia), 142,160,163 *see also: Van Diemen's Land*
Taverham (Norfolk), 143
taxes, call for reductions, 29,142
Teddington (Mddx), 45
Temple Fair, Bristol, 215
Tendring (Essex), **93,102**,110
Thanet (Isle of, Kent), 150
Thaxted (Essex), 91,**102**,112
The Herald, 29,42
The Times, 14,**33-38**,44,45,46,49,50,145,146,181,212, 216,217
theft, 5,107,160,241,242,247,254 *see also: burglary*
Thornton Heath (Surrey), 53
Thorpe-le-Soken (Essex), 112
threats, in Bucks, 143
    in Essex, 98
    in letters *see: anonymous threatening letters*
    verbal, 5,213
threshing, by hand, *2*
    flail, 2,5
    machines, 1-2
        lack of in Surrey, 27
Tilstock (Shropshire), 65,68,71
tinderbox, 103,104
tithe riot, 5,48
    and clergy, 9
    extent, *10*
    rioters occupations, 9
Tithe Commutation Act 1838, 166
tithes, 152,230
Tolpuddle (Dorset), 166
Tolpuddle Martyrs, 166
Tonbridge (Kent), 45
trade unions, 166
transportation, 17,70,90,98,101,122,124,137,142,**144**, 161,164,166,177,241-260 *see also: sentences*
    accommodation for women, 243,*243*
    deaths, 244
    reasons, 242
Transportation Act 1597, 242
trials, 47,56,71-72,93,94,97,99,100-101,105,122,124, 135-140,156,176,179,189,199,234-238

Trumpngton (Cambs), 8
turnpike tolls, 231-232,234
Twemlow's Hall and Farm (Shropshire), 70,71,75,*81*
typhus, 243

Uffington (Berks), 169
Ufton Nevett (Berks), 169
underhand, carrying of coffin, 206,207,208
unemployment, cause of Swing, 220
    due to bad weather, 29,32
    due to poor harvests, 29
    economic remedies to combat, 29
Unknown (ship), 253

Van Diemen's Land (Australia), 142,146,161,162,163, *see also: Tasmania*
Vaughan, Baron, 161-162
verbal threats, 5 *see also: threats*
Vibrio cholerae, 185
Victoria (Australia), 142,163
violence, outbreaks, in Surrey, 32-39
Virginia Water (Surrey), 36
vitriol, oil of, use, 126,131,176,177
Vyse, Col., High Sheriff of Buckinghamshire, 132

wage labour, in Surrey, 28
wage riot, 5,6,7,8,32,92,
    by county, *9*
    in Essex, 93,**93**,215
    menacing, 7-8
wage strike, 7
    death, 7
wages, 46,48,53,92,93,94,137,147,165,166,176,177 *see also: salaries*
    inadequate, 29-32,
        due to tithes, 120
    of weavers, 173,176
Wakefield (Yorks), 203
Wallasey (Cheshire), 187
Wallingford (Berks), 155,156
Wallington (Surrey), 41,53
Walton on Thames (Surrey), 47
Walton-le-Soken (Essex), 95
Wargrave (Berks), 169
Wasing (Berks), 169
Wavendon (Bucks), 127
weavers, cottages, 171,172,
    in Norwich, 171
weaving, draw-loom, 171,*173*
    hand-loom, 170-183
    of fashionable items, 171
weaving, trading methods, 172
Wellington (Shropshire), 63
Wellington, Duke, 31,44,51,120,142,154,165
Welsh rising, 220

Wem (Shropshire), 70
Wenden Lofts (Essex), **93**
Wensum (river, Norfolk), 176
West Bergholt (Essex), **102**
West Ham (Essex), **102**,113
West Hannay (Berks), 161
West Mersea (Essex), 7,93,**93**,94
Western Times, 211,212
Weston-upon-Trent (Derbys), 122
Westwick (Norfolk), 180
whipping, 72
Whitchurch (Shropshire), 14,62,64-65,69,71,72
Wickham Bishops (Essex), 113
Wilton (Wilts), 127
Wiltshire Machine Breakers: Vol 1: The Riots and Trials, Vol 2: The Rioters, 162
Wimbledon (Surrey), 36
Windlesham (Surrey), 39,51
Windsor (Berks), 152
Windsor and Eton Express, 27,28,**33-34**,156,160,164
Windsor Herald, 158
Winfarthing (Norfolk), 14
Winkfield (Berks), 156,169
Winthorpe Acadamy (Notts), 232
Witham (Essex), 87, 113
witness(es), 32,39,68,72,101,108,137,138,175,176, 180,181,185,216,217,219,234,235,236,237,238
Woking (Surrey), 32,35,37,41,43,48,50,51
Woldingham (Surrey), 43
Wollaton (Notts), 120
Wolverhampton (Staffs), 7
women, prisoners *see prisoners, women*
    protesters, 13-14,133
Wooburn (Berks), 158
work-houses, 166,190,213,219
    installation of looms, 176
    legislation, 64
Worsted (Norfolk), 180
Wotton (Surrey), 35,48,51
Writtle (Essex), 102,103
Wycombe paper-mill, rioters, 144-145
    riots, 126-149,164
Wye Valley (Bucks), 127

Yeldersley (Derbys), 120
York (prison hulk), 142,160
York, 187

FACHRS

The Family & Community Historical Research Society is all about 'hands-on' research. As the name suggests FACHRS research goes deeper than your own family history (though nearly all of our members do pursue this aspect of personal research) and moves more into the area of social history and how events may have impacted local communities and families. By engaging into research outside the immediate boundaries of your family, new skills, such as understanding wills and probate, or how to research historical newspaper articles and reports can be embraced, adding a richness to the social era around your own family's past.

Members achieve new skills or hone existing skills, by engaging in personal or team micro-research projects of an academic nature. Many members of FACHRS have an academic qualification associated with local history or social history research. However, membership of FACHRS is not restricted. We recognise that there are members who have no desire to seek a qualification but do want to engage in research and do appreciate the opportunity for hands-on support.

The benefits of being a member include:

Annual Conference

This is held in May each year, when the Society hosts a one-day event for the presentation of members' research activities and papers from noted luminary researchers.

Joining research teams

Members are able to participate in national research projects through the contribution of localised 'hands-on' research. Past projects have included research into wills and probate, the change of use from roman to arabic numbering, and assisted emigration, whilst current and future projects include the allotment movement, transport and urbanisation.

MEMBERSHIP APPLICATION FORM

I wish to become an Individual Member of the Family & Community Historical Research Society (FACHRS)

Please print clearly

First Name . . . .

Last Name . . . .

E-mail . . . .

Address . . . .

. . . .

. . . .

Post Code . . . .

Tel: . . . .
(in case we need to contact you with a query)

Membership is for a calendar year commencing 1 January

The membership fee for 2005 is £21.00

Fees may be paid by one of the following methods:

1.   Sterling cheque
2.   By credit card
3.   By direct debit

P.T.O. ☞

PAYMENT DETAILS

I wish to pay by

☐   Sterling cheque
      (payable to MANEY
      PUBLISHING)

☐   Direct Debit
      (please contact Maney
      Publishing - details below -
      and request a Direct Debit
      Form for FACHRS)

☐   By credit card as follows:

      ☐   Visa   ☐   Mastercard
      ☐   Amex

Card Number

. . . .

Expiry Date . . . .

Name on card

. . . .
                          (please print)

Signature of cardholder

. . . .

Post completed application to:-

**Family & Community Historical
Research Society**
c/o Maney Publishing
Hudson Road
Leeds LS9 7DL

Tel: 0113 249 7481
E-mail: subscriptions@maney.co.uk

Journal and Newsletter

The Society Journal, Family and Community History (FACH), is recognised by institutions around the United Kingdom as a publication of quality papers involving micro-studies into local and social history. All FACHRS members are entitled to submit articles or project reports to the editors for publication. FACH is published twice a year.

As well as issues of FACH, members also receive a copy of the Society Newsletter three times a year. This provides an opportunity for members to publish short reports on their research. In addition, it provides a medium for members who do not have Internet access to keep up-to-date with happenings within the Society.

For those with internet access and e-mail facilities, a more frequent, but much briefer e-news is sent to all those members who use e-mail.

Society Web site

This can be found at www.fachrs.com. Part of the site is open to all, but there is also a Members Only section accessible by personal user name and password, which are supplied with your membership pack on joining.

Members can post details about their own research and invite participation of fellow researchers; they can advertise any publications they have authored; take part in surveys; and provide feedback to the Committee about current and future direction of the Society, and also to the editors concerning the Journal.

*To find out more about the Society please
visit our Web site at:*

www.fachrs.com

or e-mail our Membership Secretary:

Membership.secretary@fachrs.org.uk

SWING UNMASKED DATA CD

On the CD you will find details of all the instances classed as Swing Protest identified by the research team, making this a unique collection of information connected with period. Details of 1672 identified offenders, 1849 victims and a total of 3318 individual instances of swing protest can be browsed. In over three thousand recorded instances, name searches can be made of the offenders and victims as well as a free text search relating to types of offences, parishes where the offence took place and where the instance was recorded. In some cases the occupation of the victim is also available.

The CD ROM is compatible with a PC using either Microsoft Windows™ 98SE and above or Linux and also MAC OS. Adobe Acrobat Reader is required to browse the CD ROM and a free copy of Adobe Reader™ version 7 for Windows is included on the CD ROM. MAC users can download Adobe Reader™ version 7 for MAC from the Adobe website at www.adobe.com/products/acrobat/readstep2.html

The CD can be purchased separately to Swing Unmasked, though the CD makes an excellent companion to the book.

For more details please contact:

cdsupport@fachrs.org.uk

To find out more about the Society please visit our Web site at:

www.fachrs.com

or e-mail our Membership Secretary:

Membership.secretary@fachrs.org.uk

SWING DATA CD ORDER FORM

I wish to purchase a copy of the Swing Unmasked Data CD

Please print clearly

First Name . . . .

Last Name . . . .

E-mail . . . .

Address . . . .

. . . .

. . . .

Post Code . . . .

Tel: . . . .
(in case we need to contact you with a query)

Purchase price:
- ❖ £10.00 inc UK post & packing
- ❖ Other EU Countries (airmail) £10.60 inc post & packing
- ❖ Other non-EU destinations (airmail) £11 inc post & packing
- ❖ Sterling cheques only
- ❖ Purchasers unable to send sterling cheques, please contact cdsupport@fachrs.org.uk for further details regarding payment, or write to FACHRS CD Support, FACHRS Ltd, Unit 4, 5 West Hill, Aspley Guise, Milton Keynes, MK17 8DW, UK.

For payment details see overleaf

PAYMENT DETAILS

I enclose my cheque for £_____

payable to FACHRS Ltd

for _____ copy(ies) of Swing
Unmasked Data CD

Please post completed order form to:-

**Family & Community Historical
Research Society Limited**
Unit 4, 5 West Hill
Aspley Guise
Milton Keynes MK17 8DP

Further details about the CD are available at
www.fachrs.com/swingcd.htm or email
cdsupport@fachrs.org.uk for more
information. Alternatively, please write to:

FACHRS CD Support, FACHRS Ltd, Unit 4,
5 West Hill, Aspley Guise, Milton Keynes,
MK17 8DW, UK.

For more details please contact:

cdsupport@fachrs.org.uk

*To find out more about the Society please visit
our Web site at:*

www.fachrs.com

or e-mail our Membership Secretary:

Membership.secretary@fachrs.org.uk